W9-AVF-992

FINAL FOUR

1993 NCAA

RECORDS

1939-1992

The History of the Division I Men's
Basketball Tournament, Including
First and Second Rounds, Regional,
and Tournament Records.

THE NATIONAL COLLEGIATE ATHLETIC ASSOCIATION

6201 College Boulevard
Overland Park, Kansas 66211-2422
913/339-1906
January 1993

Edited By: Steven R. Hagwell, *Publications Editor.*

Researched and Coordinated By: Gary K. Johnson, *Assistant Statistics Coordinator,* and James M. Van Valkenburg, *Director of Statistics.*

NCAA, NCAA seal, NCAA logo and NATIONAL COLLEGIATE ATHLETIC ASSOCIATION are registered marks of the Association and use in any manner is prohibited unless prior approval is obtained from the Association.

Table of Contents

NCAA Division I Men's Basketball Tournament and Final Four Records Book

THE
FINAL FOUR

Twenty years ago, UCLA's Bill Walton sank 21 of 22 shots from the field to lead the Bruins to an 87-66 victory over Memphis State in the NCAA championship game. Walton's shooting percentage of 95.5 is a Final Four record. The Bruins center was named the tournament's most outstanding player in 1972 and 1973.

CHAMPIONSHIP RESULTS

Year	Champion	Score	Runner-Up	Third Place	Fourth Place
1939	Oregon	46-33	Ohio St.	†Oklahoma	†Villanova
1940	Indiana	60-42	Kansas	†Duquesne	†Southern Cal
1941	Wisconsin	39-34	Washington St.	†Pittsburgh	†Arkansas
1942	Stanford	53-38	Dartmouth	†Colorado	†Kentucky
1943	Wyoming	46-34	Georgetown	†Texas	†DePaul
1944	Utah	42-40+	Dartmouth	†Iowa St.	†Ohio St.
1945	Oklahoma St.	49-45	New York U.	†Arkansas	†Ohio St.
1946	Oklahoma St.	43-40	North Caro.	Ohio St.	California
1947	Holy Cross	58-47	Oklahoma	Texas	CCNY
1948	Kentucky	58-42	Baylor	Holy Cross	Kansas St.
1949	Kentucky	46-36	Oklahoma St.	Illinois	Oregon St.
1950	CCNY	71-68	Bradley	North Caro. St.	Baylor
1951	Kentucky	68-58	Kansas St.	Illinois	Oklahoma St.
1952	Kansas	80-63	St. John's (N.Y.)	Illinois	Santa Clara
1953	Indiana	69-68	Kansas	Washington	Louisiana St.
1954	La Salle	92-76	Bradley	Penn St.	Southern Cal
1955	San Francisco	77-63	La Salle	Colorado	Iowa
1956	San Francisco	83-71	Iowa	Temple	Southern Methodist
1957	North Caro.	54-53‡	Kansas	San Francisco	Michigan St.
1958	Kentucky	84-72	Seattle	Temple	Kansas St.
1959	California	71-70	West Va.	Cincinnati	Louisville
1960	Ohio St.	75-55	California	Cincinnati	New York U.
1961	Cincinnati	70-65+	Ohio St.	*St. Joseph's (Pa.)	Utah
1962	Cincinnati	71-59	Ohio St.	Wake Forest	UCLA
1963	Loyola (Ill.)	60-58+	Cincinnati	Duke	Oregon St.
1964	UCLA	98-83	Duke	Michigan	Kansas St.
1965	UCLA	91-80	Michigan	Princeton	Wichita St.
1966	UTEP	72-65	Kentucky	Duke	Utah
1967	UCLA	79-64	Dayton	Houston	North Caro.
1968	UCLA	78-55	North Caro.	Ohio St.	Houston
1969	UCLA	92-72	Purdue	Drake	North Caro.
1970	UCLA	80-69	Jacksonville	New Mexico St.	St. Bonaventure
1971	UCLA	68-62	*Villanova	*Western Ky.	Kansas
1972	UCLA	81-76	Florida St.	North Caro.	Louisville
1973	UCLA	87-66	Memphis St.	Indiana	Providence
1974	North Caro. St.	76-64	Marquette	UCLA	Kansas
1975	UCLA	92-85	Kentucky	Louisville	Syracuse
1976	Indiana	86-68	Michigan	UCLA	Rutgers
1977	Marquette	67-59	North Caro.	Nevada-Las Vegas	N.C.-Charlotte
1978	Kentucky	94-88	Duke	Arkansas	Notre Dame
1979	Michigan St.	75-64	Indiana St.	DePaul	Pennsylvania
1980	Louisville	59-54	*UCLA	Purdue	Iowa
1981	Indiana	63-50	North Caro.	Virginia	Louisiana St.
1982	North Caro.	63-62	Georgetown	†Houston	†Louisville
1983	North Caro. St.	54-52	Houston	†Georgia	†Louisville
1984	Georgetown	84-75	Houston	†Kentucky	†Virginia
1985	Villanova	66-64	Georgetown	†St. John's (N.Y.)	*†Memphis St.
1986	Louisville	72-69	Duke	†Kansas	†Louisiana St.
1987	Indiana	74-73	Syracuse	†Nevada-Las Vegas	†Providence
1988	Kansas	83-79	Oklahoma	†Arizona	†Duke
1989	Michigan	80-79+	Seton Hall	†Duke	†Illinois
1990	Nevada-Las Vegas	103-73	Duke	†Arkansas	†Georgia Tech
1991	Duke	72-65	Kansas	†Nevada-Las Vegas	†North Caro.
1992	Duke	71-51	Michigan	†Cincinnati	†Indiana

†Tied for third place.
+Overtime.
‡Three overtimes.
*Record later vacated.

TOURNAMENT TRIVIA QUESTION...

What is the only school to play for the national championship in both football and basketball in the same academic school year? Answer: Oklahoma. In football, the Sooners played Miami (Florida) for the national title in the 1988 Orange Bowl, but lost, finishing third in the final wire service polls. The basketball Sooners played Kansas in the national championship game in 1988, but also lost to finish second in the nation.

FINAL FOUR SINGLE GAME
SINGLE GAME, INDIVIDUAL

Statistics for the Division I Men's Basketball tournament have been collected since 1939, the first year of the tournament. Individual rebounds were added in 1951, although team rebounds were not added until 1955. Assists were added in 1984 and blocked shots and steals were added in 1986. Scoring, rebounding, assists, blocked shots and steals are ranked on total number and per-game average; shooting, on percentage. In statistical rankings, the rounding of percentages and/or averages may indicate ties where none exist. In these cases, the numerical order of the rankings is accurate. In 1973, freshmen became eligible to compete on the varsity level.

Most Points
58, Bill Bradley, Princeton vs. Wichita St., N3d, 1965
48, Hal Lear, Temple vs. Southern Methodist, N3d, 1956
44, Bill Walton, UCLA vs. Memphis St., CH, 1973
42, Bob Houbregs, Washington vs. Louisiana St., N3d, 1953
42, *Jack Egan, St. Joseph's (Pa.) vs. Utah, N3d, 1961 (4 ot)
42, Gail Goodrich, UCLA vs. Michigan, CH, 1965
41, Jack Givens, Kentucky vs. Duke, CH, 1978
39, Oscar Robertson, Cincinnati vs. Louisville, N3d, 1959
39, Al Wood, North Caro. vs. Virginia, NSF, 1981
38, Jerry West, West Va., vs. Louisville, NSF, 1959
38, Jerry Chambers, Utah vs. UTEP, NSF, 1966
38, Freddie Banks, Nevada-Las Vegas vs. Indiana, NSF, 1987

Most Field Goals
22, Bill Bradley, Princeton vs. Wichita St., N3d, 1965
21, Bill Walton, UCLA vs. Memphis St., CH, 1973
18, Jack Givens, Kentucky vs. Duke, CH, 1978
17, Bob Houbregs, Washington vs. Louisiana St., N3d, 1953
17, Hal Lear, Temple vs. Southern Methodist, N3d, 1956
17, *Jack Egan, St. Joseph's (Pa.) vs. Utah, N3d, 1961 (4 ot)
16, Don May, Dayton vs. North Caro., NSF, 1967
16, Charlie Scott, North Caro. vs. Drake, N3d, 1969
16, Larry Bird, Indiana St. vs. DePaul, NSF, 1979
15, Lew Alcindor, UCLA vs. North Caro., CH, 1968
15, Lew Alcindor, UCLA vs. Purdue, CH, 1969
15, Ernie DiGregorio, Providence vs. Memphis St., NSF, 1973

Most Field-Goals Attempted
42, Lennie Rosenbluth, North Caro. vs. Michigan St., NSF, 1957 (3 ot)
36, Rick Mount, Purdue vs. UCLA, CH, 1969
36, Ernie DiGregorio, Providence vs. Memphis St., NSF, 1973
34, Elvin Hayes, Houston vs. Ohio St., N3d, 1968
33, *Jack Egan, St. Joseph's (Pa.) vs. Utah, N3d, 1961 (4 ot)
33, *Jerry Dunn, Western Ky. vs. Villanova, NSF, 1971 (2 ot)
32, Elgin Baylor, Seattle vs. Kentucky, CH, 1958
31, Billy McGill, Utah vs. Cincinnati, NSF, 1961
31, Jerry Chambers, Utah vs. UTEP, NSF, 1966
31, Elvin Hayes, Houston vs. UCLA, NSF, 1967

Highest Field-Goal Percentage (minimum 10 FGM)
95.5% (21-22), Bill Walton, UCLA vs. Memphis St., CH, 1973
91.7% (11-12), Bill Walton, UCLA vs. Louisville, NSF, 1972
90.9% (10-11), Jerry Lucas, Ohio St. vs. St. Joseph's (Pa.), NSF, 1961
90.9% (10-11), Billy Thompson, Louisville vs. Louisiana St., NSF, 1986
84.2% (16-19), Larry Bird, Indiana St. vs. DePaul, NSF, 1979
83.3% (10-12), Sidney Wicks, UCLA vs. New Mexico St., NSF, 1970
82.4% (14-17), Joe Barry Carroll, Purdue vs. Iowa, N3d, 1980
76.5% (13-17), Mike Gminski, Duke vs. Notre Dame, NSF, 1978
76.5% (13-17), James Worthy, North Caro. vs. Georgetown, CH, 1982
75.0% (15-20), Lew Alcindor, UCLA vs. Purdue, CH, 1969
75.0% (12-16), Anderson Hunt, Nevada-Las Vegas vs. Duke, CH, 1990

Most Three-Point Field Goals
10, Freddie Banks, Nevada-Las Vegas vs. Indiana, NSF, 1987
7, Steve Alford, Indiana vs. Syracuse, CH, 1987
7, Dave Sieger, Oklahoma vs. Kansas, CH, 1988
7, Dennis Scott, Georgia Tech vs. Nevada-Las Vegas, NSF, 1990
6, Bobby Hurley, Duke vs. Indiana, NSF, 1992
5, Glen Rice, Michigan vs. Seton Hall, CH, 1989 (ot)
5, Anderson Hunt, Nevada-Las Vegas, vs. Georgia Tech, NSF, 1990
4, six tied (most recent: two in 1991)

Most Three-Point Field Goals Attempted
19, Freddie Banks, Nevada-Las Vegas vs. Indiana, NSF, 1987
14, Dennis Scott, Georgia Tech vs. Nevada-Las Vegas, NSF, 1990
13, Dave Sieger, Oklahoma vs. Kansas, CH, 1988
12, Steve Kerr, Arizona vs. Oklahoma, NSF, 1988
12, Glen Rice, Michigan vs. Seton Hall, CH, 1989 (ot)
12, John Morton, Seton Hall vs. Michigan, CH, 1989 (ot)
11, Anderson Hunt, Nevada-Las Vegas vs. Duke, CH, 1990
11, Terry Brown, Kansas vs. Duke, CH, 1991
10, Steve Alford, Indiana vs. Syracuse, CH, 1987
9, three tied (most recent: Bobby Hurley, Duke vs. Indiana, NSF, 1992)

Highest Three-Point Field-Goal Percentage (minimum 5 3FGM)

70.0% (7-10), Steve Alford, Indiana vs. Syracuse, CH, 1987

66.7% (6-9), Bobby Hurley, Duke vs. Indiana, NSF, 1992

55.6% (5-9), Anderson Hunt, Nevada-Las Vegas vs. Georgia Tech, NSF, 1990

53.8% (7-13), Dave Sieger, Oklahoma vs. Kansas, CH, 1988

52.6% (10-19), Freddie Banks, Nevada-Las Vegas vs. Indiana, NSF, 1987

50.0% (7-14), Dennis Scott, Georgia Tech vs. Nevada-Las Vegas, NSF, 1990

41.7% (5-12), Glen Rice, Michigan vs. Seton Hall, CH, 1989 (ot)

(Note: Only ones to meet minimum.)

Most Free Throws

18, Gail Goodrich, UCLA vs. Michigan, CH, 1965

15, Oscar Robertson, Cincinnati vs. Louisville, N3d, 1959

15, Bill Buntin, Michigan vs. Kansas St., N3d, 1964

14, Hal Lear, Temple vs. Southern Methodist, N3d, 1956

14, Jerry West, West Va. vs. Louisville, NSF, 1959

14, Bill Bradley, Princeton vs. Wichita St., N3d, 1965

14, Mark Aguirre, DePaul vs. Pennsylvania, N3d, 1979

13, Don Schlundt, Indiana vs. Louisiana St., NSF, 1953

12, four tied (most recent: Christian Laettner, Duke vs. Kansas, CH, 1991)

Most Free-Throws Attempted

20, Jerry West, West Va. vs. Louisville, NSF, 1959

20, Gail Goodrich, UCLA vs. Michigan, CH, 1965

19, Oscar Robertson, Cincinnati vs. Louisville, N3d, 1959

18, Bob Pettit, Louisiana St. vs. Indiana, NSF, 1953

17, Don Schlundt, Indiana vs. Louisiana St., NSF, 1953

17, Bob Carney, Bradley vs. La Salle, CH, 1954

17, Paul Hogue, Cincinnati vs. UCLA, NSF, 1962

17, Bill Buntin, Michigan vs. Kansas St., N3d, 1964

16, Wilt Chamberlain, Kansas vs. North Caro., CH, 1957 (4 ot)

16, Lew Alcindor, UCLA vs. Drake, NSF, 1969

16, Dennis Wuycik, North Caro. vs. Louisville, N3d, 1972

Highest Free-Throw Percentage (minimum 10 FTM)

100.0% (12-12), Jim Spanarkel, Duke vs. Notre Dame, NSF, 1978

100.0% (12-12), Christian Laettner, Duke vs. Kansas, CH, 1991

100.0% (11-11), Jeff Lamp, Virginia vs. Louisiana St., N3d, 1981

100.0% (10-10), Ron King, Florida St. vs. North Caro., NSF, 1972

93.3% (14-15), Bill Bradley, Princeton vs. Wichita St., N3d, 1965

93.3% (14-15), Mark Aguirre, DePaul vs. Pennsylvania, N3d, 1979

92.9% (13-14), *Jim Lynam, St. Joseph's (Pa.) vs. Utah, N3d, 1961 (4 ot)

91.7% (11-12), Dick Estergard, Bradley vs. La Salle, CH, 1954

91.7% (11-12), Bill Walton, UCLA vs. Louisville, NSF, 1972

91.7% (11-12), Earvin "Magic" Johnson, Michigan St. vs. Pennsylvania, NSF, 1979

Most Rebounds

27, Bill Russell, San Francisco vs. Iowa, CH, 1956

24, Elvin Hayes, Houston vs. UCLA, NSF, 1967

23, Bill Russell, San Francisco vs. Southern Methodist, NSF, 1956

22, Elgin Baylor, Seattle vs. Kansas St., NSF, 1958

22, Tom Sanders, New York U. vs. Ohio St., NSF, 1960

22, Larry Kenon, Memphis St. vs. Providence, NSF, 1973

22, Akeem Olajuwon, Houston vs. Louisville, NSF, 1983

21, Bill Spivey, Kentucky vs. Kansas St., CH, 1951

21, Lew Alcindor, UCLA vs. Drake, NSF, 1969

21, Artis Gilmore, Jacksonville vs. St. Bonaventure, NSF, 1970

21, Bill Walton, UCLA vs. Louisville, NSF, 1972

Most Assists

18, Mark Wade, Nevada-Las Vegas vs. Indiana, NSF, 1987

12, Rumeal Robinson, Michigan vs. Illinois, NSF, 1989

11, Michael Jackson, Georgetown vs. St. John's (N.Y.), NSF, 1985

11, Milt Wagner, Louisville vs. Louisiana St., NSF, 1986

11, Rumeal Robinson, Michigan vs. Seton Hall, CH, 1989 (ot)

9, Alvin Franklin, Houston vs. Georgetown, CH, 1984

9, Michael Jackson, Georgetown vs. Villanova, CH, 1985

9, Bobby Hurley, Duke vs. Kansas, CH, 1991

8, five tied (most recent: Jamal Meeks, Indiana vs. Duke, NSF, 1992)

Most Blocked Shots

6, Danny Manning, Kansas vs. Duke, NSF, 1988

3, Greg Dreiling, Kansas vs. Duke, NSF, 1986

3, Rony Seikaly, Syracuse vs. Indiana, CH, 1987

3, Derrick Coleman, Syracuse vs. Indiana, CH, 1987

3, Dean Garrett, Indiana vs. Syracuse, CH, 1987

3, Armon Gilliam, Nevada-Las Vegas vs. Indiana, NSF, 1987

3, Terry Mills, Michigan vs. Seton Hall, CH, 1989 (ot)

3, Oliver Miller, Arkansas vs. Duke, NSF, 1990

3, Grant Hill, Duke vs. Indiana, NSF, 1992

3, Jamal Meeks, Indiana vs. Duke, NSF, 1992

Most Steals

7, Tommy Amaker, Duke vs. Louisville, CH, 1986

7, Mookie Blaylock, Oklahoma vs. Kansas, CH, 1988

5, Danny Manning, Kansas vs. Oklahoma, CH, 1988

5, Greg Anthony, Nevada-Las Vegas vs. Duke, CH, 1990

4, Mark Alarie, Duke vs. Kansas, NSF, 1986

4, Mark Wade, Nevada-Las Vegas vs. Indiana, NSF, 1987

4, Ernie Lewis, Providence vs. Syracuse, NSF, 1987

4, Danny Manning, Kansas vs. Duke, NSF, 1988

4, Larry Johnson, Nevada-Las Vegas vs. Duke, CH, 1990

4, Alonzo Jamison, Kansas vs. Duke, CH, 1991

4, Nick Van Exel, Cincinnati vs. Michigan, NSF, 1992

SINGLE GAME, TEAM

Most Points
127, *St. Joseph's (Pa.) vs. Utah (120), N3d, 1961 (4 ot)
120, Utah vs. St. Joseph's (Pa.) (127), N3d, 1961 (4 ot)
118, Princeton vs. Wichita St. (82), N3d, 1965
108, UCLA vs. Wichita St. (89), NSF, 1965
106, UCLA vs. Rutgers (92), N3d, 1976
106, Nevada-Las Vegas vs. N.C.-Charlotte (94), N3d, 1977
105, North Caro. vs. Louisville (91), N3d, 1972
103, Nevada-Las Vegas vs. Duke (73), CH, 1990
101, UCLA vs. Houston (69), NSF, 1968
101, Michigan St. vs. Pennsylvania (67), NSF, 1979

Fewest Points
28, Kentucky vs. Dartmouth (47), NSF, 1942
30, Duquesne vs. Indiana (39), NSF, 1940
30, Pittsburgh vs. Wisconsin (36), NSF, 1941
30, Oregon St. vs. Oklahoma St. (55), NSF, 1949
31, Iowa St. vs. Utah (40), NSF, 1944

Largest Winning Margin
36, Princeton (118) vs. Wichita St. (82), N3d, 1965
34, Cincinnati (80) vs. Oregon St. (46), NSF, 1963
34, Michigan St. (101) vs. Pennsylvania (67), NSF, 1979
32, UCLA (101) vs. Houston (69), NSF, 1968
30, Nevada-Las Vegas (103) vs. Duke (73), CH, 1990

Smallest Winning Margin
1, 11 tied (most recent: Michigan [80] vs. Seton Hall [79], CH, 1989 [ot])

Most Points Scored by Losing Team
120, Utah vs. St. Joseph's (Pa.) (127), N3d, 1961 (4 ot)
94, N.C.-Charlotte vs. Nevada-Las Vegas (106), N3d, 1977
93, Pennsylvania vs. DePaul (96), N3d, 1979
93, Nevada-Las Vegas vs. Indiana (97), NSF, 1987
92, Rutgers vs. UCLA (106), N3d, 1976

Most Field Goals
50, Utah vs. St. Joseph's (Pa.), N3d, 1961 (4 ot)
48, Princeton vs. Wichita St., N3d, 1965
47, Nevada-Las Vegas vs. N.C.-Charlotte, N3d, 1977
45, *St. Joseph's (Pa.) vs. Utah, N3d, 1961 (4 ot)
45, Drake vs. North Caro., N3d, 1969

Fewest Field Goals
9, Oklahoma St. vs. Kentucky, CH, 1949
10, Wisconsin vs. Pittsburgh, NSF, 1941
10, Kentucky vs. Dartmouth, NSF, 1942
11, Duquesne vs. Indiana, NSF, 1940
11, Oregon St. vs. Oklahoma St., NSF, 1949

Most Field Goals Attempted
105, *Western Ky. vs. Villanova, NSF, 1971 (2 ot)
103, Utah vs. St. Joseph's (Pa.), N3d, 1961 (4 ot)
101, *St. Joseph's (Pa.) vs. Utah, N3d, 1961 (4 ot)
100, Rutgers vs. UCLA, N3d, 1976
95, Houston vs. Ohio St., N3d, 1968
95, Nevada-Las Vegas vs. N.C.-Charlotte, N3d, 1977

Fewest Field Goals Attempted
28, Villanova vs. Georgetown, CH, 1985
38, Villanova vs. Memphis St., NSF, 1985
41, Georgetown vs. Louisville, NSF, 1982
41, Duke vs. Kansas, CH, 1991
42, Houston vs. Virginia, NSF, 1984 (ot)
42, St. John's (N.Y.) vs. Georgetown, NSF, 1985

Highest Field-Goal Percentage
78.6% (22-28), Villanova vs. Georgetown, CH, 1985
64.5% (40-62), UCLA vs. Memphis St., CH, 1973
63.6% (35-55), Kansas vs. Oklahoma, CH, 1988
63.3% (38-60), Ohio St. vs. St. Joseph's (Pa.), NSF, 1961
63.3% (38-60), Michigan St. vs. Pennsylvania, NSF, 1979

Lowest Field-Goal Percentage
19.5% (15-77), North Caro. St. vs. Baylor, N3d, 1950
21.5% (14-65), Washington St. vs. Wisconsin, CH, 1941
23.4% (15-64), Baylor vs. Kentucky, CH, 1948
24.5% (13-53), Kentucky vs. Georgetown, NSF, 1984
25.4% (18-71), Oklahoma St. vs. Illinois, N3d, 1951

Most Three-Point Field Goals
13, Nevada-Las Vegas vs. Indiana, NSF, 1987
10, Oklahoma vs. Kansas, CH, 1988
10, Nevada-Las Vegas vs. Georgia Tech, NSF, 1990
8, Georgia Tech vs. Nevada-Las Vegas, NSF, 1990
8, Nevada-Las Vegas vs. Duke, CH, 1990
8, Indiana vs. Duke, NSF, 1992

Fewest Three-Point Field Goals
1, Duke vs. Nevada-Las Vegas, CH, 1990
1, Michigan vs. Duke, CH, 1992
2, Indiana vs. Nevada-Las Vegas, NSF, 1987
2, Kansas vs. Duke, NSF, 1988
2, Illinois vs. Michigan, NSF, 1989

Most Three-Point Field Goals Attempted
35, Nevada-Las Vegas vs. Indiana, NSF, 1987
24, Oklahoma vs. Kansas, CH, 1988
23, Arizona vs. Oklahoma, NSF, 1988
23, Seton Hall vs. Michigan, CH, 1989 (ot)
22, Cincinnati vs. Michigan, NSF, 1992

Fewest Three-Point Field Goals Attempted
4, Indiana vs. Nevada-Las Vegas, NSF, 1987
4, Kansas vs. Duke, NSF, 1988
6, Kansas vs. Oklahoma, CH, 1988
8, five tied (most recent: Michigan vs. Cincinnati, NSF, 1992)

Highest Three-Point Field-Goal Percentage (minimum 7 3FGM)
66.7% (10-15), Nevada-Las Vegas vs. Georgia Tech, NSF, 1990
63.6% (7-11), Indiana vs. Syracuse, CH, 1987
57.1% (8-14), Nevada-Las Vegas vs. Duke, CH, 1990
53.3% (8-15), Indiana vs. Duke, NSF, 1992
41.7% (10-24), Oklahoma vs. Kansas, CH, 1988

Lowest Three-Point Field-Goal Percentage
9.1% (1-11), Duke vs. Nevada-Las Vegas, CH, 1990
9.1% (1-11), Michigan vs. Duke, CH, 1992
16.7% (3-18), North Caro. vs. Kansas, NSF, 1991
21.4% (3-14), Duke vs. Kansas, NSF, 1988
25.0% (4-16), Duke vs. Seton Hall, NSF, 1989
25.0% (2-8), Illinois vs. Michigan, NSF, 1989

Most Free Throws
37, *St. Joseph's (Pa.) vs. Utah, N3d, 1961 (4 ot)
37, Jacksonville vs. St. Bonaventure, NSF, 1970
34, DePaul vs. Pennsylvania, N3d, 1979
34, Virginia vs. Louisiana St., N3d, 1981
33, North Caro. vs. Louisville, N3d, 1972

Fewest Free Throws
1, Nevada-Las Vegas vs. North Caro., NSF, 1977
2, Dartmouth vs. Utah, CH, 1944 (ot)
2, DePaul vs. Indiana St., NSF, 1979
3, Indiana vs. UCLA, NSF, 1973
4, Dartmouth vs. Stanford, CH, 1942
4, Kansas vs. Duke, CH, 1991

Most Free Throws Attempted
45, Jacksonville vs. St. Bonaventure, NSF, 1970
44, Bradley vs. La Salle, CH, 1954
44, UCLA vs. Drake, NSF, 1969
44, North Caro. vs. Louisville, N3d, 1972
44, Syracuse vs. Providence, NSF, 1987

Fewest Free Throws Attempted
5, Dartmouth vs. Utah, CH, 1944 (ot)
5, Dartmouth vs. Stanford, CH, 1942
5, Nevada-Las Vegas vs. North Caro., NSF, 1977
5, DePaul vs. Indiana St., NSF, 1979
6, Indiana vs. UCLA, NSF, 1973

Highest Free-Throw Percentage (minimum 15 FTM)
93.8% (15-16), Ohio St. vs. Cincinnati, CH, 1961 (ot)
92.0% (23-25), Marquette vs. North Caro., CH, 1977
90.5% (19-21), Ohio St. vs. New York U., NSF, 1945 (ot)
90.5% (19-21), Duke vs. Louisville, CH, 1986
88.9% (16-18), *UCLA vs. Louisville, CH, 1980

Lowest Free-Throw Percentage
20.0% (1-5), Nevada-Las Vegas vs. North Caro., NSF, 1977
33.3% (5-15), Oklahoma St. vs. New York U., CH, 1945
35.3% (6-17), Temple vs. Iowa, NSF, 1956
37.5% (6-16), Houston vs. UCLA, NSF, 1967
40.0% (2-5), Dartmouth vs. Utah, CH, 1944 (ot)
40.0% (2-5), DePaul vs. Indiana St., NSF, 1979

Most Rebounds
76, Houston vs. North Caro., N3d, 1967
69, *Western Ky. vs. Villanova, NSF, 1971 (2 ot)
67, Kansas vs. Western Ky., N3d, 1971
65, Michigan St. vs. North Caro., NSF, 1957 (3 ot)
65, Utah vs. St. Joseph's (Pa.), N3d, 1961 (4 ot)

Fewest Rebounds
17, Villanova vs. Georgetown, CH, 1985
17, Georgetown vs. Villanova, CH, 1985

21, Memphis St. vs. UCLA, CH, 1973
21, DePaul vs. Indiana St., NSF, 1979
22, Georgetown vs. North Caro., CH, 1982

Largest Rebound Margin
25, Michigan St. (60) vs. San Francisco (35), N3d, 1957
24, Houston (76) vs. North Caro. (52), N3d, 1967
23, Seattle (56) vs. Kansas St. (33), NSF, 1958
23, New Mexico St. (57) vs. St. Bonaventure (34), N3d, 1970
21, UCLA (55) vs. Wichita St. (34), NSF, 1965

Most Assists
26, Louisville vs. Louisiana St., NSF, 1986
24, Nevada-Las Vegas vs. Duke, CH, 1990
23, Nevada-Las Vegas vs. Indiana, NSF, 1987
23, Michigan vs. Illinois, NSF, 1989
21, Duke vs. Nevada-Las Vegas, NSF, 1991

Most Blocked Shots
9, Kansas vs. Duke, NSF, 1988
7, Louisville vs. Duke, CH, 1986
7, Syracuse vs. Indiana, CH, 1987
7, Seton Hall vs. Duke, NSF, 1989
6, Duke vs. Indiana, NSF, 1992

Most Steals
16, Nevada-Las Vegas vs. Duke, CH, 1990
13, Duke vs. Louisville, CH, 1986
13, Oklahoma vs. Kansas, CH, 1988
11, four tied (most recent: Cincinnati vs. Michigan, NSF, 1992)

Most Personal Fouls
35, St. John's (N.Y.) vs. Kansas, CH, 1952
33, Providence vs. Syracuse, NSF, 1987
33, Indiana vs. Duke, NSF, 1992
32, Bradley vs. CCNY, CH, 1950
32, St. Bonaventure vs. Jacksonville, NSF, 1970

Fewest Personal Fouls
5, Stanford vs. Dartmouth, CH, 1942
6, Utah vs. Dartmouth, CH, 1944 (ot)
7, Dartmouth vs. Stanford, CH, 1942
8, Wisconsin vs. Pittsburgh, NSF, 1941
8, Washington St. vs. Wisconsin, CH, 1941

Most Players Disqualified
4, St. Bonaventure vs. Jacksonville, NSF, 1970
4, Syracuse vs. Louisville, N3d, 1975 (ot)
4, Pennsylvania vs. DePaul, N3d, 1979
4, Indiana vs. Duke, NSF, 1992
3, 11 tied (most recent: Kansas vs. Duke, NSF, 1986)

SINGLE GAME, TEAM AND TWO-TEAM SCORING BY HALVES

Most Points in a Half, One Team
65, UCLA vs. Wichita St., NSF, 1965 (1st)
65, Princeton vs. Wichita St., N3d, 1965 (2nd)
62, Seton Hall vs. Duke, NSF, 1989 (2nd)
58, Memphis St. vs. Providence, NSF, 1973 (2nd)
58, Houston vs. Louisville, NSF, 1983 (2nd)

Most Points in a Half, Both Teams
111, Louisville (57) vs. North Caro. (54), N3d, 1972 (2nd)
108, Princeton (65) vs. Wichita St. (43), N3d, 1965 (2nd)
106, UCLA (57) vs. Rutgers (49), N3d, 1976 (1st)
105, N.C.-Charlotte (55) vs. Nevada-Las Vegas (50), N3d, 1977 (1st)
104, Notre Dame (57) vs. Duke (47), NSF, 1978 (2nd)

Most Points at Half Time, One Team
65, UCLA vs. Wichita St. (38), NSF, 1965
57, UCLA vs. Rutgers (49), N3d, 1976

55, N.C.-Charlotte vs. Nevada-Las Vegas (50), N3d, 1977
54, Drake vs. North Caro. (45), N3d, 1969
53, six tied (most recent: Georgia Tech. vs. Nevada-Las Vegas [46], NSF, 1990)

Most Points at Half Time, Both Teams
106, UCLA (57) vs. Rutgers (49), N3d, 1976
105, N.C.-Charlotte (55) vs. Nevada-Las Vegas (50), N3d, 1977
103, UCLA (65) vs. Wichita St. (38), NSF, 1965
102, Louisville (53) vs. Cincinnati (49) N3d, 1959
100, Indiana (53) vs. Nevada-Las Vegas (47), NSF, 1987
100, Kansas (50) vs. Oklahoma (50), CH, 1988

Fewest Points in a Half, One Team
10, Villanova vs. Ohio St., NSF, 1939 (1st)
11, Oregon St. vs. Oklahoma St., NSF, 1949 (1st)
11, Kentucky vs. Georgetown, NSF, 1984 (2nd)
12, Pittsburgh vs. Wisconsin, NSF, 1941 (2nd)

13, Duquesne vs. Indiana, NSF, 1940 (1st)
13, Kentucky vs. Dartmouth, NSF, 1942 (1st)

Fewest Points in a Half, Both Teams
31, Duquesne (17) vs. Indiana (14), NSF, 1940 (2nd)
32, Pittsburgh (18) vs. Wisconsin (14), NSF, 1941 (1st)
32, Oklahoma St. (21) vs. Oregon St. (11), NSF, 1949 (1st)
34, Wisconsin (22) vs. Pittsburgh (12), NSF, 1941 (2nd)
34, Wyoming (18) vs. Georgetown (16), CH, 1943 (1st)

Fewest Points at Half Time, One Team
10, Villanova vs. Ohio St. (25), NSF, 1939
11, Oregon St. vs. Oklahoma St. (21), NSF, 1949
13, Duquesne vs. Indiana (25), NSF, 1940
13, Kentucky vs. Dartmouth (23), NSF, 1942
14, Wisconsin vs. Pittsburgh (18), NSF, 1941
14, Oklahoma St. vs. Kansas St. (37), NSF, 1951

Fewest Points at Half Time, Both Teams
32, Pittsburgh (18) vs. Wisconsin (14), NSF, 1941
32, Oklahoma St. (21) vs. Oregon St. (11), NSF, 1949

34, Wyoming (18) vs. Georgetown (16), CH, 1943
35, Ohio St. (25) vs. Villanova (10), NSF, 1939
35, Dartmouth (18) vs. Utah (17), CH, 1944

Largest Half-Time Lead
33, Michigan St. (50) vs. Pennsylvania (17), NSF, 1979
27, UCLA (65) vs. Wichita St. (38), NSF, 1965
23, Kansas St. (37) vs. Oklahoma St. (14), NSF, 1951
23, Purdue (53) vs. North Caro. (30), NSF, 1969
22, UCLA (53) vs. Houston (31), NSF, 1968

Largest Half-Time Deficit Overcome
11, Temple vs. Kansas St., H: 28-39, F: 67-57, N3d, 1958
9, Memphis St. vs. Providence, H: 40-49, F: 98-85, NSF, 1973
8, Loyola (Ill.) vs. Cincinnati, H: 21-29, F: 60-58 (ot), CH, 1963
8, Louisville vs. Louisiana St., H: 36-44, F: 88-77, NSF, 1986
7, three tied (most recent: Nevada-Las Vegas vs. Georgia Tech, H: 46-53, F:90-81, NSF, 1990)

SINGLE GAME, TWO-TEAM

Most Points
247, *St. Joseph's (Pa.) (127) vs. Utah (120), N3d, 1961 (4 ot)
200, Princeton (118) vs. Wichita St. (82), N3d, 1965
200, Nevada-Las Vegas (106) vs. N.C.-Charlotte (94), N3d, 1977
198, UCLA (106) vs. Rutgers (92), N3d, 1976
197, UCLA (108) vs. Wichita St. (89), NSF, 1965
196, North Caro. (105) vs. Louisville (91), N3d, 1972
190, Michigan (100) vs. Kansas St. (90), N3d, 1964
190, Indiana (97) vs. Nevada-Las Vegas (93), NSF, 1987
189, DePaul (96) vs. Pennsylvania (93), N3d, 1979
188, Drake (104) vs. North Caro. (84), N3d, 1969

Most Field Goals
95, Utah (50) vs. *St. Joseph's (Pa.) (45), N3d, 1961 (4 ot)
83, Nevada-Las Vegas (47) vs. N.C.-Charlotte (36), N3d, 1977
82, UCLA (44) vs. Rutgers (38), N3d, 1976
80, UCLA (44) vs. Wichita St. (36), NSF, 1965
79, Memphis St. (41) vs. Providence (38), NSF, 1973

Most Field Goals Attempted
204, Utah (103) vs. *St. Joseph's (Pa.) (101), N3d, 1961 (4 ot)
180, Rutgers (100) vs. UCLA (80), N3d, 1976
178, *Western Ky. (105) vs. *Villanova (73), NSF, 1971 (2 ot)
172, Houston (95) vs. Ohio St. (77), 1968
169, North Caro. (89) vs. Michigan St. (80), NSF, 1957 (3 ot)

Most Three-Point Field Goals
18, Nevada-Las Vegas (10) vs. Georgia Tech (8), NSF, 1990
15, Nevada-Las Vegas (13) vs. Indiana (2), NSF, 1987
15, Indiana (8) vs. Duke (7), NSF, 1992
14, Oklahoma (10) vs. Kansas (4), CH, 1988
13, Seton Hall (7) vs. Michigan (6), CH, 1989 (ot)
13, Kansas (7) vs. Duke (6), CH, 1991

Most Three-Point Field Goals Attempted
39, Nevada-Las Vegas (35) vs. Indiana (4), NSF, 1987
39, Seton Hall (23) vs. Michigan (16), CH, 1989 (ot)
37, Arizona (23) vs. Oklahoma (14), NSF, 1988
36, Georgia Tech (21) vs. Nevada-Las Vegas (15), NSF, 1990
32, North Caro. (18) vs. Kansas (14), NSF, 1991

Most Free Throws
60, North Caro. (33) vs. Louisville (27), N3d, 1972
57, *St. Joseph's (Pa.) (37) vs. Utah (20), N3d, 1961 (4 ot)
53, Indiana (30) vs. Louisiana St. (23), NSF, 1953
52, Jacksonville (37) vs. St. Bonaventure (15), NSF, 1970
51, Colorado (29) vs. Iowa (22), N3d, 1955

Most Free Throws Attempted
81, North Caro. (44) vs. Louisville (37), N3d, 1972
76, *St. Joseph's (Pa.) (42) vs. Utah (34), N3d, 1961 (4 ot)
70, Kentucky (38) vs. Syracuse (32), NSF, 1975
68, Bradley (44) vs. La Salle (24), CH, 1954
68, UCLA (44) vs. Drake (24), NSF, 1969
68, Florida St. (43) vs. North Caro. (25), NSF, 1972

Most Rebounds
128, Houston (76) vs. North Caro. (52), N3d, 1967
128, Utah (65) vs. *St. Joseph's (Pa.) (63), N3d, 1961 (4 ot)
123, *Western Ky. (69) vs. *Villanova (54), NSF, 1971 (2 ot)
123, Kansas (67) vs. *Western Ky. (56), N3d, 1971
119, Michigan St. (65) vs. North Caro. (54), NSF, 1957 (3 ot)
112, Ohio St. (58) vs. Houston (54), N3d, 1968
111, UCLA (57) vs. Houston (54), NSF, 1968
110, UCLA (57) vs. Rutgers (53), N3d, 1976
109, UCLA (61) vs. Purdue (48), CH, 1969
105, Temple (54) vs. Kansas St. (51), N3d, 1958
105, UCLA (54) vs. Dayton (51), CH, 1967

Most Assists
   39, Houston (20) vs. Georgetown (19), CH, 1984
   39, Louisville (26) vs. Louisiana St. (13), NSF, 1986
   39, Nevada-Las Vegas (23) vs. Indiana (16), NSF, 1987
   37, Michigan (23) vs. Illinois (14), NSF, 1989
   36, Oklahoma (19) vs. Kansas (17), CH, 1988

Most Blocked Shots
   14, Kansas (9) vs. Duke (5), NSF, 1988
   11, Seton Hall (7) vs. Duke (4), NSF, 1989
   10, Syracuse (7) vs. Indiana (3), CH, 1987
   9, Duke (6) vs. Indiana (3), NSF, 1992
   8, Duke (4) vs. Nevada-Las Vegas (4), NSF, 1991

Most Steals
   24, Oklahoma (13) vs. Kansas (11), CH, 1988
   21, Nevada-Las Vegas (16) vs. Duke (5), CH, 1990
   18, Duke (13) vs. Louisville (5), NSF, 1986
   18, Providence (11) vs. Syracuse (7), NSF, 1987
   17, three tied (most recent: two in 1992)

Most Personal Fouls
   61, Kentucky (31) vs. Syracuse (30), NSF, 1975
   57, Oklahoma St. (36) vs. Kentucky (21), CH, 1949
   55, Louisville (31) vs. North Caro. (24), N3d, 1972
   53, St. Bonaventure (32) vs. Jacksonville (21), NSF, 1970
   53, Pennsylvania (31) vs. Michigan St. (22), NSF, 1979
   53, Pennsylvania (31) vs. DePaul (22), N3d, 1979

Most Players Disqualified
   6, CCNY (3) vs. North Caro. St. (3), NSF, 1950
   6, Pennsylvania (4) vs. DePaul (2), N3d, 1979
   6, Louisiana St. (4) vs. Virginia (2), 1981
   5, four tied [most recent: Indiana (4) vs. Duke (1), NSF, 1992]

CH—National championship game.
NSF—National semifinal game.
N3d—National third-place game.
*Record later vacated.

TOURNAMENT TRIVIA QUESTION...
What are the only two schools west of the Mississippi River to win the national championship since UCLA's last title in 1975? Answer: Kansas (1988) and Nevada-Las Vegas (1990).

CHAMPIONSHIP GAME
SINGLE GAME, INDIVIDUAL

Most Points
44, Bill Walton, UCLA vs. Memphis St., 1973
42, Gail Goodrich, UCLA vs. Michigan, 1965
41, Jack Givens, Kentucky vs. Duke, 1978
37, Lew Alcindor, UCLA vs. Purdue, 1969
35, John Morton, Seton Hall vs. Michigan, 1989 (ot)
34, Lew Alcindor, UCLA vs. North Caro., 1968
34, Kevin Grevey, Kentucky vs. UCLA, 1975

Most Field Goals
21, Bill Walton, UCLA vs. Memphis St., 1973
18, Jack Givens, Kentucky vs. Duke, 1978
15, Lew Alcindor, UCLA vs. North Caro., 1968
15, Lew Alcindor, UCLA vs. Purdue, 1969
13, four tied (most recent: Danny Manning, Kansas vs. Oklahoma, 1988)

Most Field Goals Attempted
36, Rick Mount, Purdue vs. UCLA, 1969
32, Elgin Baylor, Seattle vs. Kentucky, 1958
30, Kevin Grevey, Kentucky vs. UCLA, 1975
29, Bill Spivey, Kentucky vs. Kansas St., 1951
29, Artis Gilmore, Jacksonville vs. UCLA, 1970

Highest Field-Goal Percentage (minimum 10 FGM)
95.5% (21-22), Bill Walton, UCLA vs. Memphis St., 1973
76.5% (13-17), James Worthy, North Caro. vs. Georgetown, 1982
75.0% (15-20), Lew Alcindor, UCLA vs. Purdue, 1969
75.0% (12-16), Anderson Hunt, Nevada-Las Vegas vs. Duke, 1990
72.2% (13-18), Steve Patterson, UCLA vs. Villanova, 1971

Most Three-Point Field Goals
7, Steve Alford, Indiana vs. Syracuse, 1987
7, Dave Sieger, Oklahoma vs. Kansas, 1988
5, Glen Rice, Michigan vs. Seton Hall, 1989 (ot)
4, John Morton, Seton Hall vs. Michigan, 1989 (ot)
4, Anderson Hunt, Nevada-Las Vegas vs. Duke, 1990
4, Terry Brown, Kansas vs. Duke, 1991

Most Three-Point Field Goals Attempted
13, Dave Sieger, Oklahoma vs. Kansas, 1988
12, Glen Rice, Michigan vs. Seton Hall, 1989 (ot)
12, John Morton, Seton Hall vs. Michigan, 1989 (ot)
11, Terry Brown, Kansas vs. Duke, 1991
10, Steve Alford, Indiana vs. Syracuse, 1987

Highest Three-Point Field-Goal Percentage (minimum 5 3FGM)
70.0% (7-10), Steve Alford, Indiana vs. Syracuse, 1987
53.8% (7-13), Dave Sieger, Oklahoma vs. Kansas, 1988
41.7% (5-12), Glen Rice, Michigan vs. Seton Hall, 1989 (ot)

(Note: Only ones to meet minimum.)

Most Free Throws
18, Gail Goodrich, UCLA vs. Michigan, 1965
12, Vern Hatton, Kentucky vs. Seattle, 1958
12, Christian Laettner, Duke vs. Kansas, 1991
11, Larry Finch, Memphis St. vs. UCLA, 1973
11, Wilt Chamberlain, Kansas vs. North Caro., 1957 (3 ot)
11, Dick Estergard, Bradley vs. La Salle, 1954

Most Free Throws Attempted
20, Gail Goodrich, UCLA vs. Michigan, 1965
17, Bob Carney, Bradley vs. La Salle, 1954
16, Wilt Chamberlain, Kansas vs. North Caro., 1957 (3 ot)
15, Vern Hatton, Kentucky vs. Seattle, 1958
14, Ed Warner, CCNY vs. Bradley, 1950

Highest Free-Throw Percentage (minimum 10 FTM)
100.0% (12-12), Christian Laettner, Duke vs. Kansas, 1991
91.7% (11-12), Dick Estergard, Bradley vs. La Salle, 1954
90.0% (18-20), Gail Goodrich, UCLA vs. Michigan, 1965
84.6% (11-13), Larry Finch, Memphis St. vs. UCLA, 1973
83.3% (10-12), three tied (most recent: Eugene Banks, Duke vs. Kentucky, 1978)

Most Rebounds
27, Bill Russell, San Francisco vs. Iowa, 1956
21, Bill Spivey, Kentucky vs. Kansas St., 1951
20, Lew Alcindor, UCLA vs. Purdue, 1969
20, Bill Walton, UCLA vs. Florida St., 1972
19, three tied (most recent: Derrick Coleman, Syracuse vs. Indiana, 1987)

Most Assists
11, Rumeal Robinson, Michigan vs. Seton Hall, 1989 (ot)
9, Alvin Franklin, Houston vs. Georgetown, 1984
9, Michael Jackson, Georgetown vs. Villanova, 1985
9, Bobby Hurley, Duke vs. Kansas, 1991
7, seven tied (most recent: Bobby Hurley, Duke vs. Michigan, 1992)

Most Blocked Shots
3, Rony Seikaly, Syracuse vs. Indiana, 1987
3, Derrick Coleman, Syracuse vs. Indiana, 1987
3, Dean Garrett, Indiana vs. Syracuse, 1987
3, Terry Mills, Michigan vs. Seton Hall, 1989 (ot)
2, 11 tied (most recent: two in 1992)

Most Steals
7, Tommy Amaker, Duke vs. Louisville, 1986
7, Mookie Blaylock, Oklahoma vs. Kansas, 1988
5, Danny Manning, Kansas vs. Oklahoma, 1988
5, Greg Anthony, Nevada-Las Vegas vs. Duke, 1990
4, Larry Johnson, Nevada-Las Vegas vs. Duke, 1990
4, Alonzo Jamison, Kansas vs. Duke, 1991

SINGLE GAME, TEAM

Most Points
103, Nevada-Las Vegas vs. Duke (73), 1990
98, UCLA vs. Duke (83), 1964
94, Kentucky vs. Duke (88), 1978
92, La Salle vs. Bradley (76), 1954
92, UCLA vs. Purdue (72), 1969
92, UCLA vs. Kentucky (85), 1975

Fewest Points
33, Ohio St. vs. Oregon (46), 1939
34, Washington St. vs. Wisconsin (39), 1941
34, Georgetown vs. Wyoming (46), 1943
36, Oklahoma St. vs. Kentucky (46) 1949
38, Dartmouth vs. Stanford (53), 1942

Largest Winning Margin
30, Nevada-Las Vegas (103) vs. Duke (73), 1990
23, UCLA (78) vs. North Caro.(55), 1968
21, UCLA (87) vs. Memphis St. (66), 1973
20, Ohio St. (75) vs. California (55), 1960
20, UCLA (92) vs. Purdue (72), 1969
20, Duke (71) vs. Michigan (51), 1992

Smallest Winning Margin
1, Indiana (69) vs. Kansas (68), 1953
1, North Caro. (54) vs. Kansas (53), 1957 (3 ot)
1, California (71) vs. West Va. (70), 1959
1, North Caro. (63) vs. Georgetown (62), 1982
1, Indiana (74) vs. Syracuse (73), 1987
1, Michigan (80) vs. Seton Hall (79), 1989 (ot)

Most Points Scored by Losing Team
88, Duke vs. Kentucky (94), 1978
85, Kentucky vs. UCLA (92), 1975
83, Duke vs. UCLA (98), 1964
80, Michigan vs. UCLA (91), 1965
79, Oklahoma vs. Kansas (83), 1988
79, Seton Hall vs. Michigan (80), 1989 (ot)

Most Field Goals
41, Nevada-Las Vegas vs. Duke, 1990
40, UCLA vs. Memphis St., 1973
39, Kentucky vs. Duke, 1978
38, UCLA vs. Kentucky, 1975
37, La Salle vs. Bradley, 1954

Fewest Field Goals
9, Oklahoma St. vs. Kentucky, 1949
13, North Caro. vs. Oklahoma St., 1946
14, Ohio St. vs. Oregon, 1939
14, Washington St. vs. Wisconsin, 1941
14, Georgetown vs. Wyoming, 1943

Most Field Goals Attempted
92, Purdue vs. UCLA, 1969
87, San Francisco vs. Iowa, 1956
86, Kentucky vs. UCLA, 1975
84, Loyola (Ill.) vs. Cincinnati, 1963 (ot)
80, Kansas St. vs. Kentucky, 1951
80, Jacksonville vs. UCLA, 1970

Fewest Field Goals Attempted
28, Villanova vs. Georgetown, 1985
41, Duke vs. Kansas, 1991
43, Michigan St. vs. Indiana St., 1979
46, Ohio St. vs. California, 1960
46, North Caro. St. vs. Marquette, 1974
47, three tied (most recent: North Caro. vs. Georgetown, 1982)

Highest Field-Goal Percentage
78.6% (22-28), Villanova vs. Georgetown, 1985
67.4% (31-46), Ohio St. vs. California, 1960
64.5% (40-62), UCLA vs. Memphis St., 1973
63.6% (35-55), Kansas vs. Oklahoma, 1988
61.2% (41-67), Nevada-Las Vegas vs. Duke, 1990

Lowest Field-Goal Percentage
21.5% (14-65), Washington St. vs. Wisconsin, 1941
23.4% (15-64), Baylor vs. Kentucky, 1948
25.4% (16-63), Wisconsin vs. Washington St., 1941
27.4% (23-84), Loyola (Ill.) vs. Cincinnati, 1963 (ot)
28.8% (23-80), Kansas St. vs. Kentucky, 1951

Most Three-Point Field Goals
10, Oklahoma vs. Kansas, 1988
8, Nevada-Las Vegas vs. Duke, 1990
7, Indiana vs. Syracuse, 1987
7, Seton Hall vs. Michigan, 1989 (ot)
7, Kansas vs. Duke, 1991

Fewest Three-Point Field Goals
1, Duke vs. Nevada-Las Vegas, 1990
1, Michigan vs. Duke, 1992
4, Syracuse vs. Indiana, 1987

4, Kansas vs. Oklahoma, 1988
6, Michigan vs. Seton Hall, 1989 (ot)
6, Duke vs. Kansas, 1991

Most Three-Point Field Goals Attempted
24, Oklahoma vs. Kansas, 1988
23, Seton Hall vs. Michigan, 1989 (ot)
18, Kansas vs. Duke, 1991
16, Michigan vs. Seton Hall, 1989 (ot)
14, Nevada-Las Vegas vs. Duke, 1990

Fewest Three-Point Field Goals Attempted
6, Kansas vs. Oklahoma, 1988
9, Duke vs. Michigan, 1992
10, Syracuse vs. Indiana, 1987
10, Duke vs. Kansas, 1991
11, Indiana vs. Syracuse, 1987
11, Duke vs. Nevada-Las Vegas, 1990

Highest Three-Point Field-Goal Percentage (minimum 7 3FGM)
63.6% (7-11), Indiana vs. Syracuse, 1987
57.1% (8-14), Nevada-Las Vegas vs. Duke, 1990
41.7% (10-24), Oklahoma vs. Kansas, 1988
38.9% (7-18), Kansas vs. Duke, 1991
30.4% (7-23), Seton Hall vs. Michigan, 1989 (ot)

Lowest Three-Point Field-Goal Percentage
9.1% (1-11), Duke vs. Nevada-Las Vegas, 1990
9.1% (1-11), Michigan vs. Duke, 1992
30.4% (7-23), Seton Hall vs. Michigan, 1989 (ot)
37.5% (6-16), Michigan vs. Seton Hall, 1989 (ot)
38.9% (7-18), Kansas vs. Duke, 1991

Most Free Throws
32, Bradley vs. La Salle, 1954
30, Duke vs. Kentucky, 1978
28, UTEP vs. Kentucky, 1966
28, UCLA vs. Purdue, 1969
26, Kansas vs. Indiana, 1953
26, UCLA vs. Duke, 1964

Fewest Free Throws
2, Dartmouth vs. Utah, 1944 (ot)
4, Dartmouth vs. Stanford, 1942
4, Kansas vs. Duke, 1991
5, Ohio St. vs. Oregon, 1939
5, Stanford vs. Dartmouth, 1942
5, Oklahoma St. vs. New York U., 1945

Most Free Throws Attempted
44, Bradley vs. La Salle, 1954
41, UCLA vs. Purdue, 1969
36, Kentucky vs. Seattle, 1958
35, CCNY vs. Bradley, 1950
35, UCLA vs. Jacksonville, 1970

Fewest Free Throws Attempted
5, Dartmouth vs. Utah, 1944 (ot)
5, Dartmouth vs. Stanford, 1942
8, Stanford vs. Dartmouth, 1942
8, Jacksonville vs. UCLA, 1970
8, Georgetown vs. Villanova, 1985
8, Kansas vs. Duke, 1991

Highest Free-Throw Percentage (minimum 15 FTM)
93.8% (15-16), Ohio St. vs. Cincinnati, 1961 (ot)
92.0% (23-25), Marquette vs. North Caro., 1977
90.5% (19-21), Duke vs. Louisville, 1986
88.9% (16-18), *UCLA vs. Louisville, 1980
88.2% (30-34), Duke vs. Kentucky, 1978

Lowest Free-Throw Percentage
33.3% (5-15), Oklahoma St. vs. New York U., 1945
40.0% (2-5), Dartmouth vs. Utah, 1944 (ot)
44.0% (11-25), UCLA vs. Dayton, 1967
45.5% (10-22), Indiana St. vs. Michigan St., 1979
46.2% (6-13), Georgetown vs. Wyoming, 1943

Most Rebounds
61, UCLA vs. Purdue, 1969
60, San Francisco vs. Iowa, 1956

55, Kentucky vs. Seattle, 1958
55, UCLA vs. Kentucky, 1975
54, UCLA vs. Dayton, 1967

Fewest Rebounds
17, Villanova vs. Georgetown, 1985
17, Georgetown vs. Villanova, 1985
21, Memphis St. vs. UCLA, 1973
22, Georgetown vs. North Caro., 1982
27, Duke vs. Louisville, 1986

Largest Rebound Margin
19, UCLA (40) vs. Memphis St. (21), 1973
15, Kentucky (45) vs. Kansas St. (30), 1951
14, North Caro. (42) vs. Kansas (28), 1957 (3 ot)
13, UCLA (48) vs. North Caro. (35), 1968
13, UCLA (61) vs. Purdue (48), 1969
13, UCLA (53) vs. Jacksonville (40), 1970

Most Assists
24, Nevada-Las Vegas vs. Duke, 1990
20, Houston vs. Georgetown, 1984
20, Indiana vs. Syracuse, 1987
19, Georgetown vs. Houston, 1984
19, Oklahoma vs. Kansas, 1988
19, Michigan vs. Seton Hall, 1989 (ot)

Most Blocked Shots
7, Louisville vs. Duke, 1986
7, Syracuse vs. Indiana, 1987
4, Kansas vs. Oklahoma, 1988
4, Michigan vs. Seton Hall, 1989 (ot)
4, Duke vs. Michigan, 1992

Most Steals
16, Nevada-Las Vegas vs. Duke, 1990
13, Duke vs. Louisville, 1986
13, Oklahoma vs. Kansas, 1988
11, Kansas vs. Oklahoma, 1988
10, Kansas vs. Duke, 1991

Most Personal Fouls
35, St. John's (N.Y.) vs. Kansas, 1952
32, Bradley vs. CCNY, 1950
30, Purdue vs. UCLA, 1969
29, Marquette vs. North Caro. St., 1974
28, La Salle vs. Bradley, 1954
28, Kentucky vs. UCLA, 1975

Fewest Personal Fouls
5, Stanford vs. Dartmouth, 1942
6, Utah vs. Dartmouth, 1944 (ot)
7, Dartmouth vs. Stanford, 1942
8, Washington St. vs. Wisconsin, 1941
9, Oregon vs. Ohio St., 1939
9, UCLA vs. Villanova, 1971

Most Players Disqualified
3, Bradley vs. CCNY, 1950
3, Kentucky vs. Kansas St., 1951
3, Michigan vs. UCLA, 1965
3, Purdue vs. UCLA, 1969
2, 12 tied (most recent: Duke vs. Louisville, 1986)

SINGLE GAME, TEAM AND TWO-TEAM SCORING BY HALVES

Most Points in a Half, One Team
57, Indiana vs. Michigan, 1976 (2nd)
56, Nevada-Las Vegas vs. Duke, 1990 (2nd)
50, six tied (most recent: both Kansas and Oklahoma, 1988 [1st])

Most Points in a Half, Both Teams
100, Kansas (50) vs. Oklahoma (50), 1988 (1st)
99, Duke (50) vs. Kentucky (49), 1978 (2nd)
94, UCLA (49) vs. Kentucky (45), 1975 (2nd)
94, Nevada-Las Vegas (56) vs. Duke (38), 1990

Most Points at Half Time, One Team
50, UCLA vs. Duke (38), 1964
50, UCLA vs. Purdue (41), 1969
50, UCLA vs. Florida St. (39), 1972
50, Kansas vs. Oklahoma (50), 1988
50, Oklahoma vs. Kansas (50), 1988

Most Points at Half Time, Both Teams
100, Kansas (50) vs. Oklahoma (50), 1988
91, UCLA (50) vs. Purdue (41), 1969
89, UCLA (50) vs. Florida St. (39), 1972

Fewest Points in a Half, One Team
16, Ohio St. vs. Oregon, 1939 (1st)
16, Dartmouth vs. Stanford, 1942 (1st)
16, Georgetown vs. Wyoming, 1943 (1st)
16, Oklahoma vs. Holy Cross, 1947 (2nd)

Fewest Points in a Half, Both Teams
34, Wyoming (18) vs. Georgetown (16), 1943 (1st)
35, Dartmouth (18) vs. Utah (17), 1944 (1st)
37, Oregon (21) vs. Ohio St. (16), 1939 (1st)
37, Utah (19) vs. Dartmouth (18), 1944 (2nd)

Fewest Points at Half Time, One Team
16, Ohio St. vs. Oregon (21), 1939
16, Georgetown vs. Wyoming (18), 1943
17, Utah vs. Dartmouth (18), 1944

Fewest Points at Half Time, Both Teams
34, Wyoming (18) vs. Georgetown (16), 1943
35, Dartmouth (18) vs. Utah (17), 1944
37, Oregon (21) vs. Ohio St. (16), 1939

Largest Half-Time Lead
18, Ohio St. (37) vs. California (19), 1960
18, UCLA (38) vs. Dayton (20), 1967
14, Kansas (41) vs. St. John's (N.Y.) (27), 1952

Largest Half-Time Deficit Overcome
8, Loyola (Ill.) vs. Cincinnati, H: 21-29, F: 60-58 (ot), 1963
6, Indiana vs. Michigan, H: 29-35, F: 86-68, 1976
3, three tied (most recent: Louisville vs. Duke, H: 34-37, F: 72-69, 1986)

OVERTIME GAMES

Most Overtime Periods
3, North Caro. (54) vs. Kansas (53), 1957
1, Utah (42) vs. Dartmouth (40), 1944

1, Cincinnati (70) vs. Ohio St. (65), 1961
1, Loyola (Ill.) (60) vs. Cincinnati (58), 1963
1, Michigan (80) vs. Seton Hall (79), 1989

SINGLE GAME, TWO-TEAM

Most Points
182, Kentucky (94) vs. Duke (88), 1978
181, UCLA (98) vs. Duke (83), 1964
177, UCLA (92) vs. Kentucky (85), 1975
176, Nevada-Las Vegas (103) vs. Duke (73), 1990
171, UCLA (91) vs. Michigan (80), 1965

Fewest Points
73, Washington St. (34) vs. Wisconsin (39), 1941
79, Ohio St. (33) vs. Oregon (46), 1939
80, Georgetown (34) vs. Wyoming (46), 1943
82, Dartmouth (40) vs. Utah (42), 1944 (ot)
82, Oklahoma St. (36) vs. Kentucky (46), 1949

Most Field Goals
   71, UCLA (38) vs. Kentucky (33), 1975
   68, UCLA (36) vs. Duke (32), 1964
   68, Kentucky (39) vs. Duke (29), 1978
   67, UCLA (36) vs. Florida St. (31), 1972
   67, Nevada-Las Vegas (41) vs. Duke (26), 1990

Most Field Goals Attempted
   167, San Francisco (87) vs. Iowa (80), 1956
   164, Kentucky (86) vs. UCLA (78), 1975
   151, San Francisco (83) vs. La Salle (68), 1955
   150, Purdue (92) vs. UCLA (58), 1969
   149, Kansas St. (80) vs. Kentucky (69), 1951

Most Three-Point Field Goals
   14, Oklahoma (10) vs. Kansas (4), 1988
   13, Seton Hall (7) vs. Michigan (6), 1989 (ot)
   13, Kansas (7) vs. Duke (6), 1991
   11, Indiana (7) vs. Syracuse (4), 1987

Most Three-Point Field Goals Attempted
   39, Seton Hall (23) vs. Michigan (16), 1989 (ot)
   30, Oklahoma (24) vs. Kansas (6), 1988
   28, Kansas (18) vs. Duke (10), 1991
   25, Nevada-Las Vegas (14) vs. Duke (11), 1990
   21, Indiana (11) vs. Syracuse (10), 1987

Most Free Throws
   50, Bradley (32) vs. La Salle (18), 1954
   46, Kentucky (24) vs. Seattle (22), 1958
   46, UCLA (28) vs. Purdue (18), 1969
   46, Duke (30) vs. Kentucky (16), 1978
   45, Kansas (26) vs. Indiana (19), 1953
   45, UCLA (26) vs. Duke (19), 1964

Most Free Throws Attempted
   68, Bradley (44) vs. La Salle (24), 1954
   66, Kentucky (36) vs. Seattle (30), 1958
   65, UCLA (41) vs. Purdue (24), 1969
   61, Kansas (33) vs. Indiana (28), 1953
   60, UCLA (32) vs. Duke (28), 1964

Most Rebounds
   109, UCLA (61) vs. Purdue (48), 1969
   108, San Francisco (60) vs. Iowa (48), 1956
   105, UCLA (54) vs. Dayton (51), 1967
   104, UCLA (55) vs. Kentucky (49), 1975
   101, Kentucky (55) vs. Seattle (46), 1958

Most Assists
   39, Houston (20) vs. Georgetown (19), 1984
   36, Oklahoma (19) vs. Kansas (17), 1988
   35, Nevada-Las Vegas (24) vs. Duke (11), 1990
   34, Indiana (20) vs. Syracuse (14), 1987
   33, Michigan (19) vs. Seton Hall (14), 1989 (ot)

Most Blocked Shots
   10, Syracuse (7) vs. Indiana (3), 1987
   7, Louisville (7) vs. Duke (0), 1986
   7, Kansas (4) vs. Oklahoma (3), 1988
   7, Duke (4) vs. Michigan (3), 1992
   6, Michigan (4) vs. Seton Hall (2), 1989 (ot)
   6, Nevada-Las Vegas (3) vs. Duke (3), 1990

Most Steals
   24, Oklahoma (13) vs. Kansas (11), 1988
   21, Nevada-Las Vegas (16) vs. Duke (5), 1990
   18, Duke (13) vs. Louisville (5), 1986
   17, Duke (9) vs. Michigan (8), 1992
   16, Kansas (10) vs. Duke (6), 1991

Most Personal Fouls
   57, Oklahoma St. (36) vs. Kentucky (21), 1949
   49, Bradley (32) vs. CCNY (17), 1950
   49, UCLA (25) vs. Duke (24), 1964
   49, Purdue (30) vs. UCLA (19), 1969
   48, Kentucky (26) vs. Duke (22), 1978

Most Players Disqualified
   4, Bradley (3) vs. CCNY (1), 1950
   4, Kentucky (3) vs. Kansas St. (1), 1951
   3, seven tied [most recent: North Caro. (2) vs.
      Indiana (1), 1981]
*Record later vacated.

TOURNAMENT TRIVIA QUESTION...
At the NCAA Final Four, have two teams from the same state ever played each other in the championship game? Answer: Yes, Cincinnati defeated Ohio State in both 1961 and 1962.

FINAL FOUR SEMIFINALS
SINGLE GAME, INDIVIDUAL

Most Points
39, Al Wood, North Caro. vs. Virginia, 1981
38, Jerry West, West Va., vs. Louisville, 1959
38, Jerry Chambers, Utah vs. UTEP, 1966
38, Freddie Banks, Nevada-Las Vegas vs. Indiana, 1987
36, four tied (most recent: Rick Mount, Purdue vs. North Caro., 1969)

Most Field Goals
16, Don May, Dayton vs. North Caro., 1967
16, Larry Bird, Indiana St. vs. DePaul, 1979
15, Ernie DiGregorio, Providence vs. Memphis St., 1973
14, eight tied (most recent: Armon Gilliam, Nevada-Las Vegas vs. Indiana, 1987)

Most Field Goals Attempted
42, Lennie Rosenbluth, North Caro. vs. Michigan St., 1957 (3 ot)
36, Ernie DiGregorio, Providence vs. Memphis St., 1973
33, *Jerry Dunn, Western Ky. vs. Villanova, 1971 (2 ot)
31, Billy McGill, Utah vs. Cincinnati, 1961
31, Jerry Chambers, Utah vs. UTEP, 1966
31, Elvin Hayes, Houston vs. UCLA, 1967

Highest Field-Goal Percentage (minimum 10 FGM)
91.7% (11-12), Bill Walton, UCLA vs. Louisville, 1972
90.9% (10-11), Jerry Lucas, Ohio St. vs. St. Joseph's (Pa.), 1961
90.9% (10-11), Billy Thompson, Louisville vs. Louisiana St., 1986
84.2% (16-19), Larry Bird, Indiana St. vs. DePaul, 1979
83.3% (10-12), Sidney Wicks, UCLA vs. New Mexico St., 1970

Most Three-Point Field Goals
10, Freddie Banks, Nevada-Las Vegas vs. Indiana, 1987
7, Dennis Scott, Georgia Tech vs. Nevada-Las Vegas, 1990
6, Bobby Hurley, Duke vs. Indiana, 1992
5, Anderson Hunt, Nevada-Las Vegas vs. Georgia Tech, 1990
4, three tied (most recent: Anderson Hunt, Nevada-Las Vegas vs. Duke, 1991)

Most Three-Point Field Goals Attempted
19, Freddie Banks, Nevada-Las Vegas vs. Indiana, 1987
14, Dennis Scott, Georgia Tech vs. Nevada-Las Vegas, 1990
12, Steve Kerr, Arizona vs. Oklahoma, 1988
11, Anderson Hunt, Nevada-Las Vegas vs. Duke, 1991
9, three tied (most recent: Bobby Hurley, Duke vs. Indiana, 1992)

Highest Three-Point Field-Goal Percentage (minimum 5 3FGM)
66.7% (6-9), Bobby Hurley, Duke vs. Indiana, 1992
55.5% (5-9), Anderson Hunt, Nevada-Las Vegas vs. Georgia Tech, 1990
52.6% (10-19), Freddie Banks, Nevada-Las Vegas vs. Indiana, 1987
50.0% (7-14), Dennis Scott, Georgia Tech vs. Nevada-Las Vegas, 1990
(Note: Only ones to meet minimum.)

Most Free Throws
14, Jerry West, West Va. vs. Louisville, 1959
13, Don Schlundt, Indiana vs. Louisiana St., 1953
12, Jim Spanarkel, Duke vs. Notre Dame, 1978
12, Paul Hogue, Cincinnati vs. UCLA, 1962
11, five tied (most recent: Steve Alford, Indiana vs. Nevada-Las Vegas, 1987)

Most Free Throws Attempted
20, Jerry West, West Va. vs. Louisville, 1959
18, Bob Pettit, Louisiana St. vs. Indiana, 1953
17, Don Schlundt, Indiana vs. Louisiana St., 1953
17, Paul Hogue, Cincinnati vs. UCLA, 1962
16, Lew Alcindor, UCLA vs. Drake, 1969

Highest Free-Throw Percentage (minimum 10 FTM)
100.0% (12-12), Jim Spanarkel, Duke vs. Notre Dame, 1978
100.0% (10-10), Ron King, Florida St. vs. North Caro., 1972
91.7% (11-12), Bill Walton, UCLA vs. Louisville, 1972
91.7% (11-12), Earvin "Magic" Johnson, Michigan St. vs. Pennsylvania, 1979
90.9% (10-11), Johnny Cox, Kentucky vs. Temple, 1958

Most Rebounds
24, Elvin Hayes, Houston vs. UCLA, 1967
23, Bill Russell, San Francisco vs. Southern Methodist, 1956
22, Elgin Baylor, Seattle vs. Kansas St., 1958
22, Tom Sanders, New York U. vs. Ohio St., 1960
22, Larry Kenon, Memphis St. vs. Providence, 1973
22, Akeem Olajuwon, Houston vs. Louisville, 1983

Most Assists
18, Mark Wade, Nevada-Las Vegas vs. Indiana, 1987
12, Rumeal Robinson, Michigan vs. Illinois, 1989
11, Michael Jackson, Georgetown vs. St. John's (N.Y.), 1985
11, Milt Wagner, Louisville vs. Louisiana St., 1986
8, four tied (most recent: Jamal Meeks, Indiana vs. Duke, 1992)

Most Blocked Shots
6, Danny Manning, Kansas vs. Duke, 1988
3, Greg Dreiling, Kansas vs. Duke, 1986
3, Armon Gilliam, Nevada-Las Vegas vs. Indiana, 1987
3, Oliver Miller, Arkansas vs. Duke, 1990
3, Alan Henderson, Indiana vs. Duke, 1992
3, Grant Hill, Duke vs. Indiana, 1992

Most Steals
4, Mark Alarie, Duke vs. Kansas, 1986
4, Mark Wade, Nevada-Las Vegas vs. Indiana, 1987
4, Ernie Lewis, Providence vs. Syracuse, 1987
4, Danny Manning, Kansas vs. Duke, 1988
4, Nick Van Exel, Cincinnati vs. Michigan, 1992

SINGLE GAME, TEAM

Most Points
108, UCLA vs. Wichita St. (89), 1965
101, UCLA vs. Houston (69), 1968
101, Michigan St. vs. Pennsylvania (67), 1979
98, Memphis St. vs. Providence (85), 1973
97, Indiana vs. Nevada-Las Vegas (93), 1987
97, Duke vs. Arkansas (83), 1990

Fewest Points
28, Kentucky vs. Dartmouth (47), 1942
30, Duquesne vs. Indiana (39), 1940
30, Pittsburgh vs. Wisconsin (36), 1941
30, Oregon St. vs. Oklahoma St. (55), 1949
31, Iowa St. vs. Utah (40), 1944

Largest Winning Margin
34, Cincinnati (80) vs. Oregon St. (46), 1963
34, Michigan St. (101) vs. Pennsylvania (67), 1979
32, UCLA (101) vs. Houston (69), 1968
29, Kentucky (76) vs. Illinois (47), 1949
27, Oklahoma St. (68) vs. Arkansas (41), 1945
27, Purdue (92) vs. North Caro. (65), 1969

Smallest Winning Margin
1, Kansas (43) vs. Southern Cal (42), 1940
1, Oklahoma (55) vs. Texas (54), 1947
1, Kentucky (61) vs. Temple (60), 1958
1, UCLA (75) vs. Louisville (74), 1975 (ot)
1, North Caro. (84) vs. Nevada-Las Vegas (83), 1977

Most Points Scored by Losing Team
93, Nevada-Las Vegas vs. Indiana (97), 1987
89, Wichita St. vs. UCLA (108), 1965
89, *Western Ky. vs. Villanova (92), 1971 (2 ot)
86, Notre Dame vs. Duke (90), 1978
85, Providence vs. Memphis St. (98), 1973

Most Field Goals
44, UCLA vs. Wichita St., 1965
43, UCLA vs. Houston, 1968
41, Memphis St. vs. Providence, 1973
41, Nevada-Las Vegas vs. North Caro., 1977
39, *Western Ky. vs. Villanova, 1971 (2 ot)

Fewest Field Goals
10, Wisconsin vs. Pittsburgh, 1941
10, Kentucky vs. Dartmouth, 1942
11, Duquesne vs. Indiana, 1940
11, Oregon St. vs. Oklahoma St., 1949
13, four tied (most recent: Kentucky vs. Georgetown, 1984)

Most Field Goals Attempted
105, *Western Ky. vs. Villanova, 1971 (2 ot)
91, Kentucky vs. Illinois, 1951
89, North Caro. vs. Michigan St., 1957 (3 ot)
89, UCLA vs. Wichita St., 1965
83, UCLA vs. Houston, 1968
83, Drake vs. UCLA, 1969

Fewest Field Goals Attempted
38, Villanova vs. Memphis St., 1985
41, Georgetown vs. Louisville, 1982
42, Houston vs. Virginia, 1984 (ot)
42, St. John's (N.Y.) vs. Georgetown, 1985
43, N.C.-Charlotte vs. Marquette, 1977

Highest Field-Goal Percentage
63.3% (38-60), Ohio St. vs. St. Joseph's (Pa.), 1961
63.3% (38-60), Michigan St. vs. Pennsylvania, 1979
62.5% (35-56), Indiana St. vs. DePaul, 1979
61.7% (37-60), Indiana vs. Nevada-Las Vegas, 1987
59.6% (34-57), Kansas vs. San Francisco, 1957

Lowest Field-Goal Percentage
24.5% (13-53), Kentucky vs. Georgetown, 1984
28.2% (22-78), Houston vs. UCLA, 1968
28.4% (21-74), New York U. vs. Ohio St., 1960

28.8% (23-80), Michigan St. vs. North Caro., 1957 (3 ot)
28.8% (17-59), Oregon St. vs. Cincinnati, 1963

Most Three-Point Field Goals
13, Nevada-Las Vegas vs. Indiana, 1987
10, Nevada-Las Vegas vs. Georgia Tech, 1990
8, Georgia Tech vs. Nevada-Las Vegas, 1990
8, Indiana vs. Duke, 1992
7, Duke vs. Indiana, 1992

Fewest Three-Point Field Goals
2, Indiana vs. Nevada-Las Vegas, 1987
2, Kansas vs. Duke, 1988
2, Illinois vs. Michigan, 1989
3, five tied (most recent: North Caro. vs. Kansas, 1991)

Most Three-Point Field Goals Attempted
35, Nevada-Las Vegas vs. Indiana, 1987
23, Arizona vs. Oklahoma, 1988
22, Cincinnati vs. Michigan, 1992
21, Georgia Tech vs. Nevada-Las Vegas, 1990
21, Arkansas vs. Duke, 1990

Fewest Three-Point Field Goals Attempted
4, Indiana vs. Nevada-Las Vegas, 1987
4, Kansas vs. Duke, 1988
8, five tied (most recent: Michigan vs. Cincinnati, 1992)

Highest Three-Point Field-Goal Percentage (minimum 7 3FGM)
66.7% (10-15), Nevada-Las Vegas vs. Georgia Tech, 1990
63.6% (7-11), Duke vs. Indiana, 1992
53.3% (8-15), Indiana vs. Duke, 1992
38.1% (8-21), Georgia Tech vs. Nevada-Las Vegas, 1990
37.1% (13-35), Nevada-Las Vegas vs. Indiana, 1987

Lowest Three-Point Field-Goal Percentage
16.7% (3-18), North Caro. vs. Kansas, 1991
21.4% (3-14), Duke vs. Kansas, 1988
25.0% (2-8), Illinois vs. Michigan, 1989
25.0% (4-16), Duke vs. Seton Hall, 1989
26.1% (6-23), Arizona vs. Oklahoma, 1988

Most Free Throws
37, Jacksonville vs. St. Bonaventure, 1970
32, Duke vs. Notre Dame, 1978
30, Indiana vs. Louisiana St., 1953
29, UCLA vs. Drake, 1969
29, Florida St. vs. North Caro., 1972

Fewest Free Throws
1, Nevada-Las Vegas vs. North Caro., 1977
2, DePaul vs. Indiana St., 1979
3, Indiana vs. UCLA, 1973
5, Iowa St. vs. Utah, 1944
5, Marquette vs. N.C.-Charlotte, 1977
5, Virginia vs. Houston, 1984 (ot)

Most Free Throws Attempted
45, Jacksonville vs. St. Bonaventure, 1970
44, UCLA vs. Drake, 1969
44, Syracuse vs. Providence, 1987
43, Florida St. vs. North Caro., 1972
42, Duke vs. Indiana, 1992

Fewest Free Throws Attempted
5, Nevada-Las Vegas vs. North Caro., 1977
5, DePaul vs. Indiana St., 1979
6, Indiana vs. UCLA, 1973
7, Marquette vs. N.C.-Charlotte, 1977
7, Virginia vs. Houston, 1984 (ot)

Highest Free-Throw Percentage (minimum 15 FTM)
90.5% (19-21), Ohio St. vs. New York U., 1945
87.5% (21-24), Oklahoma St. vs. Oregon St., 1949

86.5% (32-37), Duke vs. Notre Dame, 1978
85.7% (18-21), Baylor vs. Bradley, 1950
85.2% (23-27), Seton Hall vs. Duke, 1989

Lowest Free-Throw Percentage
20.0% (1-5), Nevada-Las Vegas vs. North Caro., 1977
35.3% (6-17), Temple vs. Iowa, 1956
37.5% (6-16), Houston vs. UCLA, 1967
40.0% (2-5), DePaul vs. Indiana St., 1979
46.2% (6-13), Villanova vs. Ohio St., 1939
46.2% (6-13), Southern Cal vs. Kansas, 1940

Most Rebounds
69, *Western Ky. vs. Villanova, 1971 (2 ot)
65, Michigan St. vs. North Caro., 1957 (3 ot)
57, UCLA vs. Houston, 1968
57, Kentucky vs. Syracuse, 1975
56, Seattle vs. Kansas St., 1958
56, California vs. Cincinnati, 1959

Fewest Rebounds
21, DePaul vs. Indiana St., 1979
24, St. John's (N.Y.) vs. Georgetown, 1985
25, Oklahoma St. vs. Kansas St., 1951
26, five tied (most recent: Duke vs. Nevada-Las Vegas, 1991)

Largest Rebound Margin
23, Seattle (56) vs. Kansas St. (33), 1958
22, Kentucky (49) vs. Illinois (37), 1951
21, UCLA (55) vs. Wichita St. (34), 1965
20, Michigan (52) vs. Princeton (32), 1965
19, Kansas (44) vs. San Francisco (25), 1957
19, UCLA (51) vs. Louisville (32), 1972

Most Assists
26, Louisville vs. Louisiana St., 1986
23, Nevada-Las Vegas vs. Indiana, 1987
23, Michigan vs. Illinois, 1989

21, Duke vs. Nevada-Las Vegas, 1991
20, Nevada-Las Vegas vs. Georgia Tech, 1990

Most Blocked Shots
9, Kansas vs. Duke, 1988
7, Seton Hall vs. Duke, 1989
6, Duke vs. Indiana, 1992
5, Duke vs. Kansas, 1988
4, eight tied (most recent: Cincinnati vs. Michigan, 1992)

Most Steals
11, Providence vs. Syracuse, 1987
11, North Caro. vs. Kansas, 1991
11, Cincinnati vs. Michigan, 1992
10, Duke vs. Kansas, 1986
9, Kansas vs. Duke, 1988
9, Duke vs. Arkansas, 1990

Most Personal Fouls
33, Providence vs. Syracuse, 1987
33, Indiana vs. Duke, 1992
32, St. Bonaventure vs. Jacksonville, 1970
31, Kentucky vs. Syracuse, 1975
31, Pennsylvania vs. Michigan St., 1979

Fewest Personal Fouls
8, Wisconsin vs. Pittsburgh, 1941
9, Kansas vs. Southern Cal, 1940
9, Stanford vs. Colorado, 1942
9, Oklahoma St. vs. California, 1946
10, three tied [most recent: Houston vs. Virginia, 1984 (ot)]

Most Players Disqualified
4, St. Bonaventure vs. Jacksonville, 1970
4, Indiana vs. Duke, 1992
3, eight tied (most recent: Kansas vs. Duke, 1986)

SINGLE GAME, TEAM AND TWO-TEAM SCORING BY HALVES

Most Points in a Half, One Team
65, UCLA vs. Wichita St., 1965 (1st)
62, Seton Hall vs. Duke, 1989 (2nd)
58, Memphis St. vs. Providence, 1973 (2nd)
58, Houston vs. Louisville, 1983 (2nd)

Most Points in a Half, Both Teams
104, Notre Dame (57) vs. Duke (47), 1978 (2nd)
103, UCLA (65) vs. Wichita St. (38), 1965 (1st)
103, UCLA (57) vs. Louisville (46), 1972 (2nd)

Most Points at Half Time, One Team
65, UCLA vs. Wichita St. (38), 1965
53, four tied [most recent: Georgia Tech vs. Nevada-Las Vegas (46), 1990]

Most Points at Half Time, Both Teams
103, UCLA (65) vs. Wichita St. (38), 1965
100, Indiana (53) vs. Nevada-Las Vegas (47), 1987
99, Georgia Tech (53) vs. Nevada-Las Vegas (46), 1990

Fewest Points in a Half, One Team
10, Villanova vs. Ohio St., 1939 (1st)
11, Oregon St. vs. Oklahoma St., 1949 (1st)
11, Kentucky vs. Georgetown, 1984 (2nd)

Fewest Points in a Half, Both Teams
31, Duquesne (17) vs. Indiana (14), 1940 (2nd)

32, Pittsburgh (18) vs. Wisconsin (14), 1941 (1st)
32, Oklahoma St. (21) vs. Oregon St. (11), 1949 (1st)

Fewest Points at Half Time, One Team
10, Villanova vs. Ohio St. (25), 1939
11, Oregon St. vs. Oklahoma St. (21), 1949
13, Duquesne vs. Indiana (25), 1940
13, Kentucky vs. Dartmouth (23), 1942

Fewest Points at Half Time, Both Teams
32, Pittsburgh (18) vs. Wisconsin (14), 1941
32, Oklahoma St. (21) vs. Oregon St. (11), 1949
35, Ohio St. (25) vs. Villanova (10), 1939

Largest Half-Time Lead
33, Michigan St. (50) vs. Pennsylvania (17), 1979
27, UCLA (65) vs. Wichita St. (38), 1965
23, Kansas St. (37) vs. Oklahoma St. (14), 1951
23, Purdue (53) vs. North Caro. (30), 1969

Largest Half-Time Deficit Overcome
9, Memphis St. vs. Providence, H: 40-49, F: 98-85, 1973
8, Louisville vs. Louisiana St., H: 36-44, F: 88-77, 1986
7, three tied (most recent: Nevada-Las Vegas vs. Georgia Tech, H: 46-53, F: 90-81, 1990)

SINGLE GAME, TWO-TEAM

Most Points
197, UCLA (108) vs. Wichita St. (89), 1965
190, Indiana (97) vs. Nevada-Las Vegas (93), 1987
183, Memphis St. (98) vs. Providence (85), 1973
181, *Villanova (92) vs. *Western Ky. (89), 1971 (2 ot)
180, Duke (97) vs. Arkansas (83), 1990

Most Field Goals
80, UCLA (44) vs. Wichita St. (36), 1965
79, Memphis St. (41) vs. Providence (38), 1973
75, *Western Ky. (39) vs. *Villanova (36), 1971 (2 ot)
74, Nevada-Las Vegas (41) vs. North Caro. (33), 1977
73, Kansas St. (37) vs. UCLA (36), 1964
73, Houston (41) vs. Louisville (32), 1983

Most Field Goals Attempted
178, *Western Ky. (105) vs. *Villanova (73), 1971 (2 ot)
169, North Caro. (89) vs. Michigan St. (80), 1957 (3 ot)
164, UCLA (89) vs. Wichita St. (75), 1965
162, Providence (82) vs. Memphis St. (80), 1973
158, UCLA (82) vs. Kansas St. (76), 1964

Most Three-Point Field Goals
18, Nevada-Las Vegas (10) vs. Georgia Tech (8), 1990
15, Nevada-Las Vegas (13) vs. Indiana (2), 1987
15, Indiana (8) vs. Duke (7), 1992
10, four tied [most recent: Cincinnati (6) vs. Michigan (4), 1992]

Most Three-Point Field Goals Attempted
39, Nevada-Las Vegas (35) vs. Indiana (4), 1987
37, Arizona (23) vs. Oklahoma (14), 1988
36, Georgia Tech (21) vs. Nevada-Las Vegas (15), 1990
32, North Caro. (18) vs. Kansas (14), 1991
30, Arkansas (21) vs. Duke (9), 1990
30, Cincinnati (22) vs. Michigan (8), 1992

Most Free Throws
53, Indiana (30) vs. Louisiana St. (23), 1953
52, Jacksonville (37) vs. St. Bonaventure (15), 1970
47, La Salle (24) vs. Iowa (23), 1955
47, UCLA (29) vs. Drake (18), 1969
47, Duke (28) vs. Arkansas (19), 1990

Most Free Throws Attempted
70, Kentucky (38) vs. Syracuse (32), 1975
68, UCLA (44) vs. Drake (24), 1969
68, Florida St. (43) vs. North Caro. (25), 1972
67, Jacksonville (45) vs. St. Bonaventure (22), 1970
65, Duke (39) vs. Arkansas (26), 1990

Most Rebounds
123, *Western Ky. (69) vs. *Villanova (54), 1971 (2 ot)
119, Michigan St. (65) vs. North Caro. (54), 1957 (3 ot)

111, UCLA (57) vs. Houston (54), 1968
103, North Caro. (54) vs. Ohio St. (49), 1968
102, UCLA (51) vs. Houston (51), 1967

Most Assists
39, Louisville (26) vs. Louisiana St. (13), 1986
39, Nevada-Las Vegas (23) vs. Indiana (16), 1987
37, Michigan (23) vs. Illinois (14), 1989
35, Nevada-Las Vegas (20) vs. Georgia Tech (15), 1990
34, Duke (21) vs. Nevada-Las Vegas (13), 1991

Most Blocked Shots
14, Kansas (9) vs. Duke (5), 1988
11, Seton Hall (7) vs. Duke (4), 1989
9, Duke (6) vs. Indiana (3), 1992
8, Duke (4) vs. Nevada-Las Vegas (4), 1991
7, Syracuse (4) vs. Providence (3), 1987
7, Arkansas (4) vs. Duke (3), 1990

Most Steals
18, Providence (11) vs. Syracuse (7), 1987
17, Kansas (9) vs. Duke (8), 1988
17, Cincinnati (11) vs. Michigan (6), 1992
16, Duke (9) vs. Arkansas (7), 1990
16, North Caro. (11) vs. Kansas (5), 1991

Most Personal Fouls
61, Kentucky (31) vs. Syracuse (30), 1975
53, St. Bonaventure (32) vs. Jacksonville (21), 1970
53, Pennsylvania (31) vs. Michigan St. (22), 1979
51, four tied [most recent: Indiana (33) vs. Duke (18), 1992]

Most Players Disqualified
6, CCNY (3) vs. North Caro. St. (3), 1950
5, North Caro. (3) vs. Michigan St. (2), 1957 (3 ot)
5, Indiana (4) vs. Duke (1), 1992
4, Ohio St. (3) vs. New York U. (1), 1945 (ot)
4, St. Bonaventure (4) vs. Jacksonville (0), 1970
4, Syracuse (3) vs. Kentucky (1), 1975
*Record later vacated.

TOURNAMENT TRIVIA QUESTION...
Last year, Duke finished the regular season ranked No. 1 in the nation by the wire service polls and then went on to win the national title. What was the last school before Duke to accomplish this feat? Answer: North Carolina in 1982.

FINAL FOUR TWO-GAME TOTALS
TWO-GAME, INDIVIDUAL

Most Points
87, Bill Bradley, Princeton, 1965
80, Hal Lear, Temple, 1956
70, Gail Goodrich, UCLA, 1965
70, Jerry Chambers, Utah, 1966
66, Clyde Lovellette, Kansas, 1952
66, Jerry West, West Va., 1959
65, Bob Pettit, Louisiana St., 1953
64, Rick Mount, Purdue, 1969
64, Jack Givens, Kentucky, 1978
62, Lew Alcindor, UCLA, 1969

Most Field Goals
34, Bill Bradley, Princeton, 1965
32, Hal Lear, Temple, 1956
28, Jack Givens, Kentucky, 1978
28, Bill Walton, UCLA, 1973
26, Rick Mount, Purdue, 1969

Most Field Goals Attempted
64, Rick Mount, Purdue, 1969
58, Ernie DiGregorio, Providence, 1973
57, Lennie Rosenbluth, North Caro., 1957
54, Billy McGill, Utah, 1961
54, Bill Bradley, Princeton, 1965
54, *Jim McDaniels, Western Ky., 1971

**Highest Field-Goal Percentage
(minimum 15 FGM)**
84.2% (16-19), Billy Thompson, Louisville, 1986
82.4% (28-34), Bill Walton, UCLA, 1973
74.1% (20-27), James Worthy, North Caro., 1982
71.4% (20-28), Jerry Lucas, Ohio St., 1961
71.4% (15-21), Sidney Wicks, UCLA, 1970

Most Three-Point Field Goals
9, Steve Alford, Indiana, 1987
9, Anderson Hunt, Nevada-Las Vegas, 1990
8, Dave Sieger, Oklahoma, 1988
7, Glen Rice, Michigan, 1989
7, Bobby Hurley, Duke, 1992

Most Three-Point Field Goals Attempted
19, Dave Sieger, Oklahoma, 1988
17, Terry Brown, Kansas, 1991
16, Glen Rice, Michigan, 1989
16, Anderson Hunt, Nevada-Las Vegas, 1990
15, Greg Monroe, Syracuse, 1987
15, Phil Henderson, Duke, 1990

**Highest Three-Point Field-Goal Percentage
(minimum 7 3FGM)**
64.3% (9-14), Steve Alford, Indiana, 1987
58.3% (7-12), Bobby Hurley, Duke, 1992
56.3% (9-16), Anderson Hunt, Nevada-Las Vegas, 1990
43.8% (7-16), Glen Rice, Michigan, 1989
42.1% (8-19), Dave Sieger, Oklahoma, 1988

Most Free Throws
24, Oscar Robertson, Cincinnati, 1959
24, Gail Goodrich, UCLA, 1965
22, Jerry West, West Va., 1959
21, Don Schlundt, Indiana, 1953
21, Christian Laettner, Duke, 1991

Most Free Throws Attempted
32, Jerry West, West Va., 1959
30, Oscar Robertson, Cincinnati, 1959
28, Bob Pettit, Louisiana St., 1953
28, Don Schlundt, Indiana, 1953
28, Gail Goodrich, UCLA, 1965

**Highest Free-Throw Percentage
(minimum 12 FTM)**
100.0% (15-15), Jeff Lamp, Virginia, 1981
100.0% (13-13), Ron King, Florida St., 1972
100.0% (12-12), *Kiki Vandeweghe, UCLA, 1980
95.0% (19-20), Bill Bradley, Princeton, 1965
94.4% (17-18), Jim Spanarkel, Duke, 1978

Most Rebounds
50, Bill Russell, San Francisco, 1956
41, Elgin Baylor, Seattle, 1958
41, Lew Alcindor, UCLA, 1969
41, Bill Walton, UCLA, 1972
40, Elvin Hayes, Houston, 1967
40, Akeem Olajuwon, Houston, 1983
38, Paul Hogue, Cincinnati, 1962
38, Lew Alcindor, UCLA, 1967
37, Bill Spivey, Kentucky, 1951
37, Artis Gilmore, Jacksonville, 1970

Most Assists
23, Rumeal Robinson, Michigan, 1989
20, Michael Jackson, Georgetown, 1985
16, Alvin Franklin, Houston, 1985
16, Bobby Hurley, Duke, 1991
15, Ricky Grace, Oklahoma, 1988

Most Blocked Shots
8, Danny Manning, Kansas, 1988
5, Dean Garrett, Indiana, 1987
5, Derrick Coleman, Syracuse, 1987
5, Rony Seikaly, Syracuse, 1987
5, Grant Hill, Duke, 1992

Most Steals
10, Tommy Amaker, Duke, 1986
9, Mookie Blaylock, Oklahoma, 1988
9, Danny Manning, Kansas, 1988
6, Greg Anthony, Nevada-Las Vegas, 1990
5, three tied (most recent: Chris Webber, Michigan, 1992)

TWO-GAME, TEAM

Most Points
199, UCLA, 1965
196, *St. Joseph's (Pa.), 1961
194, Princeton, 1965
193, Nevada-Las Vegas, 1990
189, Nevada-Las Vegas, 1977
188, UCLA, 1964
187, Utah, 1961
186, Drake, 1969
180, Michigan, 1964
180, North Caro., 1972
180, Kentucky, 1975

Most Field Goals
88, Nevada-Las Vegas, 1977
78, Princeton, 1965
77, Utah, 1961

77, UCLA, 1965
77, Drake, 1969

Most Field Goals Attempted
181, *Western Ky., 1971
177, *St. Joseph's (Pa.), 1961
176, Rutgers, 1976
176, Pennsylvania, 1979
175, Nevada-Las Vegas, 1977

Highest Field-Goal Percentage
62.1% (64-103), Michigan St., 1979
61.7% (71-115), UCLA, 1973
57.6% (38-66), Villanova, 1985
57.3% (63-110), Ohio St., 1961
57.0% (61-107), Kansas, 1988

Most Three-Point Field Goals
18, Nevada-Las Vegas, 1990
14, Oklahoma, 1988
13, Seton Hall, 1989
11, Kansas, 1991
10, Duke, 1991

Most Three-Point Field Goals Attempted
38, Oklahoma, 1988
35, Seton Hall, 1989
32, Kansas, 1991
29, Nevada-Las Vegas, 1990
24, Michigan, 1989

Highest Three-Point Field-Goal Percentage (minimum 9 3FGM)
62.1% (18-29), Nevada-Las Vegas, 1990
60.0% (9-15), Indiana, 1987
55.6% (10-18), Duke, 1991
55.0% (11-20), Duke, 1992
37.5% (9-24), Michigan, 1989

Most Free Throws
62, Duke, 1978
62, *St. Joseph's (Pa.), 1961
57, UCLA, 1969
56, Bradley, 1954
51, Illinois, 1951
51, Colorado, 1955

Most Free Throws Attempted
85, UCLA, 1969
72, *St. Joseph's (Pa.), 1961
71, Illinois, 1951
71, Duke, 1978
69, North Caro., 1972

Highest Free-Throw Percentage (minimum 20 FTM)
88.7% (47-53), Virginia, 1981
87.5% (28-32), Marquette, 1977
87.3% (62-71), Duke, 1978
86.1% (62-72), *St. Joseph's (Pa.), 1961
86.0% (37-43), *UCLA, 1980

Most Rebounds
127, Houston, 1967
125, Michigan St., 1957
125, *Western Ky., 1971
109, UCLA, 1969
108, Houston, 1968
107, Ohio St., 1968
106, Kentucky, 1975
105, UCLA, 1967
105, UCLA, 1968
104, Utah, 1961

Most Assists
44, Nevada-Las Vegas, 1990
42, Louisville, 1986
42, Michigan, 1989
37, Oklahoma, 1988
36, Georgetown, 1985
36, Indiana, 1987

Most Blocked Shots
13, Kansas, 1988
11, Syracuse, 1987
10, Louisville, 1986
10, Duke, 1992
9, Seton Hall, 1989

Most Steals
23, Duke, 1986
22, Nevada-Las Vegas, 1990
21, Oklahoma, 1988
20, Kansas, 1988
15, Kansas, 1991

Most Personal Fouls
62, Pennsylvania, 1979
59, Kentucky, 1975
57, St. John's (N.Y.), 1952
56, Oklahoma St., 1951
56, Syracuse, 1975

*Record later vacated.

TOURNAMENT TRIVIA QUESTION...
Who are the only two freshmen to be named the most outstanding player at the Final Four? Answer: Utah's Arnie Ferrin in 1944 and Louisville's Pervis Ellison in 1986.

FINAL FOUR HISTORY TEAM RECORDS

Most Championship Titles
10, UCLA, 1964-75
5, Indiana, 1940-87
5, Kentucky, 1948-78
2, Cincinnati, 1961-62
2, Duke, 1991-92
2, Kansas, 1952-88
2, Louisville, 1980-86
2, North Caro., 1957-82
2, North Caro. St., 1974-83
2, Oklahoma St., 1945-46
2, San Francisco, 1955-56

Most Final Four Appearances
13, UCLA, 1962-76
10, Duke, 1963-92
10, North Caro., 1946-91
9, Kansas, 1940-91
9, Kentucky, 1942-84
8, Ohio St., 1939-68
7, Indiana, 1940-92
7, Louisville, 1959-86
6, Cincinnati, 1959-92
5, Houston, 1967-84
5, Michigan, 1964-92

Most Consecutive Final Four Appearances
10, UCLA, 1967-76
5, Cincinnati, 1959-63
5, Duke, 1988-92
3, Houston, 1982-84
3, North Caro., 1967-69
3, Ohio St., 1944-46

3, Ohio St., 1960-62
3, San Francisco, 1955-57
2, 15 tied

Most Final Four Wins
22, UCLA, 1962-76
12, Kentucky, 1942-84
11, Indiana, 1940-92
10, Duke, 1963-92
9, North Caro., 1946-82
8, Kansas, 1940-91
7, Cincinnati, 1959-92
7, Ohio St., 1939-68
6, Michigan, 1964-92
5, Georgetown, 1943-85
5, Louisville, 1959-86
5, North Caro. St., 1950-83
5, Oklahoma St., 1945-51
5, San Francisco, 1955-57

Highest Final Four Winning Percentage (minimum 3 games)
84.6% (11-2), Indiana, 1940-92
84.6% (22-4), UCLA, 1962-76
83.3% (5-1), North Caro. St., 1950-83
83.3% (5-1), San Francisco, 1955-57
75.0% (12-4), Kentucky, 1942-84
75.0% (3-1), Holy Cross, 1947-48
75.0% (3-1), La Salle, 1954-55
75.0% (3-1), Marquette, 1974-77
66.7% (2-1), Villanova, 1939-85
63.6% (7-4), Cincinnati, 1959-92

FINAL FOUR MOST OUTSTANDING PLAYERS AND THEIR FINAL FOUR STATISTICS

Year	Player, School	Cl.	G	FG-A	3FG-A	FT-A	Rb.	A	Bk.	St.	PF	Pts.
1939	None selected											
1940	Marv Huffman, Indiana	Sr.	2	7		4						18
1941	John Kotz, Wisconsin	So.	2	8		6					3	22
1942	Howard Dallmar, Stanford	So.	2	8		4- 6					0	20
1943	Ken Sailors, Wyoming	Jr.	2	10		8-11					5	28
1944	Arnie Ferrin, Utah	Fr.	2	11		6						28
1945	Bob Kurland, Oklahoma St.	Jr.	2	16		5					6	37
1946	Bob Kurland, Oklahoma St.	Sr.	2	21		10-15					8	52
1947	George Kaftan, Holy Cross	So.	2	18		12-17					6	48
1948	Alex Groza, Kentucky	Jr.	2	16		5						37
1949	Alex Groza, Kentucky	Sr.	2	19		14					9	52
1950	Irwin Dambrot, CCNY	Sr.	2	12-28		4- 8					3	28
1951	None selected											
1952	Clyde Lovellette, Kansas	Sr.	2	24		18						66
1953	+B. H. Born, Kansas	Jr.	2	17		17						51
1954	Tom Gola, La Salle	Jr.	2	12		14						38
1955	Bill Russell, San Francisco	Jr.	2	19		9						47
1956	†Hal Lear, Temple	Sr.	2	32		16						80
1957	Wilt Chamberlain, Kansas	So.	2	18-35		19-27	25				3	55
1958	+Elgin Baylor, Seattle	Jr.	2	18-53		12-16	41				7	48
1959	+Jerry West, West Va.	Jr.	2	22-33		22-32	25				7	66
1960	Jerry Lucas, Ohio St.	So.	2	16-24		3- 3	23				4	35
1961	+Jerry Lucas, Ohio St.	Jr.	2	20-28		16-17	25				6	56
1962	Paul Hogue, Cincinnati	Sr.	2	23-36		12-19	38				5	58
1963	Art Heyman, Duke	Sr.	2	18-44		15-22	19				8	51
1964	Walt Hazzard, UCLA	Sr.	2	11-20		8-12	10				7	30
1965	+Bill Bradley, Princeton	Sr.	2	34-54		19-20	24				9	87
1966	‡Jerry Chambers, Utah	Sr.	2	25-47		20-24	35				6	70
1967	Lew Alcindor, UCLA	So.	2	14-23		11-24	38				1	39
1968	Lew Alcindor, UCLA	Jr.	2	22-35		9-10	34				6	53
1969	Lew Alcindor, UCLA	Sr.	2	23-34		16-25	41				5	62
1970	Sidney Wicks, UCLA	Jr.	2	15-21		9-15	34				6	39
1971	*+Howard Porter, Villanova	Sr.	2	20-41		7- 9	24				5	47
1972	Bill Walton, UCLA	So.	2	20-29		17-23	41				6	57
1973	Bill Walton, UCLA	Jr.	2	28-34		2- 5	30				8	58
1974	David Thompson, North Caro. St.	Jr.	2	19-37		11-14	17				6	49
1975	Richard Washington, UCLA	So.	2	23-42		8-11	20				8	54

Year	Player, School	Cl.	G	FG-A	3FG-A	FT-A	Rb.	A	Bk.	St.	PF	Pts.
1976	Kent Benson, Indiana	Jr.	2	17-34		7-11	18				7	41
1977	Butch Lee, Marquette	Jr.	2	11-32		8- 8	6	2	1	1	4	30
1978	Jack Givens, Kentucky	Sr.	2	28-43		8-12	17	4	1	3	6	64
1979	Earvin "Magic" Johnson, Michigan St.	So.	2	17-25		19-22	17	3	0	2	5	53
1980	Darrell Griffith, Louisville	Sr.	2	23-37		11-16	7	15	0	2	4	57
1981	Isiah Thomas, Indiana	So.	2	14-25		9-11	4	9	3	4	8	37
1982	James Worthy, North Caro.	Jr.	2	20-27		2- 7	8	9	0	4	6	42
1983	+Akeem Olajuwon, Houston	So.	2	16-29		9-14	40	3	2	5	5	41
1984	Patrick Ewing, Georgetown	Jr.	2	8-14		2- 2	18	1	15	1	7	18
1985	Ed Pinckney, Villanova	Sr.	2	8-14		12-16	15	6	3	0	6	28
1986	Pervis Ellison, Louisville	Fr.	2	15-25		6- 8	24	2	3	1	7	36
1987	Keith Smart, Indiana	Jr.	2	14-22	0- 1	7- 9	7	7	0	2	7	35
1988	Danny Manning, Kansas	Sr.	2	25-45	0- 1	6- 9	17	4	8	9	6	56
1989	Glen Rice, Michigan	Sr.	2	24-49	7-16	4- 4	16	1	0	3	3	59
1990	Anderson Hunt, Nevada-Las Vegas	So.	2	19-31	9-16	2- 4	4	9	1	1	1	49
1991	Christian Laettner, Duke	Jr.	2	12-22	1- 1	21-23	17	2	1	2	5	46
1992	Bobby Hurley, Duke	Jr.	2	10-24	7-12	8-10	3	11	0	3	6	35

+Team finished second.
†Team finished third.
‡Team finished fourth.
*Record later vacated.

FINAL WIRE SERVICE POLLS NUMBER-ONE TEAMS

Year	AP Poll	UPI Poll	NCAA Champion	Champion's Final Ranking AP	UPI
1949	Kentucky	—	Kentucky	1	—
1950	Bradley	—	CCNY	NR	—
1951	Kentucky	Kentucky	Kentucky	1	1
1952	Kentucky	Kentucky	Kansas	8	3
1953	Indiana	Indiana	Indiana	1	1
1954	Kentucky	Indiana	La Salle	2	NR
1955	San Francisco	San Francisco	San Francisco	1	1
1956	San Francisco	San Francisco	San Francisco	1	1
1957	North Caro.	North Caro.	North Caro.	1	1
1958	West Va.	West Va.	Kentucky	9	NR
1959	Kansas St.	Kansas St.	California	NR	9
1960	Cincinnati	Cincinnati	Ohio St.	3	3
1961	Ohio St.	Ohio St.	Cincinnati	2	2
1962	Ohio St.	Ohio St.	Cincinnati	2	2
1963	Cincinnati	Cincinnati	Loyola (Ill.)	3	4
1964	UCLA	UCLA	UCLA	1	1
1965	Michigan	Michigan	UCLA	2	2
1966	Kentucky	Kentucky	UTEP	3	3
1967	UCLA	UCLA	UCLA	1	1
1968	Houston	Houston	UCLA	2	2
1969	UCLA	UCLA	UCLA	1	1
1970	Kentucky	Kentucky	UCLA	2	2
1971	UCLA	UCLA	UCLA	1	1
1972	UCLA	UCLA	UCLA	1	1
1973	UCLA	UCLA	UCLA	1	1
1974	North Caro. St.	North Caro. St.	North Caro. St.	1	1
1975	UCLA	Indiana	UCLA	1	2
1976	Indiana	Indiana	Indiana	1	1
1977	Michigan	Michigan	Marquette	7	14
1978	Kentucky	Kentucky	Kentucky	1	1
1979	Indiana St.	Indiana St.	Michigan St.	3	4
1980	DePaul	DePaul	Louisville	2	4
1981	DePaul	DePaul	Indiana	9	9
1982	North Caro.	North Caro.	North Caro.	1	1
1983	Houston	Houston	North Caro. St.	16	14
1984	North Caro.	North Caro.	Georgetown	2	2
1985	Georgetown	Georgetown	Villanova	NR	NR
1986	Duke	Duke	Louisville	7	7
1987	Nevada-Las Vegas	Nevada-Las Vegas	Indiana	3	2
1988	Temple	Temple	Kansas	NR	NR
1989	Arizona	Arizona	Michigan	10	10
1990	Oklahoma	Oklahoma	Nevada-Las Vegas	3	3
1991	Nevada-Las Vegas	Nevada-Las Vegas	Duke	6	6
1992	Duke	Duke	Duke	1	1

NR—Not Ranked in Top 20 (Top 10 from 1949-67).
Note: Final poll rankings are released before the NCAA tournament.

ALL-TOURNAMENT TEAMS
(First player listed each year was the Most Outstanding Player)

1939
Not chosen

1940
Marv Huffman, Indiana
Jay McCreary, Indiana
Bob Menke, Indiana
Howard Engleman, Kansas
Bob Allen, Kansas

1941-51
Not chosen

1952
Clyde Lovellette, Kansas
John Kerr, Illinois
Dean Kelley, Kansas
Bob Zawoluk, St. John's (N.Y.)
Ron MacGilvray, St. John's (N.Y.)

1953
B. H. Born, Kansas
Bob Leonard, Indiana
Don Schlundt, Indiana
Dean Kelley, Kansas
Bob Houbregs, Washington

1954
Tom Gola, La Salle
Bob Carney, Bradley
Charlie Singley, La Salle
Jesse Arnelle, Penn St.
Roy Irvin, Southern Cal

1955
Bill Russell, San Francisco
Jim Ranglos, Colorado
Carl Cain, Iowa
Tom Gola, La Salle
K. C. Jones, San Francisco

1956
Hal Lear, Temple
Carl Cain, Iowa
Bill Logan, Iowa
Hal Perry, San Francisco
Bill Russell, San Francisco

1957
Wilt Chamberlain, Kansas
John Green, Michigan St.
Pete Brennan, North Caro.
Lennie Rosenbluth, North Caro.
Gene Brown, San Francisco

1958
Elgin Baylor, Seattle
Johnny Cox, Kentucky
Vern Hatton, Kentucky
Charley Brown, Seattle
Guy Rodgers, Temple

1959
Jerry West, West Va.
Denny Fitzpatrick, California
Darrall Imhoff, California
Oscar Robertson, Cincinnati
Don Goldstein, Louisville

1960
Jerry Lucas, Ohio St.
Darrall Imhoff, California
Oscar Robertson, Cincinnati
Mel Nowell, Ohio St.
Tom Sanders, New York U.

1961
Jerry Lucas, Ohio St.
Carl Bouldin, Cincinnati
Bob Wiesenhahn, Cincinnati
Larry Siegfried, Ohio St.
*John Egan, St. Joseph's (Pa.)

1962
Paul Hogue, Cincinnati
Tom Thacker, Cincinnati
John Havlicek, Ohio St.
Jerry Lucas, Ohio St.
Len Chappell, Wake Forest

1963
Art Heyman, Duke
Ron Bonham, Cincinnati
Tom Thacker, Cincinnati
George Wilson, Cincinnati
Les Hunter, Loyola (Ill.)

1964
Walt Hazzard, UCLA
Jeff Mullins, Duke
Willie Murrell, Kansas St.
Bill Buntin, Michigan
Gail Goodrich, UCLA

1965
Bill Bradley, Princeton
Cazzie Russell, Michigan
Gail Goodrich, UCLA
Edgar Lacey, UCLA
Kenny Washington, UCLA

1966
Jerry Chambers, Utah
Jack Marin, Duke
Louie Dampier, Kentucky
Pat Riley, Kentucky
Bobby Joe Hill, UTEP

1967
Lew Alcindor, UCLA
Don May, Dayton
Elvin Hayes, Houston
Lucius Allen, UCLA
Mike Warren, UCLA

1968
Lew Alcindor, UCLA
Larry Miller, North Caro.
Lucius Allen, UCLA
Lynn Shackelford, UCLA
Mike Warren, UCLA

1969
Lew Alcindor, UCLA
Willie McCarter, Drake
Charlie Scott, North Caro.
Rick Mount, Purdue
John Vallely, UCLA

1970
Sidney Wicks, UCLA
Artis Gilmore, Jacksonville
Jimmy Collins, New Mexico St.
Curtis Rowe, UCLA
John Vallely, UCLA

1971
*Howard Porter, Villanova
*Jim McDaniels, Western Ky.
Steve Patterson, UCLA
Sidney Wicks, UCLA
*Hank Siemiontkowski, Villanova

1972
Bill Walton, UCLA
Ron King, Florida St.
Jim Price, Louisville
Bob McAdoo, North Caro.
Keith Wilkes, UCLA

1973
Bill Walton, UCLA
Steve Downing, Indiana
Larry Finch, Memphis St.
Larry Kenon, Memphis St.
Ernie DiGregorio, Providence

1974
David Thompson, North Caro. St.
Maurice Lucas, Marquette
Tom Burleson, North Caro. St.
Monte Towe, North Caro. St.
Bill Walton, UCLA

1975
Richard Washington, UCLA
Kevin Grevey, Kentucky
Allen Murphy, Louisville
Jim Lee, Syracuse
David Meyers, UCLA

1976
Kent Benson, Indiana
Tom Abernethy, Indiana
Scott May, Indiana
Rickey Green, Michigan
Marques Johnson, UCLA

1977
Butch Lee, Marquette
Bo Ellis, Marquette
Jerome Whitehead, Marquette
Walter Davis, North Caro.
Mike O'Koren, North Caro.
Cedric Maxwell, N.C.-Charlotte

1978
Jack Givens, Kentucky
Ron Brewer, Arkansas
Mike Gminski, Duke
Jim Spanarkel, Duke
Rick Robey, Kentucky

1979
Earvin "Magic" Johnson, Michigan St.
Mark Aguirre, DePaul
Gary Garland, DePaul
Larry Bird, Indiana St.
Greg Kelser, Michigan St.

1980
Darrell Griffith, Louisville
Rodney McCray, Louisville
Joe Barry Carroll, Purdue
*Rod Foster, UCLA
*Kiki Vandeweghe, UCLA

1981
Isiah Thomas, Indiana
Jim Thomas, Indiana
Landon Turner, Indiana
Al Wood, North Caro.
Jeff Lamp, Virginia

1982
James Worthy, North Caro.
Patrick Ewing, Georgetown
Eric Floyd, Georgetown
Michael Jordan, North Caro.
Sam Perkins, North Caro.

1983

Akeem Olajuwon, Houston
Thurl Bailey, North Caro. St.
Sidney Lowe, North Caro. St.
Dereck Whittenburg, North Caro.
St.
Milt Wagner, Louisville

1984

Patrick Ewing, Georgetown
Michael Graham, Georgetown
Alvin Franklin, Houston
Akeem Olajuwon, Houston
Michael Young, Houston

1985

Ed Pinckney, Villanova
Patrick Ewing, Georgetown
Harold Jensen, Villanova
Dwayne McClain, Villanova
Gary McLain, Villanova

1986

Pervis Ellison, Louisville
Mark Alarie, Duke
Tommy Amaker, Duke
Johnny Dawkins, Duke
Billy Thompson, Louisville

*Final Four record later vacated.

1987

Keith Smart, Indiana
Steve Alford, Indiana
Armon Gilliam, Nevada-Las Vegas
Derrick Coleman, Syracuse
Sherman Douglas, Syracuse

1988

Danny Manning, Kansas
Sean Elliott, Arizona
Milt Newton, Kansas
Stacey King, Oklahoma
Dave Sieger, Oklahoma

1989

Glen Rice, Michigan
Danny Ferry, Duke
Rumeal Robinson, Michigan
Gerald Greene, Seton Hall
John Morton, Seton Hall

1990

Anderson Hunt, Nevada-Las Vegas
Phil Henderson, Duke
Dennis Scott, Georgia Tech
Stacey Augmon, Nevada-Las Vegas
Larry Johnson, Nevada-Las Vegas

1991

Christian Laettner, Duke
Bobby Hurley, Duke
Bill McCaffrey, Duke
Mark Randall, Kansas
Anderson Hunt, Nevada-Las Vegas

1992

Bobby Hurley, Duke
Grant Hill, Duke
Christian Laettner, Duke
Jalen Rose, Michigan
Chris Webber, Michigan

TOURNAMENT TRIVIA QUESTION...
Who is the only football Heisman Trophy winner to play in the Final Four? Answer: Terry Baker of Oregon State (1963).

CONSENSUS ALL-AMERICAN BASKETBALL PLAYERS
THE SAME YEAR THEY PLAYED IN THE FINAL FOUR

ARIZONA
Sean Elliott 88

ARKANSAS
John Adams 41

BRADLEY
Paul Unruh 50

CALIFORNIA
Darrall Imhoff 60

CINCINNATI
Ron Bonham 63
Oscar Robertson 59, 60
Tom Thacker 63

DARTMOUTH
Audley Brindley 44

DUKE
Johnny Dawkins 86
Danny Ferry 89
Art Heyman 63
Christian Laettner 92

GEORGETOWN
Patrick Ewing 84, 85
Eric Floyd 82

HOUSTON
Elvin Hayes 67, 68
Akeem Olajuwon 84

ILLINOIS
Rod Fletcher 52

INDIANA
Steve Alford 87
Kent Benson 76
Scott May 76
Isiah Thomas 81

INDIANA ST.
Larry Bird 79

KANSAS
Wilt Chamberlain 57
Clyde Lovellette 52
Danny Manning 88

KANSAS ST.
Bob Boozer 58

KENTUCKY
Ralph Beard 48, 49
Alex Groza 49
Bill Spivey 51

LA SALLE
Tom Gola 54, 55

LOUISVILLE
Darrell Griffith 80

LOYOLA (ILL.)
Jerry Harkness 63

MEMPHIS ST.
Keith Lee 85

MICHIGAN
Cazzie Russell 65

MICHIGAN ST.
Earvin "Magic" Johnson 79

NEVADA-LAS VEGAS
Larry Johnson 90, 91

NORTH CARO.
Phil Ford 77
Bob McAdoo 72
Larry Miller 68
Lennie Rosenbluth 57
James Worthy 82

NORTH CARO. ST.
David Thompson 74

OHIO ST.
Jimmy Hull 39
Jerry Lucas 61, 62

OKLAHOMA
Gerald Tucker 47

OKLAHOMA ST.
Bob Kurland 45, 46

OREGON
Urgel Wintermute 39

PRINCETON
Bill Bradley 65

PROVIDENCE
Ernie DiGregorio 73

PURDUE
Joe Barry Carroll 80
Rick Mount 69

ST. BONAVENTURE
Bob Lanier 70

ST. JOHN'S (N.Y.)
Chris Mullin 85

SAN FRANCISCO
Bill Russell 55, 56

SEATTLE
Elgin Baylor 58

SOUTHERN CAL
Ralph Vaughn 40

TEMPLE
Guy Rodgers 58

UCLA
Lew Alcindor 67, 68, 69
Henry Bibby 72
Gail Goodrich 65
Walt Hazzard 64
Dave Meyers 75
Bill Walton 72, 73, 74
Richard Washington 76
Sidney Wicks 71
Keith Wilkes 73, 74

VIRGINIA
Ralph Sampson 81

WAKE FOREST
Len Chappell 62

WASHINGTON
Bob Houbregs 53

WESTERN KY.
*Jim McDaniels 71

WISCONSIN
Gene Englund 41

WYOMING
Ken Sailors 43

*Final Four record later vacated.

TOURNAMENT TRIVIA QUESTION...
Duke has won the national championship the last two years. Besides UCLA, has any other school won three straight titles? Answer: No.

NCAA FINAL FOUR ALL-DECADE TEAMS
(1939-87)

All-Time Team
Lew Alcindor (Kareem Abdul-Jabbar), UCLA
  (1967-68-69)
Larry Bird, Indiana St. (1979)
Wilt Chamberlain, Kansas (1957)
Earvin "Magic" Johnson, Michigan St. (1979)
Michael Jordan, North Caro. (1982)

1939-40s
Howie Dallmar, Stanford (1942)
Jim Pollard, Stanford (1942)
Ken Sailors, Wyoming (1943)
Arnie Ferrin, Utah (1944)
Bob Kurland, Oklahoma St. (1945-46)
Gerald Tucker, Oklahoma (1947)
George Kaftan, Holy Cross (1947)
Ralph Beard, Kentucky (1948-49)
Alex Groza, Kentucky (1948-49)
Dwight Eddleman, Illinois (1949)

1950s
Clyde Lovellette, Kansas (1952)
Tom Gola, La Salle (1954)
K. C. Jones, San Francisco (1955)
Bill Russell, San Francisco (1955-56)
Wilt Chamberlain, Kansas (1957)
Lennie Rosenbluth, North Caro. (1957)
Elgin Baylor, Seattle (1958)
Guy Rodgers, Temple (1958)
Jerry West, West Va. (1959)
Oscar Robertson, Cincinnati (1959-60)

1960s
Jerry Lucas, Ohio St. (1960-61)
John Havlicek, Ohio St. (1961-62)
Gail Goodrich, UCLA (1964-65)
Walt Hazzard, UCLA (1964)
Jeff Mullins, Duke (1964)
Bill Bradley, Princeton (1965)
Cazzie Russell, Michigan (1965)
Elvin Hayes, Houston (1967-68)

Lew Alcindor, UCLA (1967-68-69)
Charlie Scott, North Caro. (1968-69)

1970s
Sidney Wicks, UCLA (1969-70)
Bill Walton, UCLA (1972-73-74)
Keith Wilkes, UCLA (1972-73-74)
David Thompson, North Caro. St. (1974)
Marques Johnson, UCLA (1975-76)
Kent Benson, Indiana (1976)
Scott May, Indiana (1976)
Jack Givens, Kentucky (1978)
Larry Bird, Indiana St. (1979)
Earvin "Magic" Johnson, Michigan St. (1979)

1980s
Darrell Griffith, Louisville (1980)
Rodney McCray, Louisville (1980)
Isiah Thomas, Indiana (1981)
Patrick Ewing, Georgetown (1982-84-85)
Michael Jordan, North Caro. (1982)
James Worthy, North Caro. (1982)
Akeem Olajuwon, Houston (1983-84)
Ed Pinckney, Villanova (1985)
Johnny Dawkins, Duke (1986)
Steve Alford, Indiana (1987)

BLUE RIBBON
SELECTION PANEL
Denny Crum, Louisville
Dean Smith, North Caro.
Joe Hall, Kentucky
Pete Newell, California
Vic Bubas, Sun Belt Conference
Dave Gavitt, Big East Conference
Jud Heathcote, Michigan St.
John Thompson, Georgetown
Henry Iba, Oklahoma St.
John Wooden, UCLA
Wayne Duke, Big Ten Conference

TOURNAMENT TRIVIA QUESTION...
Who is the only player to be named the Final Four most outstanding player three times? Answer: Lew
Alcindor (Kareem Abdul-Jabbar), UCLA, 1967-69.

Michael Jordan
North Caro.

Earvin "Magic" Johnson
Michigan St.

Larry Bird
Indiana St.

Lew Alcindor
UCLA

Wilt Chamberlain
Kansas

ALL-TIME FINAL FOUR PARTICIPANTS

TEAM (Appearances-Players)

ARIZONA (1-9)
Jud Buechler 88
Anthony Cook 88
Sean Elliott 88
Steve Kerr 88
Kenny Lofton 88
Harvey Mason 88
Craig McMillan 88
Tom Tolbert 88
Joe Turner 88

ARKANSAS (4-38)
Johnny Adams 41
O'Neal Adams 41
Chris Bennett 78
Arlyn Bowers 90
Ron Brewer 78
Tony Byles 45
Gordon Carpenter 41
Jody Copeland 45
Jim Counce 78
Mario Credit 90
Todd Day 90
Marvin Delph 78
Bill Flynt 45
John Freiberger 41
Darrell Hawkins 90
Howard Hickey 41
Lenzie Howell 90
Ron Huery 90
Charles Jolliff 45
Kenneth Kearne 45
George Kok 45
Warren Linn 90
Larry Marks 90
Lee Mayberry 90
Oliver Miller 90
Sidney Moncrief 78
Ernie Murry 90
R. C. Pitts 41
Ulysses Reed 78
Ocie Richie 45
Nobel Robbins 41
Steve Schall 78
Frank Schumchyk 45
Mike Schumchyk 45
Paul Wheeler 45
Cannon Whitby 90
Clayton Wynne 41
Alan Zahn 78

BAYLOR (2-15)
Gordon Carrington 50
Gerald Cobb 50
Bill DeWitt 48, 50
W. A. Fleetwood 50
William Harris 50
Don Heathington 48, 50
William Hickman 48, 50
Edward Hovde 50
Bill Johnson 48, 50
Norman Mullins 50
James Owens 48
Odell Preston 48, 50
Ralph Pulley 48
Jackie Robinson 48
William Srack 48, 50

BRADLEY (2-22)
Harvey Babetch 54
Elmer Behnke 50
Bob Carney 54
Mike Chianakas 50
Dick Estergard 54
Jack Gower 54

Bud Grover 50
Jim Kelly 50
John Kent 54
Barney Kilcullen 54
Ed King 54
Billy Mann 50
Dino Melchiorre 50
Gene Melchiorre 50
Lee O'Connell 54
Richard Petersen 54
Aaron Preece 50
John Riley 54
Fred Schlictman 50
Joe Stowell 50
Paul Unruh 50
Lee Utt 54

CALIFORNIA (3-29)
Bill Alexander 60
Bob Anderson 46
Ned Averbuck 60
Al Buch 59
Bob Dalton 59
Les Dean 46
Dick Doughty 59, 60
Denny Fitzpatrick 59
Tandy Gillis 60
Jack Grout 59
Bob Hogeboom 46
Lowell Holcombe 46
Darrall Imhoff 59, 60
Merv LaFaille 46
Dick Larner 46
Jerry Mann 60
Bill McClintock 59, 60
Stan Morrison 60
Art Mower 46
Ed Pearson 60
Cal Riemcke 46
Earl Shultz 60
Bernie Simpson 59
James Smith 46
Dave Stafford 60
George Walker 46
Bob Wendell 60
Andy Wolfe 46
Jim Wray 46

CINCINNATI (6-36)
Mark Altenau 61
Corie Blount 92
Ron Bonham 62, 63
Carl Bouldin 59, 60, 61
John Bryant 60
Anthony Buford 92
Jim Calhoun 61
Dick Cetrone 59
Ken Cunningham 63
Ralph Davis 59, 60
Fred Dierking 60, 61
Tarrance Gibson 92
Dale Heidotting 61, 63
Paul Hogue 60, 61, 62
Allen Jackson 61
Herb Jones 92
Mel Landfried 59
Erik Martin 92
Fritz Meyer 63
Ron Nall 59
Terry Nelson 92
Sandy Pomerantz 60
Ron Reis 60
Oscar Robertson 59, 60
Jeff Scott 92
Larry Shingleton 61, 63

Tom Sizer 60, 61, 62
Gene Smith 63
Dave Tenwick 59
Tom Thacker 61, 62, 63
Nick Van Exel 92
Bill Whitaker 59
Bob Wiesenhahn 59, 60, 61
Larry Willey 59, 60
George Wilson 62, 63
Tony Yates 61, 62, 63

CCNY (2-18)
Mason Benson 47
Herb Cohen 50
Irwin Dambrot 47, 50
Phil Farbman 47
Everett Finestone 47
Joe Galiber 47, 50
Sonny Jameson 47
Floyd Layne 50
Norman Mager 50
Paul Malamed 47
Lionel Malamed 47
Ronald Nadell 50
Edward Roman 50
Alvin Roth 50
Paul Schmones 47
Hilpy Shapiro 47
Sidney Trubowitz 47
Ed Warner 50

COLORADO (2-18)
Melvin Coffman 55
Robert Doll 42
Jim Grant 55
Burdette Halderson 55
George Hamburg 42
George Hannah 55
Horace Huggins 42
Bob Jeangerard 55
Bob Kirchner 42
Floyd Mansfield 55
Leason McCloud 42
Charlie Mock 55
Heath Nuckolls 42
Bill Peterson 55
Donald Putnam 55
Jim Ranglos 55
Wilbert Walter 55
Bob Yardley 55

DARTMOUTH (2-20)
James Briggs 42
Audley Brindley 44
Robert Gale 44
Vincent Goering 44
Harry Leggat 44
Richard McGuire 44
Gordon McKernan 42
Walter Mercer 44
John Monahan 44
George Munroe 42
Franklin Murphy 44
Robert Myers 42
Everett Nordstrom 44
William Parmer 42
Charles Pearson 42
Henry Pogue 42
James Olsen 42
Connor Shaw 42
Stanley Skaug 42
Joseph Vancisin 44

DAYTON (1-12)
Tom Heckman 67

Bob Hooper 67
Dave Inderrieden 67
Gene Klaus 67
Don May 67
Dan Obrovac 67
Dan Sadlier 67
John Samanich 67
Ned Sharpenter 67
Glinder Torain 67
Jim Wannemacher 67
Rudy Waterman 67

DePAUL (2-15)
Mark Aguirre 79
Clyde Bradshaw 79
Jimmy Cominsky 43
Mel Frailey 43
Gary Garland 79
John Jorgenson 43
Tony Kelly 43
William Madey 79
Dennis McGuire 79
George Mikan 43
James Mitchem 79
Chris Nikitas 79
Bill Ryan 43
Dick Starzyk 43
Curtis Watkins 79

DRAKE (1-12)
Don Draper 69
Ron Gwin 69
Bob Mast 69
Willie McCarter 69
Jim O'Dea 69
Garry Odom 69
Dolph Pulliam 69
Dale Teeter 69
Rick Wanamaker 69
Al Williams 69
Willie Wise 69
Gary Zeller 69

DUKE (10-64)
Alaa Abdelnaby 88, 89, 90
Mark Alarie 86
Tommy Amaker 86
Christian Ast 92
Eugene Banks 78
Tony Barone 66
Bob Bender 78
Jay Bilas 86
Kenny Blakeney 92
Robert Brickey 88, 89, 90
Clay Buckley 89, 90
Jay Buckley 63, 64
George Burgin 89
Ron Burt 66
Warren Chapman 66
Marty Clark 92
Joe Cook 88, 90
Ray Cox 63, 64
Brian Davis 89, 90, 91, 92
Johnny Dawkins 86
Kenny Dennard 78
Dennis Ferguson 63, 64
Danny Ferry 86, 88, 89
Mike Gminski 78
Scott Goetsch 78
John Harrell 78
Buzzy Harrison 63, 64
Frank Harscher 64

David Henderson 86
Phil Henderson 88, 89, 90
Ron Herbster 63, 64
Art Heyman 63
Grant Hill 91, 92
Thomas Hill 90, 91, 92
Bobby Hurley 90, 91, 92
Bob Jamieson 63
Joe Kennedy 66
Billy King 86, 88
Brent Kitching 63, 64
Tim Kolodziej 66
Greg Koubek 88, 89, 90, 91
Christian Laettner 89, 90, 91, 92
Antonio Lang 91, 92
Mike Lewis 66
Jim Liccardo 66
Ted Mann 63, 64
Jack Marin 64, 66
Bill McCaffrey 90, 91
Erik Meek 92
Jeff Mullins 63, 64
Crawford Palmer 89, 90, 91
Cherokee Parks 92
Bob Riedy 66
Fred Schmidt 63
John Smith 88, 89
Quin Snyder 88, 89
Jim Spanarkel 78
Kevin Strickland 86, 88
Jim Suddath 78
Hack Tison 63, 64
Steve Vacendak 64, 66
Bob Verga 66
Ron Wendein 66
Weldon Williams 86

DUQUESNE (1-7)
Moe Becker 40
Rudy Debnar 40
Lou Kasperik 40
Bill Lacey 40
Melvin Milkovich 40
George Reiber 40
Paul Widowitz 40

FLORIDA ST. (1-9)
Ottis Cole 72
Rowland Garrett 72
Larry Gay 72
Ron Harris 72
Ron King 72
Lawrence McCray 72
Otto Petty 72
Reggie Royals 72
Greg Samuel 72

GEORGETOWN (4-30)
Horace Broadnax 84, 85
Fred Brown 82, 84
Ralph Dalton 84, 85
Patrick Ewing 82, 84, 85
William Fenney 43
Frank Finnerty 43
Eric Floyd 82
Kevin Floyd 85
Dan Gabbianelli 43
Michael Graham 84
Mike Hancock 82
William Hassett 43
Ron Highsmith 85
Henry Hyde 43
Michael Jackson 84, 85
Anthony Jones 82
Daniel Kraus 43

Tyrone Lockhart 85
John Mahnken 43
Bill Martin 82, 84, 85
Grady Mateen 85
Perry McDonald 85
Victor Morris 84
Lloyd Potolicchio 43
James Reilly 43
Eric Smith 82
Gene Smith 82, 84
Ed Spriggs 82
Reggie Williams 84, 85
David Wingate 84, 85

GEORGIA (1-8)
James Banks 83
Richard Corhen 83
Gerald Crosby 83
Terry Fair 83
Vern Fleming 83
Derrick Floyd 83
Donald Hartry 83
Lamar Heard 83

GEORGIA TECH (1-7)
Kenny Anderson 90
Darryl Barnes 90
Karl Brown 90
Malcolm Mackey 90
Johnny McNeil 90
Brian Oliver 90
Dennis Scott 90

HOLY CROSS (2-14)
Charles Bollinger 47, 48
Bob Cousy 47, 48
Robert Curran 47, 48
Bert Dolan 48
Matthew Formon 48
Charles Graver 47
Ken Haggerty 47
George Kaftan 47, 48
Andy Laska 47, 48
Robert McMullen 47, 48
Joe Mullaney 47, 48
Dermie O'Connell 47, 48
Frank Oftring 47, 48
William Reilly 47

HOUSTON (5-37)
Marvin Alexander 84
Benny Anders 82, 83, 84
Greg Anderson 84
Stacey Belcher 84
Melvin Bell 67, 68
Andrew Benson 67
Don Chaney 67, 68
Braxton Clark 84
Eric Davis 82
Eric Dickens 84
Clyde Drexler 82, 83
Alvin Franklin 83, 84
Reid Gettys 83, 84
Derek Giles 83, 84
Tom Gribben 68
Gary Grider 67
Neimer Hamood 67, 68
Elvin Hayes 67, 68
Don Kruse 67
Theodis Lee 67, 68
Leary Lentz 67
Vern Lewis 67, 68
Elliott McVey 67
Larry Micheaux 82, 83
Akeem Olajuwon 82, 83, 84
Gary Orsak 84

David Rose 83
Lynden Rose 82
Ken Spain 67, 68
Kent Taylor 68
Renaldo Thomas 84
James Weaver 84
Bryan Williams 82, 83
Robert Williams 82
Rickie Winslow 84
Michael Young 82, 83, 84

ILLINOIS (4-33)
Nick Anderson 89
Van Anderson 49
Steve Bardo 89
Kenny Battle 89
Max Baumgardner 51
Theodore Beach 49, 51
Irving Bemoras 51, 52
James Bredar 51, 52
James Cottrell 49
Dwight Eddleman 49
William Erickson 49
Rodney Fletcher 51, 52
Richard Foley 49
Clive Follmer 51, 52
Mack Follmer 51
Roy Gatewood 49
Herbert Gerecke 51, 52
Kendall Gill 89
Fred Green 49
Lowell Hamilton 89
Max Hooper 52
John Kerr 52
Walter Kersulis 49
Marcus Liberty 89
James Marks 49
John Marks 51
Walter Osterkorn 49
Robert Peterson 51, 52
Ervin Small 89
Larry Smith 89
Don Sunderlage 49, 51
James Schuldt 51
James Wright 52

INDIANA (7-71)
Tom Abernethy 73, 76
Steve Alford 87
Eric Anderson 92
Paul Armstrong 40
Damon Bailey 92
Bob Bender 76
Quinn Buckner 73, 76
Phil Byers 53
Goethe Chambers 53
Calbert Cheaney 92
Jim Crews 73, 76
Jim DeaKyne 53
Ralph Dorsey 40
Steve Downing 73
Bob Dro 40
Steve Eyl 87
Dick Farley 53
Chet Francis 40
Chuck Franz 81
Dean Garrett 87
Greg Graham 92
Steve Green 73
Jim Gridley 40
Glen Grunwald 81
Mark Haymore 76
Alan Henderson 92
Joe Hillman 87
Marv Huffman 40
Phil Isenbarger 81
Ted Kitchel 81
Charley Kraak 53

Mike LaFave 81
John Laskowski 73
Todd Leary 92
Bob Leonard 53
Scott May 76
Jay McCreary 40
Jamal Meeks 92
Jerry Memering 73
Bill Menke 40
Bob Menke 40
Todd Meier 87
Craig Morris 73
Don Noort 73
Matt Nover 92
Paul Poff 53
Wayne Radford 76
Chris Reynolds 92
Steve Risley 81
John Ritter 73
Herman Schaefer 40
Don Schlundt 53
Jim Schooley 53
Burke Scott 53
Keith Smart 87
Kreigh Smith 87
Trent Smock 73
Ron Taylor 53
Ray Tolbert 81
Daryl Thomas 87
Isiah Thomas 81
Jim Thomas 81
Landon Turner 81
Rich Valavicius 76
Dick White 53
Bobby Wilkerson 76
Frank Wilson 73
Jim Wisman 76
Randy Wittman 81
Jack Wright 53
Andy Zimmer 40

INDIANA ST. (1-8)
Larry Bird 79
Alex Gilbert 79
Bob Heaton 79
Brad Miley 79
Rich Nemcek 79
Carl Nicks 79
Steve Reed 79
Leroy Staley 79

IOWA (3-22)
Mike Arens 80
Kenny Arnold 80
Kevin Boyle 80
Vince Brookins 80
Carl Cain 55, 56
Jon Darsee 80
McKinley Davis 55
Mark Gannon 80
Bob George 55, 56
Tom Grogan 80
Bob Hansen 80
Mike Heller 80
Mike Henry 80
Steve Krafcisin 80
Ronnie Lester 80
Bill Logan 55, 56
Augie Martel 55, 56
Jim McConnell 56
Sharm Scheuerman 55, 56
Bill Schoof 55, 56
Bill Seaberg 55, 56
Steve Waite 80

IOWA ST. (1-7)
William Block 44
Price Brookfield 44
Roy Ewoldt 44

James Myers 44
Gene Oulman 44
Robert Sauer 44
Ray Wehde 44
JACKSONVILLE (1-11)
Rusty Baldwin 70
Mike Blevins 70
Pembrook Burrows 70
Chip Dublin 70
Artis Gilmore 70
Dan Hawkins 70
Rod McIntyre 70
Rex Morgan 70
Gene Nelson 70
Ken Selke 70
Vaughn Wedeking 70
KANSAS (9-86)
Jerry Alberts 53
Bob Allen 40
Scooter Barry 88
Robert Billings 57
B. H. Born 52, 53
Roger Brown 71
Terry Brown 91
Alton Campbell 86
Randy Canfield 71
Wilt Chamberlain 57
Norman Cook 74
Edwin Dater 57
Lawrence Davenport 52, 53
Greg Douglas 71
Greg Dreiling 86
Donald Ebling 40
Gene Elstun 57
Howard Engleman 40
Leland Green 57
Dale Greenlee 74
Jeff Gueldner 88
Dick Harp 40
Keith Harris 88
Arthur Heitholt 52, 53
Charlie Hoag 52
William Hogben 40
Blaine Hollinger 57
William Hougland 52
Rodney Hull 86
Cedric Hunter 86
Thomas Hunter 40
John Keller 52
Ron Kellogg 86
Allen Kelley 52, 53
Dean Kelley 52, 53
Robert Kenney 52
Lynn Kindred 57
Maurice King 57
Bob Kivisto 71
Tom Kivisto 74
John Kline 40
Danny Knight 74
Alonzo Jamison 91
David Johanning 91
Lewis Johnson 57
Monte Johnson 57
Wallace Johnson 40
Adonis Jordan 91
William Lienhard 52
Ron Loneski 57
Clyde Lovellette 52
Mike Maddox 88, 91
Danny Manning 86, 88
Archie Marshall 86
Mark Mathews 71
Marvin Mattox 88
Ralph Miller 40
Lincoln Minor 88

Roger Morningstar 74
Aubrey Nash 71
Milt Newton 88
Clint Normore 88
John Parker 57
Harold Patterson 53
Chris Piper 86, 88
Kevin Pritchard 88
Mark Randall 91
Gil Reich 53
Patrick Richey 91
Dave Robisch 71
Pierre Russell 71
Jack Sands 40
Richard Scott 91
Dean Smith 52, 53
Tommie Smith 74
Bud Stallworth 71
Rick Suttle 74
Dave Taynor 71
Calvin Thompson 86
Sean Tunstall 91
Mark Turgeon 86
Donnie Von Moore 74
Bruce Voran 40
Kirk Wagner 91
Mark Williams 71
Steve Woodberry 91
KANSAS ST. (4-45)
Hayden Abbott 58
Sonny Ballard 58
Richard Barnard 64
Ernie Barrett 51
Clarence Brannum 48
Bob Boozer 58
Ward Clark 48
John Dean 48
Roy DeWitz 58
Steve Douglas 58
Larry Fischer 58
Wally Frank 58
John Gibson 51
Joe Gottfrid 64
Rick Harman 48
Ed Head 51
Lew Hitch 51
James Hoffman 64
Jim Holwerda 58
Harold Howey 48
James Iverson 58
Dick Knostman 51
Lloyd Krone 48
Allan Langton 48
Glen Long 58
Kenneth Mahoney 48
Don Matuszak 58
Max Moss 64
Willie Murrell 64
David Nelson 64
Ron Paradis 64
Jack Parr 58
Richard Peck 51
Louis Poma 64
Sammy Robinson 64
Robert Rousey 51
Dan Schuyler 51
Howard Shannon 48
Jeff Simons 64
Jack Stone 51
Roger Suttner 64
Joe Thornton 48
Don Upson 51
David Weatherby 48
Gary Williams 64
KENTUCKY (9-75)
Marvin Akers 42
Chuck Aleksinas 78

Ermal Allen 42
Cliff Barker 48, 49
Dale Barnstable 48, 49
Dickie Beal 84
Ralph Beard 48, 49
Bret Bearup 84
Ed Beck 58
Cliff Berger 66
Winston Bennett 84
James Blackmon 84
Sam Bowie 84
Melvin Brewer 42
Dwane Casey 78
Truman Claytor 78
Lincoln Collinsworth 58
Larry Conley 66
Jimmy Dan Conner 75
Scott Courts 78
Fred Cowan 78
Johnny Cox 58
John Crigler 58
Louie Dampier 66
Kenneth England 42
Mike Flynn 75
Gary Gamble 66
Chris Gettelfinger 78
Jack Givens 75, 78
Kevin Grevey 75
Alex Groza 48, 49
Bob Guyette 75
Cliff Hagan 51
Jerry Hale 75
Dan Hall 75
Roger Harden 84
Merion Haskins 75
Vern Hatton 58
Walter Hirsch 49
Joe Holland 48
Thad Jaracz 66
Larry Johnson 75
Wallace Jones 48, 49
James King 42
Tommy Kron 66
James Lee 75, 78
Jim LeMaster 66
James Line 48, 49
Shelby Linville 51
Kyle Macy 78
Jim Master 84
Don Mills 58
C. M. Newton 51
Mike Phillips 75, 78
Frank Ramsey 51
Lloyd Ramsey 42
Pat Riley 66
Rick Robey 75, 78
Kenneth Rollins 48
Jay Schidley 78
Adrian Smith 58
G. J. Smith 75
Carl Staker 42
Tim Stephens 78
Bill Spivey 51
Bob Tallent 66
Milton Ticco 42
Melvin Turpin 84
Lou Tsioropoulos 51
Kenny Walker 84
Reggie Warford 75
Robert Watson 51
Lucian Whitaker 51
Waller White 42
LaVon Williams 78
LA SALLE (2-10)
Frank Blatcher 54, 55
Walt Fredericks 55
Tom Gola 54, 55

Chas Greensberg 54, 55
Al Lewis 55
Bob Maples 54, 55
Frank O'Hara 54
Fran O'Malley 54, 55
Charlie Singley 54, 55
John Yodsnukis 54
LOUISIANA ST. (3-31)
Don Belcher 53
Brian Bergeron 81
Tyrone Black 81
Ricky Blanton 86
Kenneth Bridges 53
Oliver Brown 86
Howard Carter 81
Ned Clark 53
Ocie Conley 86
Greg Cook 81
Joe Costello 81
Bob Freshley 53
Johnny Jones 81
Don Loughmiller 53
Durand Macklin 81
Norman Magee 53
Ethan Martin 81
Benny McArdle 53
James McNeilly 53
Leonard Mitchell 81
Bob Pettit 53
Don Redden 86
Darrell Schultz 53
Willie Sims 81
Derrick Taylor 86
John Tudor 81
Jose Vargas 86
John Williams 86
Anthony Wilson 86
Edwin Wilson 86
Bernard Woodside 86
LOUISVILLE (7-61)
Harley Andrews 59
Harold Andrews 59
Henry Bacon 72
Ken Bradley 72
Junior Bridgeman 75
Philip Bond 75
Tony Branch 80
Danny Brown 75
Wiley Brown 80, 82
Bill Bunton 72, 75
Roger Burkman 80
George Burnette 59
Larry Carter 72
Daryl Cleveland 80
Tim Cooper 72
Wesley Cox 75
Herbert Crook 86
Greg Deuser 80
Jerry Eaves 80, 82
Pervis Ellison 86
Ricky Gallon 75
Bill Geiling 59
Don Goldstein 59
Lancaster Gordon 82, 83
Darrell Griffith 80
Bryan Hall 59
Jeff Hall 83, 86
Billy Harmon 75
Terry Howard 75
Charles Jones 82, 83
Tony Kimbro 86
Joe Kitchen 59
Mike Lawhon 72
Budd Leathers 59
Alex Mantel 59

Joe Meiman 72
Rodney McCray 80, 82, 83
Scooter McCray 82, 83
Mark McSwain 86
Allen Murphy 75
Jim Price 72
Paul Pry 72
Marty Pulliam 80
Ron Rubenstein 59
Fred Sawyer 59
Derek Smith 80, 82
Howard Stacey 59
Ron Stallings 72
Roger Tieman 59
Ron Thomas 72
Billy Thompson 83, 86
John Turner 59
Robbie Valentine 83
Al Vilcheck 72
Milt Wagner 82, 83, 86
Kevin Walls 86
Gerry Watkins 59
Chris West 83
Ike Whitfield 75
Rick Wilson 75
Poncho Wright 80, 82

LOYOLA (ILL.) (1-9)
Dan Cannaughton 63
John Egan 63
Jerry Harkness 63
Leslie Hunter 63
Ron Miller 63
Jim Reardon 63
Rich Rochelle 63
Vic Rouse 63
Chuck Wood 63

MARQUETTE (2-19)
Barry Brennan 74
John Bryant 74
Jim Boylan 77
Rick Campbell 74
Ed Daniels 74
Dave Delsman 74
Maurice Ellis 74, 77
Jerry Homan 74
Greg Johnson 74
Butch Lee 77
Maurice Lucas 74
Bill Neary 77
Gary Rosenberger 77
Earl Tatum 74
Bernard Toone 77
Paul Vollmer 74
Lloyd Walton 74
Marcus Washington 74
Jerome Whitehead 77

MEMPHIS ST. (2-21)
Ken Andrews 73
Vincent Askew 85
DeWayne Bailey 85
Willie Becton 85
William Bedford 85
Dwight Boyd 85
Bill Buford 73
Bill Cook 73
Larry Finch 73
Baskerville Holmes 85
Clarence Jones 73
Larry Kenon 73
Bill Laurie 73
Keith Lee 85
Jim Liss 73
Doug McKinney 73
Ron Robinson 73
Jerry Tetzlaff 73
Andre Turner 85

Wes Westfall 73
John Wilfong 85

MICHIGAN (5-48)
Chip Armer 92
Dennis Bankey 65
Dave Baxter 76
Tom Bergen 76
Jason Bossard 92
Wayman Britt 76
Dan Brown 65
Bill Buntin 64, 65
Demetrius Calip 89
Bob Cantrell 64
John Clawson 64, 65
Oliver Darden 64, 65
Craig Dill 65
Rickey Green 76
Mike Griffin 89
Steve Grote 76
Alan Hardy 76
Doug Herner 64
Sean Higgins 89
Juwan Howard 92
Phil Hubbard 76
Mark Hughes 89
Freddie Hunter 92
Ray Jackson 92
Bobby Jones 76
Jimmy King 92
Len Lillard 76
Tom Ludwig 65
Terry Mills 89
Jim Myers 64, 65
Rob Pelinka 92
George Pomey 64, 65
Glen Rice 89
Eric Riley 92
John Robinson 76
Rumeal Robinson 89
Jalen Rose 92
Cazzie Russell 64, 65
Chris Seter 92
Tom Staton 76
Michael Talley 92
John Thompson 65
Larry Tregoning 64, 65
Joel Thompson 76
Lloyd Schinnerer 76
Loy Vaught 89
James Voskuil 92
Chris Webber 92

MICHIGAN ST. (2-20)
Bob Anderegg 57
Chuck Bencie 57
Mike Brkovich 79
Ron Charles 79
Terry Donnelly 79
George Ferguson 57
Rob Gonzalez 79
John Green 57
Larry Hedden 57
Jamie Huffman 79
Earvin "Magic" Johnson 79
Rick Kaye 79
Greg Kelser 79
Greg Lloyd 79
Mike Longaker 79
Harry Lux 57
Jack Quiggle 57
David Scott 57
Jay Vincent 79
Pat Wilson 57

NEVADA-LAS VEGAS (4-32)
George Ackles 91
Greg Anthony 90, 91

Stacey Augmon 90, 91
Freddie Banks 87
Jarvis Basnight 87
Travis Bice 90
Lewis Brown 77
David Butler 90
Stacey Cvijanovich 90
Armon Gilliam 87
Glen Gondrezick 77
Gary Graham 87
Evric Gray 91
Eldridge Hudson 87
Anderson Hunt 90, 91
Chris Jeter 90
Larry Johnson 90, 91
James Jones 90
Larry Moffett 77
Eddie Owens 77
Gerald Paddio 87
Dave Rice 90
Rich Robinson 87
Moses Scurry 90
Robert Smith 77
Sam Smith 77
Tony Smith 77
Elmore Spencer 91
Reggie Theus 77
Mark Wade 87
David Willard 87
Barry Young 90

NEW MEXICO ST. (1-12)
John Burgess 70
Jimmy Collins 70
Charley Criss 70
Rudy Franco 70
Milton Horne 70
Sam Lacey 70
Lonnie Lefevre 70
Tom McCarthy 70
Bill Moore 70
Roy Neal 70
Chito Reyes 70
Jeff Smith 70

NEW YORK U. (2-21)
Al Barden 60
Fred Benanti 45
Russ Cunningham 60
Mike DiNapoli 60
Al Filardi 60
Don Forman 45
Marty Goldstein 45
Al Grenert 45
Rich Keith 60
Art Loche 60
Frank Mangiapane 45
Bernie Mlodinoff 60
Alvin Most 45
Leo Murphy 60
Ray Paprocky 60
Bob Regan 60
Jimmy Reiss 60
Tom Sanders 60
Dolph Schayes 45
Sid Tanenbaum 45
Herb Walsh 45

NORTH CARO. (10-90)
Don Anderson 46
Jimmy Black 81, 82
Jim Bostick 67
Jim Braddock 81, 82
Dudley Bradley 77
Pete Brennan 57
Joe Brown 67, 68, 69
Chris Brust 81, 82
Bruce Buckley 77
Pete Budko 81

Bill Bunting 67, 68, 69
Craig Carson 72
Dave Chadwick 69
Bill Chamberlain 72
Bill Chambers 72
Scott Cherry 91
Pete Chilcutt 91
Rusty Clark 67, 68, 69
Dave Colescott 77
Woody Coley 77
Bob Cunningham 57
Hubert Davis 91
Walter Davis 77
Lee Dedmon 69
Jim Delany 68, 69
John Dillon 46
Matt Doherty 81, 82
Ged Doughton 77
Don Eggleston 69
Ralph Fletcher 67, 68
Eddie Fogler 68, 69
Phil Ford 77
Rick Fox 91
Jim Fry 67, 68
Tom Gauntlett 67
Dale Gipple 69
Dick Grubar 67, 68
Kenny Harris 91
Ray Hite 72
Kim Huband 72
Don Johnston 72
Bobby Jones 72
Jim Jordan 46
Michael Jordan 82
George Karl 72
Tommy Kearns 57
Eric Kenny 81
Steve Krafcisin 77
John Kuester 77
Bob Lewis 67
Danny Lotz 57
George Lynch 91
Warren Martin 82
Bob McAdoo 72
Horace McKinney 46
Larry Miller 67, 68
Donnie Moe 67
Eric Montross 91
Mike O'Koren 77
Bob Paxton 46
Mike Pepper 81
Sam Perkins 81, 82
Buzz Peterson 82
Derrick Phelps 91
Steve Previs 72
Joe Quigg 57
Brian Reese 91
King Rice 91
Henrik Rodl 91
Lennie Rosenbluth 57
Clifford Rozier 91
Kevin Salvadori 91
Roger Scholbe 46
Charlie Scott 68, 69
Roy Searcy 57
Pat Sullivan 91
Taylor Thorne 46
Gerald Tuttle 67, 68, 69
Richard Tuttle 69
John Virgil 77
Matt Wenstorm 91
Jim White 46
Gra Whitehead 68
Jeff Wolf 77
Al Wood 81
James Worthy 81, 82
Dennis Wuycik 72

Rich Yonakor 77
Bob Young 57
Tom Zaliagris 77
N.C.-CHARLOTTE (1-12)
Ken Angel 77
Todd Crowley 77
Jeff Gruber 77
Mike Hester 77
Chad Kinch 77
Kevin King 77
Lew Massey 77
Cedric Maxwell 77
Phil Scott 77
Melvin Watkins 77
Lee Whitfield 77
Jerry Winston 77
NORTH CARO. ST. (3-25)
Thurl Bailey 83
Alvin Battle 83
Vic Bubas 50
Tom Burleson 74
Warren Cartier 50
Lorenzo Charles 83
Bob Cook 50
Dick Dickey 50
Terry Gannon 83
Joe Harand 50
Greg Hawkins 74
Paul Horvath 50
Sidney Lowe 83
Cozell McQueen 83
Mark Moeller 74
Ernie Myers 83
Sam Ranzino 50
Moe Rivers 74
Phil Spence 74
Charlie Stine 50
Tim Stoddard 74
Lee Terrill 50
David Thompson 74
Monte Towe 74
Dereck Whittenburg 83
NOTRE DAME (1-10)
Dave Batton 78
Rich Branning 78
Bruce Flowers 78
Bill Hanzlik 78
Tracy Jackson 78
Bill Laimbeer 78
Kelly Tripucka 78
Don Williams 78
Stan Wilcox 78
Orlando Woolridge 78
OHIO ST. (8-62)
Warren Amling 45, 46
Dan Andreas 68
Richard Baker 39
Craig Barclay 68
David Barker 60
Richard Boughner 39
Robert Bowen 44, 46
Gary Bradds 62
Rodney Caudill 44, 45
John Cedargren 60
Jack Dawson 39
James Doughty 62
John Dugger 44, 45
Clark Elliott 46
Ollie Fink 44
Jody Finney 68
Donald Flatt 62
Curtis Frazier 62
Richard Furry 60

Gary Gearhart 60, 61, 62
Jim Geddes 68
Donald Grate 44, 45
William Gunton 44
John Havlicek 60, 61, 62
Bill Hosket 68
Steve Howell 68
Richard Hoyt 60, 61
Jimmy Hull 39
Paul Huston 44, 45, 46
Wilbur Johnston 46
Bob Knight 60, 61, 62
Charles Kuhn 46
Jack Landes 61
Kenneth Lee 61
John Lovett 46
Jerry Lucas 60, 61, 62
Robert Lynch 39
Charles Maag 39
Doug McDonald 61, 62
Denny Meadors 68
Jed Mees 39
Gilbert Mickelson 39
Nelson Miller 61
Howard Nourse 60
Melvyn Nowell 60, 61, 62
Richard Reasbeck 61, 62
Arnold Risen 44, 45
Joe Roberts 60
William Sattler 39
John Schick 39
Bruce Schnabel 68
Don Scott 39
Larry Siegfried 60, 61
James Sims 45
Ed Smith 68
Ray Snyder 45, 46
Dave Sorenson 68
Robert Stafford 39
Mike Swain 68
Richard Taylor 62
John Underman 46
Wayne Wells 46
OKLAHOMA (3-26)
Mookie Blaylock 88
Garnett Corbin 39
Paul Courty 47
Harley Day 47
Ricky Grace 88
Harvey Grant 88
Ben Kerr 39
Stacey King 88
Jack Landon 47
Jim McNatt 39
Paul Merchant 47
Marvin Mesch 39
Vernon Mullen 39
Terrence Mullins 88
Allie Paine 47
Kenneth Pryor 47
Dick Reich 47
Gene Roop 39
Herb Scheffler 39
Dave Sieger 88
Marvin Snodgrass 39
Gerald Tucker 47
Roscoe Walker 39
Bill Waters 47
Andre Wiley 88
Matthew Zeliner 39
OKLAHOMA ST. (4-34)
Frank Allen 49

Louis Amaya 51
Sam Aubrey 46
Eugene Bell 46
A. L. Bennett 46
Joe Bradley 46, 49
Pete Darcey 51
Paul Geymann 46
Joe Halbert 45, 46
Cecil Hankins 45
Bob Harris 49
Larry Hayes 49
Jack Hobbs 49
Tom Jaquet 49
Don Johnson 51
Weldon Kern 45, 46
Bob Kurland 45, 46
Emmett McAfee 51
Gale McArthur 49, 51
John Miller 51
Bob Pager 51
J. L. Parks 45, 46, 49
Doyle Parrack 45
Morman Pilgrim 49
Gerald Rogers 51
Kendall Sheets 51
Jack Shelton 49
Keith Smith 49, 51
Mark Steinmeyer 46
Gerald Stockton 51
Maurice Ward 51
Blake Williams 45, 46
John Wylie 45
Vernon Yates 49
OREGON (1-9)
Robert Anet 39
John Dick 39
Laddie Gale 39
Robert Hardy 39
Wallace Johansen 39
Ford Mullen 39
Matt Pavalunas 39
Ted Sarpola 39
Urgel Wintermute 39
OREGON ST. (2-23)
Terry Baker 63
Dick Ballantyne 49
Rex Benner 63
Tim Campbell 63
Jim Catterall 49
Mel Counts 63
Cliff Crandall 49
Ed Fleming 49
Bill Harper 49
Dave Hayward 63
Tommy Holman 49
Jim Jarvis 63
Jim Kraus 63
Steve Pauly 63
Frank Peters 63
Alex Petersen 49
Len Rinearson 49
Gary Rossi 63
Paul Sliper 49
Ray Snyder 49
Ray Torgerson 63
Dan Torrey 49
Harvey Watt 49
PENN ST. (1-9)
Jesse Arnelle 54
Jim Blocker 54
Jim Brewer 54
Dave Edwards 54
Earl Fields 54
Ned Haag 54
Robert Rohrland 54
Jack Sherry 54

Ron Weidenhammer 54
PENNSYLVANIA (1-13)
Tom Condon 79
Ted Flick 79
Ken Hall 79
David Jackson 79
Ed Kuhl 79
Tom Leifsen 79
Tony Price 79
Angelo Reynolds 79
Vincent Ross 79
James Salters 79
Tim Smith 79
Matt White 79
Bobby Willis 79
PITTSBURGH (1-11)
Bob Artman 41
James Egan 41
James Klein 41
George Kocheran 41
Clare Malarkey 41
Sam Milanovich 41
Melvin Port 41
Larry Praffrath 41
Ed Raymond 41
Ed Straloski 41
John Swacus 41
PRINCETON (1-11)
Allen Adler 65
William Bradley 65
Robinson Brown 65
Robert Haarlow 65
Edward Hummer 65
William Kingston 65
William Koch 65
Donald Neimann 65
Donald Rodenbach 65
Donald Roth 65
Gary Walters 65
PROVIDENCE (2-22)
Al Baker 73
Marvin Barnes 73
Gary Bello 73
Delray Brooks 87
Marty Conlon 87
Fran Costello 73
Charles Crawford 73
Ernie DiGregorio 73
Billy Donovan 87
Jacek Duda 87
Rich Dunphy 73
Nehru King 73
David Kipfer 87
Ernie Lewis 87
Mark McAndrew 73
Dave Modest 73
Carlton Screen 87
David Sendeker 87
Abdul Shamsid-Deen 87
Kevin Stacom 73
Darryl Wright 87
Steve Wright 87
PURDUE (3-24)
John Anthrop 80
Roosevelt Barnes 80
Tyrone Bedford 69
Ted Benson 80
Joe Barry Carroll 80
Keith Edmonson 80
George Faerber 80
Herman Gilliam 69
Arnette Hallman 80
Jerry Johnson 69
Frank Kaufman 69

Bill Keller 69
Jon Kitchel 80
Steve Longfellow 69
Drake Morris 80
Rick Mount 69
Ted Reasoner 69
Kevin Stallings 80
Mike Scearce 80
Ralph Taylor 69
Brian Walker 80
Steve Walker 80
Larry Weatherford 69
Glenn Young 69

RUTGERS (1-8)
Abdel Anderson 76
Jim Bailey 76
Mark Conlin 76
Hollis Copeland 76
Mike Dabney 76
Steve Hefele 76
Ed Jordan 76
Phil Sellers 76

ST. BONAVENTURE (1-10)
Tom Baldwin 70
Gene Fahey 70
Matt Gantt 70
Greg Gary 70
Paul Grys 70
Paul Hoffman 70
Bill Kalbaugh 70
Mike Kull 70
Dale Tepas 70
Vic Thomas 70

ST. JOHN'S (N.Y.) (2-22)
Walter Berry 85
Terry Bross 85
Bob Cornegy 85
Jim Davis 52
Dick Duckett 52
Frank Giancontieri 52
Willie Glass 85
Mark Jackson 85
Shelton Jones 85
Ron MacGilvray 52
Jack McMahon 52
Jim McMorrow 52
Mike Moses 85
Chris Mullin 85
Carl Peterson 52
Phil Sagona 52
Ron Stewart 85
Steve Shurina 85
Solly Walker 52
Jim Walsh 52
Bill Wennington 85
Bob Zawoluk 52

ST. JOSEPH'S (PA.) (1-11)
Harry Booth 61
Dan Bugey 61
Bob Dickey 61
Jack Egan 61
Bob Gormley 61
Billy Hoy 61
Vince Kempton 61
Jim Lynam 61
Frank Majewski 61
Paul Westhead 61
Tom Wynne 61

SAN FRANCISCO (3-25)
Warren Baxter 55, 56
Carl Boldt 56
Gene Brown 56, 57

Stan Buchanan 55
Bill Bush 55
Art Day 57
Al Dunbar 57
Mike Farmer 56, 57
K. C. Jones 55
Jack King 55, 57, 56
Gordon Kirby 55
John Kolijian 57
Dick Lawless 55
Dave Lillevand 57
Bill Mallen 57
Ron Mancasola 57
Jerry Mullen 55
Tom Nelson 56
Hal Perry 55, 56
Mike Preaseau 56, 57
Bob Radanovich 57
Bill Russell 55, 56
Charles Russell 57
Bob Wiebusch 55
Rudy Zannini 55

SANTA CLARA (1-9)
Don Benedetti 52
Dallas Brock 52
Dick Garibaldi 52
Gary Gatzert 52
Bob Peters 52
Herb Schoenstein 52
Ken Sears 52
Dick Soares 52
Jim Young 52

SEATTLE (1-1)
Elgin Baylor 58
Charley Brown 58
Jerry Frizzell 58
Jim Harney 58
Thornton Humphries 58
John Kootnekoff 58
Lloyd Murphy 58
Don Ogorek 58
Jude Petrie 58
Don Piasecki 58
Francis Saunders 58
John Stepan 58
Bob Swiewarga 58
Bill Wall 58

SETON HALL (1-14)
Anthony Avent 89
Michael Cooper 89
Trevor Crowley 89
Andrew Gaze 89
Gerald Greene 89
Nick Katsikis 89
Khylem Long 89
Rene Monteserin 89
John Morton 89
Ramon Ramos 89
Jose Rebimbas 89
Frantz Volcy 89
Darryll Walker 89
Pookey Wiggington 89

SOUTHERN CAL (2-16)
Chester Carr 54
Jack Dunne 54
Richard Hammer 54
Roy Irvin 54
Keith Lambert 40
Jack Lippert 40
John Luber 40
Alan Ludecke 54
Tom McGarvin 40
Jack Morrison 40
Ralph Pausig 54
Tony Psaltis 54

Dale Sears 40
Walter Thompson 54
Ralph Vaughn 40
Richard Welsh 54

SOUTHERN METHODIST (1-8)
Rick Herrscher 56
Jim Krebs 56
Joel Krog 56
Bob McGregor 56
Buford Miller 56
Bobby Mills 56
Ronnie Morris 56
Larry Showalter 56

STANFORD (1-11)
Don Burness 42
Bill Cowden 42
Howie Dallmar 42
Jack Dana 42
John Eikelman 42
Fred Linari 42
Bud Madden 42
Leo McCaffrey 42
Fred Oliver 42
Jim Pollard 42
Ed Voss 42

SYRACUSE (2-20)
Derek Brower 87
Marty Byrnes 75
Derrick Coleman 87
Sherman Douglas 87
Rudy Hackett 75
Herman Harried 87
Larry Kelley 75
Kevin King 75
Ross Kindel 75
Jim Lee 75
Mark Meadors 75
Greg Monroe 87
Bob Parker 75
Chris Sease 75
Earnie Seibert 75
Rony Seikaly 87
Steve Shaw 75
Steve Thompson 87
Howard Triche 75
Jim Williams 75

TEMPLE (2-9)
Mel Brodsky 58
Fred Cohen 56
Dan Fleming 56, 58
Bill Kennedy 58
Hal Lear 56
Jay Norman 56, 58
Hal Reinfeld 56
Guy Rodgers 56, 58
Tink Van Patton 56, 58

TEXAS (2-11)
Frank Brahaney 43
Roy Cox 43, 47
Jack Fitzgerald 43
Tom Hamilton 47
John Hargis 43, 47
John Langdon 43, 47
Al Madsen 47
Slater Martin 47
V. C. Overall 43
Dan Wagner 47
Dudley Wright 43

UCLA (14-84)
Lew Alcindor 67, 68, 69
Lucius Allen 67, 68
Darrell Allums 80
Tony Anderson 80
Rick Betchley 70, 71
Henry Bibby 70, 71, 72

Pete Blackman 62
Kenny Booker 70, 71
Vince Carson 72, 73
Bruce Chambers 65
Jon Chapman 70, 71, 72
Joe Chrisman 67
Gary Cunningham 62
Tommy Curtis 72, 73, 74
Chuck Darrow 64
Darren Daye 80
Ralph Dollinger 74, 75, 76
John Ecker 69, 70, 71
Keith Erickson 64, 65
George Farmer 69
Larry Farmer 71, 72, 73
Rod Foster 80
Gary Franklin 72, 73, 74
John Galbraith 65
Gail Goodrich 64, 65
Fred Goss 65
John Green 62
David Greenwood 76
Roy Hamilton 76
Walt Hazzard 62, 64
Kenny Heitz 67, 68, 69
Bill Hicks 62
Andy Hill 70, 71, 72
Jack Hirsch 64
Vaughn Hoffman 64, 65
Brad Holland 76
Larry Hollyfield 72, 73
Michael Holton 80
Mike Huggins 64
Marques Johnson 74, 75, 76
Edgar Lacey 65
Greg Lee 72, 73, 74
Rich Levin 64, 65
Chris Lippert 76
Dick Lynn 67
Mike Lynn 65, 68
John Lyons 65
Andre McCarter 74, 75, 76
Doug McIntosh 64, 65
Dave Meyers 73, 74, 75
Jim Milhorn 62
Swen Nater 72, 73
Jim Nielsen 67, 68
Wilbert Olinde 74, 75, 76
Steve Patterson 69, 70, 71
Cliff Pruitt 80
Curtis Rowe 69, 70, 71
Don Saffer 67
Mike Sanders 80
Neville Saner 67, 68
Terry Schofield 69, 70, 71
Bill Seibert 69, 70
Lynn Shackelford 67, 68, 69
Gig Sims 80
Fred Slaughter 62, 64
Gavin Smith 76
Jim Spillane 74, 75, 76
Kim Stewart 62, 64
Gene Sutherland 67, 68
Bill Sweek 67, 68, 69
Ray Townsend 76
Pete Trogovich 74, 75
John Vallely 69, 70
Kiki Vandeweghe 80

Brett Vroman 76
Bill Walton 72, 73, 74
Mike Warren 67, 68
Kenny Washington 64, 65
Richard Washington 74, 75, 76
Dave Waxman 62
Bob Webb 74
Sidney Wicks 69, 70, 71
Keith Wilkes 72, 73, 74
James Wilkes 80

UTAH (3-24)
Joe Aufderheide 61
Leonard Black 66
Jerry Chambers 66
Bob Cozby 61
Bo Crain 61
Joe Day 66
Arnie Ferrin 44
Merv Jackson 66
Neil Jenson 61
Eugene Lake 66
Bob Lewis 44
Lyndon Mackay 66
Billy McGill 61
Wat Misaka 44
Joe Morton 61
Jeff Ockel 66
Jim Rhead 61
Ed Rowe 61
Rich Ruffell 61
Dick Smuin 44
Fred Sheffield 44
Rich Tate 66
Jim Thomas 61
Herb Wilkinson 44

UTEP (1-8)
Jerry Armstrong 66
Orsten Artis 66
Willie Cager 66
Harry Flournoy 66
Bobby Joe Hill 66
David Lattin 66
Nevil Shed 66
Wilie Worsley 66

VILLANOVA (3-25)
Louis Dubino 39
George Duzminski 39
Chuck Everson 85
Chris Ford 71
John Fox 71
Tom Ingelsby 71
Harold Jensen 85
John Krutulis 39
Michael Lazorchak 39
Dwayne McClain 85
Joe McDowell 71
Gary McLain 85
James Montgomery 39
Paul Nugent 39
Ed Pinckney 85
Mark Plansky 85
Howard Porter 71
Harold Pressley 85
Lloyd Rice 39
Ernest Robinson 39
Hank Siemiontkowski 71
William Sinnott 39
Clarence Smith 71
Dwight Wilbur 85
Charles Yund 39

VIRGINIA (2-16)
Rick Carlisle 84
Louis Collins 81
Kenton Edelin 84
Terry Gates 81
Jeff Jones 81
Jeff Klein 81
Jeff Lamp 81
Lewis Lattimore 81
Jim Miller 84
Olden Polynice 84
Lee Raker 81
Craig Robinson 81
Ralph Sampson 81
Tom Sheehey 84
Ricky Stokes 81, 84
Othell Wilson 81, 84

WAKE FOREST (1-12)
James Brooks 62

Richard Carmichael 62
Len Chappell 62
Frank Christie 62
Bryan Hassell 62
Harry Hull 62
Al Koehler 62
Tommy McCoy 62
Billy Packer 62
Dave Wiedeman 62
Bob Wollard 62
Ted Zawacki 62

WASHINGTON (1-10)
Don Apeland 53
Joe Cipriano 53
Will Elliott 53
Roland Halle 53
Bob Houbregs 53
Charles Koon 53
Doug McClary 53
Mike McCutchen 53
Dean Parsons 53
Steve Roake 53

WASHINGTON ST. (1-10)
Albert Akins 41
Vern Butts 41
Kirk Gebert 41
Dale Gentry 41
Marv Gilberg 41
John Hooper 41
Owen Hunt 41
Paul Lindenmann 41
Arnold Sundquist 41
Harold Zimmerman 41

WEST VA. (1-12)
Willie Akers 59
Marvin Bolyard 59
Robert Clousson 59
Paul Goode 59
Lee Patrone 59
Joseph Posch 59
Ronnie Retton 59
James Ritchie 59
Howard Schertzinger 59

Bob Smith 59
Nick Visnic 59
Jerry West 59

WESTERN KY. (1-9)
Rex Bailey 71
Jerry Dunn 71
Steve Eaton 71
Clarence Glover 71
Danny Johnson 71
Jim McDaniels 71
Jim Rose 71
Gary Sundmacker 71
Chuck Witt 71

WICHITA ST. (1-11)
John Criss 65
Gerald Davis 65
Dave Leach 65
Larry Nosich 65
Kelly Pete 65
Melvin Reed 65
Gerard Reimond 65
Vernon Smith 65
Jamie Thompson 65
Al Trope 65
Manny Zafinos 65

WISCONSIN (1-10)
Bob Alwin 41
Gene Englund 41
Charles Epperson 41
John Kotz 41
Fred Rehm 41
Ed Schiewe 41
Warren Schrage 41
Harlo Scott 41
Ted Strain 41
Don Timmerman 41

WYOMING (1-8)
Jimmy Collins 43
Milo Komenich 43
Jim Reese 43
Ted Roney 43
Ken Sailors 43
Floyd Volker 43
Don Waite 43
James Weir 43

TOURNAMENT TRIVIA QUESTION...
What is the only school to make the Final Four in its one and only NCAA tournament appearance?
Answer: Indiana State in 1979.

FINAL FOUR GAME OFFICIALS

1939
Lyle Clarno*
John Getchell*

1940
Gil MacDonald*
Ted O'Sullivan*

1941
Wally Cameron*
Bill Haarlow*

1942
Glenn Adams*
Ab Curtis*

1943
Matty Begovich*
Pat Kennedy*

1944
Paul Menton*
James Osborne*

1945
Glenn Adams*
James Beiersdorfer
Edward Boyle
Ab Curtis*

1946
Jocko Collins*
Pat Kennedy*
John Nucatola
William Orwig

1947
Hagan Anderson*
Bill Haarlow
Pat Kennedy*
William Orwig

1948
Matty Begovich
Bill Haarlow*
Gil MacDonald*
James Osborne

1949
Ab Curtis
Hal Lee*
Tim McCullough*
Cliff Ogden

1950
Lou Eisenstein*
Ronald Gibbs*
Remy Meyer
John Morrow

1951
No officials listed

1952
Lou Eisenstein*
Cliff Ogden*

1953
Joe Conway
Alex George
Al Lightner*

Cliff Ogden
Shaw*

1954
Hagan Anderson*
Dick Ball Sr.
Dean*
Jim Enright

1955
Phil Fox
Mike Milner
Mohr
Cliff Ogden

1956
No officials listed

1957
Hagan Anderson*
Joe Conway*
Al Lightner
Cliff Ogden

1958
Joe Conway
Al Mercer
Red Mihalik
John Morrow

1959
Tommy Bell
Red Mihalik

1960
No officials listed

1961
Curtis Filiberti*
Phil Fox*
Tom Glennon
Lenny Wirtz

1962
No officials listed

1963
No officials listed

1964
Charles Fouty
Tom Glennon*
Steve Honzo
Red Mihalik*

1965
Steve Honzo*
Bob Korte
Floyd Magnuson
Red Mihalik*

1966
Bill Bussenius
Steve Honzo*
Thornton Jenkins*
Lenny Wirtz

1967
No officials listed

1968
Bill Bussenius

Charles Fouty*
Steve Honzo*
Thornton Jenkins

1969
Irv Brown*
Michael
  DiTomasso*
Charles Fouty
John Overby

1970
Otis Allmond
Rudy Marich
Bobby Scott*
Art White
Lenny Wirtz*

1971
Jim Bain*
Irv Brown*
Steve Honzo
Art White

1972
Irv Brown*
Reggie Copeland
Jim Hernjack
Bobby Scott*

1973
Jack Ditty
Jim Howell*
Joe Shosid*
Art White

1974
Irv Brown*
Paul Galvan
Jim Howell*
Rich Weiler

1975
Paul Galvan
Hank Nichols*
Lou Soriano
Bob Wortman*

1976
Jim Bain
Irv Brown*
Charles Fouty
Bob Wortman*

1977
Irv Brown
Reggie Copeland*
Charles Fouty
Paul Galvan*

1978
Jim Bain*
Roy Clymer*
Jim Howell
Dale Kelley

1979
Frank Buckiewicz
Gary Muncy*

Hank Nichols*
Joe Silvester
Rich Weiler
Lenny Wirtz*

1980
Robert Herrold
Larry Lembo*
Hank Nichols*
Bob Rhodes
Booker Turner
Rich Weiler*

1981
Bobby Dibbler
Jim Howell
Dale Kelley
Ken Lauderdale*
Lou Moser*
Booker Turner*

1982
John Dabrow*
Bobby Dibbler*
Joe Forte
Hank Nichols*
Tom Rucker
Bob Wortman

1983
Joe Forte*
Paul Housman*
Larry Lembo
Hank Nichols*
Booker Turner
Rich Weiler

1984
Jim Clark
Hank Nichols
Dick Paparo
Ron Spitler*
Mike Tanco*
Booker Turner*

1985
Jim Burr
John Clougherty*
Bobby Dibbler*
Willis McJunkin
Don Rutledge*
Charles Vacca

1986
John Clougherty
Tom Fincken
Joe Forte
Paul Galvan
Hank Nichols*
Dick Paparo
Pete Pavia*
Don Rutledge*
Lenny Wirtz

1987
John Clougherty
Nolan Fine*

Joe Forte*
Paul Galvan
Luis Grillo
Rusty Herring
Dick Paparo
Don Rutledge
Joe Silvester*

1988
Jim Burr
John Clougherty*
Joe Forte
Luis Grillo
Tim Higgins*
Ed Hightower*
Paul Housman
Larry Lembo
Booker Turner

1989
John Clougherty*
Mickey Crowley*
Tom Harrington
Ed Hightower
Ted Hillary
David Jones
Larry Lembo
Tom Rucker*
Don Rutledge

1990
Jim Bain
Richie Ballesteros*
Frank Bosone
Jim Burr
Gerry Donaghy
Tim Higgins*
Ed Hightower*
Dick Paparo
Jim Stupin

1991
Jim Burr*
John Clougherty
Mickey Crowley*
Gerry Donaghy
Ed Hightower
Tom O'Neill
Pete Pavia
Charles Range*
Ted Valentine

1992
Jim Burr
John Clougherty
Gerry Donaghy*
Tom Harrington*
Tim Higgins
Ed Hightower
Dave Libbey*
Don Rutledge
Ted Valentine

*Officiated the championship game.

TOURNAMENT TRIVIA QUESTION...
Name the last undefeated team to win the NCAA tournament? Answer: Indiana in 1976 (32-0).

EARLY ROUNDS

Thirty-five years ago, Oscar Robertson scored 56 points to lead Cincinnati ov[er] [A]rkansas, 97-62, in the Midwest regional consolation game. Robertson's single[-]game output is the most by an individual in a Midwest region game. The "Big C" [a]veraged 32.4 points a game in 10 tournament games from 1958 to 1960.

REGIONAL RECORDS
SINGLE GAME, INDIVIDUAL

Most Points
56, Oscar Robertson, Cincinnati vs. Arkansas, MW R3d, 1958
52, Austin Carr, Notre Dame vs. Kentucky, SE RSF, 1970
47, Austin Carr, Notre Dame vs. Houston, MW R3d, 1971
46, Dave Corzine, DePaul vs. Louisville, MW RSF, 1978
45, Bob Houbregs, Washington vs. Seattle, West RSF 1953
45, Austin Carr, Notre Dame vs. Iowa, SE R3d, 1970

Most Field Goals
22, Austin Carr, Notre Dame vs. Kentucky, SE RSF, 1970
21, Oscar Robertson, Cincinnati vs. Arkansas, MW R3d, 1958
21, Austin Carr, Notre Dame vs. Iowa, SE R3d, 1970
20, Bob Houbregs, Washington vs. Seattle, West RSF 1953
19, Oscar Robertson, Cincinnati vs. Kansas, MW RF, 1960
19, Jeff Mullins, Duke vs. Villanova, East RSF, 1964

Most Field Goals Attempted
42, Dwight Lamar, Southwestern La. vs. Louisville, MW RSF, 1972
40, Austin Carr, Notre Dame vs. Houston, MW R3d, 1971
39, Austin Carr, Notre Dame vs. Iowa, SE R3d, 1970
38, Bob Cousy, Holy Cross vs. North Caro. St., East RF, 1950
36, Oscar Robertson, Cincinnati vs. Arkansas, MW R3d, 1958

Highest Field-Goal Percentage (minimum 10 FGM)
100.0% (10-10), Marvin Barnes, Providence vs. Pennsylvania, East RSF, 1973
100.0% (10-10), Christian Laettner, Duke vs. Kentucky, East RF, 1992 (ot)
92.3% (12-13), Dennis Holman, Southern Methodist vs. Cincinnati, MW R3d, 1966
91.7% (11-12), Pembrook Burrows, Jacksonville vs. Iowa, SE RSF, 1970
90.9% (10-11), Akeem Olajuwon, Houston vs. Villanova, MW RF, 1983

Most Three-Point Field Goals
8, Glen Rice, Michigan vs. North Caro., SE RSF, 1989
8, Bo Kimble, Loyola (Cal.) vs. Nevada-Las Vegas, West RF, 1990
7, Tim McCalister, Oklahoma vs. Iowa, West RSF, 1987 (ot)
7, Sean Higgins, Michigan vs. Virginia, SE RF, 1989
6, Barry Booker, Vanderbilt vs. Kansas, MW RSF, 1988
6, Phil Henderson, Duke vs. UCLA, East RSF, 1990

Most Three-Point Field Goals Attempted
16, Jeff Fryer, Loyola (Cal.) vs. Nevada-Las Vegas, West RF, 1990
14, Anfernee Hardaway, Memphis St. vs. Georgia Tech, MW RSF, 1992 (ot)
13, Freddie Banks, Nevada-Las Vegas vs. Iowa, West RF, 1987
13, Barry Booker, Vanderbilt vs. Kansas, MW RSF, 1988
12, four tied (most recent: two in 1990)

Highest Three-Point Field-Goal Percentage (minimum 5 3FGM)
100.0% (5-5), Hubert Davis, North Caro. vs. Eastern Mich., East RSF, 1991
83.3% (5-6), Billy Donovan, Providence vs. Alabama, SE RSF, 1987
83.3% (5-6), Dwayne Bryant, Georgetown vs. North Caro. St., East RSF, 1989
71.4% (5-7), Ken Atkinson, Richmond vs. Temple, East RSF, 1988
70.0% (7-10), Sean Higgins, Michigan vs. Virginia, SE RF, 1989

Most Free Throws
23, Bob Carney, Bradley vs. Colorado, MW RSF, 1954
18, John O'Brien, Seattle vs. Wyoming, West R3d, 1953
17, Roger Newman, Kentucky vs. Ohio St., SE RF, 1961
17, Barry Kramer, New York U. vs. West Va., East R3d, 1963
16, five tied (most recent: two in 1987)

Most Free Throws Attempted
26, Bob Carney, Bradley vs. Colorado, MW RSF, 1954
24, Donnie Gaunce, Morehead St. vs. Iowa, SE RSF, 1956
22, John O'Brien, Seattle vs. Wyoming, West R3d, 1953
22, Wilt Chamberlain, Kansas vs. Oklahoma City, MW RF, 1957
22, Roger Newman, Kentucky vs. Ohio St., SE RF, 1961

Highest Free-Throw Percentage (minimum 10 FTM)
100.0% (13-13), Bill Bradley, Princeton vs. Providence, East RF, 1965
100.0% (13-13), Mike Maloy, Davidson vs. St. John's (N.Y.), East RSF, 1969
100.0% (12-12), Dan Issel, Kentucky vs. Miami (Ohio), SE R3d, 1969
100.0% (12-12), Larry Finch, Memphis St. vs. Kansas St., MW RF, 1973
100.0% (12-12), Michael Jackson, Georgetown vs. Nevada-Las Vegas, West RSF, 1984

Most Rebounds
34, Fred Cohen, Temple vs. Connecticut, East RSF, 1956
31, Nate Thurmond, Bowling Green vs. Mississippi St., SE R3d, 1963
30, Jerry Lucas, Ohio St. vs. Kentucky, SE RF, 1961
28, Elvin Hayes, Houston vs. Pacific (Cal.), West R3d, 1966
27, John Green, Michigan St. vs. Notre Dame, SE RSF, 1957

Most Assists
13, Rumeal Robinson, Michigan vs. North Caro., SE RSF, 1989
13, Anderson Hunt, Nevada-Las Vegas vs. Loyola (Cal.), West RF, 1990
12, five tied (most recent: Steve Henson, Kansas St. vs. Purdue, MW RSF, 1988)

Most Blocked Shots
9, David Robinson, Navy vs. Cleveland St., East RSF, 1986
8, Mark Strickland, Temple vs. Oklahoma St., East RSF, 1991
7, Pervis Ellison, Louisville vs. Illinois, MW RSF, 1989
6, Tim Perry, Temple vs. Duke, East RF, 1988

5, Alonzo Mourning, Georgetown vs. North Caro. St., East RSF, 1989
5, Chris Webber, Michigan vs. Ohio St., SE RF, 1992 (ot)

Most Steals
7, Ricky Grace, Oklahoma vs. Iowa, West RSF, 1987 (ot)
6, John Evans, Rhode Island vs. Duke, East RSF, 1988

6, Anderson Hunt, Nevada-Las Vegas vs. Loyola (Cal.), West RF, 1990
6, Jason Buchanan, St. John's (N.Y.) vs. Ohio St., MW RSF, 1991
5, three tied (most recent: Greg Anthony, Nevada-Las Vegas vs. Seton Hall, West RF, 1991)

SINGLE GAME, TEAM

Most Points
131, Nevada-Las Vegas vs. Loyola (Cal.) (101), West RF, 1990
121, Iowa vs. Notre Dame (106), SE R3d, 1970
119, Houston vs. Notre Dame (106), MW R3d, 1971
118, Notre Dame vs. Vanderbilt (88), SE R3d, 1974
114, Arizona vs. Nevada-Las Vegas (109), RSF, West 1976 (ot)

Fewest Points
20, North Caro. vs. Pittsburgh (26), East RF, 1941
24, Springfield vs. Indiana (48), East RF, 1940
26, Pittsburgh vs. North Caro. (20), East RF, 1941
29, Western Ky. vs. Duquesne (30), East RF, 1940
29, Baylor vs. Oklahoma St. (44), West RF, 1946

Largest Winning Margin
49, UCLA (109) vs. Wyoming, (60), West RSF, 1967
47, Duke (101) vs. Connecticut (54), East RF, 1964
43, *Villanova (90) vs. Pennsylvania (47), East RF, 1971
40, Cincinnati (99) vs. DePaul (59), MW RSF, 1960
40, Princeton (109) vs. Providence (69), East RF, 1965
40, Louisville (93) vs. Kansas St. (53), MW R3d, 1968

Most Points Scored by Losing Team
109, Nevada-Las Vegas vs. Arizona (114), West RSF, 1976 (ot)
106, Notre Dame vs. Iowa (121), SE R3d, 1970
106, Notre Dame vs. Houston (119), MW R3d, 1971
103, Iowa vs. Jacksonville (104), SE RSF, 1970
103, Kentucky vs. Duke (104), East RF, 1992 (ot)

Most Field Goals
52, Iowa vs. Notre Dame, SE R3d, 1970
51, UCLA vs. Dayton, West RSF, 1974 (3 ot)
51, Nevada-Las Vegas vs. Loyola (Cal.), West RF, 1990
50, Kentucky vs. Austin Peay, SE RSF, 1973 (ot)
49, Notre Dame vs. Vanderbilt, SE R3d, 1974

Most Field Goals Attempted
106, Indiana vs. Miami (Ohio), SE R3d, 1958
103, St. Joseph's (Pa.) vs. West Va., East R3d, 1960
102, Notre Dame vs. Houston, MW R3d, 1971
100, Houston vs. Pacific (Cal.), West R3d, 1966
99, Brigham Young vs. Oklahoma City, West R3d, 1965
99, *Austin Peay vs. Kentucky, SE RSF, 1973 (ot)

Highest Field-Goal Percentage
74.4% (29-39), Georgetown vs. Oregon St., West RF, 1982
68.8% (33-48), Providence vs. Alabama, SE RSF, 1987

68.6% (35-51), Indiana vs. St. Joseph's (Pa.), SE RF, 1981
68.3% (41-60), Princeton vs. Providence, East RF, 1965
66.7% (30-45), Notre Dame vs. North Caro., East RSF, 1977

Lowest Field-Goal Percentage
12.7% (8-63), Springfield vs. Indiana, East RSF, 1940
13.9% (10-72), Harvard vs. Ohio St., East RSF, 1946
20.6% (13-63), Arkansas vs. Oregon St., West RSF, 1949
22.9% (16-70), St. John's (N.Y.) vs. Kentucky, East RSF, 1951
24.4% (20-82), Holy Cross vs. Ohio St., East R3d, 1950

Most Three-Point Field Goals
17, Loyola (Cal.) vs. Nevada-Las Vegas, West RF, 1990
14, Providence vs. Alabama, SE RSF, 1987
13, Michigan vs. North Caro., SE RSF, 1989
12, Kentucky vs. Duke, East RF, 1992 (ot)
11, three tied (most recent: Michigan vs. Virginia, SE RF, 1989)

Most Three-Point Field Goals Attempted
41, Loyola (Cal.) vs. Nevada-Las Vegas, West RF, 1990
30, Nevada-Las Vegas vs. Iowa, West RF, 1987
28, Loyola (Cal.) vs. Alabama, West RSF, 1990
24, Michigan vs. North Caro., SE RSF, 1989
24, Temple vs. North Caro., East RF, 1991

Highest Three-Point Field-Goal Percentage (minimum 7 3FGM)
80.0% (8-10), Kansas St. vs. Purdue, MW RSF, 1988
72.7% (8-11), Duke vs. Indiana, MW RSF, 1987
70.0% (7-10), St. John's (N.Y.) vs. Duke, MW RF, 1991
63.6% (14-22), Providence vs. Alabama, SE RSF, 1987
58.3% (7-12), Duke vs. Connecticut, MW RSF, 1991
58.3% (7-12), UCLA vs. New Mexico St., West RSF, 1992

Most Free Throws
41, Utah vs. Santa Clara, West R3d, 1960
39, Seattle vs. Utah, West R3d, 1955
38, Bradley vs. Colorado, MW RSF, 1954
38, Loyola (Ill.) vs. Kentucky, SE R3d, 1964
36, New York U. vs. St. Joseph's (Pa.), East R3d, 1962

Most Free Throws Attempted
53, Morehead St. vs. Iowa, SE RSF, 1956
52, Iowa vs. Morehead St., SE RSF, 1956
50, West Va. vs. St. Joseph's (Pa.), East RSF, 1959
49, New York U. vs. St. Joseph's (Pa.), East R3d, 1962
48, Utah vs. Santa Clara, West R3d, 1960

Highest Free-Throw Percentage (minimum 15 FTM)

100.0% (22-22), Fordham vs. South Caro., East R3d, 1971

100.0% (17-17), Villanova vs. Kentucky, SE RSF, 1988

95.5% (21-22), Vanderbilt vs. Marquette, SE RSF, 1974

95.2% (20-21), Notre Dame vs. Vanderbilt, SE R3d, 1974

95.0% (19-20), North Caro. St. vs. St. John's (N.Y.), East R3d, 1951

95.0% (19-20), Iowa vs. Georgetown, East RF, 1980

Most Rebounds

76, Temple vs. Connecticut, East RSF, 1956

76, Houston vs. Texas Christian, MW RF, 1968

76, UCLA vs. Weber St., West RSF, 1972

72, UCLA vs. Seattle, West R3d, 1956

72, Seattle vs. Utah St., West R3d, 1964

Largest Rebound Margin

33, Cincinnati (68) vs. Texas Tech (35), MW RSF, 1961

29, Utah (59) vs. Loyola (Cal.) (30), West RSF, 1961

28, Seattle (72) vs. Utah St. (44), West R3d, 1964

28, Indiana St. (50) vs. Oklahoma (22), MW RSF, 1979

27, Memphis St. (60) vs. South Caro. (33), MW RSF, 1973

Most Assists

35, Nevada-Las Vegas vs. Loyola (Cal.), West RF, 1990

26, Louisiana Tech vs. Oklahoma, MW RSF, 1985

25, North Caro. vs. Louisville, West RSF, 1986

25, Nevada-Las Vegas vs. Auburn, West RSF, 1986

25, Oklahoma vs. Louisville, SE RSF, 1988

Most Blocked Shots

13, Louisville vs. Illinois, MW RSF, 1989

11, Duke vs. Temple, East RF, 1988

10, Providence vs. Georgetown, SE RF, 1987

9, five tied (most recent: UTEP vs. Cincinnati, MW RSF, 1992)

Most Steals

17, Duke vs. St. John's (N.Y.), MW RF, 1991

15, Arkansas vs. Texas, MW RF, 1990

14, Oklahoma vs. Iowa, West RSF, 1987 (ot)

14, Loyola (Cal.) vs. Nevada-Las Vegas, West RF, 1990

14, Nevada-Las Vegas vs. Seton Hall, West RF, 1991

14, St. John's (N.Y.) vs. Ohio St., MW RSF, 1991

Most Personal Fouls

41, Dayton vs. Illinois, East RSF, 1952

36, UCLA vs. Seattle, West R3d, 1956

36, Seattle vs. UCLA, West RSF, 1964

35, Iowa vs. Morehead St., SE RSF, 1956

35, DePaul vs. Va. Military, East RSF, 1976 (ot)

Most Players Disqualified

5, St. Joseph's (Pa.) vs. West Va., East RSF, 1959

5, DePaul vs. Va. Military, East RSF, 1976 (ot)

5, Syracuse vs. Virginia, East RSF, 1984

4, 11 tied (most recent: Boston College vs. Houston, MW RF, 1982)

SINGLE GAME, TWO-TEAM

Most Points

232, Nevada-Las Vegas (131) vs. Loyola (Cal.) (101), West RF, 1990

227, Iowa (121) vs. Notre Dame (106), SE R3d, 1970

225, Houston (119) vs. Notre Dame (106), MW R3d, 1971

223, Arizona (114) vs. Nevada-Las Vegas (109), West RSF, 1976 (ot)

214, Oklahoma City (112) vs. Brigham Young (102), West R3d, 1965

Most Field Goals

97, Iowa (52) vs. Notre Dame (45), SE R3d, 1970

96, Kentucky (50) vs. Austin Peay (46), SE RSF, 1973 (ot)

91, UCLA (51) vs. Dayton (40), West RSF, 1974 (3 ot)

86, Nevada-Las Vegas (51) vs. Loyola (Cal.) (35), West RF, 1990

Most Field Goals Attempted

196, Austin Peay (99) vs. Kentucky (97), SE RSF, 1973 (ot)

195, Iowa (98) vs. Notre Dame (97), SE R3d, 1970

194, Indiana (106) vs. Miami (Ohio) (88), SE RSF, 1958

194, Houston (100) vs. Pacific (Cal.) (94), West R3d, 1966

180, Loyola (Cal.) (94) vs. Nevada-Las Vegas (86), West RF, 1990

Most Three-Point Field Goals

24, Loyola (Cal.) (17) vs. Nevada-Las Vegas (7), West RF, 1990

21, Providence (14) vs. Alabama (7), SE RSF, 1987

20, Michigan (13) vs. North Caro. (7), SE RSF, 1989

20, Kentucky (12) vs. Duke (8), East RF, 1992 (ot)

Most Three-Point Field Goals Attempted

59, Loyola (Cal.) (41) vs. Nevada-Las Vegas (18), West RF, 1990

45, Alabama (23) vs. Providence (22), SE RSF, 1987

Most Free Throws

68, Iowa (35) vs. Morehead St. (33), SE RSF, 1956

68, Oklahoma City (35) vs. Kansas St. (33), MW RSF, 1956

64, Bradley (38) vs. Colorado (26), West RSF, 1954

63, Seattle (39) vs. Utah (24), West R3d, 1955

63, La Salle (35) vs. Canisius (28), East RF, 1955

Most Free Throws Attempted

105, Morehead St. (53) vs. Iowa (52), SE RSF, 1956

92, Oklahoma City (48) vs. Kansas St. (44), MW RSF, 1956

92, Seattle (52) vs. UCLA (40), West R3d, 1956

89, New York U. (49) vs. St. Joseph's (Pa.) (40), East R3d, 1962

Most Rebounds

132, Pacific (Cal.) (67) vs. Houston (65), West R3d, 1966

131, Houston (76) vs. Texas Christian (55), MW RF, 1968

130, UCLA (76) vs. Weber St. (54), West RSF, 1972

128, UCLA (72) vs. Seattle (56), West R3d, 1956

126, UCLA (64) vs. Seattle (62), West RSF, 1964

126, Drake (66) vs. Notre Dame (60), MW RSF, 1971 (ot)

Most Assists

58, Nevada-Las Vegas (35) vs. Loyola (Cal.) (23), West RF, 1990

47, North Caro. (25) vs. Louisville (22), West RSF, 1986

47, Kentucky (24) vs. Duke (23), East RF, 1992 (ot)

Most Blocked Shots
15, Louisville (13) vs. Illinois (2), MW RSF, 1989
14, Providence (10) vs. Georgetown (4), SE RF, 1987
14, Nevada-Las Vegas (9) vs. Arizona (5), West RSF, 1989
14, North Caro. (8) vs. Eastern Mich. (6), East RSF, 1991

Most Steals
27, Loyola (Cal.) (14) vs. Nevada-Las Vegas (13), West RF, 1990
26, Duke (17), vs. St. John's (N.Y.) (9), MW RF, 1991
23, St. John's (N.Y.) (14) vs. Ohio St. (9), MW RSF, 1991

21, Memphis St. (12) vs. Georgia Tech (9), MW RSF, 1992 (ot)
20, Oklahoma (14) vs. Iowa (6), West RSF, 1987 (ot)
20, Kentucky (12) vs. Duke (8), East RF, 1992 (ot)

Most Personal Fouls
65, Seattle (36) vs. UCLA (29), West RSF, 1964

RF—Regional final game.
RSF—Regional semifinal game.
R3d—Regional third-place game.
East—East region.
SE—Southeast/Mideast region.
MW—Midwest region.
West—West/Far West region.
*Record later vacated.

FIRST AND SECOND ROUNDS
SINGLE GAME, INDIVIDUAL

Most Points
61, Austin Carr, Notre Dame vs. Ohio, SE 1st, 1970
52, Austin Carr, Notre Dame vs. Texas Christian, MW 1st, 1971
50, David Robinson, Navy vs. Michigan, East 1st, 1987
49, Elvin Hayes, Houston vs. Loyola (Ill.), MW 1st, 1968
45, Bo Kimble, Loyola (Cal.) vs. New Mexico St., West 1st, 1990

Most Field Goals
25, Austin Carr, Notre Dame vs. Ohio, SE 1st, 1970
20, Elvin Hayes, Houston vs. Loyola (Ill.), MW 1st, 1968
20, Austin Carr, Notre Dame vs. Texas Christian, MW 1st, 1971
22, David Robinson, Navy vs. Michigan, East 1st, 1987
17, five tied [most recent: Bo Kimble, Loyola (Cal.) vs. New Mexico St., West 1st, 1990]

Most Field Goals Attempted
44, Austin Carr, Notre Dame vs. Ohio, SE 1st, 1970
37, David Robinson, Navy vs. Michigan, East 1st, 1987
36, Ronald "Popeye" Jones, Murray St. vs. Michigan St., SE 1st, 1990 (ot)
35, Rich Laurel, Hofstra vs. Notre Dame, East 1st, 1977
35, Bo Kimble, Loyola (Cal.) vs. New Mexico St., West 1st, 1990

Highest Field-Goal Percentage (minimum 10 FGM)
100.0% (11-11), Kenny Walker, Kentucky vs. Western Ky., SE 2nd, 1986
100.0% (10-10), Joey Wright, Texas vs. St. John's (N.Y.), MW 2nd, 1991
90.9% (10-11), Dwayne McClain, Villanova vs. Marshall, SE 1st, 1984
90.9% (10-11), Byron Houston, Oklahoma St. vs. North Caro. St., East 2nd, 1991
90.9% (10-11), Oliver Miller, Arkansas vs. Murray St., MW 1st, 1992

Most Three-Point Field Goals
11, Jeff Fryer, Loyola (Cal.) vs. Michigan, West 2nd, 1990
9, Garde Thompson, Michigan vs. Navy, East, 1st, 1987
8, Gerald Paddio, Nevada-Las Vegas vs. Iowa, West 2nd, 1988
8, Brad Soucie, Eastern Mich. vs. Pittsburgh, MW 1st, 1988

8, Jamie Mercurio, Miami (Ohio) vs. North Caro., SE 1st, 1992

Most Three-Point Field Goals Attempted
22, Jeff Fryer, Loyola (Cal.) vs. Arkansas, MW 1st, 1989
20, Chris Walker, Villanova vs. Louisiana St., SE 1st, 1990
19, Gerald Paddio, Nevada-Las Vegas vs. Iowa, West 2nd, 1988
16, Carlos Sample, Southern-B.R. vs. North Caro., SE 1st, 1989
15, four tied (most recent: Randy Woods, La Salle vs. Seton Hall, East 1st, 1992)

Highest Three-Point Field-Goal Percentage (minimum 5 3FGM)
100.0% (6-6), Mike Buck, Middle Tenn. St. vs. Florida St., SE 1st, 1989
100.0% (6-6), Migjen Bakalli, North Caro. St. vs. Southern Miss., East 1st, 1991
100.0% (5-5), Mitch Richmond, Kansas St. vs. Georgia, West 1st, 1987 (ot)
87.5% (7-8), William Scott, Kansas St. vs. DePaul, MW 2nd, 1988
83.3% (5-6), four tied (most recent: two in 1991)

Most Free Throws
23, Travis Mays, Texas vs. Georgia, MW 1st, 1990
21, David Robinson, Navy vs. Syracuse, East 2nd, 1986
19, Tom Hammonds, Georgia Tech vs. Iowa St., East 1st, 1988
18, Jon Rose, Connecticut vs. Boston U., East 1st, 1959
17, Tyrone Hill, Xavier (Ohio) vs. Kansas St., MW 1st, 1990

Most Free Throws Attempted
27, David Robinson, Navy vs. Syracuse, East 2nd, 1986
27, Travis Mays, Texas vs. Georgia, MW 1st, 1990
21, Adrian Dantley, Notre Dame vs. Kansas, MW 1st, 1975
21, John Bagley, Boston College vs. Wake Forest, SE 2nd, 1981
21, Vernon Maxwell, Florida vs. North Caro. St., East 1st, 1987
21, Tom Hammonds, Georgia Tech vs. Iowa St., East 1st, 1988

Highest Free-Throw Percentage (minimum 12 FTM)
100.0% (16-16), Bill Bradley, Princeton vs. St. Joseph's (Pa.), East 1st, 1963
100.0% (16-16), Fennis Dembo, Wyoming vs.

UCLA, West 2nd, 1987

100.0% (13-13), Al Gooden, Ball St. vs. Boston College, SE 1st, 1981

100.0% (12-12), nine tied (most recent: two in 1992)

Most Rebounds

29, Toby Kimball, Connecticut vs. St. Joseph's (Pa.), East 1st, 1965

27, Paul Silas, Creighton vs. Oklahoma City, MW 1st, 1964

27, Elvin Hayes, Houston vs. Loyola (Ill.), MW 1st, 1968

24, Paul Silas, Creighton vs. Memphis St., MW 1st, 1962

24, Eddie Jackson, Oklahoma City vs. Creighton, MW 1st, 1964

Most Assists

15, Kenny Patterson, DePaul vs. Syracuse, East 1st, 1985

15, Keith Smart, Indiana vs. Auburn, MW 2nd, 1987

14, Dicky Beal, Kentucky vs. Brigham Young, SE 2nd, 1984

14, Carl Wright, Southern Methodist vs. Miami (Ohio), West 1st, 1984

14, John Crotty, Virginia vs. Middle Tenn. St., SE 2nd, 1989

14, Pooh Richardson, UCLA vs. Iowa St., SE 1st, 1989

Most Blocked Shots

11, Shaquille O'Neal, Louisiana St. vs. Brigham Young, West 1st, 1992

10, Shawn Bradley, Brigham Young vs. Virginia, West 1st, 1991

8, Tim Perry, Temple vs. Lehigh, East 1st, 1988

8, Acie Earl, Iowa vs. Duke, East 2nd, 1992

7, six tied (most recent: two in 1989)

Most Steals

7, Tommy Amaker, Duke vs. Old Dominion, East 2nd, 1986

7, Reggie Miller, UCLA vs. Wyoming, West 2nd, 1987

7, Delray Brooks, Providence vs. Austin Peay, SE 2nd, 1987

7, Scott Burrell, Connecticut vs. Xavier (Ohio), MW 2nd, 1991

6, eight tied (most recent: Clarence Ceasar, Louisiana St. vs. Brigham Young, West 1st, 1992)

SINGLE GAME, TEAM

Most Points

149, Loyola (Cal.) vs. Michigan (115), West 2nd, 1990

124, Oklahoma vs. Louisiana Tech (81), SE 2nd, 1989

123, North Caro. vs. Loyola (Cal.) (97), West 2nd, 1988

121, Nevada-Las Vegas vs. San Francisco (95), West 1st, 1977

120, Arkansas vs. Loyola (Cal.) (101), MW 1st, 1989

Fewest Points

38, Ohio vs. Kansas (49), SE 1st, 1985

40, Ohio vs. Kentucky (57), SE 2nd, 1983

42, Loyola (La.) vs. Oklahoma St. (59), MW 1st, 1958

42, Tennessee Tech vs. Loyola (Ill.) (111), SE 1st, 1963

42, Pennsylvania vs. Duke (52), SE 2nd, 1980

Largest Winning Margin

69, Loyola (Ill.) (111) vs. Tennessee Tech (42), SE 1st, 1963

49, Syracuse (101) vs. Brown (52), East 1st, 1986

47, DePaul (99) vs. Eastern Ky. (52), SE 1st, 1965

43, Oklahoma (124) vs. Louisiana Tech (81), SE 2nd, 1989

42, Notre Dame (108) vs. Austin Peay (66), SE 1st, 1974

Most Points Scored by Losing Team

115, Wyoming vs. Loyola (Cal.) (119), West 1st, 1988

115, Michigan vs. Loyola (Cal.) (149), West 2nd, 1990

101, Marshall vs. Southwestern La. (112), MW 1st, 1972

101, Loyola (Cal.) vs. Arkansas (120), MW 1st, 1989

98, Notre Dame vs. Houston (99), MW 1st, 1965

98, Iowa St. vs. Kentucky (106), East 2nd, 1992

Most Field Goals

50, Notre Dame vs. Austin Peay, SE 1st, 1974

49, North Caro. vs. Loyola (Cal.), West 2nd, 1988

49, Nevada-Las Vegas vs. San Francisco, West 1st, 1977

49, Loyola (Cal.) vs. Michigan, West 2nd, 1990

48, Oklahoma vs. Louisiana Tech, SE 2nd, 1989

Most Field Goals Attempted

112, Marshall vs. Southwestern La., MW 1st, 1972

103, Loyola (Cal.) vs. North Caro., West 2nd, 1988

101, Holy Cross vs. North Caro. St., East 1st, 1950

99, Oral Roberts vs. Louisville, MW 1st, 1974

98, Oklahoma vs. Louisiana Tech, SE 2nd, 1989

98, Arkansas vs. Loyola (Cal.), MW 1st, 1989

Highest Field-Goal Percentage

80.0% (28-35), Oklahoma St. vs. Tulane, SE 2nd, 1992

79.0% (49-62), North Caro. vs. Loyola (Cal.), West 2nd, 1988

75.0% (33-44), Northeastern vs. Va. Commonwealth, East 1st, 1984

73.2% (30-41), North Caro. St. vs. UTEP, West 2nd, 1985

72.7% (40-55), *Alabama vs. New Orleans, SE 2nd, 1987

Lowest Field-Goal Percentage

22.0% (18-82), Tennessee Tech vs. Loyola (Ill.), SE 1st, 1963

25.0% (17-68), Massachusetts vs. New York U., East 1st, 1962

25.3% (19-75), Brown vs. Syracuse, East 1st, 1986

26.2% (17-65), Texas A&M vs. Washington, West 1st, 1951

26.7% (16-60), Howard vs. Wyoming, West 1st, 1981

Most Three-Point Field Goals

21, Loyola (Cal.) vs. Michigan, West 2nd, 1990

13, Loyola (Cal.) vs. North Caro., West 2nd, 1988

13, St. Francis (Pa.) vs. Arizona, West 1st, 1991

13, Texas vs. Iowa, East 1st, 1992

13, Brigham Young vs. Louisiana St., West 1st, 1992

13, East Tenn. St. vs. Arizona, SE 1st, 1992

Most Three-Point Field Goals Attempted

40, Loyola (Cal.) vs. Michigan, West 2nd, 1990

39, Loyola (Cal.) vs. North Caro., West 2nd, 1988

39, Loyola (Cal.) vs. Arkansas, MW 1st, 1989

35, La Salle vs. Clemson, East 2nd, 1990

33, three tied (most recent: Brigham Young vs. Louisiana St., West 1st, 1992)

Highest Three-Point Field-Goal Percentage (minimum 7 3FGM)

88.9% (8-9), Kansas St. vs. Georgia, West 1st, 1987 (ot)

81.8% (9-11), *Alabama vs. North Caro. A&T, SE 1st, 1987

76.9% (10-13), Kansas St. vs. DePaul, MW 2nd, 1988

72.7% (8-11), Alabama vs. Colorado St., West 1st, 1990

70.0% (7-10), five tied (most recent: Iowa vs. East Tenn. St., MW 1st, 1991)

Most Free Throws

41, Navy vs. Syracuse, East 2nd, 1986

39, UTEP vs. Tulsa, West 1st, 1985

37, Morehead St. vs. Pittsburgh, SE 1st, 1957

37, Xavier (Ohio) vs. Kansas St., MW 1st, 1990

36, Georgia Tech vs. Iowa St., East 1st, 1988

36, UCLA vs. Louisville, West 2nd, 1992

Most Free Throws Attempted

55, UTEP vs. Tulsa, West 1st, 1985

54, Morehead St. vs. Pittsburgh, SE 1st, 1957

52, Weber St. vs. Hawaii, West 1st, 1972

52, Navy vs. Syracuse, East 2nd, 1986

50, Notre Dame vs. Kansas, MW 1st, 1975

Highest Free-Throw Percentage (minimum 15 FTM)

100.0% (17-17), Dayton vs. Villanova, SE 1st, 1985

95.8% (23-24), Oklahoma St. vs. Loyola (La.), MW 1st, 1958

95.2% (20-21), Iowa vs. North Caro. St., East 2nd, 1989

94.7% (18-19), Nevada-Las Vegas vs. Kansas St., West 2nd, 1987

94.4% (17-18), Michigan St. vs. Cincinnati, MW 2nd, 1992

Most Rebounds

86, Notre Dame vs. Tennessee Tech, SE 1st, 1958

70, Western Ky. vs. Miami (Fla.), SE 1st, 1960

68, Utah vs. Southern Cal, West 1st, 1960

68, Marshall vs. Southwestern La., MW 1st, 1972

66, Loyola (Ill.) vs. Tennessee Tech, SE 1st, 1963

66, Arizona St. vs. Loyola (Cal.), West 1st, 1980

Largest Rebound Margin

42, Notre Dame (86) vs. Tennessee Tech (44), SE 1st, 1958

35, St. John's (N.Y.) (56) vs. Connecticut (21), East 1st, 1951

30, Louisiana Tech (56) vs. Pittsburgh (26), MW 1st, 1985

29, West Va. (63) vs. Dartmouth (34), East 1st, 1959

29, Indiana (52) vs. Robert Morris (23), SE 1st, 1982

Most Assists

36, North Caro. vs. Loyola (Cal.), West 2nd, 1988

33, Loyola (Cal.) vs. Michigan, West 2nd, 1990

32, Arkansas vs. Georgia St., SE 1st, 1991

32, Kansas vs. Howard, MW 1st, 1992

32, Michigan vs. East Tenn. St., SE 2nd, 1992

Most Blocked Shots

13, Brigham Young vs. Virginia, West 1st, 1991

12, Clemson vs. St. Mary's (Cal.), West 1st, 1989

12, Louisiana St. vs. Brigham Young, West 1st, 1992

11, Arizona vs. UTEP, West 1st, 1987 (ot)

11, North Caro. St. vs. Iowa, East 2nd, 1989

Most Steals

19, Providence vs. Austin Peay, SE 2nd, 1987

19, Connecticut vs. Boston U., East 1st, 1990

18, Xavier (Ohio) vs. Kansas, MW 1st, 1988

17, Seton Hall vs. Pepperdine, West 1st, 1991

16, seven tied (most recent: Kentucky vs. Old Dominion, East 1st, 1992)

Most Personal Fouls

39, Kansas vs. Notre Dame, MW 1st, 1975

36, North Caro. vs. Texas A&M, MW 2nd, 1980

35, Hawaii vs. Weber St., West 1st, 1972

35, DePaul vs. Boston College, MW 2nd, 1982

34, four tied (most recent: two in 1987)

Most Players Disqualified

6, Kansas vs. Notre Dame, MW 1st, 1975

5, DePaul vs. Boston College, MW 2nd, 1982

5, Wyoming vs. Loyola (Cal.), West 1st, 1988

4, 13 tied (most recent: Florida St. vs. Iowa, West 1st, 1988)

SINGLE GAME, TWO-TEAM

Most Points

264, Loyola (Cal.) (149) vs. Michigan (115), West 2nd, 1990

234, Loyola (Cal.) (119) vs. Wyoming (115), West 1st, 1988

221, Arkansas (120) vs. Loyola (Cal.) (101), MW 1st, 1989

220, North Caro. (123) vs. Loyola (Cal.) (97), West 2nd, 1988

216, Nevada-Las Vegas (121) vs. San Francisco (95), West 1st, 1977

Most Field Goals Made

94, Loyola (Cal.) (49) vs. Michigan (45), West 2nd, 1990

84, La Salle (42) vs. Villanova (42), East 1st, 1978

Most Field Goals Attempted

184, Ohio (94) vs. Notre Dame (90), SE 1st, 1970

174, Loyola (Cal.) (89) vs. Michigan (85), West 2nd, 1990

Most Three-Point Field Goals

25, Loyola (Cal.) (21) vs. Michigan (4), West 2nd, 1990

21, St. Francis (Pa.) (13) vs. Arizona (8), West 1st, 1991

20, North Caro. St. (12) vs. Southern Miss. (8), East 1st, 1991

19, Pittsburgh (10) vs. Kansas (9), SE 2nd, 1991

19, Stanford (10) vs. Alabama (9), SE 1st, 1992

19, Seton Hall (10) vs. La Salle (9), East 1st, 1992

Most Three-Point Field Goals Attempted

56, La Salle (33) vs. Southern Miss. (23), East 1st, 1990

54, La Salle (30) vs. Seton Hall (24), East 1st, 1992

53, Loyola (Cal.) (40) vs. Michigan (13), West 2nd, 1990

48, Loyola (Cal.) (39) vs. Arkansas (9), MW 1st, 1989

47, Texas Southern (33) vs. Georgetown (14), MW 1st, 1990

47, North Caro. St. (25) vs. Southern Miss. (22), East 1st, 1991

Most Free Throws Made

69, Morehead St. (37) vs. Pittsburgh (32), SE 1st, 1957

Most Free Throws Attempted

97, Morehead St. (54) vs. Pittsburgh (43), SE 1st, 1957

91, Manhattan (49) vs. West Va. (42), East 1st, 1958

Most Rebounds

134, Marshall (68) vs. Southwestern La. (66), MW 1st, 1972

130, Notre Dame (86) vs. Tennessee Tech (44), SE 1st, 1958

121, Utah (68) vs. Southern Cal (53), West 1st, 1960

119, Massachusetts (60) vs. New York U. (59), East 1st, 1962

119, Loyola (Cal.) (65) vs. Arkansas (54), MW 1st, 1989

Most Assists

55, Michigan (30) vs. Florida (25), West 2nd, 1988

54, Loyola (Cal.) (33) vs. Michigan (21), West 2nd, 1990

51, Wake Forest (27) vs. Alabama (24), SE 2nd, 1991

48, Arkansas (32) vs. Georgia St. (16), SE 1st, 1991

47, three tied (most recent: two in 1992)

Most Blocked Shots

18, Iowa (10) vs. Duke (8), East 2nd, 1992

16, Oklahoma (9) vs. Louisiana Tech (7), SE 2nd, 1989

15, Georgia (8) vs. Texas (7), MW 1st, 1990

15, Arkansas (8) vs. Georgia St. (7), SE 1st, 1991

14, Brigham Young (13) vs. Virginia (1), West 1st, 1991

14, Nevada-Las Vegas (8) vs. Georgetown (6), West 2nd, 1991

Most Steals

26, Providence (19) vs. Austin Peay (7), SE 2nd, 1987

26, Arkansas (16) vs. Georgia St. (10), SE 1st, 1991

25, South Caro. St. (13) vs. Duke (12), East 1st, 1989

25, East Tenn. St. (14) vs. Iowa (11), MW 1st, 1991

Most Personal Fouls

61, West Va. (32) vs. Manhattan (29), East 1st, 1958

54, West Va. (29) vs. Missouri (25), East 1st, 1992

54, Kentucky (29) vs. Iowa St. (25), East 2nd, 1992

2nd—Second-round game.
1st—First-round game.
OR—Opening-round game.
East—East region.
SE—Southeast/Mideast region.
MW—Midwest region.
West—West/Far West region.
*Record later vacated.

BASKETBALL FACTS...

What two colleges met in the first basketball game between two schools? A good question with at least three different answers, depending on how you look at it. On February 9, 1895, the first game was played between two college teams as the Minnesota School of Agriculture defeated Hamline, 9-3. However, nine players were allowed on the court at the same time for both teams. Also, the School of Agriculture included students of both college and high-school age. So many people say that game doesn't count. The first college basketball game with five players on a side was played on January 16, 1896, when Chicago defeated Iowa, 15-12, in Iowa City. Both teams' starting five played the whole game. However, Iowa's starters were composed of a YMCA team that all happened to be students at the university, so does this game count as a true college game? And finally, some basketball historians say that the first true collegiate men's game was played between Yale and Pennsylvania in 1897. Yale soundly defeated Penn, 32-10. Remember, vote for only one.

EAST REGION
SINGLE GAME, INDIVIDUAL

Most Points
50, David Robinson, Navy vs. Michigan, 1st, 1987
44, Rod Thorn, West Va. vs. St. Joseph's (Pa.), RSF, 1963
43, Jeff Mullins, Duke vs. Villanova, RSF, 1964
42, John Clune, Navy vs. Connecticut, 1st, 1954
41, Don Schlundt, Indiana vs. Notre Dame, RF, 1953
41, Bill Bradley, Princeton vs. Providence, RF, 1965

Most Field Goals
22, David Robinson, Navy vs. Michigan, 1st, 1987
19, Jeff Mullins, Duke vs. Villanova, RSF, 1964
18, Hal Lear, Temple vs. Connecticut, RSF, 1956
18, Tom Rikers, South Caro. vs. Fordham, R3d, 1971
16, nine tied (most recent: Derrick Chievous, Missouri vs. Rhode Island, 1st, 1988)

Most Field Goals Attempted
38, Bob Cousy, Holy Cross vs. North Caro. St., RF, 1950
37, David Robinson, Navy vs. Michigan, 1st, 1987
35, Rich Laurel, Hofstra vs. Notre Dame, 1st, 1977
34, Reggie Lewis, Northeastern vs. Oklahoma, 1st, 1986
32, Lafester Rhodes, Iowa St. vs. Georgia Tech, 1st, 1988

Highest Field-Goal Percentage (minimum 10 FGM)
100.0% (10-10), Marvin Barnes, Providence vs. Pennsylvania, RSF, 1973
100.0% (10-10), Christian Laettner, Duke vs. Kentucky, RF, 1992 (ot)
88.2% (15-17), Reggie Lewis, Northeastern vs. Va. Commonwealth, 1st, 1984
86.7% (13-15), Truman Claytor, Kentucky vs. Va. Military, RSF, 1977
86.7% (13-15), Erich Santifer, Syracuse vs. Villanova, 2nd, 1980

Most Three-Point Field Goals
9, Garde Thompson, Michigan vs. Navy, 1st, 1987
7, Chris Fleming, Richmond vs. Temple, 2nd, 1991
7, Mark Mocnik, Campbell vs. Duke, 1st, 1992
6, nine tied (most recent: two in 1992)

Most Three-Point Field Goals Attempted
15, Steve Henson, Kansas St. vs. Minnesota, 1st, 1989
15, Jeff Robinson, Siena vs. Minnesota, 2nd, 1989
15, Randy Woods, La Salle vs. Seton Hall, 1st, 1992
13, four tied (most recent: Mark Mocnik, Campbell vs. Duke, 1st, 1992)

Highest Three-Point Field-Goal Percentage (minimum 5 3FGM)
100.0% (6-6), Migjen Bakalli, North Caro. St. vs. Southern Miss., 1st, 1991
83.3% (5-6), Dennis Scott, Georgia Tech vs. Iowa St., 1st, 1988
83.3% (5-6), Dwayne Bryant, Georgetown vs. North Caro., RSF, 1989
83.3% (5-6), Terry Brown, Kansas vs. UCLA, 2nd, 1990
75.0% (9-12), Garde Thompson, Michigan vs. Navy, 1st, 1987

75.0% (6-8), Doug Lee, Purdue vs. Northeastern, 1st, 1987

Most Free Throws
21, David Robinson, Navy vs. Syracuse, 2nd, 1986
19, Tom Hammonds, Georgia Tech vs. Iowa St., 1st, 1988
18, Jon Rose, Connecticut vs. Boston U., 1st, 1959
17, Barry Kramer, New York U. vs. West Va., R3d, 1963
16, Bill Bradley, Princeton vs. St. Joseph's (Pa.), 1st, 1963
16, Len Chappell, Wake Forest vs. St. Joseph's (Pa.), RSF, 1962

Most Free Throws Attempted
27, David Robinson, Navy vs. Syracuse, 2nd, 1986
21, Vernon Maxwell, Florida vs. North Caro. St., 1st, 1987
21, Tom Hammonds, Georgia Tech vs. Iowa St., 1st, 1988
20, Barry Kramer, New York U. vs. West Va., R3d, 1963
20, Len Chappell, Wake Forest vs. St. Joseph's (Pa.), RSF, 1962

Highest Free-Throw Percentage (minimum 10 FTM)
100.0% (16-16), Bill Bradley, Princeton vs. St. Joseph's (Pa.), 1st, 1963
100.0% (13-13), Bill Bradley, Princeton vs. Providence, RF, 1965
100.0% (13-13), Mike Maloy, Davidson vs. St. John's (N.Y.), RSF, 1969
100.0% (12-12), Calvin Duncan, Va. Commonwealth vs. La Salle, 1st, 1983
100.0% (11-11), Willie Burton, Minnesota vs. Kansas St., 1st, 1989

Most Rebounds
34, Fred Cohen, Temple vs. Connecticut, RSF, 1956
29, Toby Kimball, Connecticut vs. St. Joseph's (Pa.), 1st, 1965
24, Tom Burleson, North Caro. St. vs. Providence, RSF, 1974
23, Cliff Anderson, St. Joseph's (Pa.) vs. North Caro. St., R3d, 1965
21, five tied (most recent: Marvin Barnes, Providence vs. Furman, R3d, 1974)

Most Assists
15, Kenny Patterson, DePaul vs. Syracuse, 1st, 1985
12, nine tied (most recent: two in 1988)

Most Blocked Shots
9, David Robinson, Navy vs. Cleveland St., RSF, 1986
8, Tim Perry, Temple vs. Lehigh, 1st, 1988
8, Mark Strickland, Temple vs. Oklahoma St., RSF, 1991 (ot)
8, Acie Earl, Iowa vs. Duke, 2nd, 1992
7, four tied (most recent: two in 1989)

Most Steals
7, Tommy Amaker, Duke vs. Old Dominion, 2nd, 1986
6, John Evans, Rhode Island vs. Duke, RSF, 1988
6, Rick Dadika, Rutgers vs. Iowa, 1st, 1989
6, Phil Henderson, Duke vs. Richmond, 1st, 1990
6, Monroe Brown, Penn St. vs. UCLA, 1st, 1991

SINGLE GAME, TEAM

Most Points
114, North Caro. St. vs. Southern Miss. (85), 1st, 1991
113, North Caro. vs. Pennsylvania (82), 1st, 1987
110, North Caro. vs. Boston College (90), R3d, 1975
109, Princeton vs. Providence (69), RF, 1965
109, North Caro. vs. Michigan (97), 2nd, 1987

Fewest Points
20, North Caro. vs. Pittsburgh (26), RF, 1941
24, Springfield vs. Indiana (48), RF, 1940
26, Pittsburgh vs. North Caro. (20), RF, 1941
29, Western Ky. vs. Duquesne (30), RF, 1940
30, Brown vs. Villanova (43), RF, 1939
30, Duquesne vs. Western Ky. (29), RF, 1940

Largest Winning Margin
49, Syracuse (101) vs. Brown (52), 1st, 1986
47, Duke (101) vs. Connecticut (54), RF, 1964
43, *Villanova (90) vs. Pennsylvania (47), RF, 1971
40, Princeton (109) vs. Providence (69), RF, 1965
35, three tied (most recent: North Caro. (101) vs. Northeastern (66), 1st, 1991)

Most Points Scored by Losing Team
100, St. Joseph's (Pa.) vs. West Va., (106), R3d, 1960
98, Iowa St. vs. Kentucky (106), 2nd, 1992
97, La Salle vs. Villanova (103), 1st, 1978
97, Michigan vs. North Caro. (109), 2nd, 1987
96, Iowa vs. North Caro. St., (102), 2nd, 1989 (2 ot)

Most Field Goals
44, Fordham vs. Furman, 1st, 1971
44, North Caro. vs. Boston College, R3d, 1975
43, Duke vs. Connecticut, RF, 1964
43, Providence vs. Maryland, R3d, 1973
42, La Salle vs. Villanova, 1st, 1978
42, Villanova vs. La Salle, 1st, 1978

Most Field Goals Attempted
103, St. Joseph's (Pa.) vs. West Va., R3d, 1960
101, Holy Cross vs. North Caro. St., 1st, 1950
94, Furman vs. Providence, R3d, 1974
92, West Va. vs. St. Joseph's (Pa.), RSF, 1959
89, three tied (most recent: Furman vs. Boston College, 1st, 1975)

Highest Field-Goal Percentage
75.0% (33-44), Northeastern vs. Va. Commonwealth, 1st, 1984
71.4% (25-35), Georgetown vs. Notre Dame, 2nd, 1989
68.3% (41-60), Princeton vs. Providence, RF, 1965
67.3% (33-49), Pennsylvania vs. Providence, 1st, 1972
67.3% (33-49), Villanova vs. Houston, 1st, 1981

Lowest Field-Goal Percentage
12.7% (8-63), Springfield vs. Indiana, RSF, 1940
13.9% (10-72), Harvard vs. Ohio St., RSF, 1946
22.9% (16-70), St. John's (N.Y.) vs. Kentucky, RSF, 1951
24.4% (20-82), Holy Cross vs. Ohio St., R3d, 1950
25.0% (17-68), Massachusetts vs. New York U., 1st, 1962

Most Three-Point Field Goals
13, Texas vs. Iowa, 1st, 1992
12, Michigan vs. Navy, 1st, 1987
12, North Caro. St. vs. Southern Miss., 1st, 1991
12, Kentucky vs. Duke, RF, 1992 (ot)
11, three tied (most recent: two in 1992)

Most Three-Point Field Goals Attempted
35, La Salle vs. Clemson, 2nd, 1990
33, La Salle vs. Southern Miss., 1st, 1990
32, Siena vs. Minnesota, 2nd, 1989
31, Tennessee vs. West Va., 1st, 1989
31, Texas vs. Iowa, 1st, 1992

Highest Three-Point Field-Goal Percentage (minimum 7 3FGM)
70.0% (7-10), Rhode Island vs. Syracuse, 2nd, 1988
66.7% (8-12), Minnesota vs. Kansas St., 1st, 1989
64.3% (9-14), Purdue vs. Northeastern, 1st, 1987
64.3% (9-14), Iowa vs. Rutgers, 1st, 1989
60.0% (12-20), Michigan vs. Navy, 1st, 1987

Most Free Throws
41, Navy vs. Syracuse, 2nd, 1986
36, New York U. vs. St. Joseph's (Pa.), R3d, 1962
36, Georgia Tech vs. Iowa St., 1st, 1988
35, La Salle vs. Canisius, RF, 1955
35, Manhattan vs. West Va., 1st, 1958

Most Free Throws Attempted
52, Navy vs. Syracuse, 2nd, 1986
50, West Va. vs. St. Joseph's (Pa.), RSF, 1959
49, Manhattan vs. West Va., 1st, 1958
49, New York U. vs. St. Joseph's (Pa.), R3d, 1962
46, West Va. vs. St. Joseph's (Pa.), R3d, 1960

Highest Free-Throw Percentage (minimum 15 FTM)
100.0% (22-22), Fordham vs. South Caro., R3d, 1971
95.2% (20-21), Iowa vs. North Caro. St., 2nd, 1989 (2 ot)
95.0% (19-20), North Caro. St. vs. St. John's (N.Y.), R3d, 1951
95.0% (19-20), Iowa vs. Georgetown, RF, 1980
94.1% (16-17), Notre Dame vs. Georgetown, 2nd, 1989

Most Rebounds
76, Temple vs. Connecticut, RSF, 1956
65, West Va. vs. St. Joseph's (Pa.), RSF, 1959
65, North Caro. vs. Princeton, RSF, 1967 (ot)
63, West Va. vs. Dartmouth, 1st, 1959
63, West Va. vs. St. Joseph's (Pa.), R3d, 1960
63, Syracuse vs. Brown, 1st, 1986

Largest Rebound Margin
35, St. John's (N.Y.) (56) vs. Connecticut (21), 1st, 1951
29, West Va. (63) vs. Dartmouth (34), 1st, 1959
26, North Caro. (60) vs. Pittsburgh (34), RF, 1974
24, Davidson (59) vs. Rhode Island (35), 1st, 1966
24, Syracuse (63) vs. Brown (39), 1st, 1986

Most Assists
31, Syracuse vs. Brown, 1st, 1986
30, North Caro. vs. Pennsylvania, 1st, 1987
27, Richmond vs. Rider, OR, 1984
27, North Caro. vs. Villanova, 2nd, 1991
26, four tied (most recent: two in 1992)

Most Blocked Shots
11, Duke vs. Temple, RF, 1988
11, North Caro. St. vs. Iowa, 2nd, 1989 (2 ot)
9, Navy vs. Cleveland St., RSF, 1986
9, Temple vs. Lehigh, 1st, 1988
9, Syracuse vs. North Caro. A&T, 1st, 1988
9, Temple vs. Oklahoma St., RSF, 1991 (ot)

Most Steals
19, Connecticut vs. Boston U., 1st, 1990

16, Connecticut vs. California, 2nd, 1990
16, UCLA vs. Kansas, 2nd, 1990
16, Kentucky vs. Old Dominion, 1st, 1992
14, La Salle vs. Southern Miss., 1st, 1990
14, St. John's (N.Y.) vs. Duke, 2nd, 1990

Most Personal Fouls
41, Dayton vs. Illinois, RSF, 1952
35, DePaul vs. Va. Military, RSF, 1976 (ot)
34, Syracuse vs. Virginia, RSF, 1984

34, Syracuse vs. Navy, 2nd, 1986
34, Northeastern vs. Purdue, 1st, 1987

Most Players Disqualified
5, Dayton vs. Illinois, RSF, 1952
5, St. Joseph's (Pa.) vs. West Va., RSF, 1959
5, DePaul vs. Va. Military, RSF, 1976 (ot)
5, Syracuse vs. Virginia, RSF, 1984
4, 11 tied (most recent: Northeastern vs. Purdue, 1st, 1987)

SINGLE GAME, TWO-TEAM

Most Points
207, Duke (104) vs. Kentucky (103), RF, 1992 (ot)
206, West Va. (106) vs. St. Joseph's (Pa.) (100), R3d, 1960
206, North Caro. (109) vs. Michigan (97), 2nd, 1987
204, Kentucky (106) vs. Iowa St. (98), 2nd, 1992
200, North Caro. (110) vs. Boston College (90), R3d, 1975
200, Villanova (103) vs. La Salle (97), 1st, 1978

Most Field Goals
84, La Salle (42) vs. Villanova (42), 1st, 1978

Most Field Goals Attempted
188, St. Joseph's (Pa.) (103) vs. West Va. (85), R3d, 1960

Most Three-Point Field Goals
20, North Caro. St. (12) vs. Southern Miss. (8), 1st, 1991
20, Kentucky (12) vs. Duke (8), RF, 1992 (ot)
19, Seton Hall (10) vs. La Salle (9), 1st, 1992
18, Siena (11) vs. Stanford (7), 1st, 1989
17, Richmond (12) vs. Temple (5), 2nd, 1991

Most Three-Point Field Goals Attempted
56, La Salle (33) vs. Southern Miss. (23), 1st, 1990
54, La Salle (30) vs. Seton Hall (24), 1st, 1992
47, North Caro. St. (25) vs. Southern Miss. (22), 1st, 1991
46, Oklahoma St. (27) vs. North Caro. St. (19), 2nd, 1991
45, Texas (31) vs. Iowa (14), 1st, 1992

Most Free Throws
63, La Salle (35) vs. Canisius (28), RF, 1955
60, Purdue (31) vs. Northeastern (29), 1st, 1987

Most Free Throws Attempted
91, Manhattan (49) vs. West Va. (42), 1st, 1958
89, New York U. (49) vs. St. Joseph's (Pa.) (40), R3d, 1962

83, Purdue (45) vs. Northeastern (38), 1st, 1987

Most Rebounds
124, West Va. (63) vs. St. Joseph's (Pa.) (61), R3d, 1960
120, West Va. (65) vs. St. Joseph's (Pa.) (55), RSF, 1959
119, Manhattan (60) vs. Dartmouth (59), RSF, 1958
119, Massachusetts (60) vs. New York U. (59), 1st, 1962
118, North Caro. (65) vs. Princeton (53), 2nd, 1967 (ot)

Most Assists
47, Kentucky (24) vs. Duke (23), RF, 1992 (ot)
45, Florida (26) vs. Purdue (19), 2nd, 1987

Most Blocked Shots
18, Iowa (10) vs. Duke (8), 2nd, 1992
17, Duke (11) vs. Temple (6), RF, 1988
14, North Caro. (8) vs. Eastern Mich. (6), RSF, 1991
13, four tied [most recent: North Caro. (7) vs. Temple (6), RF, 1991]

Most Steals
25, South Caro. St. (13) vs. Duke (12), 1st, 1989
23, Connecticut (19) vs. Boston U. (4), 1st, 1990
23, Kentucky (16) vs. Old Dominion (7), 1st, 1992
22, UCLA (16) vs. Kansas (6), 2nd, 1990
22, Northeastern (13) vs. North Caro. (9), 1st, 1991

Most Personal Fouls
61, West Va. (32) vs. Manhattan (29), 1st, 1958

RF—Regional final game.
RSF—Regional semifinal game.
R3d—Regional third-place game.
2nd—Second-round game.
1st—First-round game.
OR—Opening-round game.
*Record later vacated.

BASKETBALL FACTS...

In December 1891, Dr. James Naismith, an instructor at the School for Christian Workers (now Springfield College) in Springfield, Massachusetts, invented the game of basketball. The first published rules appeared in January 1892, and the first game played in public was two months later between the students and teachers at Springfield. Two-hundred "fans" saw the students crush the teachers, 5-1, as football legend Amos Alonzo Stagg scored the only point for the losing team.

SOUTHEAST REGION
SINGLE GAME, INDIVIDUAL

Most Points
61, Austin Carr, Notre Dame vs. Ohio, 1st, 1970
52, Austin Carr, Notre Dame vs. Kentucky, RSF, 1970
45, Austin Carr, Notre Dame vs. Iowa, R3d, 1970
44, Dan Issel, Kentucky vs. Notre Dame, RSF, 1970
44, Hersey Hawkins, Bradley vs. Auburn, 1st, 1988

Most Field Goals
25, Austin Carr, Notre Dame vs. Ohio, 1st, 1970
22, Austin Carr, Notre Dame vs. Kentucky, RSF, 1970
21, Austin Carr, Notre Dame vs. Iowa, R3d, 1970
17, Dan Issel, Kentucky vs. Notre Dame, RSF, 1970
17, Rickey Green, Michigan vs. Holy Cross, 1st, 1977

Most Field Goals Attempted
44, Austin Carr, Notre Dame vs. Ohio, 1st, 1970
39, Austin Carr, Notre Dame vs. Iowa, R3d, 1970
36, Ronald "Popeye" Jones, Murray St. vs. Michigan St., 1st, 1990 (ot)
35, Austin Carr, Notre Dame vs. Kentucky, RSF, 1970
35, *Jim McDaniels, Western Ky. vs. Ohio St., RF, 1971 (ot)

Highest Field-Goal Percentage
(minimum 10 FGM)
100.0% (11-11), Kenny Walker, Kentucky vs. Western Ky., 2nd, 1986
91.7% (11-12), Pembrook Burrows, Jacksonville vs. Iowa, RSF, 1970
90.9% (10-11), Dwayne McClain, Villanova vs. Marshall, 1st, 1984
86.7% (13-15), Brian Penny, Coastal Caro. vs. Indiana, 1st, 1991
84.6% (11-13), five tied [most recent: Eric Montross, North Caro. vs. Miami (Ohio), 1st, 1992]

Most Three-Point Field Goals
8, Glen Rice, Michigan vs. North Caro., RSF, 1989
8, Jamie Mercurio, Miami (Ohio) vs. North Caro., 1st, 1992
7, Sean Higgins, Michigan vs. Virginia, RF, 1989
7, Dennis Scott, Georgia Tech vs. Minnesota, RF, 1990
6, six tied (most recent: Chris Walker, Villanova vs. Louisiana St., 1st, 1990)

Most Three-Point Field Goals Attempted
20, Chris Walker, Villanova vs. Louisiana St., 1st, 1990
16, Carlos Sample, Southern-B.R. vs. North Caro., 1st, 1989
14, Ernie Lewis, Providence vs. Austin Peay, 2nd, 1987 (ot)
14, Jamie Mercurio, Miami (Ohio) vs. North Caro., 1st, 1992
13, three tied (most recent: James Robinson, Alabama vs. North Caro., 2nd, 1992)

Highest Three-Point Field-Goal Percentage
(minimum 5 3FGM)
100.0% (6-6), Mike Buck, Middle Tenn. St. vs. Florida St., 1st, 1989
83.3% (5-6), Billy Donovan, Providence vs. Alabama, RSF, 1987
83.3% (5-6), Richard Morgan, Virginia vs. Middle Tenn. St., 2nd, 1989
83.3% (5-6), Brian Penny, Coastal Caro. vs. Indiana, 1st, 1991

83.3% (5-6), Gary Waites, Alabama vs. Wake Forest, 2nd, 1991

Most Free Throws
17, Roger Newman, Kentucky vs. Ohio St., RF, 1961
16, John Riser, Pittsburgh vs. Kentucky, RSF, 1957
16, Reggie Williams, Georgetown vs. Kansas, RSF, 1987
16, Billy Donovan, Providence vs. Georgetown, RF, 1987
15, John Bagley, Boston College vs. Wake Forest, 2nd, 1981

Most Free Throws Attempted
24, Donnie Gaunce, Morehead St. vs. Iowa, RSF, 1956
22, Roger Newman, Kentucky vs. Ohio St., RF, 1961
21, John Bagley, Boston College vs. Wake Forest, 2nd, 1981
20, Clarence Kea, Lamar vs. Detroit Mercy, 1st, 1979
18, Reggie Williams, Georgetown vs. Kansas, RSF, 1987
18, Billy Donovan, Providence vs. Georgetown, RF, 1987

Highest Free-Throw Percentage
(minimum 11 FTM)
100.0% (13-13), Al Gooden, Ball St. vs. Boston College, 1st, 1981
100.0% (12-12), Dan Issel, Kentucky vs. Miami (Ohio), R3d, 1969
100.0% (12-12), Bryant Smith, Virginia vs. Middle Tenn. St., 2nd, 1989
100.0% (11-11), four tied [most recent: Hubert Davis, North Caro. vs. Miami (Ohio), 1st, 1992]

Most Rebounds
31, Nate Thurmond, Bowling Green vs. Mississippi St., R3d, 1963
30, Jerry Lucas, Ohio St. vs. Kentucky, RF, 1961
27, John Green, Michigan St. vs. Notre Dame, RSF, 1957
26, Howard Jolliff, Ohio vs. Georgia Tech, RSF, 1960
26, Phil Hubbard, Michigan vs. Detroit Mercy, RSF, 1978

Most Assists
14, Dicky Beal, Kentucky vs. Brigham Young, 2nd, 1984
14, John Crotty, Virginia vs. Middle Tenn. St., 2nd, 1989
14, Pooh Richardson, UCLA vs. Iowa St., 1st, 1989
13, Rumeal Robinson, Michigan vs. North Caro., RSF, 1989
12, four tied (most recent: John Crotty, Virginia vs. Syracuse, 2nd, 1990)

Most Blocked Shots
6, Zavian Smith, Georgia St. vs. Arkansas, 1st, 1991
5, *Derrick McKey, Alabama vs. New Orleans, 2nd, 1987
5, Chris Webber, Michigan vs. Ohio St., RF, 1992 (ot)
4, 13 tied (most recent: three in 1992)

Most Steals
7, Delray Brooks, Providence vs. Austin Peay, 2nd, 1987 (ot)
6, Byron Dinkins, N.C.-Charlotte vs. Brigham Young, 1st, 1988 (ot)
5, 11 tied (most recent: two in 1992)

SINGLE GAME, TEAM

Most Points
124, Oklahoma vs. Louisiana Tech (81), 2nd, 1989
121, Iowa vs. Notre Dame (106), R3d, 1970
118, Notre Dame vs. Vanderbilt (88), R3d, 1974
117, Arkansas vs. Georgia St. (76), 1st, 1991
112, Notre Dame vs. Ohio (82), 1st, 1970

Fewest Points
38, Ohio vs. Kansas (49), 1st, 1985
40, Ohio vs. Kentucky (57), 2nd, 1983
41, Boston College vs. St. Joseph's (Pa.) (42), RSF, 1981
42, Tennessee Tech vs. Loyola (III.) (111), 1st, 1963
42, Pennsylvania vs. Duke (52), 2nd, 1980
42, St. Joseph's (Pa.) vs. Boston College (41), RSF, 1981

Largest Winning Margin
69, Loyola (III.) (111) vs. Tennessee Tech (42), 1st, 1963
47, DePaul (99) vs. Eastern Ky. (52), 1st, 1965
43, Oklahoma (124) vs. Louisiana Tech (81), 2nd, 1989
42, Notre Dame (108) vs. Austin Peay (66), 1st, 1974
41, Arkansas (117) vs. Georgia St. (76), 1st, 1991

Most Points Scored by Losing Team
106, Notre Dame vs. Iowa (121), R3d, 1970
103, Iowa vs. Jacksonville (104), RSF, 1970
100, Kentucky vs. Jacksonville (106), RF, 1970
100, *Austin Peay vs. Kentucky (106), RSF, 1973 (ot)
99, Notre Dame vs. Kentucky (109), RSF, 1970

Most Field Goals
52, Iowa vs. Notre Dame, R3d, 1970
50, Kentucky vs. Austin Peay, RSF, 1973 (ot)
50, Notre Dame vs. Austin Peay, 1st, 1974
49, Notre Dame vs. Vanderbilt, R3d, 1974
48, Oklahoma vs. Louisiana Tech, 2nd, 1989

Most Field Goals Attempted
106, Indiana vs. Miami (Ohio), R3d, 1958
99, *Austin Peay vs. Kentucky, RSF, 1973 (ot)
98, Kentucky vs. Miami (Ohio), RSF, 1958
98, Iowa vs. Notre Dame, R3d, 1970
98, Oklahoma vs. Louisiana Tech, 2nd, 1989

Highest Field-Goal Percentage
80.0% (28-35), Oklahoma St. vs. Tulane, 2nd, 1992
72.7% (40-55), *Alabama vs. New Orleans, 2nd, 1987
71.4% (30-42), Villanova vs. Marshall, 1st, 1984
68.8% (33-48), Providence vs. Alabama, RSF, 1987
68.6% (35-51), Indiana vs. St. Joseph's (Pa.), RF, 1981

Lowest Field-Goal Percentage
22.0% (18-82), Tennessee Tech vs. Loyola (III.), 1st, 1963
26.3% (21-80), Bowling Green vs. Mississippi St., R3d, 1963
27.4% (23-84), Tennessee Tech vs. Notre Dame, 1st, 1958
28.2% (22-78), Notre Dame vs. Kentucky, RF, 1958
29.0% (20-69), Alabama vs. North Caro., 2nd, 1992

Most Three-Point Field Goals
14, Providence vs. Alabama, RSF, 1987
13, Michigan vs. North Caro., RSF, 1989
13, East Tenn. St. vs. Arizona, 1st, 1992
12, East Tenn. St. vs. Michigan, 2nd, 1992

11, five tied [most recent: Miami (Ohio) vs. North Caro., 1st, 1992]

Most Three-Point Field Goals Attempted
31, East Tenn. St. vs. Michigan, 2nd, 1992
28, Southern-B.R. vs. North Caro., 1st, 1989
28, East Tenn. St. vs. Georgia Tech, 1st, 1990
28, Villanova vs. Louisiana St., 1st, 1990
28, Alabama vs. North Caro., 2nd, 1992

Highest Three-Point Field-Goal Percentage (minimum 7 3FGM)
81.8% (9-11), *Alabama vs. North Caro. A&T, 1st, 1987
70.0% (7-10), Virginia vs. Providence, 1st, 1989
70.0% (7-10), Virginia vs. Middle Tenn. St., 2nd, 1989
63.6% (14-22), Providence vs. Alabama, RSF, 1987
63.6% (7-11), *Alabama vs. New Orleans, 2nd, 1987

Most Free Throws
38, Loyola (III.) vs. Kentucky, R3d, 1964
37, Morehead St. vs. Pittsburgh, 1st, 1957
35, Iowa vs. Morehead St., RSF, 1956
35, Ala.-Birmingham vs. Western Ky., 1st, 1981
34, Navy vs. Louisiana St., 1st, 1985

Most Free Throws Attempted
54, Morehead St. vs. Pittsburgh, 1st, 1957
53, Morehead St. vs. Iowa, RSF, 1956
52, Iowa vs. Morehead St., RSF, 1956
45, Purdue vs. Indiana, RSF, 1980
44, Loyola (III.) vs. Kentucky, R3d, 1964

Highest Free-Throw Percentage (minimum 15 FTM)
100.0% (17-17), Dayton vs. Villanova, 1st, 1985
100.0% (17-17), Villanova vs. Kentucky, RSF, 1988
95.5% (21-22), Vanderbilt vs. Marquette, RSF, 1974
95.2% (20-21), Notre Dame vs. Vanderbilt, R3d, 1974
93.8% (15-16), Alabama vs. North Caro. A&T, 1st, 1987
93.8% (15-16), Rutgers vs. Arizona St., 1st, 1991

Most Rebounds
86, Notre Dame vs. Tennessee Tech, 1st, 1958
70, Western Ky. vs. Miami (Fla.), 1st, 1960
66, Michigan St. vs. Notre Dame, RSF, 1957
66, Loyola (III.) vs. Tennessee Tech, 1st, 1963
66, Western Ky. vs. Dayton, R3d, 1966

Largest Rebound Margin
42, Notre Dame (86) vs. Tennessee Tech (44), 1st, 1958
29, Indiana (52) vs. Robert Morris (23), 1st, 1982
27, Western Ky. (70) vs. Miami (Fla.) (43), 1st, 1960
26, Michigan St. (66) vs. Notre Dame (40), RSF, 1957
26, Michigan (56) vs. Dayton (30), RSF, 1965

Most Assists
32, Arkansas vs. Georgia St., 1st, 1991
32, Michigan vs. East Tenn. St., 2nd, 1992
31, Oklahoma vs. Auburn, 2nd, 1988
29, Louisville vs. Brigham Young, 2nd, 1988
28, Oklahoma St. vs. Ga. Southern, 1st, 1992

Most Blocked Shots
10, Providence vs. Georgetown, RF, 1987
10, Louisiana St. vs. Georgia Tech, 2nd, 1990
9, Oklahoma vs. Louisiana Tech, 2nd, 1989
8, four tied (most recent: two in 1992)

Most Steals
   19, Providence vs. Austin Peay, 2nd, 1987 (ot)
   16, Oklahoma vs. Auburn, 2nd, 1988
   16, Oklahoma vs. Louisiana Tech, 2nd, 1989
   16, Arkansas vs. Georgia St., 1st, 1991
   14, Georgetown vs. Bucknell, 1st, 1987

Most Personal Fouls
   35, Iowa vs. Morehead St., RSF, 1956
   33, Indiana vs. Purdue, RSF, 1980

   32, Kentucky vs. Florida St., 2nd, 1980
   32, Louisiana St. vs. Navy, 1st, 1985
   31, three tied (most recent: Arizona vs. East
      Tenn. St., 1st, 1992)

Most Players Disqualified
   4, Kentucky vs. Marquette, RSF, 1969
   4, Kentucky vs. Jacksonville, RF, 1970
   3, 16 tied (most recent: two in 1992)

SINGLE GAME, TWO-TEAM

Most Points
   227, Iowa (121) vs. Notre Dame (106), R3d,
      1970
   208, Kentucky (109) vs. Notre Dame (99), RSF,
      1970
   207, Jacksonville (104) vs. Iowa (103), RSF,
      1970
   206, four tied [most recent: Oklahoma (108) vs.
      Louisville (98), RSF, 1988]

Most Field Goals
   97, Iowa (52) vs. Notre Dame (45), R3d, 1970
   96, Kentucky (50) vs. Austin Peay (46), RSF,
      1973 (ot)

Most Field Goals Attempted
   196, Austin Peay (99) vs. Kentucky (97), RSF,
      1973 (ot)
   195, Iowa (98) vs. Notre Dame (97), R3d, 1970
   194, Indiana (106) vs. Miami (Ohio) (88), R3d,
      1958

Most Three-Point Field Goals
   21, Providence (14) vs. Alabama (7), RSF, 1987
   20, Michigan (13) vs. North Caro. (7), RSF, 1989
   19, Pittsburgh (10) vs. Kansas (9), 2nd, 1991
   19, Stanford (10) vs. Alabama (9), 1st, 1992

Most Three-Point Field Goals Attempted
   46, Georgia (27) vs. Pittsburgh (19), 1st, 1991
      (ot)
   45, Alabama (23) vs. Providence (22), RSF,
      1987

Most Free Throws
   68, Iowa (35) vs. Morehead St. (33), RSF, 1956

Most Free Throws Attempted
   105, Morehead St. (53) vs. Iowa (52), RSF, 1956
   97, Morehead St. (54) vs. Pittsburgh (43), 1st,
      1957

Most Rebounds
   130, Notre Dame (86) vs. Tennessee Tech (44),
      1st, 1958

   122, Miami (Ohio) (65) vs. Indiana (57), R3d,
      1958
   118, Notre Dame (62) vs. Ohio (56), 1st, 1970
   117, Jacksonville (59) vs. Western Ky. (58), 1st,
      1971
   116, Indiana (61) vs. Virginia Tech (55), 2nd,
      1967

Most Assists
   51, Wake Forest (27) vs. Alabama (24), 2nd,
      1991
   48, Arkansas (32) vs. Georgia St. (16), 1st, 1991
   47, Arkansas (24) vs. Arizona St. (23), 2nd, 1991
   47, Michigan (32) vs. East Tenn. St. (15), 2nd,
      1992
   46, Oklahoma St. (28) vs. Ga. Southern (18),
      1st, 1992

Most Blocked Shots
   16, Oklahoma (9) vs. Louisiana Tech (7), 2nd,
      1989
   15, Arkansas (8) vs. Georgia St. (7), 1st, 1991
   14, Providence (10) vs. Georgetown (4), RF,
      1987

Most Steals
   26, Providence (19) vs. Austin Peay (7), 2nd,
      1987 (ot)
   26, Arkansas (16) vs. Georgia St. (10), 1st, 1991

Most Personal Fouls
   55, Providence (29) vs. Austin Peay (26), 2nd,
      1987 (ot)
   53, Arizona (31) vs. East Tenn. St. (22), 1st, 1992

RF—Regional final game.
RSF—Regional semifinal game.
R3d—Regional third-place game.
2nd—Second-round game.
1st—First-round game.
OR—Opening-round game.
*Record later vacated.

TOURNAMENT FACTS...

Eight times in history the NCAA basketball champions also won a football bowl game the same
academic school year. They are as follows:

Year	School	Bowl	Date of Bowl
1944-45	Oklahoma State	Cotton	1-1-45
1945-46	Oklahoma State	Sugar	1-1-46
1947-48	Kentucky	Great Lakes	12-6-47
1950-51	Kentucky	Sugar	1-1-51
1965-66	UTEP	Sun	12-31-65
1973-74	North Carolina State	Liberty	12-17-73
1981-82	North Carolina	Gator	12-28-81
1988-89	Michigan	Rose	1-2-89

MIDWEST REGION
SINGLE GAME, INDIVIDUAL

Most Points
56, Oscar Robertson, Cincinnati vs. Arkansas, R3d, 1958
52, Austin Carr, Notre Dame vs. Texas Christian, 1st, 1971
49, Elvin Hayes, Houston vs. Loyola (Ill.), 1st, 1968
47, Austin Carr, Notre Dame vs. Houston, R3d, 1971
46, Dave Corzine, DePaul vs. Louisville, RSF, 1978 (2 ot)

Most Field Goals
21, Oscar Robertson, Cincinnati vs. Arkansas, R3d, 1958
20, Austin Carr, Notre Dame vs. Texas Christian, 1st, 1971
20, Elvin Hayes, Houston vs. Loyola (Ill.), 1st, 1968
19, Oscar Robertson, Cincinnati vs. Kansas, RF, 1960
18, Willie Smith, Missouri vs. Michigan, RF, 1976
18, Dave Corzine, DePaul vs. Louisville, RSF, 1978 (2 ot)

Most Field Goals Attempted
42, *Dwight Lamar, Southwestern La. vs. Louisville, RSF, 1972
40, Austin Carr, Notre Dame vs. Houston, R3d, 1971
36, Oscar Robertson, Cincinnati vs. Arkansas, R3d, 1958
35, Willie Smith, Missouri vs. Michigan, RF, 1976
34, four tied (most recent: *Dwight Lamar, Southwestern La. vs. Houston, 1st, 1973)

**Highest Field-Goal Percentage
(minimum 10 FGM)**
92.3% (12-13), Dennis Holman, Southern Methodist vs. Cincinnati, R3d, 1966
90.9% (10-11), Akeem Olajuwon, Houston vs. Villanova, RF, 1983
90.9% (10-11), Oliver Miller, Arkansas vs. Murray St., 1st, 1992
87.5% (14-16), Akeem Olajuwon, Houston vs. Wake Forest, RF, 1984
87.5% (14-16), Wayman Tisdale, Oklahoma vs. Illinois St., 2nd, 1985

Most Three-Point Field Goals
8, Brad Soucie, Eastern Mich. vs. Pittsburgh, 1st, 1988
7, Darryl Joe, Louisiana St. vs. Georgia Tech, 1st, 1987
7, Steve Alford, Indiana vs. Auburn, 2nd, 1987
7, William Scott, Kansas St. vs. DePaul, 2nd, 1988
6, five tied (most recent: two in 1992)

Most Three-Point Field Goals Attempted
22, Jeff Fryer, Loyola (Cal.) vs. Arkansas, 1st, 1989
14, Brad Soucie, Eastern Mich. vs. Pittsburgh, 1st, 1988
14, Anfernee Hardaway, Memphis St. vs. Georgia Tech, RSF, 1992 (ot)
13, Barry Booker, Vanderbilt vs. Kansas, RSF, 1988
13, Carl Brown, Ark.-Lit. Rock vs. Louisville, 1st, 1989

**Highest Three-Point Field-Goal Percentage
(minimum 5 3FGM)**
87.5% (7-8), William Scott, Kansas St. vs. DePaul, 2nd, 1988

77.8% (7-9), Darryl Joe, Louisiana St. vs. Georgia Tech, 1st, 1987
71.4% (5-7), Kendall Gill, Illinois vs. Dayton, 1st, 1990
71.4% (5-7), Rick Fox, North Caro. vs. Oklahoma, 2nd, 1990
66.7% (6-9), Frank Allen, Murray St. vs. Arkansas, 1st, 1992
66.7% (6-9), Jon Barry, Georgia Tech vs. Southern Cal, 1st, 1992

Most Free Throws
23, Bob Carney, Bradley vs. Colorado, RSF, 1954
23, Travis Mays, Texas vs. Georgia, 1st, 1990
17, Tyrone Hill, Xavier (Ohio) vs. Kansas St., 1st, 1990
16, Byron Larkin, Xavier (Ohio) vs. Missouri, 1st, 1987
15, Jim Krebs, Southern Methodist vs. St. Louis, R3d, 1957
15, Adrian Dantley, Notre Dame vs. Kansas, 1st, 1975

Most Free Throws Attempted
27, Travis Mays, Texas vs. Georgia, 1st, 1990
26, Bob Carney, Bradley vs. Colorado, RSF, 1954
22, Wilt Chamberlain, Kansas vs. Oklahoma City, RF, 1957
21, Adrian Dantley, Notre Dame vs. Kansas, 1st, 1975
20, Byron Larkin, Xavier (Ohio) vs. Missouri, 1st, 1987

**Highest Free-Throw Percentage
(minimum 11 FTM)**
100.0% (12-12), Arlen Clark, Oklahoma St. vs. Loyola (Ill.), 1st, 1958
100.0% (12-12), Larry Finch, Memphis St. vs. Kansas St., RF, 1973
100.0% (12-12), Wesley Cox, Louisville vs. Oral Roberts, 1st, 1974
100.0% (11-11), Bob Hickman, Kansas vs. Texas, RSF, 1960
100.0% (11-11), Les Craft, Kansas St. vs. Northern Ill., 1st, 1982

Most Rebounds
27, Paul Silas, Creighton vs. Oklahoma City, 1st, 1964
27, Elvin Hayes, Houston vs. Loyola (Ill.), 1st, 1968
25, Elvin Hayes, Houston vs. Texas Christian, RF, 1968
24, five tied (most recent: Sam Lacey, New Mexico St. vs. Drake, RF, 1970)

Most Assists
15, Keith Smart, Indiana vs. Auburn, 2nd, 1987
13, Rod Strickland, DePaul vs. Wichita St., 1st, 1988
13, Keith Jennings, East Tenn. St. vs. Iowa, 1st, 1991
12, *Andre Turner, Memphis St. vs. Oklahoma, RF, 1985
12, Steve Henson, Kansas St. vs. Purdue, RSF, 1988
12, Keith Wilson, Arkansas vs. Loyola (Cal.), 1st, 1989

Most Blocked Shots
7, Tim Perry, Temple vs. Southern-B.R., 1st, 1987
7, Pervis Ellison, Louisville vs. Illinois, RSF, 1989
5, Shaquille O'Neal, Louisiana St. vs. Connecticut, 1st, 1991

5, Charles Outlaw, Houston vs. Georgia Tech, 1st, 1992

5, David Van Dyke, UTEP vs. Kansas, 2nd, 1992

Most Steals

7, Scott Burrell, Connecticut vs. Xavier (Ohio), 2nd, 1991

6, Rodney Douglas, Memphis St. vs. Baylor, 1st, 1988

6, Lance Blanks, Texas vs. Missouri, 1st, 1989

6, Grant Hill, Duke vs. Iowa, 2nd, 1991

6, Jason Buchanan, St. John's (N.Y.) vs. Ohio St., RSF, 1991

SINGLE GAME, TEAM

Most Points

120, Arkansas vs. Loyola (Cal.) (101), 1st, 1989

119, Houston vs. Notre Dame (106), R3d, 1971

112, *Southwestern La. vs. Marshall (101), 1st, 1972

108, Missouri vs. Texas (89), 2nd, 1989

107, Kansas St. vs. Houston (98), R3d, 1970

107, Indiana vs. Auburn (90), 2nd, 1987

Fewest Points

42, Loyola (La.) vs. Oklahoma St. (59), 1st, 1958

43, Temple vs. Kansas (65), 2nd, 1986

46, five tied [most recent: Florida vs. Colorado St. (68), 1st, 1989]

Largest Winning Margin

40, Cincinnati (99) vs. DePaul (59), RSF, 1960

40, Louisville (93) vs. Kansas St. (53), R3d, 1968

38, Cincinnati (85) vs. Delaware (47), 1st, 1992

37, Seattle (88) vs. Wyoming (51), 1st, 1958

35, Cincinnati (97) vs. Arkansas (62), R3d, 1958

35, Houston (103) vs. Texas Christian (68), RF, 1968

Most Points Scored by Losing Team

106, Notre Dame vs. Houston (119), R3d, 1971

101, Marshall vs. Southwestern La. (112), 1st, 1972

101, Loyola (Cal.) vs. Arkansas (120), 1st, 1989

98, Notre Dame vs. Houston (99), 1st, 1965

98, Houston vs. Kansas St. (107), R3d, 1970

Most Field Goals

47, Houston vs. Notre Dame, R3d, 1971

47, Kansas St. vs. Houston, R3d, 1970

47, Arkansas vs. Loyola (Cal.), 1st, 1989

45, Louisiana St. vs. Lamar, 2nd, 1981

44, New Mexico St. vs. Rice, 1st, 1970

Most Field Goals Attempted

112, Marshall vs. Southwestern La., 1st, 1972

102, Notre Dame vs. Houston, R3d, 1971

99, Oral Roberts vs. Louisville, 1st, 1974

98, Arkansas vs. Loyola (Cal.), 1st, 1989

94, three tied (most recent: Kansas St. vs. Houston, R3d, 1970)

Highest Field-Goal Percentage

68.0% (34-50), Arkansas vs. Wake Forest, 1st, 1977

66.0% (35-53), Oklahoma vs. Illinois St., 2nd, 1985

65.5% (38-58), Houston vs. Alcorn St., 1st, 1982

65.5% (36-55), Maryland vs. Creighton, 1st, 1975

64.9% (24-37), Villanova vs. Lamar, 2nd, 1983

Lowest Field-Goal Percentage

19.4% (14-72), Creighton vs. Cincinnati, RSF, 1962

25.3% (22-87), Arkansas vs. Cincinnati, R3d, 1958

27.0% (20-74), Texas Southern vs. Georgetown, 1st, 1990

27.4% (20-73), Southern-B.R. vs. Temple, 1st, 1987

27.9% (19-68), Purdue vs. Memphis St., 2nd, 1984

Most Three-Point Field Goals

12, Eastern Mich. vs. Pittsburgh, 1st, 1988

10, Kansas St. vs. DePaul, 2nd, 1988

10, Dayton vs. Illinois, 1st, 1990

9, eight tied (most recent: three in 1992)

Most Three-Point Field Goals Attempted

39, Loyola (Cal.) vs. Arkansas, 1st, 1989

33, Texas Southern vs. Georgetown, 1st, 1990

26, Houston vs. Georgia Tech, 1st, 1992

25, Pittsburgh vs. Ball St., 1st, 1989

25, Dayton vs. Illinois, 1st, 1990

25, East Tenn. St. vs. Iowa, 1st, 1991

Highest Three-Point Field-Goal Percentage (minimum 7 3FGM)

80.0% (8-10), Kansas St. vs. Purdue, RSF, 1988

76.9% (10-13), Kansas St. vs. DePaul, 2nd, 1988

72.7% (8-11), Duke vs. Indiana, RSF, 1987

70.0% (7-10), North Caro. vs. Oklahoma, 2nd, 1990

70.0% (7-10), Iowa vs. East Tenn. St., 1st, 1991

70.0% (7-10), St. John's (N.Y.) vs. Duke, RF, 1991

Most Free Throws

38, Bradley vs. Colorado, RSF, 1954

37, Xavier (Ohio) vs. Kansas St., 1st, 1990

35, Notre Dame vs. Kansas, 1st, 1975

34, Southern Methodist vs. Oklahoma City, RF, 1956

33, Houston vs. Boston College, RF, 1982

Most Free Throws Attempted

50, Notre Dame vs. Kansas, 1st, 1975

48, Oklahoma City vs. Kansas St., RSF, 1956

48, Texas A&M vs. North Caro., 2nd, 1980

45, New Mexico St. vs. Drake, RF, 1970

45, Texas vs. Georgia, 1st, 1990

Highest Free-Throw Percentage (minimum 15 FTM)

95.8% (23-24), Oklahoma St. vs. Loyola (La.), 1st, 1958

95.0% (19-20), Wichita St. vs. DePaul, 1st, 1988

94.4% (17-18), Michigan St. vs. Cincinnati, 2nd, 1992

92.3% (24-26), Temple vs. Southern-B.R., 1st, 1987

92.3% (24-26), Southern Cal vs. Northeast La., 1st, 1992

Most Rebounds

76, Houston vs. Texas Christian, RF, 1968

71, Kansas St. vs. Houston, R3d, 1970

68, Cincinnati vs. Texas Tech, RSF, 1961

68, Marshall vs. Southwestern La., 1st, 1972

67, Kansas St. vs. New Mexico St., RSF, 1970

Largest Rebound Margin

33, Cincinnati (68) vs. Texas Tech (35), RSF, 1961

30, Louisiana Tech (56) vs. Pittsburgh (26), 1st, 1985

28, Indiana St. (50) vs. Oklahoma (22), RSF, 1979

27, Memphis St. (60) vs. South Caro. (33), RSF, 1973

23, UTEP (55) vs. Oklahoma City (32), 1st, 1966

Most Assists

32, Kansas vs. Howard, 1st, 1992

30, Purdue vs. Memphis St., 2nd, 1988

30, Arkansas vs. Loyola (Cal.), 1st, 1989

29, Pittsburgh vs. Eastern Mich., 1st, 1988

28, Louisville vs. Arkansas, 2nd, 1989

Most Blocked Shots
13, Louisville vs. Illinois, RSF, 1989
9, UTEP vs. Cincinnati, RSF, 1992
8, Temple vs. Southern-B.R., 1st, 1987
8, Louisville vs. Arkansas, 2nd, 1989
8, Georgia vs. Texas, 1st, 1990
8, Memphis St. vs. Georgia Tech, RSF, 1992 (ot)

Most Steals
18, Xavier (Ohio) vs. Kansas, 1st, 1988
17, Duke vs. St. John's (N.Y.), RF, 1991
15, Dayton vs. Illinois, 1st, 1990
15, Arkansas vs. Texas, RF, 1990

14, four tied (most recent: three in 1991)

Most Personal Fouls
39, Kansas vs. Notre Dame, 1st, 1975
36, North Caro. vs. Texas A&M, 2nd, 1980
35, DePaul vs. Boston College, 2nd, 1982
33, Boston College vs. Houston, RF, 1982
33, Loyola (Cal.) vs. Arkansas, 1st, 1989

Most Players Disqualified
6, Kansas vs. Notre Dame, 1st, 1975
5, DePaul vs. Boston College, 2nd, 1982
4, seven tied (most recent: Boston College vs. Houston, RF, 1982)

SINGLE GAME, TWO-TEAM

Most Points
225, Houston (119) vs. Notre Dame (106), R3d, 1971
213, Southwestern La. (112) vs. Marshall (101), 1st, 1972
205, Kansas St. (107) vs. Houston (98), R3d, 1970
197, Houston (99) vs. Notre Dame (98), 1st, 1965
197, Indiana (107) vs. Auburn (90), 2nd, 1987

Most Field Goals
86, Houston (47) vs. Notre Dame (39), R3d, 1971
86, Kansas St. (47) vs. Houston (39), RSF, 1971

Most Field Goals Attempted
186, Notre Dame (102) vs. Houston (84), R3d, 1971

Most Three-Point Field Goals
17, Georgia Tech (9) vs. Southern Cal (8), 2nd, 1992
16, Dayton (10) vs. Illinois (6), 1st, 1990
16, Connecticut (9) vs. Duke (7), RSF, 1991
15, East Tenn. St. (8) vs. Iowa (7), 1st, 1991
14, Louisiana St. (9) vs. Georgia Tech (5), 1st, 1987
14, North Caro. (7) vs. Oklahoma (7), 2nd, 1990

Most Three-Point Field Goals Attempted
48, Loyola (Cal.) (39) vs. Arkansas (9), 1st, 1989
47, Texas Southern (33) vs. Georgetown (14), 1st, 1990
46, Dayton (25) vs. Illinois (21), 1st, 1990
41, Houston (26) vs. Georgia Tech (15), 1st, 1992
37, Dayton (19) vs. Arkansas (18), 2nd, 1990

Most Free Throws
68, Oklahoma City (35) vs. Kansas St. (33), RSF, 1956

Most Free Throws Attempted
92, Oklahoma City (48) vs. Kansas St. (44), RSF, 1956
80, Oklahoma City (40) vs. Texas (40), R3d, 1963
78, Southern Methodist (46) vs. Houston (32), RSF, 1956
77, Oklahoma Ctiy (39) vs. Memphis St. (38), 1st, 1956

Most Rebounds
134, Marshall (68) vs. Southwestern La. (66), 1st, 1972
131, Houston (76) vs. Texas Christian (55), RF, 1968
126, Drake (66) vs. Notre Dame (60), RSF, 1971 (ot)
124, Kansas St. (71) vs. Houston (53), R3d, 1970
121, Notre Dame (66) vs. Houston (55), R3d, 1971

Most Assists
47, Georgia Tech (27) vs. Southern Cal (20), 2nd, 1992
46, Kansas (32) vs. Howard (14), 1st, 1992
44, Louisiana Tech (26) vs. Oklahoma (18), RSF, 1985 (ot)
43, Arkansas (26) vs. Murray St. (17), 1st, 1992
40, Arkansas (23) vs. Memphis St. (17), 2nd, 1992

Most Blocked Shots
15, Louisville (13) vs. Illinois (2), RSF, 1989
15, Georgia (8) vs. Texas (7), 1st, 1990
13, Memphis St. (8) vs. Georgia Tech (5), RSF, 1992 (ot)
11, Arkansas (7) vs. Dayton (4), 2nd, 1990
11, Louisiana St. (6) vs. Connecticut (5), 1st, 1991
11, Houston (6) vs. Georgia Tech (5), 1st, 1992

Most Steals
26, Duke (17) vs. St. John's (N.Y.) (9) RF, 1991
25, East Tenn. St. (14) vs. Iowa (11), 1st, 1991
23, St. John's (N.Y.) (14) vs. Ohio St. (9), RSF, 1991
22, Texas A&M (12) vs. Duke (10), 1st, 1987
22, Missouri (12) vs. Texas (10), 2nd, 1989

Most Personal Fouls
59, Loyola (Cal.) (33) vs. Arkansas (26), 1st, 1989
57, Texas (30) vs. Oklahoma City (27), R3d, 1963

RF—Regional final game.
RSF—Regional semifinal game.
R3d—Regional third-place game.
2nd—Second-round game.
1st—First-round game.
OR—Opening-round game.
*Record later vacated.

WEST REGION
SINGLE GAME, INDIVIDUAL

Most Points
45, Bob Houbregs, Washington vs. Seattle, RSF, 1953
45, Bo Kimble, Loyola (Cal.) vs. New Mexico St., 1st, 1990
44, Clyde Lovellette, Kansas vs. St. Louis, RF, 1952
42, John O'Brien, Seattle vs. Idaho St., 1st, 1953
42, Bo Kimble, Loyola (Cal.) vs. Nevada-Las Vegas, RF, 1990

Most Field Goals
20, Bob Houbregs, Washington vs. Seattle, RSF, 1953
17, seven tied [most recent: Bo Kimble, Loyola (Cal.) vs. New Mexico St., 1st, 1990]

Most Field Goals Attempted
35, Bob Houbregs, Washington vs. Seattle, RSF, 1953
35, Marv Roberts, Utah St. vs. UCLA, RF, 1970
35, Bo Kimble, Loyola (Cal.) vs. New Mexico St., 1st, 1990
32, Chris Jackson, Louisiana St. vs. UTEP, 1st, 1989
32, Bo Kimble, Loyola (Cal.) vs. Nevada-Las Vegas, RF, 1990

Highest Field-Goal Percentage (minimum 10 FGM)
88.2% (15-17), Dennis Awtrey, Santa Clara vs. Long Beach St., R3d, 1970
85.7% (12-14), Brad Daugherty, North Caro. vs. Utah, 1st, 1986
84.6% (11-13), Randy Reed, Kansas St. vs. San Francisco, 1st, 1981
84.6% (11-13), Kevin Gamble, Iowa vs. Oklahoma, RSF, 1987 (ot)
83.3% (10-12), Alan Taylor, Brigham Young vs. Clemson, 2nd, 1980
83.3% (10-12), Bill Wennington, St. John's (N.Y.) vs. Southern-B.R., 1st, 1985

Most Three-Point Field Goals
11, Jeff Fryer, Loyola (Cal.) vs. Michigan, 2nd, 1990
8, Gerald Paddio, Nevada-Las Vegas vs. Iowa, 2nd, 1988
8, Bo Kimble, Loyola (Cal.) vs. Nevada-Las Vegas, RF, 1990
7, four tied [most recent: Jeff Fryer, Loyola (Cal.) vs. North Caro., 2nd, 1988]

Most Three-Point Field Goals Attempted
19, Gerald Paddio, Nevada-Las Vegas vs. Iowa, 2nd, 1988
16, Jeff Fryer, Loyola (Cal.) vs. Nevada-Las Vegas, RF, 1990
15, Jeff Fryer, Loyola (Cal.) vs. Michigan, 2nd, 1990
14, Jeff Fryer, Loyola (Cal.) vs. North Caro., 2nd, 1988
14, Jeff Fryer, Loyola (Cal.) vs. New Mexico St., 1st, 1990

Highest Three-Point Field-Goal Percentage (minimum 5 3FGM)
100.0% (5-5), Mitch Richmond, Kansas St. vs. Georgia, 1st, 1987 (ot)
75.0% (6-8), Robert Horry, Alabama vs. Colorado St., 1st, 1990
73.3% (11-15), Jeff Fryer, Loyola (Cal.) vs. Michigan, 2nd, 1990
72.7% (8-11), Bo Kimble, Loyola (Cal.) vs. Nevada-Las Vegas, RF, 1990
71.4% (5-7), five tied (most recent: two in 1991)

Most Free Throws
18, John O'Brien, Seattle vs. Wyoming, R3d, 1953
16, Conrad Wells, Idaho St. vs. Brigham Young, R3d, 1957
16, Fennis Dembo, Wyoming vs. UCLA, 2nd, 1987
16, B. J. Armstrong, Iowa vs. Florida St., 1st, 1988
15, four tied (most recent: Don MacLean, UCLA vs. Robert Morris, 1st, 1992)

Most Free Throws Attempted
22, John O'Brien, Seattle vs. Wyoming, R3d, 1953
20, B. J. Armstrong, Iowa vs. Florida St., 1st, 1988
19, Roosevelt Chapman, Dayton vs. Oklahoma, 2nd, 1984
18, Billy McGill, Utah vs. Southern Cal, 1st, 1960
18, Mel Counts, Oregon St. vs. Seattle, 1st, 1964
18, Roy Hamilton, UCLA vs. Kansas, 1st, 1978

Highest Free-Throw Percentage (minimum 12 FTM)
100.0% (16-16), Fennis Dembo, Wyoming vs. UCLA, 2nd, 1987
100.0% (12-12), Willie Worsley, UTEP vs. Seattle, 1st, 1967
100.0% (12-12), Ken Owens, Idaho vs. Iowa, 2nd, 1982 (ot)
100.0% (12-12), Wayman Tisdale, Oklahoma vs. Dayton, 2nd, 1984
100.0% (12-12), Michael Jackson, Georgetown vs. Nevada-Las Vegas, RSF, 1984
100.0% (12-12), John Morton, Seton Hall vs. UTEP, 1st, 1988
100.0% (12-12), Shaquille O'Neal, Louisiana St. vs. Indiana, 2nd, 1992

Most Rebounds
28, Elvin Hayes, Houston vs. Pacific (Cal.), R3d, 1966
23, Keith Swagerty, Pacific (Cal.) vs. Houston, R3d, 1966
23, Lew Alcindor, UCLA vs. New Mexico St., RSF, 1968
23, Kresimir Cosic, Brigham Young vs. UCLA, RSF, 1971
22, James Ware, Oklahoma City vs. San Francisco, RSF, 1965

Most Assists
14, Carl Wright, Southern Methodist vs. Miami (Ohio), 1st, 1984
13, Mark Wade, Nevada-Las Vegas vs. Kansas St., 2nd, 1987
13, James Sanders, Alabama vs. Arizona, 2nd, 1990
12, 10 tied (most recent: Joey Brown, Georgetown vs. South Fla., 1st, 1992)

Most Blocked Shots
11, Shaquille O'Neal, Louisiana St. vs. Brigham Young, 1st, 1992
10, Shawn Bradley, Brigham Young vs. Virginia, 1st, 1991
7, Anthony Cook, Arizona vs. UTEP, 1st, 1987 (ot)
6, Elmore Spencer, Nevada-Las Vegas vs. Montana, 1st, 1991
6, Elmore Spencer, Nevada-Las Vegas vs. Georgetown, 2nd, 1991
4, 10 tied (most recent: two in 1991)

Most Steals
7, Reggie Miller, UCLA vs. Wyoming, 2nd, 1987
7, Ricky Grace, Oklahoma vs. Iowa, RSF, 1987
(ot)
6, Anderson Hunt, Nevada-Las Vegas vs. Loyola (Cal.), RF, 1990

6, Clarence Ceasar, Louisiana St. vs. Brigham Young, 1st, 1992
5, 12 tied (most recent: three in 1991)

SINGLE GAME, TEAM

Most Points
149, Loyola (Cal.) vs. Michigan (115), 2nd, 1990
131, Nevada-Las Vegas vs. Loyola (Cal.) (101), RF, 1990
123, North Caro. vs. Loyola (Cal.) (97), 2nd, 1988
121, Nevada-Las Vegas vs. San Francisco (95), 1st, 1977
119, Loyola (Cal.) vs. Wyoming (115), 1st, 1988

Fewest Points
29, Baylor vs. Oklahoma St. (44), RF, 1946
32, Colorado vs. Southern Cal (38), RF, 1940
35, Missouri vs. Utah (45), RF, 1944
36, Southern Methodist vs. Georgetown (37), RSF, 1984
37, Utah vs. Oklahoma St. (62), RF, 1945
37, Georgetown vs. Southern Methodist (36), RSF, 1984

Largest Winning Margin
49, UCLA (109) vs. Wyoming, (60), RSF, 1967
40, Arizona (90) vs. Cornell (50), 1st, 1988
39, Indiana (94) vs. Eastern Ill. (55), 1st, 1992
38, UCLA (90) vs. Santa Clara (52), RF, 1969
35, Wyoming (78) vs. Howard (43), 1st, 1981

Most Points Scored by Losing Team
115, Wyoming vs. Loyola (Cal.) (119), 1st, 1988
115, Michigan vs. Loyola (Cal.) (149), 2nd, 1990
109, Nevada-Las Vegas vs. Arizona (114), RSF, 1976 (ot)
102, Brigham Young vs. Oklahoma City (112), R3d, 1965
101, Loyola (Cal.) vs. Nevada-Las Vegas (131), RF, 1990

Most Field Goals
51, UCLA vs. Dayton, RSF, 1974 (3 ot)
51, Nevada-Las Vegas vs. Loyola (Cal.), RF, 1990
49, North Caro. vs. Loyola (Cal.), 2nd, 1988
49, Nevada-Las Vegas vs. San Francisco, 1st, 1977
49, Loyola (Cal.) vs. Michigan, 2nd, 1990

Most Field Goals Attempted
103, Loyola (Cal.) vs. North Caro., 2nd, 1988
100, Houston vs. Pacific (Cal.), R3d, 1966
99, Brigham Young vs. Oklahoma City, R3d, 1965
97, UCLA vs. Dayton, RSF, 1974 (3 ot)
96, Nevada-Las Vegas vs. Arizona, RSF, 1976 (ot)

Highest Field-Goal Percentage
79.0% (49-62), North Caro. vs. Loyola (Cal.), 2nd, 1988
74.4% (29-39), Georgetown vs. Oregon St., RF, 1982
73.2% (30-41), North Caro. St. vs. UTEP, 2nd, 1985
70.5% (31-44), Washington vs. Duke, 2nd, 1984
68.4% (39-57), San Francisco vs. Brigham Young, 2nd, 1979

Lowest Field-Goal Percentage
20.6% (13-63), Arkansas vs. Oregon St., RSF, 1949
26.1% (24-92), UCLA vs. Brigham Young, R3d, 1950
26.2% (17-65), Texas A&M vs. Washington, 1st, 1951

26.3% (15-57), Idaho St. vs. Brigham Young, R3d, 1957
26.7% (16-60), Howard vs. Wyoming, 1st, 1981

Most Three-Point Field Goals
21, Loyola (Cal.) vs. Michigan, 2nd, 1990
17, Loyola (Cal.) vs. Nevada-Las Vegas, RF, 1990
13, Loyola (Cal.) vs. North Caro., 2nd, 1988
13, St. Francis (Pa.) vs. Arizona, 1st, 1991
13, Brigham Young vs. Louisiana St., 1st, 1992

Most Three-Point Field Goals Attempted
41, Loyola (Cal.) vs. Nevada-Las Vegas, RF, 1990
40, Loyola (Cal.) vs. Michigan, 2nd, 1990
39, Loyola (Cal.) vs. North Caro., 2nd, 1988
33, Brigham Young vs. Louisiana St., 1st, 1992
30, Nevada-Las Vegas vs. Iowa, RF, 1987

Highest Three-Point Field-Goal Percentage (minimum 7 3FGM)
88.9% (8-9), Kansas St. vs. Georgia, 1st, 1987 (ot)
72.7% (8-11), Alabama vs. Colorado St., 1st, 1990
70.0% (7-10), Indiana vs. UTEP, 2nd, 1989
63.6% (7-11), Indiana vs. Eastern Ill., 1st, 1992
58.3% (7-12), UCLA vs. New Mexico St., RSF, 1992

Most Free Throws
41, Utah vs. Santa Clara, R3d, 1960
39, Seattle vs. Utah, R3d, 1955
39, UTEP vs. Tulsa, 1st, 1985
36, UCLA vs. Louisville, 2nd, 1992
33, six tied (most recent: Indiana vs. UCLA, RF, 1992)

Most Free Throws Attempted
55, UTEP vs. Tulsa, 1st, 1985
52, Weber St. vs. Hawaii, 1st, 1972
48, Utah vs. Santa Clara, R3d, 1960
46, Arizona vs. Nevada-Las Vegas, RSF, 1976 (ot)
46, Iowa vs. Nevada-Las Vegas, 2nd, 1988
46, Utah vs. Michigan St., 2nd, 1991 (2 ot)

Highest Free-Throw Percentage (minimum 15 FTM)
94.7% (18-19), Seattle vs. California, RF, 1958 (ot)
94.7% (18-19), Nevada-Las Vegas vs. Kansas St., 2nd, 1987
91.7% (22-24), Arizona vs. Cornell, 1st, 1988
91.3% (21-23), DePaul vs. Air Force, 1st, 1960
90.9% (20-22), Loyola (Cal.) vs. New Mexico St., 1st, 1990

Most Rebounds
76, UCLA vs. Weber St., RSF, 1972
72, UCLA vs. Seattle, R3d, 1956
72, Seattle vs. Utah St., R3d, 1964
70, Arizona St. vs. Southern Cal, RSF, 1961
68, Utah vs. Southern Cal, 1st, 1960

Largest Rebound Margin
29, Utah (59) vs. Loyola (Cal.) (30), RSF, 1961
28, Seattle (72) vs. Utah St. (44), R3d, 1964
27, New Mexico St. (62) vs. Brigham Young (35), 1st, 1969
23, Nevada-Las Vegas (57) vs. Boise St. (34), 1st, 1976

23, Arizona St. (66) vs. Loyola (Cal.) (43), 1st,
  1980
Most Assists
  36, North Caro. vs. Loyola (Cal.), 2nd, 1988
  35, Nevada-Las Vegas vs. Loyola (Cal.), RF,
  1990
  33, Loyola (Cal.) vs. Michigan, 2nd, 1990
  30, Michigan vs. Florida, 2nd, 1988
  29, Wyoming vs. Loyola (Cal.), 1st, 1988
Most Blocked Shots
  13, Brigham Young vs. Virginia, 1st, 1991
  12, Clemson vs. St. Mary's (Cal.), 1st, 1989
  12, Louisiana St. vs. Brigham Young, 1st, 1992
  11, Arizona vs. UTEP, 1st, 1987 (ot)
  10, Seton Hall vs. Creighton, 2nd, 1991
Most Steals
  17, Seton Hall vs. Pepperdine, 1st, 1991
  16, Loyola (Cal.) vs. Wyoming, 1st, 1988
  14, Oklahoma vs. Iowa, RSF, 1987 (ot)

14, Loyola (Cal.) vs. Nevada-Las Vegas, RF,
  1990
14, Nevada-Las Vegas vs. Seton Hall, RF, 1991
Most Personal Fouls
  36, UCLA vs. Seattle, R3d, 1956
  35, Hawaii vs. Weber St., 1st, 1972
  34, Nevada-Las Vegas vs. Arizona, RSF, 1976
  (ot)
  34, Tulsa vs. UTEP, 1st, 1985
  34, UTEP vs. Arizona, 1st, 1987 (ot)

Most Players Disqualified
  5, Wyoming vs. Loyola (Cal.), 1st, 1988
  4, Hawaii vs. Weber St., 1st, 1972
  4, Nevada-Las Vegas vs. Arizona, RSF, 1976
  (ot)
  4, Iowa vs. Idaho, 2nd, 1982 (ot)
  4, UTEP vs. Arizona, 1st, 1987 (ot)
  4, Florida St. vs. Iowa, 1st, 1988

SINGLE GAME, TWO-TEAM

Most Points
  264, Loyola (Cal.) (149) vs. Michigan (115),
  2nd, 1990
  234, Loyola (Cal.) (119) vs. Wyoming (115), 1st,
  1988
  232, Nevada-Las Vegas (131) vs. Loyola (Cal.)
  (101), RF, 1990
  223, Arizona (114) vs. Nevada-Las Vegas (109),
  RSF, 1976 (ot)
  220, North Caro. (123) vs. Loyola (Cal.) (97),
  2nd, 1988
Most Field Goals
  94, Loyola (Cal.) (49) vs. Michigan (45), 2nd,
  1990
  91, UCLA (51) vs. Dayton (40), RSF, 1974 (3 ot)
Most Field Goals Attempted
  194, Houston (100) vs. Pacific (Cal.) (94), R3d,
  1966
Most Three-Point Field Goals
  25, Loyola (Cal.) (21) vs. Michigan (4), 2nd,
  1990
  24, Loyola (Cal.) (17) vs. Nevada-Las Vegas (7),
  RF, 1990
  21, St. Francis (Pa.) (13) vs. Arizona (8), 1st,
  1991
  18, Brigham Young (13) vs. Louisiana St. (5),
  1st, 1992
  17, Evansville (12) vs. Oregon St. (5), 1st, 1989
  (ot)
Most Three-Point Field Goals Attempted
  59, Loyola (Cal.) (41) vs. Nevada-Las Vegas
  (18), RF, 1990
  53, Loyola (Cal.) (40) vs. Michigan (13), 2nd,
  1990
  46, Nevada-Las Vegas (23) vs. Ark.-Lit. Rock
  (23), 1st, 1990
  44, Brigham Young (33) vs. Louisiana St. (11),
  1st, 1992
  43, Loyola (Cal.) (28) vs. New Mexico St. (15),
  1st, 1990
Most Free Throws
  64, Bradley (38) vs. Colorado (26), RSF, 1954
  63, Seattle (39) vs. Utah (24), R3d, 1955
Most Free Throws Attempted
  92, Seattle (52) vs. UCLA (40), R3d, 1956
  84, Seattle (45) vs. UCLA (39), RSF, 1964

Most Rebounds
  132, Pacific (Cal.) (67) vs. Houston (65), R3d,
  1966
  130, UCLA (76) vs. Weber St. (54), RSF, 1972
  128, UCLA (72) vs. Seattle (56), R3d, 1956
  124, UCLA (62) vs. Seattle (62), RSF, 1964
  122, UCLA (66) vs. Brigham Young (56), RSF,
  1965

Most Assists
  58, Nevada-Las Vegas (35) vs. Loyola (Cal.)
  (23), RF, 1990
  55, Michigan (30) vs. Florida (25), 2nd, 1988
  54, Loyola (Cal.) (33) vs. Michigan (21), 2nd,
  1990
  47, North Caro. (25) vs. Louisville (22), RSF,
  1986

Most Blocked Shots
  14, Nevada-Las Vegas (9) vs. Arizona (5), RSF,
  1989
  14, Brigham Young (13) vs. Virginia (1), 1st,
  1991
  14, Nevada-Las Vegas (8) vs. Georgetown (6),
  2nd, 1991
  13, six tied (most recent: Louisiana St. vs.
  Brigham Young, 1st, 1992)

Most Steals
  27, Loyola (Cal.) (14) vs. Nevada-Las Vegas
  (13), RF, 1990
  24, Seton Hall (17) vs. Pepperdine (7), 1st, 1991
  22, Loyola (Cal.) (12) vs. New Mexico St., (10),
  1st, 1990
  20, Oklahoma (14) vs. Iowa (6), RSF, 1987 (ot)
  20, Louisiana St. (10) vs. Brigham Young (10),
  1st, 1992

Most Personal Fouls
  60, UCLA (36) vs. Seattle (24), R3d, 1956
  60, Seattle (31) vs. UCLA (29), RSF, 1964

RF—Regional final game.
RSF—Regional semifinal game.
R3d—Regional third-place game.
2nd—Second-round game.
1st—First-round game.
OR—Opening-round game.
*Record later vacated.

THE
TOURNAMENT

Five years ago, Danny Manning was named the tournament's most outstanding player as he led the underdog Kansas Jayhawks to the national championship. Manning blocked a Final Four record six shots against Duke in the national semifinals, then scored 31 points to help Kansas to an 83-79 win over Big Eight-rival Oklahoma in the title game.

TOURNAMENT
SINGLE GAME, INDIVIDUAL

Most Points
- 61, Austin Carr, Notre Dame vs. Ohio, SE 1st, 1970
- 58, Bill Bradley, Princeton vs. Wichita St., N3d, 1965
- 56, Oscar Robertson, Cincinnati vs. Arkansas, MW R3d, 1958
- 52, Austin Carr, Notre Dame vs. Kentucky, SE RSF, 1970
- 52, Austin Carr, Notre Dame vs. Texas Christian, MW 1st, 1971
- 50, David Robinson, Navy vs. Michigan, East 1st, 1987
- 49, Elvin Hayes, Houston vs. Loyola (Ill.), MW 1st, 1968
- 48, Hal Lear, Temple vs. Southern Methodist, N3d, 1956
- 47, Austin Carr, Notre Dame vs. Houston, MW R3d, 1971
- 46, Dave Corzine, DePaul vs. Louisville, MW RSF, 1978
- 45, Bob Houbregs, Washington vs. Seattle, West RSF, 1953
- 45, Austin Carr, Notre Dame vs. Iowa, SE R3d, 1970
- 45, Bo Kimble, Loyola (Cal.) vs. New Mexico St., West 1st, 1990
- 44, Clyde Lovellette, Kansas vs. St. Louis, West RF, 1952
- 44, Rod Thorn, West Va. vs. St. Joseph's (Pa.), East RSF, 1963
- 44, Dan Issel, Kentucky vs. Notre Dame, SE RSF, 1963
- 44, Bill Walton, UCLA vs. Memphis St., CH, 1973
- 44, Hersey Hawkins, Bradley vs. Auburn, SE 1st, 1988
- 44, Travis Mays, Texas vs. Georgia, MW 1st, 1990
- 43, Oscar Robertson, Cincinnati vs. Kansas, MW RF, 1960
- 43, Jeff Mullins, Duke vs. Villanova, East RSF, 1964
- 43, Willie Smith, Missouri vs. Michigan, MW RF, 1976

Most Points by Two Teammates
- 85, Austin Carr (61) and Collis Jones (24), Notre Dame vs. Ohio, SE 1st, 1970
- 78, Austin Carr (52) and Collis Jones (26), Notre Dame vs. Texas Christian, MW, 1971
- 78, Jeff Fryer (41) and Bo Kimble (37), Loyola (Cal.) vs. Michigan, West 2nd, 1990
- 74, Bill Bradley (58) and Don Rodenbach (16), Princeton vs. Wichita St., N3d, 1965
- 74, Austin Carr (52) and Collis Jones (22), Notre Dame vs. Kentucky, SE RSF, 1970

Most Points by Two Opposing Players
- 96, Austin Carr (52), Notre Dame, and Dan Issel (44), Kentucky, SE RSF, 1970
- 85, Austin Carr (61), Notre Dame, and John Canine (24), Ohio, SE 1st, 1970
- 85, Austin Carr (47), Notre Dame, and Poo Welch (38), Houston, MW R3d, 1971
- 83, David Robinson (50), Navy, and Garde Thompson (33), Michigan, East 1st, 1987
- 77, Travis Mays (44), Texas, and Alec Kessler (33), Georgia, MW 1st, 1990

Most Field Goals
- 25, Austin Carr, Notre Dame vs. Ohio, SE 1st, 1970
- 22, Bill Bradley, Princeton vs. Wichita St., N3d, 1965

- 22, Austin Carr, Notre Dame vs. Kentucky, SE RSF, 1970
- 22, David Robinson, Navy vs. Michigan, East 1st, 1987
- 21, Oscar Robertson, Cincinnati vs. Arkansas, MW R3d, 1958
- 21, Austin Carr, Notre Dame vs. Iowa, SE R3d, 1970
- 21, Bill Walton, UCLA vs. Memphis St., CH, 1973
- 20, Bob Houbregs, Washington vs. Seattle, West RSF, 1953
- 20, Elvin Hayes, Houston vs. Loyola (Ill.), MW 1st, 1968
- 20, Austin Carr, Notre Dame vs. Texas Christian, MW 1st, 1971

Most Field Goals Attempted
- 44, Austin Carr, Notre Dame vs. Ohio, SE 1st, 1970
- 42, Lennie Rosenbluth, North Caro. vs. Michigan St., NSF, 1957 (3 ot)
- 42, *Dwight Lamar, Southwestern La. vs. Louisville, MW RSF, 1972
- 40, Austin Carr, Notre Dame vs. Houston, MW R3d, 1971
- 39, Austin Carr, Notre Dame vs. Iowa, SE R3d, 1970
- 38, Bob Cousy, Holy Cross vs. North Caro. St., East RF, 1950
- 37, David Robinson, Navy vs. Michigan, East 1st, 1987
- 36, Oscar Robertson, Cincinnati vs. Arkansas, MW R3d, 1958
- 36, Rick Mount, Purdue vs. UCLA, CH, 1969
- 36, Ernie DiGregorio, Providence vs. Memphis St., NSF, 1973
- 36, Ronald "Popeye" Jones, Murray St. vs. Michigan St., SE 1st, 1990 (ot)

Highest Field-Goal Percentage (minimum 10 FGM)
- 100.0% (11-11), Kenny Walker, Kentucky vs. Western Ky., SE 2nd, 1986
- 100.0% (10-10), Marvin Barnes, Providence vs. Pennsylvania, East RSF, 1973
- 100.0% (10-10), Christian Laettner, Duke vs. Kentucky, East RF, 1992 (ot)
- 95.5% (21-22), Bill Walton, UCLA vs. Memphis St., CH, 1973
- 92.3% (12-13), Dennis Holman, Southern Methodist vs. Cincinnati, MW R3d, 1966
- 91.7% (11-12), Pembrook Burrows, Jacksonville vs. Iowa, SE RSF, 1970
- 90.9% (10-11), Jerry Lucas, Ohio St. vs. St. Joseph's (Pa.), NSF, 1961
- 90.9% (10-11), Akeem Olajuwon, Houston vs. Villanova, MW RF, 1983
- 90.9% (10-11), Dwayne McClain, Villanova vs. Marshall, SE 1st, 1984
- 90.9% (10-11), Billy Thompson, Louisville vs. Louisiana St., NSF, 1986
- 90.9% (10-11), Oliver Miller, Arkansas vs. Murray St., MW 1st, 1992

Most Three-Point Field Goals
- 11, Jeff Fryer, Loyola (Cal.) vs. Michigan, West 2nd, 1990
- 10, Freddie Banks, Nevada-Las Vegas vs. Indiana, NSF, 1987
- 9, Garde Thompson, Michigan vs. Navy, East 1st, 1987
- 8, Gerald Paddio, Nevada-Las Vegas vs. Iowa, West 2nd, 1988

8, Brad Soucie, Eastern Mich. vs. Pittsburgh, MW 1st, 1988

8, Glen Rice, Michigan vs. North Caro., SE RSF, 1989

8, Bo Kimble, Loyola (Cal.) vs. Nevada-Las Vegas, West 2nd, 1990

8, Jamie Mercurio, Miami (Ohio) vs. North Caro., SE 1st, 1992

7, 12 tied (most recent: Chris Fleming, Richmond vs. Temple, East 2nd, 1991)

Most Three-Point Field Goals Attempted

22, Jeff Fryer, Loyola (Cal.) vs. Arkansas, MW 1st, 1989

20, Chris Walker, Villanova vs. Louisiana St., SE 1st, 1990

19, Freddie Banks, Nevada-Las Vegas vs. Indiana, NSF, 1987

19, Gerald Paddio, Nevada-Las Vegas vs. Iowa, West 2nd, 1988

16, Carlos Sample, Southern-B.R. vs. North Caro., SE 1st, 1989

16, Jeff Fryer, Loyola (Cal.) vs. Nevada-Las Vegas, West RF, 1990

15, Steve Henson, Kansas St. vs. Minnesota, East 1st, 1989

15, Jeff Robinson, Siena vs. Minnesota, East 2nd, 1989

15, Jeff Fryer, Loyola (Cal.) vs. Michigan, West 2nd, 1990

15, Randy Woods, La Salle vs. Seton Hall, East 1st, 1992

Highest Three-Point Field-Goal Percentage (minimum 5 3FGM)

100.0% (6-6), Mike Buck, Middle Tenn. St. vs. Florida St., SE 1st, 1989

100.0% (6-6), Migjen Bakalli, North Caro. St. vs. Southern Miss., East 1st, 1991

100.0% (5-5), Mitch Richmond, Kansas St. vs. Georgia, West 1st, 1987 (ot)

100.0% (5-5), Hubert Davis, North Caro. vs. Eastern Mich., East RSF, 1991

87.5% (7-8), William Scott, Kansas St. vs. DePaul, MW 2nd, 1988

83.3% (5-6), Billy Donovan, Providence vs. Alabama, SE RSF, 1987

83.3% (5-6), Dennis Scott, Georgia Tech vs. Iowa St., East 1st, 1988

83.3% (5-6), Richard Morgan, Virginia vs. Middle Tenn. St., SE 2nd, 1989

83.3% (5-6), Dwayne Bryant, Georgetown vs. North Caro. St., East RSF, 1989

83.3% (5-6), Brian Penny, Coastal Caro. vs. Indiana, SE 1st, 1991

83.3% (5-6), Gary Waites, Alabama vs. Wake Forest, SE 2nd, 1991

Most Free Throws

23, Bob Carney, Bradley vs. Colorado, MW RSF, 1954

23, Travis Mays, Texas vs. Georgia, MW 1st, 1990

21, David Robinson, Navy vs. Syracuse, East 2nd, 1986

19, Tom Hammonds, Georgia Tech vs. Iowa St., East 1st, 1988

18, John O'Brien, Seattle vs. Wyoming, West R3d, 1953

18, Jon Rose, Connecticut vs. Boston U., East 1st, 1959

18, Gail Goodrich, UCLA vs. Michigan, CH, 1965

17, Roger Newman, Kentucky vs. Ohio St., SE RF, 1961

17, Barry Kramer, New York U. vs. West Va., East R3d, 1963

17, Tyrone Hill, Xavier (Ohio) vs. Kansas St., MW 1st, 1990

Most Free Throws Attempted

27, David Robinson, Navy vs. Syracuse, East 2nd, 1986

27, Travis Mays, Texas vs. Georgia, MW 1st, 1990

26, Bob Carney, Bradley vs. Colorado, MW RSF, 1954

24, Donnie Gaunce, Morehead St. vs. Iowa, SE RSF, 1956

22, John O'Brien, Seattle vs. Wyoming, West R3d, 1953

22, Wilt Chamberlain, Kansas vs. Oklahoma City, MW RF, 1957

22, Roger Newman, Kentucky vs. Ohio St., SE RF, 1961

21, Adrian Dantley, Notre Dame vs. Kansas, MW 1st, 1975

21, John Bagley, Boston College vs. Wake Forest, SE 2nd, 1981

21, Vernon Maxwell, Florida vs. North Caro. St., East 1st, 1987

21, Tom Hammonds, Georgia Tech vs. Iowa St., East 1st, 1988

Highest Free-Throw Percentage (minimum 10 FTM)

100.0% (16-16), Bill Bradley, Princeton vs. St. Joseph's (Pa.), East 1st, 1963

100.0% (16-16), Fennis Dembo, Wyoming vs. UCLA, West 2nd, 1987

100.0% (13-13), Bill Bradley, Princeton vs. Providence, East RF, 1965

100.0% (13-13), Mike Maloy, Davidson vs. St. John's (N.Y.), East RSF, 1969

100.0% (13-13), Al Gooden, Ball St. vs. Boston College, SE 1st, 1981

100.0% (12-12), 15 tied (most recent: two in 1992)

Most Rebounds

34, Fred Cohen, Temple vs. Connecticut, East RSF, 1956

31, Nate Thurmond, Bowling Green vs. Mississippi St., SE R3d, 1963

30, Jerry Lucas, Ohio St. vs. Kentucky, SE RF, 1961

29, Toby Kimball, Connecticut vs. St. Joseph's (Pa.), East 1st, 1965

28, Elvin Hayes, Houston vs. Pacific (Cal.), West R3d, 1966

27, Bill Russell, San Francisco vs. Iowa, CH, 1956

27, John Green, Michigan St. vs. Notre Dame, SE RSF, 1957

27, Paul Silas, Creighton vs. Oklahoma City, MW 1st, 1964

27, Elvin Hayes, Houston vs. Loyola (Ill.), MW 1st, 1968

26, Howard Jolliff, Ohio vs. Georgia Tech, SE RSF, 1960

26, Phil Hubbard, Michigan vs. Detroit Mercy, SE RSF, 1977

25, Jerry Lucas, Ohio St. vs. Western Ky., SE RSF, 1960

25, Elvin Hayes, Houston vs. Texas Christian, MW RF, 1968

24, K. E. Kirchner, Texas Christian vs. DePaul, MW R3d, 1959

24, Paul Silas, Creighton vs. Memphis St., MW 1st, 1962

24, Eddie Jackson, Oklahoma City vs. Creighton, MW 1st, 1964

24, Elvin Hayes, Houston vs. UCLA, NSF, 1967

24, Elvin Hayes, Houston vs. Louisville, RSF, 1968

24, Sam Lacey, New Mexico St. vs. Drake, MW RF, 1970

24, Tom Burleson, North Caro. St. vs. Providence, East RSF, 1974

Most Assists

18, Mark Wade, Nevada-Las Vegas vs. Indiana, NSF, 1987

15, Kenny Patterson, DePaul vs. Syracuse, East 1st, 1985

15, Keith Smart, Indiana vs. Auburn, MW 2nd, 1987

14, Dicky Beal, Kentucky vs. Brigham Young, SE 2nd, 1984

14, Carl Wright, Southern Methodist vs. Miami (Ohio), West 1st, 1984

14, John Crotty, Virginia vs. Middle Tenn. St., SE 2nd, 1989

14, Pooh Richardson, UCLA vs. Iowa St., SE 1st, 1989

13, six tied (most recent: Keith Jennings, East Tenn. St. vs. Iowa, MW 1st, 1991)

Most Blocked Shots

11, Shaquille O'Neal, Louisiana St. vs. Brigham Young, West 1st, 1992

10, Shawn Bradley, Brigham Young vs. Virginia, West 1st, 1991

9, David Robinson, Navy vs. Cleveland St., East RSF, 1986

8, Tim Perry, Temple vs. Lehigh, East 1st, 1988

8, Mark Strickland, Temple vs. Oklahoma St., East RSF, 1991 (ot)

8, Acie Earl, Iowa vs. Duke, East 2nd, 1992

7, seven tied (most recent: three in 1989)

Most Steals

7, Tommy Amaker, Duke vs. Old Dominion, East 2nd, 1986

7, Tommy Amaker, Duke vs. Louisville, CH, 1986

7, Reggie Miller, UCLA vs. Wyoming, West 2nd, 1987

7, Delray Brooks, Providence vs. Austin Peay, SE 2nd, 1987

7, Ricky Grace, Oklahoma vs. Iowa, West RSF, 1987 (ot)

7, Mookie Blaylock, Oklahoma vs. Kansas, CH, 1988

7, Scott Burrell, Connecticut vs. Xavier (Ohio), MW 2nd, 1991

6, 11 tied (most recent: Clarence Ceasar, Louisiana St. vs. Brigham Young, West 1st, 1992)

TOURNAMENT TRIVIA QUESTION...

What was the first year two teams from the same conference played in the NCAA tournament? Answer: Most basketball experts would answer 1975, the year the bracket was expanded to 32 teams and teams other than the conference champion could be chosen at large from the same conference for the first time. However, in 1944, the Southwest Conference champion was Arkansas, which was unable to participate because of an automobile accident involving several of the Razorbacks' players. Since the first round was being held in Kansas City, Missouri, Missouri made the late entry to fill out the tournament bracket and take the place of Arkansas. Missouri joined fellow Big Six (later became Big Eight) member and champion, Iowa State, to become the first teams from the same conference in the tournament field.

SERIES, INDIVIDUAL
(Three Game Minimum for Averages and Percentages)

Most Points
184, Glen Rice, Michigan, 1989 (6 games)
177, Bill Bradley, Princeton, 1965 (5)
167, Elvin Hayes, Houston, 1968 (5)
163, Danny Manning, Kansas, 1988 (6)
160, Hal Lear, Temple, 1956 (5)
160, Jerry West, West Va., 1959 (5)
158, Austin Carr, Notre Dame, 1970 (3)
158, Joe Barry Carroll, Purdue, 1980 (6)
153, Johnny Dawkins, Duke, 1986 (6)
153, Dennis Scott, Georgia Tech, 1990 (5)

Highest Scoring Average
52.7 (158 points in 3 games), Austin Carr, Notre Dame, 1970
41.7 (125 in 3), Austin Carr, Notre Dame, 1971
35.8 (143 in 4), Jerry Chambers, Utah, 1966
35.8 (143 in 4), Bo Kimble, Loyola (Cal.), 1990
35.4 (177 in 5), Bill Bradley, Princeton, 1965
35.3 (141 in 4), Clyde Lovellette, Kansas, 1952
35.0 (140 in 4), Gail Goodrich, UCLA, 1965
35.0 (105 in 3), Jerry West, West Va., 1960
34.8 (139 in 4), Bob Houbregs, Washington, 1953
33.4 (167 in 5), Elvin Hayes, Houston, 1968

Most Field Goals
75, Glen Rice, Michigan, 1989 (6 games)
70, Elvin Hayes, Houston, 1968 (5)
69, Danny Manning, Kansas, 1988 (6)
68, Austin Carr, Notre Dame, 1970 (3)
66, Johnny Dawkins, Duke, 1986 (6)
65, Bill Bradley, Princeton, 1965 (5)
63, Hal Lear, Temple, 1956 (5)
63, Joe Barry Carroll, Purdue, 1980 (6)
63, Stacey King, Oklahoma, 1988 (6)
61, *Jim McDaniels, Western Ky., 1971 (5)

Most Field Goals Attempted
138, *Jim McDaniels, Western Ky., 1971 (5 games)
137, Elvin Hayes, Houston, 1968 (5)
131, Glen Rice, Michigan, 1989 (6)
125, Danny Manning, Kansas, 1988 (6)
124, Lennie Rosenbluth, North Caro., 1957 (5)
121, Ernie DiGregorio, Providence, 1973 (5)
121, Bo Kimble, Loyola (Cal.), 1990 (4)
118, Austin Carr, Notre Dame, 1970 (3)
116, Rick Mount, Purdue, 1969 (4)
115, Dennis Scott, Georgia Tech, 1990 (5)

Highest Field-Goal Percentage
(minimum 5 FGM per game)
78.8% (26-33), Christian Laettner, Duke, 1989 (5 games)
78.6% (22-28), Heyward Dotson, Columbia, 1968 (3)
78.3% (18-23), *Winston Bennett, Kentucky, 1988 (3)
78.0% (32-41), Kevin Gamble, Iowa, 1987 (4)
77.1% (27-35), Mark Dressler, Missouri, 1980 (3)
76.9% (20-26), Robert Werdann, St. John's (N.Y.), 1991 (4)
76.5% (26-34), Alex Gilbert, Indiana St., 1979 (5)
76.3% (45-59), Bill Walton, UCLA, 1973 (4)
75.0% (24-32), Eric Montross, North Caro., 1992 (3)
74.2% (23-31), Ralph Sampson, Virginia, 1983 (4)

Most Three-Point Field Goals
27, Glen Rice, Michigan, 1989 (6 games)
26, Freddie Banks, Nevada-Las Vegas, 1987 (5)
24, Dennis Scott, Georgia Tech, 1990 (5)
23, Jeff Fryer, Loyola (Cal.), 1990 (4)

21, Steve Alford, Indiana, 1987 (6)
21, William Scott, Kansas St., 1988 (4)
19, Dave Sieger, Oklahoma, 1988 (6)
17, Phil Henderson, Duke, 1990 (6)
16, Andrew Gaze, Seton Hall, 1989 (6)
15, four tied [most recent: Bobby Hurley, Duke, 1992 (6)]

Most Three-Point Field Goals Attempted
65, Freddie Banks, Nevada-Las Vegas, 1987 (5 games)
55, Jeff Fryer, Loyola (Cal.), 1990 (4)
54, Dennis Scott, Georgia Tech, 1990 (5)
49, Glen Rice, Michigan, 1989 (6)
46, Dave Sieger, Oklahoma, 1988 (6)
45, Terry Brown, Kansas, 1991 (6)
44, Phil Henderson, Duke, 1990 (6)
42, Anderson Hunt, Nevada-Las Vegas, 1990 (6)
39, Gerald Paddio, Nevada-Las Vegas, 1987 (5)
38, Anderson Hunt, Nevada-Las Vegas, 1991 (5)

Highest Three-Point Field-Goal Percentage
(minimum 1.5 3FGM per game)
100.0% (6-6), Ranzino Smith, North Caro., 1987 (4 games)
80.0% (8-10), John Crotty, Virginia, 1989 (4)
77.8% (7-9), Corey Williams, Oklahoma St., 1992 (3)
66.7% (6-9), Dwayne Bryant, Georgetown, 1989 (4)
66.7% (8-12), John Leahy, Seton Hall, 1992 (3)
63.6% (14-22), Billy Donovan, Providence, 1987 (5)
63.6% (7-11), Glen Rice, Michigan, 1988 (3)
63.6% (7-11), Sean Sutton, Oklahoma St., 1992 (3)
61.8% (21-34), Steve Alford, Indiana, 1987 (6)
61.8% (21-34), William Scott, Kansas St., 1988 (4)

Most Free Throws
55, Bob Carney, Bradley, 1954 (5 games)
49, Don Schlundt, Indiana, 1953 (4)
49, Christian Laettner, Duke, 1991 (6)
47, Bill Bradley, Princeton, 1965 (5)
46, Jerry West, West Va., 1959 (5)
45, Cedric Maxwell, N.C.-Charlotte, 1977 (5)
44, Len Chappell, Wake Forest, 1962 (5)
43, Travis Mays, Texas, 1990 (4)
42, Gail Goodrich, UCLA, 1965 (4)
42, Christian Laettner, Duke, 1990 (6)

Most Free Throws Attempted
71, Jerry West, West Va., 1959 (5 games)
70, Bob Carney, Bradley, 1954 (5)
63, Don Schlundt, Indiana, 1953 (4)
62, Len Chappell, Wake Forest, 1962 (5)
62, Wilt Chamberlain, Kansas, 1957 (4)
55, David Robinson, Navy, 1986 (4)
54, Christian Laettner, Duke, 1991 (6)
53, Cedric Maxwell, N.C.-Charlotte, 1977 (5)
53, Ed Pinckney, Villanova, 1985 (6)
52, Christian Laettner, Duke, 1990 (6)

Highest Perfect Free-Throw Percentage
(minimum 2.5 FTM per game)
100.0% (23-23), Richard Morgan, Virginia, 1989 (4 games)
100.0% (19-19), *Derrick McKey, Alabama, 1987 (3)
100.0% (18-18), Mike Vreeswyk, Temple, 1988 (4)
100.0% (17-17), Oliver Robinson, Ala.-Birmingham, 1981 (3)

100.0% (15-15), John Pinone, Villanova, 1983 (3)
100.0% (15-15), LaBradford Smith, Louisville, 1988 (3)
100.0% (15-15), John Pelphrey, Kentucky, 1992 (4)
100.0% (14-14), *Jim Farmer, Alabama, 1987 (3)
100.0% (11-11), Tom Greis, Villanova, 1988 (4)
100.0% (10-10), Ron Haigler, Pennsylvania, 1973 (3)
100.0% (10-10), Gene Harmon, Creighton, 1974 (3)
100.0% (10-10), Cliff Rees, Navy, 1986 (4)
100.0% (10-10), Jeff Lebo, North Caro., 1988 (4)

Highest Free-Throw Percentage (minimum 20 FTM)
100.0% (23-23), Richard Morgan, Virginia, 1989 (4 games)
96.3% (26-27), Sidney Moncrief, Arkansas, 1979 (3)
96.2% (25-26), Jeff Lamp, Virginia, 1981 (5)
96.0% (24-25), Dwayne McClain, Villanova, 1985 (6)
95.5% (21-22), Steve Alford, Indiana, 1984 (3)
95.2% (20-21), Phil Ford, North Caro., 1977 (5)
92.2% (47-51), Bill Bradley, Princeton, 1965 (5)
92.1% (35-38), Don MacLean, UCLA, 1992 (4)
91.7% (33-36), Milt Wagner, Louisville, 1986 (6)
91.7% (22-24), Monte Towe, North Caro. St., 1974 (4)
91.7% (22-24), LaBradford Smith, Louisville, 1989 (3)

Most Rebounds
97, Elvin Hayes, Houston, 1968 (5 games)
93, Artis Gilmore, Jacksonville, 1970 (5)
91, Elgin Baylor, Seattle, 1958 (5)
90, Sam Lacey, New Mexico St., 1970 (5)
89, *Clarence Glover, Western Ky., 1971 (5)
86, Len Chappell, Wake Forest, 1962 (5)
83, Tom Sanders, New York U., 1960 (5)
82, Don May, Dayton, 1967 (5)
77, John Green, Michigan St., 1957 (4)
75, Elvin Hayes, Houston, 1967 (5)
75, Lew Alcindor, UCLA, 1968 (4)
75, Larry Johnson, Nevada-Las Vegas, 1990 (6)
73, Jerry Lucas, Ohio St., 1961 (4)
73, Jerry West, West Va., 1959 (5)
73, Derrick Coleman, Syracuse, 1987 (6)
70, Nate Thurmond, Bowling Green, 1963 (3)
70, Vic Rouse, Loyola (Ill.), 1963 (5)
69, Paul Hogue, Cincinnati, 1962 (4)
67, Ken Spain, Houston, 1968 (5)
67, Larry Bird, Indiana St., 1979 (5)

Highest Rebound Average
23.3 (70 rebounds in 3 games), Nate Thurmond, Bowling Green, 1963
21.3 (64 in 3), Howard Jolliff, Ohio, 1960

19.4 (97 in 5), Elvin Hayes, Houston, 1968
19.3 (77 in 4), John Green, Michigan St., 1957
19.0 (57 in 3), Paul Silas, Creighton, 1964
18.8 (75 in 4), Lew Alcindor, UCLA, 1968
18.6 (93 in 5), Artis Gilmore, Jacksonville, 1970
18.3 (73 in 4), Jerry Lucas, Ohio St., 1961
18.3 (55 in 3), James Ware, Oklahoma City, 1965
18.2 (91 in 5), Elgin Baylor, Seattle, 1958
18.0 (90 in 5), Sam Lacey, New Mexico St., 1970
17.8 (89 in 5), *Clarence Glover, Western Ky., 1971
17.7 (53 in 3), Mel Counts, Oregon St., 1962
17.3 (69 in 4), Paul Hogue, Cincinnati, 1962
17.2 (86 in 5), Len Chappell, Wake Forest, 1962
17.0 (51 in 3), Len Chappell, Wake Forest, 1961
17.0 (51 in 3), Marvin Barnes, Providence, 1974
16.7 (50 in 3), Elvin Hayes, Houston, 1966
16.7 (50 in 3), Errol Palmer, DePaul, 1965
16.6 (83 in 5), Tom Sanders, New York U., 1960

Most Assists
61, Mark Wade, Nevada-Las Vegas, 1987 (5 games)
56, Rumeal Robinson, Michigan, 1989 (6)
49, Sherman Douglas, Syracuse, 1987 (6)
47, Bobby Hurley, Duke, 1992 (6)
45, Michael Jackson, Georgetown, 1985 (6)
43, Bobby Hurley, Duke, 1991 (6)
42, Cedric Hunter, Kansas, 1986 (5)
42, Billy Donovan, Providence, 1987 (5)
42, Jamal Meeks, Indiana, 1992 (5)
41, Ricky Grace, Oklahoma, 1988 (6)

Most Blocked Shots
23, David Robinson, Navy, 1986 (4 games)
20, Tim Perry, Temple, 1988 (4)
19, Alonzo Mourning, Georgetown, 1989 (4)
17, Chris Webber, Michigan, 1992 (6)
16, Derrick Coleman, Syracuse, 1987 (6)
16, Shaquille O'Neal, Louisiana St., 1992 (2)
15, Dean Garrett, Indiana, 1987 (6)
15, Elmore Spencer, Nevada-Las Vegas, 1991 (5)
14, Danny Manning, Kansas, 1988 (6)
13, Pervis Ellison, Louisville, 1989 (3)
13, Mark Strickland, Temple, 1991 (4)

Most Steals
23, Mookie Blaylock, Oklahoma, 1988 (6 games)
18, Tommy Amaker, Duke, 1986 (6)
18, Mark Wade, Nevada-Las Vegas, 1987 (5)
18, Lee Mayberry, Arkansas, 1990 (5)
17, Kendall Gill, Illinois, 1989 (5)
16, Derrick Taylor, Louisiana St., 1986 (5)
16, Dave Sieger, Oklahoma, 1988 (6)
15, Grant Hill, Duke, 1991 (6)
14, Ricky Grace, Oklahoma, 1987 (3)
14, Ricky Grace, Oklahoma, 1988 (6)
14, Nick Anderson, Illinois, 1989 (5)

CAREER, INDIVIDUAL
(Two-Year Minimum for Averages and Percentages)

Most Points
407, Christian Laettner, Duke, 1989-90-91-92 (23 games)
358, Elvin Hayes, Houston, 1966-67-68 (13)
328, Danny Manning, Kansas, 1985-86-87-88 (16)
324, Oscar Robertson, Cincinnati, 1958-59-60 (10)
308, Glen Rice, Michigan, 1986-87-88-89 (13)
304, Lew Alcindor, UCLA, 1967-68-69 (12)
303, Bill Bradley, Princeton, 1963-64-65 (9)
289, Austin Carr, Notre Dame, 1969-70-71 (7)
275, Jerry West, West Va., 1958-59-60 (9)
269, Danny Ferry, Duke, 1986-87-88-89 (19)

266, Jerry Lucas, Ohio St., 1960-61-62 (12)
260, Reggie Williams, Georgetown, 1984-85-86-87 (17)
256, Patrick Ewing, Georgetown, 1982-83-84-85 (18)
254, Bill Walton, UCLA, 1972-73-74 (12)
246, Stacey King, Oklahoma, 1987-88-89 (12)
242, Stacey Augmon, Nevada-Las Vegas, 1988-89-90-91 (17)
240, Todd Day, Arkansas, 1989-90-91-92 (13)
237, Sam Perkins, North Caro., 1981-82-83-84 (15)
236, Sean Elliott, Arizona, 1986-87-88-89 (10)
235, Gail Goodrich, UCLA, 1963-64-65 (10)

Highest Scoring Average (minimum 6 games)
41.3 (289 points in 7 games), Austin Carr, Notre Dame, 1969-70-71
33.7 (303 in 9), Bill Bradley, Princeton, 1963-64-65
32.4 (324 in 10), Oscar Robertson, Cincinnati, 1958-59-60
30.6 (275 in 9), Jerry West, West Va., 1958-59-60
30.5 (183 in 6), Bob Pettit, Louisiana St., 1953-54
29.3 (176 in 6), Dan Issel, Kentucky, 1968-69-70
29.3 (176 in 6), *Jim McDaniels, Western Ky., 1970-71
29.2 (175 in 6), *Dwight Lamar, Southwestern La., 1972-73
29.1 (204 in 7), Bo Kimble, Loyola (Cal.), 1988-89-90
28.6 (200 in 7), David Robinson, Navy, 1985-86-87
27.7 (166 in 6), Billy McGill, Utah, 1960-61
27.6 (221 in 8), Len Chappell, Wake Forest, 1961-62
27.5 (358 in 13), Elvin Hayes, Houston, 1966-67-68
27.4 (192 in 7), Bob Houbregs, Washington, 1951-53
27.0 (162 in 6), Don Schlundt, Indiana, 1953-54
25.7 (180 in 7), Kenny Anderson, Georgia Tech, 1990-91
25.4 (203 in 8), Adrian Dantley, Notre Dame, 1974-75-76
25.3 (304 in 12), Lew Alcindor, UCLA, 1967-68-69
25.2 (151 in 6), Barry Kramer, New York U., 1962-63
25.2 (151 in 6), Bob Lanier, St. Bonaventure, 1968-70

Most Field Goals
152, Elvin Hayes, Houston, 1966-67-68 (13 games)
140, Danny Manning, Kansas, 1985-86-87-88 (16)
128, Glen Rice, Michigan, 1986-87-88-89 (13)
128, Christian Laettner, Duke, 1989-90-91-92 (23)
117, Oscar Robertson, Cincinnati, 1958-59-60 (10)
117, Austin Carr, Notre Dame, 1969-70-71 (7)

Most Field Goals Attempted
310, Elvin Hayes, Houston, 1966-67-68 (13 games)
257, Danny Manning, Kansas, 1985-86-87-88 (16)
235, Oscar Robertson, Cincinnati, 1958-59-60 (10)
225, Austin Carr, Notre Dame, 1969-70-71 (7)
224, Glen Rice, Michigan, 1986-87-88-89 (13)

Highest Field-Goal Percentage
(minimum 70 FGM)
68.6% (109-159), Bill Walton, UCLA, 1972-73-74 (12 games)
68.4% (78-114), Stephen Thompson, Syracuse 1987-88-89-90 (15)
68.0% (70-103), Brad Daugherty, North Caro., 1983-84-85-86 (12)
65.1% (95-146), Akeem Olajuwon, Houston, 1982-83-84 (15)
64.2% (115-179), Lew Alcindor, UCLA, 1967-68-69 (12)

Most Three-Point Field Goals
38, Jeff Fryer, Loyola (Cal.), 1988-89-90 (7 games)
35, Glen Rice, Michigan, 1986-87-88-89 (13)
34, Anderson Hunt, Nevada-Las Vegas, 1989-90-91 (15)

33, Dennis Scott, Georgia Tech, 1988-89-90 (8)
30, Bobby Hurley, Duke, 1990-91-92 (18)

Most Three-Point Field Goals Attempted
103, Anderson Hunt, Nevada-Las Vegas, 1989-90-91 (15 games)
97, Jeff Fryer, Loyola (Cal.), 1988-89-90 (7)
76, Dennis Scott, Georgia Tech, 1988-89-90 (8)
71, Bobby Hurley, Duke, 1990-91-92 (18)
67, Todd Day, Arkansas, 1989-90-91-92 (13)

Highest Three-Point Field-Goal Percentage
(minimum 20 FGM)
65.0% (26-40), William Scott, Kansas St., 1987-88 (5 games)
61.8% (21-34), Steve Alford, Indiana, 1984-86-87 (10)
56.5% (35-62), Glen Rice, Michigan, 1986-87-88-89 (13)

Most Free Throws
142, Christian Laettner, Duke, 1989-90-91-92 (23 games)
90, Oscar Robertson, Cincinnati, 1958-59-60 (10)
87, Bill Bradley, Princeton, 1963-64-65 (9)
83, Ed Pinckney, Villanova, 1982-83-84-85 (14)
81, Jerry West, West Va., 1958-59-60 (9)

Most Free Throws Attempted
167, Christian Laettner, Duke, 1989-90-91-92 (23 games)
119, Lew Alcindor, UCLA, 1967-68-69 (12)
116, Oscar Robertson, Cincinnati, 1958-59-60 (10)
115, Ed Pinckney, Villanova, 1982-83-84-85 (14)
114, Jerry West, West Va., 1958-59-60 (9)

Highest Free-Throw Percentage
(minimum 30 FTM)
95.7% (45-47), LaBradford Smith, Louisville, 1988-89-90 (8 games)
94.9% (37-39), Phil Ford, North Caro., 1975-76-77-78 (10)
92.7% (38-41), Rodney Monroe, North Caro. St., 1988-89-91 (6)
90.9% (30-33), Howard Komives, Bowling Green, 1962-63 (4)
90.7% (39-43), Hubert Davis, North Caro., 1989-90-91-92 (12)

Highest Free-Throw Percentage
(minimum 50 FTM)
90.6% (87-96), Bill Bradley, Princeton, 1963-64-65 (9 games)
90.6% (58-64), Steve Alford, Indiana, 1984-86-87 (10)
89.8% (53-59), Johnny Cox, Kentucky, 1957-58-59 (8)
85.0% (142-167), Christian Laettner, Duke, 1989-90-91-92 (23)
84.7% (50-59), Don MacLean, UCLA, 1989-90-91-92 (10)

Most Rebounds
222, Elvin Hayes, Houston, 1966-67-68 (13 games)
201, Lew Alcindor, UCLA, 1967-68-69 (12)
197, Jerry Lucas, Ohio St., 1960-61-62 (12)
176, Bill Walton, UCLA, 1972-73-74 (12)
169, Christian Laettner, Duke, 1989-90-91-92 (23)
160, Paul Hogue, Cincinnati, 1960-61-62 (12)
157, Sam Lacey, New Mexico St., 1968-69-70 (11)
155, Derrick Coleman, Syracuse, 1987-88-89-90 (14)

153, Akeem Olajuwon, Houston, 1982-83-84 (15)
144, Patrick Ewing, Georgetown, 1982-83-84-85 (18)
138, Marques Johnson, UCLA, 1974-75-76-77 (16)
137, Len Chappell, Wake Forest, 1961-62 (8)
135, Ed Pinckney, Villanova, 1982-83-84-85 (14)
131, Oscar Robertson, Cincinnati, 1958-59-60 (10)
131, Curtis Rowe, UCLA, 1969-70-71 (12)
131, Danny Ferry, Duke, 1986-87-88-89 (19)
129, Sam Perkins, North Caro., 1981-82-83-84 (15)
127, Mel Counts, Oregon St., 1962-63-64 (9)
126, Larry Johnson, Nevada-Las Vegas, 1990-91 (11)
124, Jerry West, West Va., 1958-59-60 (9)

Highest Rebounding Average (minimum 6 games)
19.7 (118 rebounds in 6 games), John Green, Michigan St., 1957-59
19.2 (115 in 6), Artis Gilmore, Jacksonville, 1970-71
18.5 (111 in 6), Paul Silas, Creighton, 1962-64
17.1 (137 in 8), Len Chappell, Wake Forest, 1961-62
17.1 (222 in 13), Elvin Hayes, Houston, 1966-67-68
16.8 (201 in 12), Lew Alcindor, UCLA, 1967-68-69
16.4 (197 in 12), Jerry Lucas, Ohio St., 1960-61-62
14.7 (176 in 12), Bill Walton, UCLA, 1972-73-74
14.3 (157 in 11), Sam Lacey, New Mexico St., 1968-69-70
14.2 (85 in 6), Bob Lanier, St. Bonaventure, 1968-70

Most Assists
129, Bobby Hurley, Duke, 1990-91-92 (18 games)
106, Sherman Douglas, Syracuse, 1986-87-88-89 (14)
100, Greg Anthony, Nevada-Las Vegas, 1989-90-91 (15)
93, Mark Wade, Nevada-Las Vegas, 1986-87 (8)
93, Rumeal Robinson, Michigan, 1988-89-90 (11)

Most Blocked Shots
37, Alonzo Mourning, Georgetown, 1989-90-91-92 (10 games)
34, Tim Perry, Temple, 1985-86-87-88 (10)
33, Rony Seikaly, Syracuse, 1985-86-87-88 (12)
32, Pervis Ellison, Louisville, 1986-88-89 (12)
29, Shaquille O'Neal, Louisiana St., 1990-91-92 (5)

Most Steals
32, Mookie Blaylock, Oklahoma, 1988-89 (9 games)
32, Christian Laettner, Duke, 1989-90-91-92 (23)
31, Lee Mayberry, Arkansas, 1989-90-91-92 (13)
30, Greg Anthony, Nevada-Las Vegas, 1989-90-91 (15)
30, Stacey Augmon, Nevada-Las Vegas, 1988-89-90-91 (17)

Most Games Played
23, Christian Laettner, Duke, 1989-90-91-92
22, Greg Koubek, Duke, 1988-89-90-91
22, Brian Davis, Duke, 1989-90-91-92
19, Danny Ferry, Duke, 1986-87-88-89
19, Alaa Abdelnaby, Duke, 1987-88-89-90
19, Robert Brickey, Duke, 1987-88-89-90

SINGLE GAME, TEAM

Most Points
149, Loyola (Cal.) vs. Michigan (115), West 2nd, 1990
131, Nevada-Las Vegas vs. Loyola (Cal.) (101), West RF, 1990
127, *St. Joseph's (Pa.) vs. Utah (120), N3d, 1961 (4 ot)
124, Oklahoma, vs. Louisiana Tech (81), SE 2nd, 1989
123, North Caro. vs. Loyola (Cal.) (97), West 2nd, 1988
121, Iowa vs. Notre Dame (106), SE R3d, 1970
121, Nevada-Las Vegas vs. San Francisco (95), West 1st, 1977
120, Utah vs. St. Joseph's (Pa.) (127), N3d, 1961 (4 ot)
120, Arkansas vs. Loyola (Cal.) (101), MW 1st, 1989
119, Houston vs. Notre Dame (106), MW R3d, 1971
119, Loyola (Cal.) vs. Wyoming (115), West 1st, 1988

Fewest Points
20, North Caro. vs. Pittsburgh (26), East RF, 1941
24, Springfield vs. Indiana (48), East RF, 1940
26, Pittsburgh vs. North Caro. (20), East RF, 1941
28, Kentucky vs. Dartmouth (47), NSF, 1942
29, Western Ky. vs. Duquesne (30), East RF, 1940
29, Baylor vs. Oklahoma St. (44), West RF, 1946
30, Brown vs. Villanova (43), East RF, 1939
30, Duquesne vs. Western Ky. (29), East RF.

1940
30, Duquesne vs. Indiana (39), NSF, 1940
30, Pittsburgh vs. Wisconsin (36), NSF, 1941
30, Oregon St. vs. Oklahoma St. (55), NSF, 1949

Largest Winning Margin
69, Loyola (Ill.) (111) vs. Tennessee Tech (42), SE 1st, 1963
49, UCLA (109) vs. Wyoming, (60), West RSF, 1967
49, Syracuse (101) vs. Brown (52), East 1st, 1986
47, Duke (101) vs. Connecticut (54), East RF, 1964
47, DePaul (99) vs. Eastern Ky. (52), SE 1st, 1965
43, *Villanova (90) vs. Pennsylvania (47), East RF, 1971
43, Oklahoma (124) vs. Louisiana Tech (81), SE 2nd, 1989
42, Notre Dame (108) vs. Austin Peay (66), SE 1st, 1974
41, Arkansas (117) vs. Georgia St. (76), SE 1st, 1991
40, five tied [most recent: Arizona (90) vs. Cornell (50), West 1st, 1988]

Smallest Winning Margin
1, 115 tied (most recent: two in 1992)

Most Points Scored by Losing Team
120, Utah vs. St. Joseph's (Pa.) (127), N3d, 1961 (4 ot)
115, Wyoming vs. Loyola (Cal.) (119), West 1st, 1988
115, Michigan vs. Loyola (Cal.) (149), West 2nd, 1990

109, Nevada-Las Vegas vs. Arizona (114), West RSF, 1976 (ot)
106, Notre Dame vs. Iowa (121), SE R3d, 1970
106, Notre Dame vs. Houston (119), MW R3d, 1971
103, Iowa vs. Jacksonville (104), SE RSF, 1970
103, Kentucky vs. Duke (104), East RF, 1992 (ot)
102, Brigham Young vs. Oklahoma City (112), West R3d, 1965
101, Marshall vs. Southwestern La. (112), MW 1st, 1972
101, Loyola (Cal.) vs. Arkansas (120), MW 1st, 1989
101, Loyola (Cal.) vs. Nevada-Las Vegas (131), West RF, 1990

Most Field Goals
52, Iowa vs. Notre Dame, SE R3d, 1970
51, UCLA vs. Dayton, West RSF, 1974 (3 ot)
51, Nevada-Las Vegas vs. Loyola (Cal.), West RF, 1990
50, Utah vs. St. Joseph's (Pa.), N3d, 1961 (4 ot)
50, Kentucky vs. Austin Peay, SE RSF, 1973 (ot)
50, Notre Dame vs. Austin Peay, SE 1st, 1974
49, Notre Dame vs. Vanderbilt, SE R3d, 1974
49, Nevada-Las Vegas vs. San Francisco, West 1st, 1977
49, North Caro. vs. Loyola (Cal.), West 2nd, 1988
49, Loyola (Cal.) vs. Michigan, West 2nd, 1990

Fewest Field Goals
8, Springfield vs. Indiana, East 1st, 1940
9, Pittsburgh vs. North Caro., East RSF, 1941
9, North Caro. vs. Pittsburgh, East RSF, 1941
9, Oklahoma St. vs. Kentucky, CH, 1949
10, Wisconsin vs. Pittsburgh, NSF, 1941
10, Kentucky vs. Dartmouth, NSF, 1942
10, Harvard vs. Ohio St., East 1st, 1946
11, eight tied (most recent: Oregon St. vs. Oklahoma St., NSF, 1949)

Most Field Goals Attempted
112, Marshall vs. Southwestern La., MW 1st, 1972
106, Indiana vs. Miami (Ohio), SE R3d, 1958
105, *Western Ky. vs. Villanova, NSF, 1971 (2 ot)
103, St. Joseph's (Pa.) vs. West Va., East R3d, 1960
103, Utah vs. St. Joseph's (Pa.), N3d, 1961 (4 ot)
103, Loyola (Cal.) vs. North Caro., West 2nd, 1988
102, Notre Dame vs. Houston, MW R3d, 1971
101, Holy Cross vs. North Caro. St., East 1st, 1950
101, *St. Joseph's (Pa.) vs. Utah, N3d, 1961 (4 ot)
100, Houston vs. Pacific (Cal.), West R3d, 1966
100, Rutgers vs. UCLA, N3d, 1976

Highest Field-Goal Percentage
80.0% (28-35), Oklahoma St. vs. Tulane, SE 2nd, 1992
79.0% (49-62), North Caro. vs. Loyola (Cal.), West 2nd, 1988
78.6% (22-28), Villanova vs. Georgetown, CH, 1985
75.0% (33-44), Northeastern vs. Va. Commonwealth, East 1st, 1984
74.4% (29-39), Georgetown vs. Oregon St., West RF, 1982
73.2% (30-41), North Caro. St. vs. UTEP, West 2nd, 1985
72.7% (40-55), *Alabama vs. New Orleans, SE 2nd, 1987
71.4% (30-42), Villanova vs. Marshall, SE 1st, 1984
71.4% (25-35), Georgetown vs. Notre Dame, East 2nd, 1989

70.5% (31-44), Washington vs. Duke, West 2nd, 1984

Lowest Field-Goal Percentage
12.7% (8-63), Springfield vs. Indiana, East RSF, 1940
13.9% (10-72), Harvard vs. Ohio St., East RSF, 1946
19.4% (14-72), Creighton vs. Cincinnati, MW RSF, 1962
19.5% (15-77), North Caro. St. vs. Baylor, N3d, 1950
20.6% (13-63), Arkansas vs. Oregon St., West RSF, 1949
22.0% (18-82), Tennessee Tech vs. Loyola (Ill.), SE 1st, 1963
22.9% (16-70), St. John's (N.Y.) vs. Kentucky, East RSF, 1951
24.4% (20-82), Holy Cross vs. Ohio St., East R3d, 1950
24.5% (13-53), Kentucky vs. Georgetown, NSF, 1984
25.0% (17-68), Massachusetts vs. New York U., East 1st, 1962

Most Three-Point Field Goals
21, Loyola (Cal.) vs. Michigan, West 2nd, 1990
17, Loyola (Cal.) vs. Nevada-Las Vegas, West RF, 1990
14, Providence vs. Alabama, SE RSF, 1987
13, Nevada-Las Vegas vs. Indiana, NSF, 1987
13, Loyola (Cal.) vs. North Caro., West 2nd, 1988
13, Michigan vs. North Caro., SE RSF, 1989
13, St. Francis (Pa.) vs. Arizona, West 1st, 1991
13, Texas vs. Iowa, East 1st, 1992
13, Brigham Young vs. Louisiana St., West 1st, 1992
13, East Tenn. St. vs. Arizona, SE 1st, 1992

Most Three-Point Field Goals Attempted
41, Loyola (Cal.) vs. Nevada-Las Vegas, West RF, 1990
40, Loyola (Cal.) vs. Michigan, West 2nd, 1990
39, Loyola (Cal.) vs. North Caro., West 2nd, 1988
39, Loyola (Cal.) vs. Arkansas, MW 1st, 1989
35, Nevada-Las Vegas vs. Indiana, NSF, 1987
35, La Salle vs. Clemson, East 2nd, 1990
33, La Salle vs. Southern Miss., East 1st, 1990
33, Texas Southern vs. Georgetown, MW 1st, 1990
33, Brigham Young vs. Louisiana St., West 1st, 1992
32, Siena vs. Minnesota, East 2nd, 1989

Highest Three-Point Field-Goal Percentage (minimum 7 3FGM)
88.9% (8-9), Kansas St. vs. Georgia, West 1st, 1987 (ot)
81.8% (9-11), *Alabama vs. North Caro. A&T, SE 1st, 1987
80.0% (8-10), Kansas St. vs. Purdue, MW RSF, 1988
76.9% (10-13), Kansas St. vs. DePaul, MW 2nd, 1988
72.7% (8-11), Duke vs. Indiana, MW RSF, 1987
72.7% (8-11), Alabama vs. Colorado St., West 1st, 1990
70.0% (7-10), seven tied (most recent: two in 1991)

Most Free Throws
41, Utah vs. Santa Clara, West R3d, 1960
41, Navy vs. Syracuse, East 2nd, 1986
39, Seattle vs. Utah, West R3d, 1955
39, UTEP vs. Tulsa, West 1st, 1985
38, Bradley vs. Colorado, MW RSF, 1954
38, Loyola (Ill.) vs. Kentucky, SE R3d, 1964
37, Morehead St. vs. Pittsburgh, SE 1st, 1957

37, *St. Joseph's (Pa.) vs. Utah, N3d, 1961 (4 ot)
37, Jacksonville vs. St. Bonaventure, NSF, 1970
37, Xavier (Ohio) vs. Kansas St., MW 1st, 1990

Most Free Throws Attempted
55, UTEP vs. Tulsa, West 1st, 1985
54, Morehead St. vs. Pittsburgh, SE 1st, 1957
53, Morehead St. vs. Iowa, SE RSF, 1956
52, Iowa vs. Morehead St., SE RSF, 1956
52, Weber St. vs. Hawaii, West 1st, 1972
52, Navy vs. Syracuse, East 2nd, 1986
50, West Va. vs. St. Joseph's (Pa.), East RSF, 1959
50, Notre Dame vs. Kansas, MW 1st, 1975
49, Manhattan vs. West Va., East 1st, 1958
49, New York U. vs. St. Joseph's (Pa.), East R3d, 1962

Highest Free-Throw Percentage
(minimum 15 FTM)
100.0% (22-22), Fordham vs. South Caro., East R3d, 1971
100.0% (17-17), Dayton vs. Villanova, SE 1st, 1985
100.0% (17-17), Villanova vs. Kentucky, SE RSF, 1988
95.8% (23-24), Oklahoma St. vs. Loyola (La.), MW 1st, 1958
95.5% (21-22), Vanderbilt vs. Marquette, SE RSF, 1974
95.2% (20-21), Notre Dame vs. Vanderbilt, SE R3d, 1974
95.2% (20-21), Iowa vs. North Caro. St., East 2nd, 1989 (2 ot)
95.0% (19-20), North Caro. St. vs. St. John's (N.Y.), East R3d, 1951
95.0% (19-20), Iowa vs. Georgetown, East RF, 1980
94.7% (18-19), Seattle vs. California, West RF, 1958
94.7% (18-19), Nevada-Las Vegas vs. Kansas St., West 2nd, 1987

Most Rebounds
86, Notre Dame vs. Tennessee Tech, SE 1st, 1958
76, Temple vs. Connecticut, East RSF, 1956
76, Houston vs. North Caro., N3d, 1967
76, Houston vs. Texas Christian, MW RF, 1968
76, UCLA vs. Weber St., West RSF, 1972
72, UCLA vs. Seattle, West R3d, 1956
72, Seattle vs. Utah St., West R3d, 1964
71, Kansas St. vs. Houston, MW R3d, 1970
70, Western Ky. vs. Miami (Fla.), SE 1st, 1960
70, Arizona St. vs. Southern Cal, West RSF, 1961

Largest Rebound Margin
42, Notre Dame (86) vs. Tennessee Tech (44), SE 1st, 1958
35, St. John's (N.Y.) (56) vs. Connecticut (21), East 1st, 1951
33, Cincinnati (68) vs. Texas Tech (35), MW RSF, 1961
30, Louisiana Tech (56) vs. Pittsburgh (26), MW 1st, 1985
29, West Va. (63) vs. Dartmouth (34), East 1st, 1959
29, Utah (59) vs. Loyola (Cal.) (30), West RSF, 1961

29, Indiana (52) vs. Robert Morris (23), SE 1st, 1982
28, Seattle (72) vs. Utah St. (44), West R3d, 1964
28, Indiana St. (50) vs. Oklahoma (22), MW RSF, 1979
27, three tied [most recent: Memphis St. (60) vs. South Caro. (33), MW RSF, 1973]

Most Assists
36, North Caro. vs. Loyola (Cal.), West 2nd, 1988
35, Nevada-Las Vegas vs. Loyola (Cal.), West RF, 1990
33, Loyola (Cal.) vs. Michigan, West 2nd, 1990
32, Arkansas vs. Georgia St., SE 1st, 1991
32, Kansas vs. Howard, MW 1st, 1992
32, Michigan vs. East Tenn. St., SE 2nd, 1992
31, Syracuse vs. Brown, East 1st, 1986
31, Oklahoma vs. Auburn, SE 2nd, 1988
30, North Caro. vs. Pennsylvania, East 1st, 1987
30, Michigan vs. Florida, West 2nd, 1988
30, Purdue vs. Memphis St., MW 2nd, 1988
30, Arkansas vs. Loyola (Cal.), MW 1st, 1989

Most Blocked Shots
13, Louisville vs. Illinois, MW RSF, 1989
13, Brigham Young vs. Virginia, 1st, 1991
12, Clemson vs. St. Mary's (Cal.), West 1st, 1989
12, Louisiana St. vs. Brigham Young, West 1st, 1992
11, Arizona vs. UTEP, West 1st, 1987 (ot)
11, Duke vs. Temple, East RF, 1988
11, North Caro. St. vs. Iowa, East 2nd, 1989
10, Providence vs. Georgetown, SE RF, 1987
10, Louisiana St. vs. Georgia Tech, SE 2nd, 1990
10, Seton Hall vs. Creighton, West 2nd, 1991
10, Iowa vs. Duke, East 2nd, 1992

Most Steals
19, Providence vs. Austin Peay, SE 2nd, 1987 (ot)
19, Connecticut vs. Boston U., East 1st, 1990
18, Xavier (Ohio) vs. Kansas, MW 1st, 1988
17, Seton Hall vs. Pepperdine, West 1st, 1991
17, Duke vs. St. John's (N.Y.), MW RF, 1991
16, eight tied (most recent: Kentucky vs. Old Dominion, East 1st, 1992)

Most Personal Fouls
41, Dayton vs. Illinois, East RSF, 1952
39, Kansas vs. Notre Dame, MW 1st, 1975
36, UCLA vs. Seattle, West R3d, 1956
36, North Caro. vs. Texas A&M, MW 2nd, 1980
35, Iowa vs. Morehead St., SE RSF, 1956
35, Hawaii vs. Weber St., West 1st, 1972
35, DePaul vs. Va. Military, East RSF, 1976 (ot)
35, DePaul vs. Boston College, MW 2nd, 1982
34, six tied (most recent: two in 1987)

Most Players Disqualified
6, Kansas vs. Notre Dame, MW 1st, 1975
5, St. Joseph's (Pa.) vs. West Va., East RSF, 1959
5, DePaul vs. Va. Military, East RSF, 1976 (ot)
5, DePaul vs. Boston College, MW 2nd, 1982
5, Syracuse vs. Virginia, East RSF, 1984
5, Wyoming vs. Loyola (Cal.), West 1st, 1988
4, 29 tied (most recent: Indiana vs. Duke, NSF, 1992)

SINGLE GAME, TWO-TEAM

Most Points
264, Loyola (Cal.) (149) vs. Michigan (115), West 2nd, 1990
247, *St. Joseph's (Pa.) (127) vs. Utah (120), N3d, 1961 (4 ot)
234, Loyola (Cal.) (119) vs. Wyoming (115), West 1st, 1988

232, Nevada-Las Vegas (131) vs. Loyola (Cal.) (101), West RF, 1990
227, Iowa (121) vs. Notre Dame (106), SE R3d, 1970
225, Houston (119) vs. Notre Dame (106), MW R3d, 1971

223, Arizona (114) vs. Nevada-Las Vegas (109), West RSF, 1976 (ot)
221, Arkansas (120) vs. Loyola (Cal.) (101), MW 1st, 1989
220, North Caro. (123) vs. Loyola (Cal.) (97), West 2nd, 1988
216, Nevada-Las Vegas (121) vs. San Francisco (95), 1st, 1977

Most Field Goals
97, Iowa (52) vs. Notre Dame (45), SE R3d, 1970
96, Kentucky (50) vs. Austin Peay (46), SE RSF, 1973 (ot)
95, Utah (50) vs. *St. Joseph's (Pa.) (45), N3d, 1961 (4 ot)
94, Loyola (Cal.) (49) vs. Michigan (45), West 2nd, 1990
91, UCLA (51) vs. Dayton (40), West RSF, 1974 (3 ot)

Most Field Goals Attempted
204, Utah (103) vs. *St. Joseph's (Pa.) (101), N3d, 1961 (4 ot)
196, Austin Peay (99) vs. Kentucky (97), SE RSF, 1973 (ot)
195, Iowa (98) vs. Notre Dame (97), SE R3d, 1970
194, Indiana (106) vs. Miami (Ohio) (88), SE R3d, 1958
194, Houston (100) vs. Pacific (Cal.) (94), West R3d, 1966

Most Three-Point Field Goals
25, Loyola (Cal.) (21) vs. Michigan (4), West 2nd, 1990
24, Loyola (Cal.) (17) vs. Nevada-Las Vegas (7), West RF, 1990
21, Providence (14) vs. Alabama (7), SE RSF, 1987
21, St. Francis (Pa.) (13) vs. Arizona (8), West 1st, 1991
20, three tied [most recent: Kentucky (12) vs. Duke (8), East RF, 1992 (ot)]

Most Three-Point Field Goals Attempted
59, Loyola (Cal.) (41) vs. Nevada-Las Vegas (18), West RF, 1990
56, La Salle (33) vs. Southern Miss. (23), East 1st, 1990
54, La Salle (30) vs. Seton Hall (24), East 1st, 1992
53, Loyola (Cal.) (40) vs. Michigan (13), West 2nd, 1990
48, Loyola (Cal.) (39) vs. North Caro. (9), West 2nd, 1988
48, Loyola (Cal.) (39) vs. Arkansas (9), MW 1st, 1989

Most Free Throws
69, Morehead St. (37) vs. Pittsburgh (32), SE 1st, 1957
68, Iowa (35) vs. Morehead St. (33), SE RSF, 1956

68, Oklahoma City (35) vs. Kansas St. (33), MW RSF, 1956
64, Bradley (38) vs. Colorado (26), West RSF, 1954
63, Seattle (39) vs. Utah (24), West R3d, 1955

Most Free Throws Attempted
105, Morehead St. (53) vs. Iowa (52), SE RSF, 1956
97, Morehead St. (54) vs. Pittsburgh (43), SE 1st, 1957
92, Oklahoma City (48) vs. Kansas St. (44), MW RSF, 1956
92, Seattle (52) vs. UCLA (40), West R3d, 1956
91, Manhattan (49) vs. West Va. (42), East 1st, 1958

Most Rebounds
134, Marshall (68) vs. *Southwestern La. (66), MW 1st, 1972
132, Pacific (Cal.) (67) vs. Houston (65), West R3d, 1966
131, Houston (76) vs. Texas Christian (55), MW RF, 1968
130, Notre Dame (86) vs. Tennessee Tech (44), SE 1st, 1958
130, UCLA (76) vs. Weber St. (54), West RSF, 1972
128, UCLA (72) vs. Seattle (56), West R3d, 1956
128, Utah (65) vs. *St. Joseph's (Pa.) (63), N3d, 1961 (4 ot)
128, Houston (76) vs. North Caro. (52), N3d, 1967
126, Drake (66), vs. Notre Dame (60), MW RSF, 1971 (ot)
124, UCLA (62) vs. Seattle (62), West RSF, 1964

Most Assists
58, Nevada-Las Vegas (35) vs. Loyola (Cal.) (23), West RF, 1990
55, Michigan (30) vs. Florida (25), West 2nd, 1988
54, Loyola (Cal.) (33) vs. Michigan (21), West 2nd, 1990

Most Blocked Shots
18, Iowa (10) vs. Duke (8), East 2nd, 1992
17, Duke (11) vs. Temple (6), East RF, 1988

Most Steals
27, Loyola (Cal.) (14) vs. Nevada-Las Vegas (13), West RF, 1990
26, Providence (19) vs. Austin Peay (7), SE 2nd, 1987 (ot)
26, Arkansas (16) vs. Georgia St. (10), SE 1st, 1991
26, Duke (17) vs. St. John's (N.Y.) (9), MW RF, 1991

Most Personal Fouls
60, Seattle (31) vs. UCLA (29), West RSF, 1964

SINGLE GAME, TEAM—OVERTIMES

Most Overtime Periods
4, Canisius (79) vs. North Caro. St. (78), East 1st, 1956
4, *St. Joseph's (Pa.) (127) vs. Utah (120), N3d, 1961
3, North Caro. (54) vs. Kansas (53), CH, 1957
3, North Caro. (74) vs. Michigan St. (70), NSF, 1957
3, UCLA (111) vs. Dayton (100), West RSF, 1974
3, Villanova (76) vs. Northeastern (72), East 2nd, 1982

Most Points in Overtimes
38, *St. Joseph's (Pa.) vs. Utah, N3d, 1961 (4 ot)
31, Utah vs. St. Joseph's (Pa.), N3d, 1961 (4 ot)

31, UCLA vs. Dayton, West RSF, 1974 (3 ot)
27, North Caro. St. vs. Iowa, East 2nd, 1989 (2 ot)
25, Texas A&M vs. North Caro., MW 2nd, 1980 (2 ot)
25, Louisiana St. vs. Purdue, SE 1st, 1986 (2 ot)

Most Points in Overtimes, Both Teams
69, *St. Joseph's (Pa.) (38) vs. Utah (31), N3d, 1961 (4 ot)
51, UCLA (31) vs. Dayton (20), West RSF, 1974 (3 ot)
48, North Caro. St. (27) vs. Iowa (21), East 2nd, 1989 (2 ot)

43, Louisiana St. (25) vs. Purdue (18), SE 1st, 1986 (2 ot)

42, North Caro. St. (22) vs. Pepperdine (20), West 1st, 1983 (2 ot)

Most Points in One Overtime Period

25, Texas A&M vs. North Caro., MW 2nd, 1980 (2nd ot)

22, Utah vs. Missouri, MW 1st, 1978

21, Louisiana St. vs. Purdue, SE 1st, 1986 (2nd ot)

19, seven tied (most recent: Temple vs. Oklahoma St., East RSF, 1991)

Most Points in One Overtime Period, Both Teams

37, Utah (22) vs. Missouri (15), MW 1st, 1978

35, Louisiana St. (21) vs. Purdue (14), SE 1st, 1986 (2nd ot)

34, Iowa (18) vs. Oklahoma (16), West RSF, 1987

33, Texas A&M (25) vs. North Caro. (8), MW 2nd, 1980 (2nd ot)

32, North Caro. St. (19) vs. Iowa (13), East 2nd, 1989 (2nd ot)

Least Points in One Overtime Period

0, nine tied (most recent: Va. Commonwealth vs. Tennessee, East 2nd, 1981)

Least Points in One Overtime Period, Both Teams

0, Canisius vs. North Caro. St., East 1st, 1956 (3rd ot)

0, North Caro. vs. Kansas, CH, 1957 (2nd ot)

0, Texas A&M vs. North Caro., MW 2nd, 1980 (1st ot)

1, Southern Cal (1) vs. Santa Clara (0), West RF, 1956 (2nd ot)

2, Tennessee (2) vs. Va. Commonwealth (0), East 2nd, 1981 (1st ot)

Largest Winning Margin in an Overtime Game

17, Texas A&M (78) vs. North Caro. (61), MW 2nd, 1980 (2 ot)

14, North Caro. St. (80) vs. Ark.-Lit. Rock (66), MW 2nd, 1986 (2 ot)

12, UCLA (103) vs. Michigan (91), West 1st, 1975

12, Louisville (80) vs. Kentucky (68), ME RF, 1983

11, three tied [most recent: Temple (61) vs. Jacksonville (50), MW 1st, 1986]

Most Overtime Games by One Team in One Tournament

3, Syracuse, 1975

2, 10 tied (most recent: Michigan St., 1990)

Most Overtime Periods by One Team in One Tournament

6, North Caro., 1957 (2 games)

5, UCLA, 1974 (2 games)

3, 12 tied [most recent: Villanova and Northeastern, 1982 (1 game)]

SINGLE GAME, TEAM MISCELLANEOUS

Most Players in Double Figures, One Team

7, Indiana vs. George Mason, West 1st, 1989

7, Nevada-Las Vegas vs. Ark.-Lit. Rock, West 1st, 1990

6, 15 tied (most recent: Kentucky vs. Old Dominion, East 1st, 1992)

Most Players in Double Figures, Both Teams

12, Notre Dame (6) vs. Houston (6), West 1st, 1965

11, eight tied [most recent: Michigan (6) vs. Loyola (Cal.) (5), West 2nd, 1990]

Most Players with 20+ Points, One Team

4, Fordham vs. South Caro., East R3d, 1971

4, Syracuse vs. Western Ky., East 2nd, 1987

4, Loyola (Cal.) vs. Michigan, West 2nd, 1990

4, Nevada-Las Vegas vs. Loyola (Cal.), West RF, 1990

Most Players with 20+ Points, Both Teams

6, 10 tied (most recent: two in 1990)

Most Players Scored, One Team

14, Iowa vs. Santa Clara, West 1st, 1987

13, Indiana vs. St. Joseph's (Pa.), SE RF, 1981

13, Indiana vs. Fairfield, MW 1st, 1987

Most Players Scored, Both Teams

24, Brown (12) vs. Syracuse (12), East 1st, 1986

24, Iowa (14) vs. Santa Clara (10), West 1st, 1987

22, Duke (12) vs. Connecticut (10), East RF, 1964

Fewest Players Scored, One Team

3, Utah St. vs. San Francisco, West RSF, 1964

4, 12 tied (most recent: Indiana vs. Syracuse, CH, 1987)

Fewest Players Scored, Both Teams

9, Connecticut (4) vs. Temple (5), East 1st, 1964

9, Michigan St. (4) vs. Washington (5), MW 1st, 1986

10, 13 tied [most recent: Indiana (4) vs. Syracuse (6), CH, 1987]

Most Players Used, One Team

15, 11 tied (most recent: three tied in 1986)

Most Players Used, Both Teams

29, Arizona St. (15) vs. Loyola (Cal.) (14), West 1st, 1980

27, Brown (15) vs. Syracuse (12), East 1st, 1986

27, Iowa (14) vs. Santa Clara (13), West 1st, 1987

Fewest Players Used, One Team

5, nine tied (most recent: DePaul twice in 1979, vs. Southern Cal, West 2nd, and vs. Indiana St., NSF)

Fewest Players Used, Both Teams

12, five tied [most recent: St. Joseph's (Pa.) (6) vs. DePaul (6), SE 2nd, 1981]

SERIES, TEAM
(Three-Game Minimum for Averages and Percentages)

Most Points

571, Nevada-Las Vegas, 1990 (6 games)

552, Oklahoma, 1988 (6)

540, Michigan, 1989 (6)

535, Indiana, 1987 (6)

513, Louisville, 1986 (6)

Highest Scoring Average

105.8, (423 points in 4 games), Loyola (Cal.), 1990

105.7, (317 in 3), Notre Dame, 1970

101.0, (505 in 5), Nevada-Las Vegas, 1977

100.0, (400 in 4), UCLA, 1965

98.7, (296 in 3), *Southwestern La., 1972

Most Field Goals
218, Nevada-Las Vegas, 1977 (5 games)
217, Nevada-Las Vegas, 1990 (6)
217, Michigan, 1989 (6)
206, Oklahoma, 1988 (6)
203, Louisville, 1986 (6)

Most Field Goals Attempted
442, *Western Ky., 1971 (5 games)
441, Nevada-Las Vegas, 1977 (5)
418, Houston, 1968 (5)
412, Oklahoma, 1988 (6)
410, Nevada-Las Vegas, 1990 (6)

Highest Field-Goal Percentage
60.4% (113-187), North Caro., 1975 (3 games)
59.6% (96-161), Michigan, 1988 (3)
59.0% (92-156), Michigan St., 1978 (3)
58.6% (99-169), *Alabama, 1987 (3)
58.1% (83-143), Arkansas, 1979 (3)

Most Three-Point Field Goals
56, Loyola (Cal.), 1990 (4 games)
45, Providence, 1987 (5)
43, Nevada-Las Vegas, 1987 (5)
43, Michigan, 1989 (6)
41, Oklahoma, 1988 (6)

Most Three-Point Field Goals Attempted
137, Loyola (Cal.), 1990 (4 games)
132, Nevada-Las Vegas, 1987 (5)
105, Oklahoma, 1988 (6)
102, Nevada-Las Vegas, 1990 (6)
 98, Georgia Tech, 1990 (5)

Highest Three-Point Field-Goal Percentage (minimum 12 3FGM)
60.9% (14-23), Indiana, 1989 (3 games)
59.3% (16-27), St. John's (N.Y.), 1991 (4)
54.0% (27-50), Virginia, 1989 (4)
52.5% (21-40), Indiana, 1987 (6)

Highest Three-Point Field-Goal Percentage (minimum 30 3FGM)
50.8% (33-65), Kansas St., 1988 (4 games)

Most Free Throws
146, Bradley, 1954 (5 games)
136, *UCLA, 1980 (6)
136, Duke, 1990 (5)
136, Duke, 1992 (6)
130, Southern Methodist, 1956 (5)

Most Free Throws Attempted
194, Bradley, 1954 (5 games)
192, West Va., 1959 (5)
183, Duke, 1990 (5)
183, Duke, 1992 (6)
178, Purdue, 1980 (6)

Highest Free-Throw Percentage
87.0% (47-54), St. John's (N.Y.), 1969 (3 games)
85.5% (47-55), Notre Dame, 1987 (3)
84.8% (50-59), *Alabama, 1987 (3)
84.4% (76-90), Temple, 1988 (4)
83.7% (36-43), Georgia Tech, 1992 (3)

Most Rebounds
306, Houston, 1968 (5 games)
289, *Western Ky., 1971 (5)
268, New Mexico St., 1970 (5)
262, Nevada-Las Vegas, 1990 (6)

Most Assists
140, Nevada-Las Vegas, 1990 (6 games)
136, Oklahoma, 1988 (6)
125, Michigan, 1989 (6)
120, Louisville, 1986 (6)
115, Kansas, 1988 (6)

Most Blocked Shots
33, Nevada-Las Vegas, 1990 (6 games)
32, Nevada-Las Vegas, 1991 (5)
31, Duke, 1992 (6)
30, Syracuse, 1987 (6)
29, Seton Hall, 1989 (6)
29, Michigan, 1992 (6)

Most Steals
72, Oklahoma, 1988 (6 games)
57, Arkansas, 1990 (5)
55, Duke, 1991 (6)
54, Nevada-Las Vegas, 1990 (6)
52, Duke, 1992 (6)

Most Personal Fouls
150, Pennsylvania, 1979 (6 games)
135, Providence, 1987 (5)
128, Kentucky, 1975 (5)
124, Michigan, 1989 (6)
123, Nevada-Las Vegas, 1977 (5)

CH—National championship game.
NSF—National semifinal game.
N3d—National third-place game.
RF—Regional final game.
RSF—Regional semifinal game.
R3d—Regional third-place game.
2nd—Second-round game.
1st—First-round game.
OR—Opening-round game.
East—East region.
SE—Southeast/Mideast region.
MW—Midwest region.
West—West/Far West region.
*Record later vacated.

TOURNAMENT TRIVIA QUESTION...
The highest-rated televised collegiate basketball game was the 1979 NCAA championship game between Michigan State and Indiana State. Each team had a star player which caused the big attraction to the game. Who were they? Answer: Earvin "Magic" Johnson of Michigan State and Larry Bird of Indiana State.

TOURNAMENT HISTORY TEAM RECORDS

Most Tournament Appearances
33, Kentucky, 1942–92
27, UCLA, 1950–92
26, North Caro., 1941–92
24, Notre Dame, 1953–90
22, Louisville, 1951–92
22, St. John's (N.Y.), 1951–92
21, Indiana, 1940–92
21, Kansas, 1940–92
20, DePaul, 1943–92
20, Kansas St., 1948–90
20, Syracuse, 1957–92
20, Villanova, 1939–91

Most Consecutive Tournament Appearances
18, North Caro., 1975–92
14, Georgetown, 1979–92
13, UCLA, 1967–79
10, Marquette, 1971–80
10, Syracuse, 1983–92
9, Arkansas, 1977–85
9, Duke, 1984–92
9, Louisiana St., 1984–92
9, Nevada-Las Vegas, 1983–91
8, Arizona, 1985–92
8, Idaho St., 1953–60
8, Georgia Tech, 1985–92
8, Illinois, 1983–90
8, Kentucky, 1980–87
8, Louisville, 1977–84
8, Notre Dame, 1974–81
8, Oklahoma, 1983–90
8, Syracuse, 1973–80

Current Most Consecutive Tournament Appearances
18, North Caro., 1975–92

14, Georgetown, 1979–92
10, Syracuse, 1983–92
9, Duke, 1984–92
9, Louisiana St., 1984–92
8, Arizona, 1985–92
8, Georgia Tech, 1985–92
7, Indiana, 1986–92
5, Arkansas, 1988–92
4, Alabama, 1989–92
4, East Tenn. St., 1989–92
4, Texas, 1989–92
4, UCLA, 1989–92

Most Tournament Wins
62, UCLA, 1950–92
56, Kentucky, 1942–92
56, North Caro., 1941–92
50, Duke, 1955–92
45, Indiana, 1940–92
43, Kansas, 1940–92
39, Louisville, 1951–92
32, Michigan, 1953–92
31, Ohio St., 1939–92
31, Villanova, 1939–91

Highest Tournament Winning Percentage (minimum 20 games)
76.9% (50–15), Duke, 1955–92
74.7% (62–21), UCLA, 1950–92
73.8% (45–16), Indiana, 1940–92
73.2% (30–11), Nevada-Las Vegas, 1975–92
70.6% (24–10), Cincinnati, 1958–92
69.6% (32–14), Michigan, 1948–92
67.5% (56–27), North Caro., 1941–92
67.2% (43–21), Kansas, 1940–92
65.9% (27–14), North Caro. St., 1950–91
65.5% (19–10), Oklahoma St., 1945–92

Note: On all percentages of the year-by-year leaders, a player must have played in at least 50 percent of the maximum tournament games. Thus, there is a two-game minimum from 1939–52 and a three-game minimum from 1953 to present.

INDIVIDUAL SCORING LEADERS

Year	Player, School	G	FG	FT	Pts.	Avg.
1939	Jim Hull, Ohio St.	3	22	14	58	19.3
1940	Howard Engleman, Kansas	3	18	3	39	13.0
1941	John Adams, Arkansas	2	21	6	48	24.0
1942	Chet Palmer, Rice	2	19	5	43	21.5
	Jim Pollard, Stanford	2	20	3	43	21.5
1943	John Hargis, Texas	2	21	17	59	29.5
1944	Aud Brindley, Dartmouth	3	24	4	52	17.3
1945	Bob Kurland, Oklahoma St.	3	30	5	65	21.7
1946	Bob Kurland, Oklahoma St.	3	28	16	72	24.0
1947	George Kaftan, Holy Cross	3	25	13	63	21.0
1948	Alex Groza, Kentucky	3	23	8	54	18.0
1949	Alex Groza, Kentucky	3	31	20	82	27.3
1950	Sam Ranzino, North Caro. St.	3	25	25	75	25.0
1951	Don Sunderlage, Illinois	4	28	27	83	20.8
1952	Clyde Lovellette, Kansas	4	53	35	141	35.3
1953	Bob Houbregs, Washington	4	57	25	139	34.8
1954	Tom Gola, La Salle	5	38	38	114	22.8
1955	Bill Russell, San Francisco	5	49	20	118	23.6
1956	Hal Lear, Temple	5	63	34	160	32.0
1957	Lennie Rosenbluth, North Caro.	5	53	34	140	28.0
1958	Elgin Baylor, Seattle	5	48	39	135	27.0
1959	Jerry West, West Va.	5	57	46	160	32.0
1960	Oscar Robertson, Cincinnati	4	47	28	122	30.5
1961	Billy McGill, Utah	4	49	21	119	29.8
1962	Len Chappell, Wake Forest	5	45	44	134	26.8
1963	Mel Counts, Oregon St.	5	50	23	123	24.6
1964	Jeff Mullins, Duke	4	50	16	116	29.0
1965	Bill Bradley, Princeton	5	65	47	177	35.4
1966	Jerry Chambers, Utah	4	55	33	143	35.8

Year	Player, School	G	FG	FT	Pts.	Avg.
1967	Elvin Hayes, Houston	5	57	14	128	25.6
1968	Elvin Hayes, Houston	5	70	27	167	33.4
1969	Rick Mount, Purdue	4	49	24	122	30.5
1970	Austin Carr, Notre Dame	3	68	22	158	52.7
1971	*Jim McDaniels, Western Ky.	5	61	25	147	29.4
	Austin Carr, Notre Dame	3	48	29	125	41.7
1972	Jim Price, Louisville	4	41	21	103	25.8
1973	Ernie DiGregorio, Providence	5	59	10	128	25.6
1974	David Thompson, North Caro. St.	4	38	21	97	24.3
1975	Jim Lee, Syracuse	5	51	17	119	23.8
1976	Scott May, Indiana	5	45	23	113	22.6
1977	Cedric Maxwell, N.C.-Charlotte	5	39	45	123	24.6
1978	Mike Gminski, Duke	5	45	19	109	21.8
1979	Tony Price, Pennsylvania	6	58	26	142	23.7
1980	Joe Barry Carroll, Purdue	6	63	32	158	26.3
1981	Al Wood, North Caro.	5	44	21	109	21.8
1982	Rob Williams, Houston	5	30	28	88	17.6
1983	Dereck Whittenburg, North Caro. St.	6	47	26	120	20.0
1984	Roosevelt Chapman, Dayton	4	35	35	105	26.3
1985	Chris Mullin, St. John's (N.Y.)	5	39	32	110	22.0
1986	Johnny Dawkins, Duke	6	66	21	153	25.5

Year	Player, School	G	FG	3FG	FT	Pts.	Avg.
1987	Steve Alford, Indiana	6	42	21	33	138	23.0
	Rony Seikaly, Syracuse	6	53	0	32	138	23.0
1988	Danny Manning, Kansas	6	69	2	23	163	27.2
1989	Glen Rice, Michigan	6	75	7	27	184	30.7
1990	Dennis Scott, Georgia Tech	5	51	24	27	153	30.6
1991	Christian Laettner, Duke	6	37	2	49	125	20.8
1992	Christian Laettner, Duke	6	39	7	30	115	19.2

*Record later vacated.

HIGHEST SCORING AVERAGE

Year	Player, School	G	FG	FT	Pts.	Avg.
1939	Jim Hull, Ohio St.	3	22	14	58	19.3
1940	Howard Engleman, Kansas	3	18	3	39	13.0
	Bob Kinney, Rice	2	12	2	26	13.0
1941	John Adams, Arkansas	2	21	6	48	24.0
1942	Chet Palmer, Rice	2	19	5	43	21.5
	Jim Pollard, Stanford	2	20	3	43	21.5
1943	John Hargis, Texas	2	21	17	59	29.5
1944	Nick Bozolich, Pepperdine	2	17	11	45	22.5
1945	Dick Wilkins, Oregon	2	19	6	44	22.0
1946	Bob Kurland, Oklahoma St.	3	28	16	72	24.0
1947	George Kaftan, Holy Cross	3	25	13	63	21.0
1948	Jack Nichols, Washington	2	13	13	39	19.5
1949	Alex Groza, Kentucky	3	31	20	82	27.3
1950	Sam Ranzino, North Caro. St.	3	25	25	75	25.0
1951	William Kukoy, North Caro. St.	3	25	19	69	23.0
1952	Clyde Lovellette, Kansas	4	53	35	141	35.3
1953	Bob Houbregs, Washington	4	57	25	139	34.8
1954	John Clune, Navy	3	30	19	79	26.3
1955	Terry Rand, Marquette	3	31	11	73	24.3
1956	Hal Lear, Temple	5	63	34	160	32.0
1957	Wilt Chamberlain, Kansas	4	40	41	121	30.3
1958	Wayne Embry, Miami (Ohio)	3	32	19	83	27.7
1959	Jerry West, West Va.	5	57	46	160	32.0
1960	Jerry West, West Va.	3	35	35	105	35.0
1961	Billy McGill, Utah	4	49	21	119	29.8
1962	Len Chappell, Wake Forest	5	45	44	134	26.8
1963	Barry Kramer, New York U.	3	31	38	100	33.3
1964	Jeff Mullins, Duke	4	50	16	116	29.0
1965	Bill Bradley, Princeton	5	65	47	177	35.4
1966	Jerry Chambers, Utah	4	55	33	143	35.8
1967	Lew Alcindor, UCLA	4	39	28	106	26.5
1968	Elvin Hayes, Houston	5	70	27	167	33.4
1969	Rick Mount, Purdue	4	49	24	122	30.5
1970	Austin Carr, Notre Dame	3	68	22	158	52.7
1971	Austin Carr, Notre Dame	3	48	29	125	41.7
1972	*Dwight Lamar, Southwestern La.	3	41	18	100	33.3
	Jim Price, Louisville	4	41	21	103	25.8

Year	Player, School	G	FG	FT	Pts.	Avg.
1973	Larry Finch, Memphis St.	4	34	39	107	26.8
1974	John Shumate, Notre Dame	3	35	16	86	28.7
1975	Adrian Dantley, Notre Dame	3	29	34	92	30.7
1976	Willie Smith, Missouri	3	38	18	94	31.3
1977	Cedric Maxwell, N.C.-Charlotte	5	39	45	123	24.6
1978	Dave Corzine, DePaul	3	33	16	82	27.3
1979	Larry Bird, Indiana St.	5	52	32	136	27.2
1980	Joe Barry Carroll, Purdue	6	63	32	158	26.3
1981	Al Wood, North Caro.	5	44	21	109	21.8
1982	Oliver Robinson, Ala.-Birmingham	3	27	12	66	22.0
1983	Greg Stokes, Iowa	3	24	13	61	20.3
1984	Roosevelt Chapman, Dayton	4	35	35	105	26.3
1985	Kenny Walker, Kentucky	3	28	19	75	25.0
1986	David Robinson, Navy	4	35	40	110	27.5

Year	Player, School	G	FG	3FG	FT	Pts.	Avg.
1987	Fennis Dembo, Wyoming	3	25	11	23	84	28.0
1988	Danny Manning, Kansas	6	69	2	23	163	27.2
1989	Glen Rice, Michigan	6	75	7	27	184	30.7
1990	Bo Kimble, Loyola (Cal.)	4	51	15	26	143	35.8
1991	Terry Dehere, Seton Hall	4	34	12	17	97	24.3
1992	Jamal Mashburn, Kentucky	4	34	6	22	96	24.0

*Record later vacated.

HIGHEST FIELD-GOAL PERCENTAGE
(Minimum: 5 field goals made per game)

Year	Player, School	G	FGM	FGA	Pct.
1950	Dick Schnittker, Ohio St.	2	15	29	51.7
1951	Don Sunderlage, Illinois	4	28	62	45.2
1963	William Humphrey, Texas	3	16	22	72.7
1964	Jay Buckley, Duke	4	24	39	61.5
1965	Dave Mills, DePaul	3	16	21	76.2
1966	Henry Finkel, Dayton	3	37	61	60.7
1967	Ken Talley, Virginia Tech	3	20	30	66.7
1968	Heyward Dotson, Columbia	3	22	28	78.6
1969	Jarrett Durham, Duquesne	3	26	38	68.4
1970	Pembrook Burrows, Jacksonville	5	24	33	72.7
1971	Jim Chones, Marquette	3	29	48	60.4
1972	*Wilbert Loftin, Southwestern La.	3	16	23	69.6
	Bill Walton, UCLA	4	28	41	68.3
1973	Bill Walton, UCLA	4	45	59	76.3
1974	John Shumate, Notre Dame	3	35	50	70.0
1975	Mitch Kupchak, North Caro.	3	29	40	72.5
1976	Ron Carter, Va. Military	3	22	37	59.5
1977	Rick Robey, Kentucky	3	16	22	72.7
1978	Greg Kelser, Michigan St.	3	29	40	72.5
1979	Alex Gilbert, Indiana St.	5	26	34	76.5
1980	Mark Dressler, Missouri	3	27	35	77.1
1981	Randy Reed, Kansas St.	4	22	33	66.7
1982	Larry Micheaux, Houston	5	29	45	64.4
1983	Ralph Sampson, Virginia	3	23	31	74.2
1984	Kelvin Johnson, Richmond	3	29	38	76.3
1985	Brad Daugherty, North Caro.	4	29	40	72.5
1986	Kenny Walker, Kentucky	4	35	50	70.0
1987	Kevin Gamble, Iowa	4	32	41	78.0
1988	*Winston Bennett, Kentucky	3	18	23	78.3
	Tim Perry, Temple	4	26	36	72.2
1989	Christian Laettner, Duke	5	26	33	78.8
1990	Alaa Abdelnaby, Duke	6	42	64	65.6
1991	Robert Werdann, St. John's (N.Y.)	4	20	26	76.9
1992	Eric Montross, North Caro.	3	24	32	75.0

MOST THREE-POINT FIELD GOALS MADE

Year	Player, School	G	3FGM
1987	Freddie Banks, Nevada-Las Vegas	5	26
1988	William Scott, Kansas St.	4	21
1989	Glen Rice, Michigan	6	27
1990	Dennis Scott, Georgia Tech	5	24
1991	Terry Brown, Kansas	6	14
1992	Bobby Hurley, Duke	6	15

HIGHEST THREE-POINT FIELD-GOAL PERCENTAGE
(Minimum: 1.5 three-point field goals made per game)

Year	Player, School	G	3FGM	3FGA	Pct.
1987	Ranzino Smith, North Caro.	4	6	6	100.0
1988	Glen Rice, Michigan	3	7	11	63.6
1989	John Crotty, Virginia	4	8	10	80.0
1990	Kevin Lynch, Minnesota	4	9	16	56.3
1991	Jason Buchanan, St. John's (N.Y.)	4	8	13	61.5
1992	Corey Williams, Oklahoma St.	3	7	9	77.8

HIGHEST FREE-THROW PERCENTAGE
(Minimum: 10 free throws made and 2.5 free throws made per game)

Year	Player, School	G	FTM	FTA	Pct.
1941	Gene Englund, Wisconsin	3	16	19	84.2
1942	Charles Black, Kansas	2	10	14	71.4
1943	Bill Hassett, Georgetown	3	10	13	76.9
1945	Arnold Risen, Ohio St.	2	11	16	68.8
1946	Jack Underman, Ohio St.	3	18	21	85.7
1947	Gerald Tucker, Oklahoma	3	16	19	84.2
1948	Howard Shannon, Kansas St.	2	15	15	100.0
1949	Jack Shelton, Oklahoma St.	3	19	22	86.4
1950	Floyd Layne, CCNY	3	12	15	80.0
	Gene Melchiorre, Bradley	3	12	15	80.0
1951	Bill Kukoy, North Caro. St.	3	19	22	86.4
1952	Jim Young, Santa Clara	3	13	16	81.3
1953	Ron Perry, Holy Cross	3	18	20	90.0
1954	Jack Clune, Navy	3	19	22	86.4
1955	Tom Gola, La Salle	5	37	42	88.1
1956	Bobby Mills, Southern Methodist	5	32	40	80.0
1957	John Riser, Pittsburgh	3	30	36	83.3
1958	Johnny Cox, Kentucky	4	21	23	91.3
1959	Howie Carl, DePaul	3	16	18	88.9
1960	Darrall Imhoff, California	5	22	24	91.7
1961	John Turner, Louisville	3	19	21	90.5
1962	Gary Cunningham, UCLA	4	17	19	89.5
	Mel Counts, Oregon St.	3	17	19	89.5
1963	Howard Komives, Bowling Green	3	29	32	90.6
1964	Wayne Estes, Utah St.	3	21	23	91.3
1965	Bill Bradley, Princeton	5	47	51	92.2
1966	Mike Lewis, Duke	4	17	18	94.4
1967	Steve Adelman, Boston College	3	14	16	87.5
1968	Harley Swift, East Tenn. St.	3	18	18	100.0
1969	Rick Mount, Purdue	4	24	27	88.9
1970	Chip Dublin, Jacksonville	5	19	20	95.0
1971	Henry Bibby, UCLA	4	17	17	100.0
1972	Larry McNeill, Marquette	3	11	12	91.7
1973	Ron Haigler, Pennsylvania	3	10	10	100.0
1974	Gene Harmon, Creighton	3	10	10	100.0
1975	Phil Ford, North Caro.	3	17	18	94.4
1976	Will Bynum, Va. Military	3	22	26	84.6
1977	Phil Ford, North Caro.	5	20	21	95.2
1978	Mike Gminski, Duke	5	19	21	90.5
1979	Sidney Moncrief, Arkansas	3	26	27	96.3
1980	*Cliff Pruitt, UCLA	6	14	15	93.3
	Eric Floyd, Georgetown	3	12	14	85.7
1981	Oliver Robinson, Ala.-Birmingham	3	17	17	100.0
1982	Oliver Robinson, Ala.-Birmingham	3	12	13	92.3
1983	John Pinone, Villanova	3	15	15	100.0
1984	Steve Alford, Indiana	3	21	22	95.5
1985	Dwayne McClain, Villanova	6	24	25	96.0
1986	Cliff Rees, Navy	4	10	10	100.0
1987	*Derrick McKey, Alabama	3	19	19	100.0
	*Jim Farmer, Alabama	3	14	14	100.0
	Reggie Williams, Georgetown	4	27	30	90.0
1988	Mike Vreeswyk, Temple	4	18	18	100.0
	LaBradford Smith, Louisville	3	15	15	100.0
	Tom Greis, Villanova	4	11	11	100.0
	Jeff Lebo, North Caro.	4	10	10	100.0
1989	Richard Morgan, Virginia	4	23	23	100.0
1990	Bo Kimble, Loyola (Cal.)	4	26	29	89.7
1991	Brian Davis, Duke	5	19	20	95.0
1992	John Pelphrey, Kentucky	4	15	15	100.0

INDIVIDUAL REBOUNDING LEADERS

Year	Player, School	G	Reb.	Avg.
1951	Bill Spivey, Kentucky	4	65	16.3
1957	John Green, Michigan St.	4	77	19.3
1958	Elgin Baylor, Seattle	5	91	18.2
1959	Jerry West, West Va.	5	73	14.6
1960	Tom Sanders, New York U.	5	83	16.6
1961	Jerry Lucas, Ohio St.	4	73	18.3
1962	Len Chappell, Wake Forest	5	86	17.2
1963	Nate Thurmond, Bowling Green	3	70	23.3
	Vic Rouse, Loyola (Ill.)	5	70	14.0
1964	Paul Silas, Creighton	3	57	19.0
1965	Bill Bradley, Princeton	5	57	11.4
1966	Jerry Chambers, Utah	4	56	14.0
1967	Don May, Dayton	5	82	16.4
1968	Elvin Hayes, Houston	5	97	19.4
1969	Lew Alcindor, UCLA	4	64	16.0
1970	Artis Gilmore, Jacksonville	5	93	18.6
1971	*Clarence Glover, Western Ky.	5	89	17.8
	Sidney Wicks, UCLA	4	52	13.0
1972	Bill Walton, UCLA	4	64	16.0
1973	Bill Walton, UCLA	4	58	14.5
1974	Tom Burleson, North Caro. St.	4	61	15.3
1975	Richard Washington, UCLA	5	60	12.0
1976	Phil Hubbard, Michigan	5	61	10.2
1977	Cedric Maxwell, N.C.-Charlotte	5	64	12.8
1978	Eugene Banks, Duke	5	50	10.0
1979	Larry Bird, Indiana St.	5	67	13.4
1980	Mike Sanders, UCLA	6	60	10.0
1981	Cliff Levingston, Wichita St.	4	53	13.3
1982	Clyde Drexler, Houston	5	42	8.4
1983	Akeem Olajuwon, Houston	5	65	13.0
1984	Akeem Olajuwon, Houston	5	57	11.4
1985	Ed Pinckney, Villanova	6	48	8.0
1986	Pervis Ellison, Louisville	6	57	9.5
1987	Derrick Coleman, Syracuse	6	73	12.2
1988	Danny Manning, Kansas	6	56	9.3
1989	Daryll Walker, Seton Hall	6	58	9.7
1990	Larry Johnson, Nevada-Las Vegas	6	75	12.5
1991	Larry Johnson, Nevada-Las Vegas	5	51	10.2
1992	Chris Webber, Michgian	6	58	9.7

HIGHEST REBOUNDING AVERAGE

Year	Player, School	G	Reb.	Avg.
1951	Bill Spivey, Kentucky	4	65	16.3
1957	John Green, Michigan St.	4	77	19.3
1958	Elgin Baylor, Seattle	5	91	18.2
1959	Oscar Robertson, Cincinnati	4	63	15.8
1960	Howard Jolliff, Ohio	3	64	21.3
1961	Jerry Lucas, Ohio St.	4	73	18.3
1962	Mel Counts, Oregon St.	3	53	17.7
1963	Nate Thurmond, Bowling Green	3	70	23.3
1964	Paul Silas, Creighton	3	57	19.0
1965	James Ware, Oklahoma City	3	55	18.3
1966	Elvin Hayes, Houston	3	50	16.7
1967	Don May, Dayton	5	82	16.4
1968	Elvin Hayes, Houston	5	97	19.4
1969	Lew Alcindor, UCLA	4	64	16.0
1970	Artis Gilmore, Jacksonville	5	93	18.6
1971	*Clarence Glover, Western Ky.	5	89	17.8
	Collis Jones, Notre Dame	3	49	16.3
1972	Bill Walton, UCLA	4	64	16.0
1973	Bill Walton, UCLA	4	58	14.5
1974	Marvin Barnes, Providence	3	51	17.0
1975	Mike Franklin, Cincinnati	3	49	16.3
1976	Al Fleming, Arizona	3	39	13.0
1977	Phil Hubbard, Michigan	3	45	15.0
1978	Greg Kelser, Michigan St.	3	37	12.3
1979	Larry Bird, Indiana St.	5	67	13.4
1980	Durand Macklin, Louisiana St.	3	31	10.3
1981	Cliff Levingston, Wichita St.	4	53	13.3
1982	Ed Pinckney, Villanova	3	30	10.0

Year	Player, School	G	Reb.	Avg.
1983	Akeem Olajuwon, Houston	5	65	13.0
1984	*Keith Lee, Memphis St.	3	37	12.3
	Akeem Olajuwon, Houston	5	57	11.4
1985	Karl Malone, Louisiana Tech	3	40	13.3
1986	David Robinson, Navy	4	47	11.8
1987	Derrick Coleman, Syracuse	6	73	12.2
1988	Pervis Ellison, Louisville	3	33	11.0
1989	Pervis Ellison, Louisville	3	31	10.3
	Stacey King, Oklahoma	3	31	10.3
1990	Dale Davis, Clemson	3	44	14.7
1991	Byron Houston, Oklahoma St.	3	36	12.0
	Perry Clark, Ohio St.	3	36	12.0
1992	Doug Edwards, Florida St.	3	32	10.7

INDIVIDUAL ASSISTS LEADERS

Year	Player, School	G	Ast.
1984	Reid Gettys, Houston	5	36
1985	Michael Jackson, Georgetown	6	45
1986	Cedric Hunter, Kansas	5	42
1987	Mark Wade, Nevada-Las Vegas	5	61
1988	Ricky Grace, Oklahoma	6	41
1989	Rumeal Robinson, Michigan	6	56
1990	Bobby Hurley, Duke	6	39
1991	Bobby Hurley, Duke	6	43
1992	Bobby Hurley, Duke	6	47

INDIVIDUAL BLOCKED SHOTS LEADERS

Year	Player, School	G	Blk.
1986	David Robinson, Navy	4	23
1987	Derrick Coleman, Syracuse	6	16
1988	Tim Perry, Temple	4	20
1989	Alonzo Mourning, Georgetown	4	19
1990	Larry Johnson, Nevada-Las Vegas	6	11
1991	Elmore Spencer, Nevada-Las Vegas	5	15
1992	Chris Webber, Michigan	6	17

INDIVIDUAL STEALS LEADERS

Year	Player, School	G	St.
1986	Tommy Amaker, Duke	6	18
1987	Mark Wade, Nevada-Las Vegas	5	18
1988	Mookie Blaylock, Oklahoma	6	23
1989	Kendall Gill, Illinois	5	17
1990	Lee Mayberry, Arkansas	5	18
1991	Grant Hill, Duke	6	15
1992	John Pelphrey, Kentucky	4	13
	Christian Laettner, Duke	6	13

*Record later vacated.

ENTERING THE NCAA TOURNAMENT, THESE TEAMS...

...Were Undefeated.

Year	Team (Coach)	Record	How It Did
1951	Columbia (Lou Rossini)	21-0	0-1
1956	San Francisco (Phil Woolpert)	25-0	4-0, CHAMPION
1957	North Caro. (Frank McGuire)	27-0	5-0, CHAMPION
1961	Ohio St. (Fred Taylor)	24-0	3-1, Final Four—2nd
1964	UCLA (John Wooden)	26-0	4-0, CHAMPION
1967	UCLA (John Wooden)	26-0	4-0, CHAMPION
1968	Houston (Guy Lewis)	28-0	3-2, Final Four—4th
1968	St. Bonaventure (Larry Weise)	22-0	1-2
1971	Marquette (Al McGuire)	26-0	2-1, Regional 3rd
1971	Pennsylvania (Dick Harter)	26-0	2-1, Regional 2nd
1972	UCLA (John Wooden)	26-0	4-0, CHAMPION
1973	UCLA (John Wooden)	26-0	4-0, CHAMPION
1975	Indiana (Bob Knight)	29-0	2-1, Regional 2nd
1976	Indiana (Bob Knight)	27-0	5-0, CHAMPION
1976	Rutgers (Tom Young)	28-0	3-2, Final Four—4th
1979	Indiana St. (Bill Hodges)	29-0	4-1, Final Four—2nd
1991	Nevada-Las Vegas (Jerry Tarkanian)	30-0	4-1, Final Four—tie 3rd

...Had One Loss.

Year	Team (Coach)	Record	How It Did
1942	Colorado (Frosty Cox)	15-1	1-1, Final Four—tie 3rd
1944	Dartmouth (Earl Brown)	17-1	2-1, Final Four—2nd
1946	Harvard (Floyd Stahl)	20-1	0-2
1947	Texas (Jack Gray)	24-1	2-1, Final Four—3rd
1947	Navy (Ben Carnevale)	16-1	0-2
1948	Columbia (Gordon Ridings)	20-1	0-2
1953	Louisiana St. (Harry Rabenhorst)	20-1	2-2, Final Four—4th
†1953	Lebanon Valley (George Marquette)	18-1	1-2
1954	Seattle (Al Brightman)	26-1	0-1
1955	San Francisco (Phil Woolpert)	23-1	5-0, CHAMPION
†1955	Williams (Alex Shaw)	17-1	0-1
†1956	Wayne St. (Mich.) (Joel Mason)	17-1	1-2
1958	West Va. (Fred Schaus)	26-1	0-1
1958	San Francisco (Phil Woolpert)	24-1	1-1
1959	Kansas St. (Tex Winter)	24-1	1-1, Regional 2nd
1960	California (Pete Newell)	24-1	4-1, Final Four—2nd
1960	Cincinnati (George Smith)	25-1	3-1, Final Four—3rd
1962	Ohio St. (Fred Taylor)	23-1	3-1, Final Four—2nd
1963	Cincinnati (Ed Jucker)	23-1	3-1, Final Four—2nd
1965	Providence (Joe Mullaney)	22-1	2-1, Regional 2nd
1965	St. Joseph's (Pa.) (Jack Ramsay)	25-1	1-2
1966	UTEP (Don Haskins)	23-1	5-0, CHAMPION
1966	Kentucky (Adolph Rupp)	24-1	3-1, Final Four—2nd
1967	Toledo (Bob Nichols)	23-1	0-1
1968	UCLA (John Wooden)	25-1	4-0, CHAMPION
1969	UCLA (John Wooden)	25-1	4-0, CHAMPION
1969	Santa Clara (Dick Garibaldi)	26-1	1-1, Regional 2nd
1970	Jacksonville (Joe Williams)	23-1	4-1, Final Four—2nd
1970	Kentucky (Adolph Rupp)	25-1	1-1, Regional 2nd
1970	Pennsylvania (Dick Harter)	25-1	0-1
1970	St. Bonaventure (Larry Weise)	22-1	3-2, Final Four—4th
1971	UCLA (John Wooden)	25-1	4-0, CHAMPION
1971	Kansas (Ted Owens)	25-1	2-2, Final Four—4th
1973	Long Beach St. (Jerry Tarkanian)	22-1	2-1, Regional 2nd
1973	Southwestern La. (Beryl Shipley)	22-1	1-2
1974	North Caro. St. (Norm Sloan)	26-1	4-0, CHAMPION
1976	Nevada-Las Vegas (Jerry Tarkanian)	28-1	1-1
1976	Marquette (Al McGuire)	25-1	2-1, Regional 2nd
1977	San Francisco (Bob Gaillard)	29-1	0-1
1977	Arkansas (Eddie Sutton)	29-1	0-1
1980	Alcorn St. (Davey Whitney)	27-1	1-1
1980	DePaul (Ray Meyer)	26-1	0-1
1981	DePaul (Ray Meyer)	27-1	0-1
1981	Oregon St. (Ralph Miller)	26-1	0-1
1982	DePaul (Ray Meyer)	26-1	0-1
1987	Nevada-Las Vegas (Jerry Tarkanian)	33-1	4-1, Final Four—tie 3rd
1988	Temple (John Chaney)	29-1	3-1, Regional 2nd
1990	La Salle (Bill Morris)	29-1	1-1

†Before the advent of the College Division (now Division II), the tournament committee had the option of selecting teams below Division I.
*Record later vacated.

...Had Two Losses.

Year	Team (Coach)	Record	How It Did
1940	Rice (Buster Brannon)	21-2	1-1, Regional 2nd
1940	Duquesne (Charles Davies)	19-2	1-1, Final Four—tie 3rd
1940	Southern Cal (Sam Barry)	19-2	1-1, Final Four—tie 3rd
1940	Springfield (Ed Hickox)	16-2	0-1, Regional 2nd
1940	Colorado (Forrest Cox)	17-2	0-2, Regional 2nd
1941	Arkansas (Glen Rose)	19-2	1-1, Final Four—tie 3rd
1942	Penn St. (John Lawther)	17-2	1-1, Regional 2nd
1943	Wyoming (Everett Shelton)	28-2	3-0, CHAMPION
1943	Dartmouth (Osborne Cowles)	19-2	1-1, Regional 2nd
1945	Utah (Vadal Peterson)	17-2	0-2, Regional 2nd
1946	Oklahoma St. (Henry Iba)	28-2	3-0, CHAMPION
1946	New York U. (Howard Cann)	18-2	1-1, Regional 2nd
1948	Kentucky (Adolph Rupp)	31-2	3-0, CHAMPION
1949	Kentucky (Adolph Rupp)	29-2	3-0, CHAMPION
1950	Holy Cross (Buster Sheary)	27-2	0-2
1951	Kentucky (Adolph Rupp)	28-2	4-0, CHAMPION
1952	Kentucky (Adolph Rupp)	28-2	1-1, Regional 2nd

Year	Team (Coach)	Record	How It Did
1952	Kansas (Phog Allen)	22-2	4-0, CHAMPION
1953	Washington (Tippy Dye)	25-2	3-1, Final Four—3rd
1954	Connecticut (Hugh Greer)	23-2	0-1
1954	Notre Dame (John Jordan)	20-2	2-1, Regional 2nd
1955	Marquette (Jack Nagle)	22-2	2-1, Regional 2nd
1955	Kentucky (Adolph Rupp)	22-2	1-1
1956	Southern Methodist (Doc Hayes)	22-2	3-2, Final Four—4th
1957	Kansas (Dick Harp)	21-2	3-1, Final Four—2nd
1957	Idaho St. (John Grayson)	24-2	1-2
1958	Temple (Harry Litwack)	24-2	3-1, Final Four—3rd
1958	Cincinnati (George Smith)	24-2	1-1
1959	Kentucky (Adolph Rupp)	23-2	1-1
1960	Utah (Jack Gardner)	24-2	2-1
1962	Cincinnati (Ed Jucker)	25-2	4-0, CHAMPION
1962	Kentucky (Adolph Rupp)	22-2	1-1, Regional 2nd
1963	Loyola (Ill.) (George Ireland)	24-2	5-0, CHAMPION
1963	Duke (Vic Bubas)	24-2	3-1, Final Four—3rd
1963	Arizona St. (Ned Wulk)	24-2	2-1, Regional 2nd
1964	UTEP (Don Haskins)	23-2	2-1
1965	UCLA (John Wooden)	24-2	4-0, CHAMPION
1965	Connecticut (Fred Shabel)	23-2	0-1
1966	Western Ky. (Johnny Oldham)	23-2	2-1
1966	Loyola (Ill.) (George Ireland)	22-2	0-1
1967	Princeton (Bill van Breda Kolff)	23-2	2-1
1967	Western Ky. (Johnny Oldham)	23-2	0-1
1967	Boston College (Bob Cousy)	19-2	2-1, Regional 2nd
1969	Davidson (Lefty Driesell)	25-2	2-1, Regional 2nd
1969	Weber St. (Phil Johnson)	25-2	2-1
1970	UCLA (John Wooden)	24-2	4-0, CHAMPION
1970	New Mexico St. (Lou Henson)	23-2	4-1, Final Four—3rd
1970	Western Ky. (Johnny Oldham)	22-2	0-1
1971	Fordham (Digger Phelps)	24-2	2-1
1972	Pennsylvania (Chuck Daly)	23-2	2-1, Regional 2nd
1972	Hawaii (Red Rocha)	24-2	0-1
1972	Marquette (Al McGuire)	24-2	1-2
1973	Long Beach St. (Jerry Tarkanian)	24-2	2-1
1973	Providence (Dave Gavitt)	24-2	3-2, Final Four—4th
1974	Notre Dame (Digger Phelps)	24-2	2-1
1975	Louisville (Denny Crum)	24-2	4-1, Final Four—3rd
1976	Western Mich. (Eldon Miller)	24-2	1-1
1977	Nevada-Las Vegas (Jerry Tarkanian)	25-2	4-1, Final Four—3rd
1977	Detroit Mercy (Dick Vitale)	25-2	1-1
1978	Kentucky (Joe Hall)	25-2	5-0, CHAMPION
1978	DePaul (Ray Meyer)	25-2	2-1, Regional 2nd
1978	UCLA (Gary Cunningham)	24-2	1-1
1980	Weber St. (Neil McCarthy)	26-2	0-1
1982	North Caro. (Dean Smith)	27-2	5-0, CHAMPION
1982	Fresno St. (Boyd Grant)	26-2	1-1
1982	Idaho (Don Monson)	26-2	1-1
1983	Houston (Guy Lewis)	27-2	4-1, Final Four—2nd
1983	Nevada-Las Vegas (Jerry Tarkanian)	28-2	0-1
1984	DePaul (Ray Meyer)	26-2	1-1
1984	North Caro. (Dean Smith)	27-2	1-1
1985	Georgetown (John Thompson)	30-2	5-1, Final Four—2nd
1985	Louisiana Tech (Andy Russo)	27-2	2-1
1986	Duke (Mike Krzyzewski)	32-2	5-1, Final Four—2nd
1986	Bradley (Dick Versace)	31-2	1-1
1987	DePaul (Joey Meyer)	26-2	2-1
1988	Arizona (Lute Olson)	31-2	4-1, Final Four—tie 3rd
1988	North Caro. A&T (Don Corbett)	26-2	0-1
1989	Ball St. (Rick Majerus)	28-2	1-1
1991	Princeton (Pete Carril)	24-2	0-1
1992	Duke (Mike Krzyzewski)	28-2	6-0, CHAMPION

...Had a .500 Record.

Year	Team (Coach)	Record	How It Qualified	How It Did
1958	Wyoming (Everett Shelton)	13-13	Skyline Conference champion 10-4	0-1
1965	West Va. (George King)	14-14	won Southern Conference tournament	0-1
1972	East Caro. (Tom Quinn)	14-14	won Southern Conference tournament	0-1

Year	Team (Coach)	Record	How It Qualified	How It Did
1985	Pennsylvania (Craig Littlepage)	13-13	Ivy League champion 10-4	0-1
1987	Fairfield (Mitch Buonaguro)	15-15	won Metro Atlantic Conference tournament	0-1
1987	Idaho St. (Jim Boutin)	15-15	won Big Sky Conference tournament	0-1

...Had a Losing Record.

Year	Team (Coach)	Record	How It Qualified	How It Did
1955	Bradley (Bob Vanatta)	7-19	‡Independent	2-1, Regional 2nd
1955	Oklahoma City (Doyle Parrack)	9-17	‡Independent	0-1
1961	Geo. Washington (Bill Reinhart)	9-16	won Southern Conference tournament	0-1
1974	Texas (Leon Black)	12-14	Southwest Conference champion 11-3	0-1
1978	Missouri (Norm Stewart)	14-15	won Big Eight Conference tournament	0-1
1985	Lehigh (Tom Schneider)	12-18	won East Coast Conference tournament	0-1
1986	Montana St. (Stu Starner)	14-16	won Big Sky Conference tournament	0-1

‡District 5 committee restricted to District 5 independents (only two in the district) to fill out bracket; this rule was changed for the 1956 tournament.

BY THE NUMBERS

(Year-by-year numbers: Teams in Division I, tournament automatic qualifiers, teams entered in NCAA tournament, tournament games played, overtime games, one-, two- and three-point wins, close games, 100 points scored in game.)

Year	AA	BB	CC	DD	EE	FF	GG	HH	JJ	KK
1939	.		8	8	0	0	1	0	1	0
1940	.		8	8	1	2	0	0	3	0
1941	.		8	9	0	3	0	0	3	0
1942	.		8	9	0	0	3	0	3	0
1943	.		8	9	0	0	1	1	2	0
1944	.		8	9	1	0	1	0	1	0
1945	.		8	9	1	0	0	2	3	0
1946	.		8	10	1	0	0	2	2	0
1947	.		8	10	0	2	2	0	4	0
1948	.	160	8	10	0	0	1	0	1	0
1949	.	148	8	10	0	1	0	0	1	0
1950	.	145	8	10	0	2	1	1	4	0
1951	.	153	10	16	18	0	2	0	2	0
1952	.	156	10	16	20	0	2	2	4	0
1953	.	158	14	22	26	0	1	3	0	4	0
1954	.	160	15	24	28	2	2	5	0	7	0
1955	.	162	15	24	28	0	3	2	1	6	1
1956	.	168	17	25	29	2	2	4	0	6	1
1957	.	167	16	23	27	3	3	1	0	6	0
1958	.	173	16	24	28	2	1	1	1	4	0
1959	.	174	16	23	27	0	3	1	1	5	1
1960	.	175	14	25	29	1	1	1	1	3	3
1961	.	173	15	24	28	2	1	4	0	7	2
1962	.	178	15	25	29	3	2	5	1	10	0
1963	.	178	15	25	29	2	2	1	2	6	1
1964	.	179	15	25	29	0	0	2	0	2	4
1965	.	182	15	23	27	2	2	4	0	8	8
1966	.	182	15	22	26	2	2	3	1	6	2
1967	.	185	15	23	27	3	3	4	0	9	1
1968	.	189	14	23	27	1	2	1	0	3	4
1969	.	193	15	25	29	1	2	5	3	10	1
1970	.	196	15	25	29	0	2	0	1	3	13
1971	.	203	15	25	29	3	2	4	4	11	6
1972	.	210	16	25	29	1	0	2	0	3	4
1973	.	216	16	25	29	1	3	1	1	6	5
1974	.	233	16	25	29	4	1	1	5	9	5
1975	.	233	15	32	36	6	2	3	3	13	2
1976	.	235	16	32	32	4	3	2	0	8	4
1977	.	245	16	32	32	2	3	2	1	8	3
1978	.	254	16	32	32	4	5	2	4	12	2
1979	.	257	23	40	40	2	1	6	3	11	1
1980	.	261	24	48	48	5	3	2	4	11	0
1981	.	264	24	48	48	2	7	5	3	15	0

Year	AA	BB	CC	DD	EE	FF	GG	HH	JJ	KK
1982 .	272	24	48	47	2	7	2	2	12	1
1983 .	274	24	52	51	2	5	7	4	17	0
1984 .	276	24	53	52	3	7	8	2	17	1
1985 .	282	30	64	63	3	5	8	5	18	0
1986 .	283	30	64	63	5	2	7	2	15	1
1987 .	290	30	64	63	5	6	4	5	17	7
1988 .	290	30	64	63	2	1	0	9	12	10
1989 .	293	30	64	63	3	4	3	4	13	9
1990 .	292	30	64	63	5	7	10	6	24	9
1991 .	295	29	64	63	4	1	3	5	11	4
1992 .	298	30	64	63	4	2	4	2	11	7

AA—Teams in Division I men's basketball.
BB—Number of automatic qualifiers for the NCAA tournament.
CC—Teams entered into the NCAA tournament.
DD—Tournament games played.
EE—Overtime tournament games.
FF—One-point wins in tournament play.
GG—Two-point wins in tournament play.
HH—Three-point wins in tournament play.
JJ—Close games (overtime games plus any regulation game won by less than three points).
KK—Number of times 100 points scored in a game.

CONFERENCE WON-LOST RECORDS—THROUGH 1992
(Using Current Conference Membership)

Conference	Teams	App.	Won	Lost	Pct.	CH	2d	3d	Final 4th	FF	RR
Atlantic Coast........	9	111	202	109	.650	6	9	11	2	28	21
Atlantic 10............	8	65	56	72	.438	0	1	3	2	6	5
Big East.............	10	132	165	138	.545	2	7	4	2	15	23
Big Eight.............	8	95	130	100	.565	4	8	5	6	23	22
Big Sky..............	6	32	14	36	.280	0	0	0	0	0	1
Big South...........	3	4	0	4	.000	0	0	0	0	0	0
Big Ten..............	10	115	196	112	.636	9	8	13	3	33	18
Big West.............	9	52	56	57	.496	1	0	4	0	5	7
Colonial.............	5	15	9	15	.375	0	0	0	0	0	0
East Coast...........	1	2	0	2	.000	0	0	0	0	0	0
Great Midwest........	6	71	92	75	.551	3	3	6	0	12	7
Ivy..................	8	49	35	59	.372	0	2	1	1	4	9
Metro................	7	41	51	44	.537	2	0	3	3	8	1
Metro Atlantic........	7	14	10	16	.385	0	0	0	0	0	2
Midwestern..........	8	46	45	46	.495	2	2	1	0	5	2
Mid-American........	9	41	17	45	.274	0	0	0	0	0	1
Mid-Continent........	4	5	2	5	.286	0	0	0	0	0	0
Mid-Eastern..........	4	11	0	11	.000	0	0	0	0	0	0
Missouri Valley.......	10	43	37	45	.451	0	3	1	1	5	6
North Atlantic........	4	13	5	13	.278	0	0	0	0	0	1
Northeast............	6	13	1	13	.071	0	0	0	0	0	0
Ohio Valley...........	6	27	9	29	.237	0	0	0	0	0	0
Pacific-10............	10	98	137	97	.585	13	3	5	5	26	19
Patriot..............	6	24	17	26	.395	1	0	1	0	2	5
Southeastern.........	12	113	137	117	.539	5	2	8	2	17	21
Southern.............	8	32	12	35	.255	0	0	0	0	0	3
Southland...........	4	8	0	8	.000	0	0	0	0	0	0
Southwest...........	8	67	63	82	.434	0	3	4	3	10	7
Southwestern........	4	12	3	12	.200	0	0	0	0	0	0
Sun Belt.............	8	41	32	43	.427	0	1	1	0	2	1
Trans America........	2	3	0	3	.000	0	0	0	0	0	0
West Coast...........	7	43	40	44	.476	2	0	1	1	4	11
Western Athletic......	10	78	56	90	.384	3	0	0	2	5	11
Independents.........	1	24	25	28	.472	0	0	0	1	1	4
Others..............	17	47	35	58	.376	1	2	0	2	5	8
TOTAL...............	245	1,587	1,689	1,689	.500	54	54	72	36	216	216

Notes: Third-place games were played from 1946 through 1981. Results from the other years are treated as third-place ties. The "Teams" column represents the number of teams in that conference that have appeared in the NCAA tournament.

App.—Appearances.
Pct.—Winning percentage.
CH—Champion.
2d—Second place.

3d—Third place.
4th—Fourth place.
FF—Final Four appearances.
RR—Regional runner-up.

CONFERENCE WON-LOST RECORDS—THROUGH 1992
(Using Actual Conference Membership for Each Season)

EAST

Conference, Former Names, Years	App.	Won	Lost	Pct.	CH	2d	3d	4th	FF	RR
Atlantic Coast, 1954-92	97	188	94	.667	6	7	10	2	25	17
Atlantic 10; Eastern Eight, 1977-92	28	25	28	.472	0	0	0	0	0	3
Big East, 1980-92	63	106	61	.635	2	4	2	0	8	11
Colonial; ECAC South, 1975-92	18	11	18	.379	0	0	0	0	0	1
East Coast; Middle Atlantic, 1959-92	33	12	37	.245	0	0	1	0	1	2
ECAC Upstate, 1975-79	4	4	5	.444	0	0	1	0	1	0
Ivy Group; Eastern Intercollegiate, 1939-92	47	35	56	.385	0	2	1	1	4	7
Little Three (New England), 1955	1	0	1	.000	0	0	0	0	0	0
Metro Atlantic, 1984-92	9	1	9	.100	0	0	0	0	0	0
North Atlantic; ECAC North Atlantic, 1975-92	18	6	19	.240	0	0	0	0	0	0
Northeast; ECAC Northeast; ECAC Metro, 1975-92	18	5	19	.208	0	0	1	0	1	0
Patriot, 1991-92	1	0	1	.000	0	0	0	0	0	0
Western New York Little Three, 1955-57	3	6	3	.667	0	0	0	0	0	2
Yankee, 1951-76	14	3	15	.167	0	0	0	0	0	1

SOUTHEAST

Conference, Former Names, Years	App.	Won	Lost	Pct.	CH	2d	3d	4th	FF	RR
Big South, 1991-92	2	0	2	.000	0	0	0	0	0	0
Florida Intercollegiate, 1960	1	0	1	.000	0	0	0	0	0	0
Kentucky Intercollegiate, 1940	1	0	1	.000	0	0	0	0	0	1
Metro, 1976-92	38	42	36	.538	2	0	3	0	5	0
Mid-Eastern, 1981-90	11	0	11	.000	0	0	0	0	0	0
Ohio Valley, 1949-92	39	20	43	.317	0	0	1	0	1	0
Southeastern, 1939-92	92	113	94	.546	5	2	4	2	13	19
Southern, 1939-92	46	26	50	.342	0	2	1	0	3	6
Sun Belt, 1977-92	27	18	28	.391	0	0	0	1	1	1
Trans America, 1981-92	12	1	12	.077	0	0	0	0	0	0

MIDWEST

Conference, Former Names, Years	App.	Won	Lost	Pct.	CH	2d	3d	4th	FF	RR
American South, 1987-91	3	1	3	.250	0	0	0	0	0	0
Big Eight; Big Seven; Big Six, 1939-92	85	114	90	.559	2	7	3	6	18	17
Big Ten; Big Nine; Western, 1939-92	109	189	104	.645	9	8	13	2	32	17
Great Midwest, 1992	3	7	3	.700	0	0	1	0	1	1
Indiana Collegiate, 1962	1	2	1	.667	0	0	0	0	0	0
Mid-American, 1953-92	42	17	46	.270	0	0	0	0	0	1
Mid-Continent, 1986-92	9	4	9	.308	0	0	0	0	0	0
Midwestern, 1982-92	13	8	13	.381	0	0	0	0	0	0
Missouri Valley, 1939-92	56	65	60	.520	4	5	4	3	16	8
Presidents Athletic, 1956	1	1	2	.333	0	0	0	0	0	0
Southland, 1969-92	17	12	18	.400	0	0	0	0	0	0
Southwest, 1939-92	73	70	85	.452	0	3	7	2	12	10
Southwestern, 1980-90	12	3	12	.200	0	0	0	0	0	0

WEST

Conference, Former Names, Years	App.	Won	Lost	Pct.	CH	2d	3d	4th	FF	RR
Big Sky, 1968-92	25	8	27	.229	0	0	0	0	0	1
Big West; Pacific Coast Athletic Association, 1970-92	32	36	32	.529	1	0	2	0	3	4
Border, 1951-62	12	2	12	.143	0	0	0	0	0	1
Pacific-10; Pacific-8; Pacific Coast, 1939-92	83	121	80	.602	13	3	5	4	25	13
Rocky Mountain, 1951-60	9	6	11	.353	0	0	0	0	0	0
Skyline Eight; Mountain States, 1939-62	24	20	34	.370	2	0	1	1	4	12
West Coast; California Basketball Association, 1953-92	44	42	44	.488	2	0	1	0	3	11
Western Athletic, 1963-92	49	35	55	.389	0	0	0	1	1	4

OTHERS

Conference, Former Names, Years	App.	Won	Lost	Pct.	CH	2d	3d	4th	FF	RR
Independents, 1939-92	262	304	304	.500	6	11	10	11	38	45
TOTAL	1,587	1,689	1,689	.500	54	54	72	36	216	216

Note: Third-place games were played from 1946 through 1981. Results from the other years are treated as third-place ties.

App.—Appearances.
Pct.—Winning percentage.
CH—Champion.
2d—Second place.
3d—Third place.
4th—Fourth place.
FF—Final Four appearances.
RR—Regional runner-up.

HIGHEST-RATED TELEVISED
COLLEGE BASKETBALL GAMES

	Date	Game	Round	Network	Rating/Share	Homes
1.	3/26/79	Michigan St. vs. Indiana St.	CH	NBC	24.1/38	17,950,000
2.	4/ 1/85	Georgetown vs. Villanova	CH	CBS	23.3/33	19,800,000
3.	4/ 6/92	Duke vs. Michigan	CH	CBS	22.7/35	20,900,000
4.	4/ 4/83	North Caro. St. vs. Houston	CH	CBS	22.3/32	18,580,000
5.	3/29/82	North Caro. vs. Georgetown	CH	CBS	21.6/31	17,600,000
6.	4/ 3/89	Michigan vs. Seton Hall	CH	CBS	21.3/33	19,260,000
7.	3/31/75	UCLA vs. Kentucky	CH	NBC	21.3/33	14,590,000
8.	3/31/86	Louisville vs. Duke	CH	CBS	20.7/31	17,780,000
9.	3/30/81	Indiana vs. North Caro.	CH	NBC	20.7/29	16,100,000
10.	3/26/73	UCLA vs. Memphis St.	CH	NBC	20.5/32	13,280,000
11.	3/29/76	Indiana vs. Michigan	CH	NBC	20.4/31	14,200,000
12.	4/ 2/90	Nevada-Las Vegas vs. Duke	CH	CBS	20.0/31	18,400,000
13.	3/27/78	Kentucky vs. Duke	CH	NBC	19.9/31	14,510,000
14.	3/25/74	North Caro. St. vs. Marquette	CH	NBC	19.9/30	13,170,000
15.	3/24/80	Louisville vs. UCLA	CH	NBC	19.8/30	15,110,000
16.	4/ 2/84	Georgetown vs. Houston	CH	CBS	19.7/29	16,510,000
17.	3/30/87	Syracuse vs. Indiana	CH	CBS	19.6/28	17,100,100
18.	4/ 1/91	Duke vs. Kansas	CH	CBS	19.4/30	18,060,000
19.	3/28/77	Marquette vs. North Caro.	CH	NBC	19.3/29	13,740,000
20.	4/ 4/88	Kansas vs. Oklahoma	CH	CBS	18.8/30	16,660,000
21.	4/ 2/83	Houston vs. Louisville	NSF	CBS	17.8/35	14,827,000
22.	3/24/79	Indiana St. vs. DePaul	NSF	NBC	17.2/39	12,810,000
23.	3/30/85	Georgetown vs. St. John's (N.Y.)	NSF	CBS	17.1/33	14,500,000
24.	4/ 4/92	Duke vs. Indiana	NSF	CBS	16.8/30	15,473,000
25.	1/26/74	UCLA vs. Notre Dame	RS	TVS	16.3/—	10,790,000

MOST-WATCHED COLLEGE BASKETBALL
TELECASTS (BY HOMES)

	Date	Game	Round	Network	Rating/Share	Homes
1.	4/ 6/92	Duke vs. Michigan	CH	CBS	22.7/35	20,900,000
2.	4/ 1/85	Georgetown vs. Villanova	CH	CBS	23.3/33	19,800,000
3.	4/ 3/89	Michigan vs. Seton Hall	CH	CBS	21.3/33	19,260,000
4.	4/ 4/83	North Caro. St. vs. Houston	CH	CBS	22.3/32	18,580,000
5.	4/ 2/90	Nevada-Las Vegas vs. Duke	CH	CBS	20.0/31	18,400,000
6.	4/ 1/91	Duke vs. Kansas	CH	CBS	19.4/30	18,060,000
7.	3/26/79	Michigan St. vs. Indiana St.	CH	NBC	24.1/38	17,950,000
8.	3/31/86	Louisville vs. Duke	CH	CBS	20.7/31	17,780,000
9.	3/29/82	North Caro. vs. Georgetown	CH	CBS	21.6/31	17,600,000
10.	3/30/87	Syracuse vs. Indiana	CH	CBS	19.6/28	17,100,000
11.	4/ 4/88	Kansas vs. Oklahoma	CH	CBS	18.8/30	16,660,000
12.	4/ 2/84	Georgetown vs. Houston	CH	CBS	19.7/29	16,510,000
13.	3/30/81	Indiana vs. North Caro.	CH	NBC	20.7/29	16,100,000
14.	4/ 4/92	Duke vs. Indiana	NSF	CBS	16.8/30	15,473,000
15.	3/24/80	Louisville vs. UCLA	CH	NBC	19.8/30	15,110,000
16.	4/ 2/83	Houston vs. Louisville	NSF	CBS	17.8/35	14,827,000
17.	3/30/91	Duke vs. Nevada-Las Vegas	NSF	CBS	15.7/29	14,620,000
18.	3/31/75	UCLA vs. Kentucky	CH	NBC	21.3/33	14,590,000
19.	3/27/78	Kentucky vs. Duke	CH	NBC	19.9/31	14,510,000
20.	3/30/85	Georgetown vs. St. John's (N.Y.)	NSF	CBS	17.1/33	14,500,000
21.	3/29/76	Indiana vs. Michigan	CH	NBC	20.4/31	14,200,000
22.	3/28/77	Marquette vs. North Caro.	CH	NBC	19.3/29	13,740,000
23.	3/31/84	Georgetown vs. Kentucky	NSF	CBS	16.0/32	13,400,000
24.	3/26/73	UCLA vs. Memphis St.	CH	NBC	20.5/32	13,280,000
25.	3/25/74	North Caro. St. vs. Marquette	CH	NBC	19.9/30	13,170,000

CH—National championship game.
NSF—National semifinal game.
RS—Regular-season game.

TOURNAMENT TRIVIA QUESTION...
Who is the only player to lead the nation in scoring while playing for the NCAA champion? Answer: Clyde Lovellette of Kansas averaged 28.4 points a game in 1952 to lead the nation in scoring.

TOURNAMENT GAME MILESTONES

**Game
Number**

1   Villanova defeated Brown, 42-30, on March 17, 1939, in Philadelphia, Pennsylvania. In the second game of the double-header, Ohio State defeated Wake Forest, 64-52.

50   Dartmouth defeated Ohio State, 60-53, in the Eastern regional final on March 28, 1944, in New York, New York.

100   Illinois defeated Oregon State, 57-53, in the national third-place game in March 1949 at Seattle, Washington.

200   Bradley defeated Southern California, 74-72, in the national semifinal game on March 19, 1954, at Kansas City, Missouri.

300   Temple defeated Maryland, 71-67, in the fifth of eight regional semifinal games on March 14, 1958. The East region game took place in Charlotte, North Carolina.

400   Wake Forest defeated Yale, 92-82 in overtime, in the first game of the 1962 Tournament. The East region game took place in Philadelphia, Pennsylvania, and was the first of seven first-round games played on March 12.

500   Providence defeated St. Joseph's (Pennsylvania), 81-73 in overtime, in an East region semifinal game at College Park, Maryland, on March 12, 1965. The game was the fifth of eight regional semifinal games that day.

600   New Mexico State defeated Brigham Young, 74-62, on March 8, 1969, in Las Cruces, New Mexico. The West region game was the seventh of nine first-round games played that day.

700   Southwestern Louisiana defeated Texas, 100-70, in Ames, Iowa, in a regional consolation game on March 1, 1972. The Midwest region game was the third of four regional third-place games played that day, along with four regional finals.

800   Kentucky defeated Syracuse, 95-79, in the national semifinal game on March 29, 1975, played in San Diego, California.

900   St. John's (New York) defeated Temple, 75-70, on March 9 in the first game of the 1979 tournament. The East region game took place in Raleigh, North Carolina.

1,000   Villanova defeated Houston, 90-72, on March 13, 1981, in Charlotte, North Carolina. The East region game was the fifth of eight first-round games played that day.

1,100   Iowa defeated Utah State, 64-59, on March 18, 1983, in Louisville, Kentucky. The Midwest region game was the sixth of eight first-round games played that day.

1,200   Illinois State defeated Southern California, 58-55, on March 14, 1985, in Tulsa, Oklahoma. The Midwest region game was the 15th of 16 first-round games played that day.

1,300   Louisville defeated North Carolina, 94-79, on March 20, 1986, in Houston, Texas. The West region semifinal game was the fourth of four games played that day.

1,400   Maryland defeated UC Santa Barbara, 92-82, on March 18, 1988, in Cincinnati, Ohio. The Southeast region game was the 10th of 16 first-round games played that day.

1,500   Michigan defeated Seton Hall, 80-79 in overtime, for the national championship on April 3, 1989, in Seattle, Washington. It was the first time in tournament history that a first-year head coach—Steve Fisher—won the national title.

1,600   Temple defeated Richmond, 77-64, on March 16, 1991, in East Rutherford, New Jersey. The East region game was the fifth of eight second-round games played that day.

TOURNAMENT HISTORY

1939 The first National Collegiate men's basketball tournament was held. For the first 12 years, district playoffs often were held with the winner entering an eight-team field for the championship. The district games were not considered a part of the tournament. The winners of the East and West regionals were the only two teams to advance to the final site.

1940 The National Association of Basketball Coaches held its annual convention at the site of the national finals for the first time. It has been held in conjunction with the tournament ever since.

1946 The championship game was televised locally for the first time in New York City by WCBS-TV as Oklahoma State defeated North Carolina, 43-40. The initial viewing audience was estimated to be 500,000.

  This was the first time four teams advanced to the final site. With only East and West regionals, the two regional champions played for the national title while the regional runners-up played for third place.

1951 The field was expanded to 16 teams, with 10 conference champions qualifying automatically for the first time. Those 10 conferences were: Big Seven, Big Ten, Border, Eastern (Ivy), Missouri Valley, Pacific Coast, Skyline, Southeastern, Southern and Southwest.

1952 Tournament games were televised regionally for the first time.

  The number of regional sites changed from two to four, with the four winners advancing to the finals.

1953 The bracket expanded from 16 teams to 22 and fluctuated between 22 and 25 teams until 1974.

1954 The Tuesday-Wednesday format for semifinals and the final game was changed to Friday-Saturday.

  The championship game was televised nationally for the first time as La Salle defeated Bradley, 94-76, in Kansas City, Missouri.

1957 The largest media group to date assembled for the finals in Kansas City, Missouri. Coverage included an 11-station television network, 64 newspaper writers and live radio broadcasts on 73 stations in 11 states.

1963 A contract to run through 1968 was worked out with Sports Network for the championship game to be televised nationally. Television rights totaled $140,000.

  For the first time, sites for the tournament competition were selected two years in advance.

1966 Net income for the entire tournament exceeded $500,000 for the first time.

  A television-blackout provision requiring a 48-hour advance sellout was adopted.

1969 The Friday-Saturday format for semifinals and the final game changed to Thursday-Saturday.

  NBC was selected to televise the championship at television rights totaling $547,500, exceeding $500,000 for the first time. The tournament's net income of $1,032,915 was the first time above the million-dollar mark.

1971 NBC recorded the largest audience ever for a basketball network telecast during the semifinals as 9,320,000 homes saw the game.

1973 The Thursday-Saturday format for semifinals and the final game changed to Saturday-Monday.

  Television rights totaled $1,165,755, exceeding $1,000,000 for the first time. NBC reported that the championship game was the highest-rated basketball telecast of all time. The contest received a rating of 20.5 and was seen by 13,580,000 television households reaching a total audience of 39 million persons. Also for the first time, the championship game was televised in prime time.

TVS, with the approval of NBC, agreed to televise those games not carried by NBC for a two-year period at the rights fee of $65,000 per year.

First-round byes were determined on the basis of an evaluation of the conference's won-lost record over the past 10 years in National Collegiate Championship play.

The first public draw to fill oversubscribed orders for Final Four game tickets was administered by the committee for the 1974 championship.

1974 The bracket rotation was changed for the first time, eliminating East vs. West bracketing in effect since 1939. East played West and Mideast played Midwest in the national semifinals.

The Eastern Collegiate Athletic Conference was divided to receive multiple automatic qualification berths in the tournament.

1975 A 32-team bracket was adopted and teams other than the conference champion could be chosen at large from the same conference for the first time.

Dressing rooms opened to media representatives after a 10-minute cooling-off period.

1976 The rights for the NCAA Radio Network were awarded to Host Communications, Inc., of Lexington, Kentucky.

Regional third-place games were eliminated.

For the first time, two teams from the same conference (Big Ten) played in the national championship game, with Indiana defeating Michigan.

1977 NBC televised 23 hours and 18 minutes of tournament programming.

1978 A seeding process was used for the first time for individual teams. A maximum of four automatic-qualifying conference teams were seeded in each of the four regional brackets. These teams were seeded based on their respective conferences' won-lost percentages in tournament play during the past five years. At-large seeding in each region was based on current won-lost records, strength of schedule and eligibility status of student-athletes for postseason competition.

NBC televised the four regional championship games and a first-round double-header on Saturday and Sunday. NCAA Productions televised all regional semifinal games and all other tournament games.

Complimentary tickets for all NCAA championships were eliminated.

1979 The bracket was expanded to 40 teams and all teams were seeded for the first time.

NBC received a record one-game rating with a 24.1 in Michigan State's national championship victory over Indiana State. The 38 share and the 18 million homes viewing were both records at the time.

The Division I Men's Basketball Committee assigned three-man officiating crews for all tournament games.

A public "lottery" for the drawing of Final Four game tickets was first held.

1980 The bracket was expanded to 48 teams, which included 24 automatic qualifiers and 24 at-large teams. The top 16 seeds received byes to the second round.

The limit of two teams from the same conference being allowed in the tournament was lifted. This gave the committee maximum flexibility to balance the bracket as well as to select the best possible at-large entrants.

1981 Principles for the seeding and placement of teams to develop a balanced tournament bracket were implemented. They included establishing 12 levels that transcended each of the four regions; dividing each region into three sections with four levels each; only one conference team could be placed in each regional section; and placing teams in their geographical area or on their home court if the first three principles are not compromised.

A computer ranking system was used as an aid in evaluating teams in the preparation for making at-large selections.

It became policy that "no more than 50 percent of the tournament berths shall be filled by automatic qualifiers."

Virginia defeated Louisiana State in the last third-place game conducted at the Final Four site.

1982 CBS was awarded the television rights for 16 exposures to the championship for three years.

The "selection show" was shown on live national television for the first time.

North Carolina's national championship win against Georgetown received a 21.6 rating and was the 11th-ranked prime time program for that week. CBS also achieved second-round record ratings with an 11.8 rating and 27 share on Saturday, and an 11.3 rating and 28 share on Sunday.

Host Communications, Inc., and the CBS Radio Network coproduced the NCAA Radio Network.

1983 An opening round was added that required the representatives of eight automatic-qualifying conferences to compete for four positions in the 52-team tournament bracket. This concept permitted the committee to retain a 48-team bracket evenly balanced with 24 automatic qualifiers and 24 at-large selections, yet award automatic qualification to each of the 28 conferences that received it the year before. The 16 top-seeded teams received byes to the second round of the tournament.

The current format was established that begins the tournament the third weekend in March, regional championships on the fourth Saturday and Sunday, and the national semifinals and final the following Saturday and Monday.

North Carolina State's national championship victory over Houston attracted what then was a record 18.6 million homes to the CBS telecast. The game had a 22.3 rating (third best) and a 32 share. It was the fifth-ranked prime time television program for that week.

A national semifinal record also was set in Houston's victory over Louisville. The game had a 17.8 rating and 35 share and was viewed by 14,800,000 homes on CBS.

The committee determined that a facility in which the final session is held must have a minimum of 17,000 seats

1984 One additional opening-round game was established, requiring 10 automatic-qualifying conferences to compete for five positions in the 53-team bracket that included 24 automatic qualifiers and 24 at-large selections.

For the first time, awards were presented to all participating teams in the championship.

1985 The tournament bracket was expanded to include 64 teams, which eliminated all first-round byes.

The committee realigned each region and renamed the Mideast region the Southeast region. Specifically, the Southern and Mid-Eastern conferences were moved from the East to the Southeast region; the Big Ten, Mid-American and Southwestern conferences moved from the Southeast to the Midwest; the Metro and Trans America conferences were moved from the Midwest to the Southeast, and the Southland and Southwest conferences were moved from the Midwest to the West region.

The number of automatic qualifiers was capped at 30 for a five-year period (1986-90).

CBS had a record 19.8 million homes view Villanova's national championship victory over Georgetown. This game attracted a 23.3 rating (second best) and a 33 share. The game was the second-rated prime time program on television for that week.

The East regional championship game (with Georgetown defeating Georgia Tech) set television records for that level of tournament competition with a 12.6 rating, a 32 share and 10.7 million homes tuned to CBS.

The NCAA Radio Network reached an all-time high radio audience for any sports event when the Villanova-Georgetown game attracted 21 million listeners.

CBS began a second three-year contract that included 19 exposures.

1986   CBS televised 40 hours, 51 minutes of tournament programming.

The NCAA Radio Network included a record 426 stations, including 92 of the top 100 markets.

Regional competition will be played at neutral sites. From now on, if an institution selected to host this level of competition is a participant in the tournament, it will be bracketed in another region.

Three separate three-man officiating crews were assigned to the two national semifinals and the championship final.

1987   The National Association of Basketball Coaches reaffirmed its endorsement of the policy that permits an institution to participate on its home court in the first and second rounds of competition.

Championship team members were awarded 10-karat gold rings, while the other three teams in the Final Four received silver rings.

All 64 teams selected for the championship were subject to drug testing for the first time.

1988   CBS began a third three-year contract. All regional semifinal games were televised in prime time.

Separate three-man officiating crews were assigned to all competition at regional and national championship sites.

1989   The NCAA Executive Committee expanded a moratorium enacted in 1984 limiting the bracket to 30 automatic-qualifying conference champions and 34 at-large teams through the 1998 championship.

An NCAA Executive Regulation was amended to strengthen criteria governing automatic qualification for conferences.

Bracket rotation was established, with East vs. West, Midwest vs. Southeast in 1989; East vs. Southeast, West vs. Midwest in 1990, and East vs. Midwest, Southeast vs. West in 1991.

Awards for the national runner-up were presented in the dressing room immediately after the championship game.

Host Communications, Inc., began a three-year contract for rights to the NCAA Radio Network and programs for all sites.

Neutral courts were used in all rounds of the championship.

1990   The general public was limited to purchasing two tickets to future Final Fours.

The basketball committee defined "home court" as an arena in which a team has played no more than 50 percent of its regular season schedule, excluding conference tournament games.

The NCAA Executive Committee approved "play-in" concept to identify the 30 automatic-qualifying conferences in December 1989. The Ratings Percentage Index (RPI) administered by the NCAA was computed for the nonconference schedules of all eligible conferences. Those with the lowest ranking must compete for the available automatic-qualifying positions. The "play-in" was implemented in 1991 with 33 eligible conferences. Six conference representatives played for three automatic-qualifying berths in the 64-team bracket.

1991   CBS Sports began a new seven-year contract for $1,000,000,000, which included live coverage of all sessions of the championship.

The definition of "home court" was amended to include playing no more than three games of a regular-season schedule, excluding conference tournaments, in one arena.

1992   Duke University won its second consecutive national championship, the first team to successfully defend its title since UCLA in 1973.

TOURNAMENT TRIVIA QUESTION...

Name the only eight schools to finish in the top four in the nation in both basketball and football in the same academic school year? Answer: This exclusive list is Arkansas 1977-78, Georgia 1982-83, Illinois 1951-52, Michigan 1964-65, Notre Dame 1977-78, Ohio State 1961-62, Oklahoma 1987-88 and Southern Cal 1939-40.

NCAA DIVISION I MEN'S TOURNAMENT
ALL-TIME RECORD OF EACH COLLEGE
COACH-BY-COACH, 1939-1992
(240 COLLEGES)

	Yrs.	Won	Lost	CH	2d	3d%	4th	RR
AIR FORCE								
Bob Spear (DePauw '41) 60, 62.........................	2	0	2	0	0	0	0	0
TOTAL	2	0	2	0	0	0	0	0
AKRON								
Bob Huggins (West Va. '77) 86.........................	1	0	1	0	0	0	0	0
TOTAL	1	0	1	0	0	0	0	0
ALABAMA*								
C. M. Newton (Kentucky '52) 75, 76....................	2	1	2	0	0	0	0	0
Wimp Sanderson (North Ala. '59) 82, 83, 84, 85,								
86, 87, 89, 90, 91, 92...............................	10	12	10	0	0	0	0	0
TOTAL	12	13	12	0	0	0	0	0
ALA.-BIRMINGHAM								
Gene Bartow (Northeast Mo. St. '53) 81, 82RR, 83, 84,								
85, 86, 87, 90.......................................	8	6	8	0	0	0	0	1
TOTAL	8	6	8	0	0	0	0	1
ALCORN ST.								
Davey Whitney (Kentucky St. '53) 80, 82, 83, 84........	4	3	4	0	0	0	0	0
TOTAL	4	3	4	0	0	0	0	0
APPALACHIAN ST.								
Bobby Cremins (South Caro. '70) 79...................	1	0	1	0	0	0	0	0
TOTAL	1	0	1	0	0	0	0	0
ARIZONA								
Fred Enke (Minnesota '21) 51...........................	1	0	1	0	0	0	0	0
Fred Snowden [Wayne St. (Mich.) '58] 76RR, 77.......	2	2	2	0	0	0	0	1
Luther "Lute" Olson (Augsburg '57) 85, 86, 87,								
88-tie 3d, 89, 90, 91, 92.............................	8	9	8	0	0	1	0	0
TOTAL	11	11	11	0	0	1	0	1
ARIZONA ST.								
Ned Wulk (Wis.-La Crosse '42) 58, 61RR, 62, 63RR, 64,								
73, 75RR, 80, 81....................................	9	8	10	0	0	0	0	3
Bill Frieder (Michigan '64) 91.........................	1	1	1	0	0	0	0	0
TOTAL	10	9	11	0	0	0	0	3
ARKANSAS								
Eugene Lambert (Arkansas '29) 45-tie 3d, 49RR........	2	2	2	0	0	1	0	1
Glen Rose (Arkansas '28) 41-tie 3d, 58...............	2	1	3	0	0	1	0	0
Eddie Sutton (Oklahoma St. '59) 77, 78-3d, 79RR, 80,								
81, 82, 83, 84, 85....................................	9	10	9	0	0	1	0	1
Nolan Richardson (UTEP '65) 88, 89, 90-tie 3d, 91RR,								
92..	5	9	5	0	0	1	0	1
TOTAL	18	22	19	0	0	4	0	3
ARK.-LIT. ROCK								
Mike Newell (Sam Houston St. '73) 86, 89, 90..........	3	1	3	0	0	0	0	0
TOTAL	3	1	3	0	0	0	0	0
AUBURN								
Sonny Smith (Milligan '58) 84, 85, 86RR, 87, 88........	5	7	5	0	0	0	0	1
TOTAL	5	7	5	0	0	0	0	1
AUSTIN PEAY*								
Lake Kelly (Georgia Tech '56) 73, 74, 87...............	3	2	4	0	0	0	0	0
TOTAL	3	2	4	0	0	0	0	0
BALL ST.								
Steve Yoder (Ill. Wesleyan '62) 81.....................	1	0	1	0	0	0	0	0
Al Brown (Purdue '64) 86..............................	1	0	1	0	0	0	0	0
Rick Majerus (Marquette '70) 89.......................	1	1	1	0	0	0	0	0
Dick Hunsaker (Weber St. '77) 90......................	1	2	1	0	0	0	0	0
TOTAL	4	3	4	0	0	0	0	0
BAYLOR								
R. E. "Bill" Henderson (Howard Payne '25) 46RR,								
48-2d, 50-4th..	3	3	5	0	1	0	1	1
Gene Iba (Tulsa '63) 88...............................	1	0	1	0	0	0	0	0
TOTAL	4	3	6	0	1	0	1	1
BOISE ST.								
Doran "Bus" Connor (Idaho St. '55) 76.................	1	0	1	0	0	0	0	0
Bob Dye (Idaho St. '62) 88............................	1	0	1	0	0	0	0	0
TOTAL	2	0	2	0	0	0	0	0

	Yrs.	Won	Lost	CH	2d	3d%	4th	RR
BOSTON COLLEGE								
Donald Martin (Georgetown '41) 58	1	0	1	0	0	0	0	0
Bob Cousy (Holy Cross '48) 67RR, 68	2	2	2	0	0	0	0	1
Bob Zuffelato (Central Conn. St. '59) 75	1	1	2	0	0	0	0	0
Tom Davis (Wis.-Platteville '60) 81, 82RR	2	5	2	0	0	0	0	1
Gary Williams (Maryland '67) 83, 85	2	3	2	0	0	0	0	0
TOTAL	8	11	9	0	0	0	0	2
BOSTON U.								
Matt Zunic (Geo. Washington '42) 59RR	1	2	1	0	0	0	0	1
Rick Pitino (Massachusetts '74) 83	1	0	1	0	0	0	0	0
Mike Jarvis (Northeastern '68) 88, 90	2	0	2	0	0	0	0	0
TOTAL	4	2	4	0	0	0	0	1
BOWLING GREEN								
Harold Anderson (Otterbein '24) 59, 62, 63	3	1	4	0	0	0	0	0
Bill Fitch (Coe '54) 68	1	0	1	0	0	0	0	0
TOTAL	4	1	5	0	0	0	0	0
BRADLEY								
Forrest "Forddy" Anderson (Stanford '42) 50-2d, 54-2d	2	6	2	0	2	0	0	0
Bob Vanatta (Central Methodist '45) 55RR	1	2	1	0	0	0	0	1
Dick Versace (Wisconsin '64) 80, 86	2	1	2	0	0	0	0	0
Stan Albeck (Bradley '55) 88	1	0	1	0	0	0	0	0
TOTAL	6	9	6	0	2	0	0	1
BRIGHAM YOUNG								
Stan Watts (Brigham Young '38) 50RR, 51RR, 57, 65, 69, 71, 72	7	4	10	0	0	0	0	2
Frank Arnold (Idaho St. '56) 79, 80, 81RR	3	3	3	0	0	0	0	1
Ladell Andersen (Utah St. '51) 84, 87, 88	3	2	3	0	0	0	0	0
Roger Reid (Weber St. '67) 90, 91, 92	3	1	3	0	0	0	0	0
TOTAL	16	10	19	0	0	0	0	3
BROWN								
George Allen (West Va. '35) 39RR	1	0	1	0	0	0	0	1
Mike Cingiser (Brown '62) 86	1	0	1	0	0	0	0	0
TOTAL	2	0	2	0	0	0	0	1
BUCKNELL								
Charles Woollum (William & Mary '62) 87, 89	2	0	2	0	0	0	0	0
TOTAL	2	0	2	0	0	0	0	0
BUTLER								
Paul "Tony" Hinkle (Chicago '21) 62	1	2	1	0	0	0	0	0
TOTAL	1	2	1	0	0	0	0	0
CALIFORNIA								
Clarence "Nibs" Price (California '14) 46-4th	1	1	2	0	0	0	1	0
Pete Newell [Loyola (Cal.)] '40) 57RR, 58RR, 59-CH, 60-2d	4	10	3	1	1	0	0	2
Lou Campanelli (Montclair St. '60) 90	1	1	1	0	0	0	0	0
TOTAL	6	12	6	1	1	0	1	2
UC SANTA BARB.								
Jerry Pimm (Southern Cal '61) 88, 90	2	1	2	0	0	0	0	0
TOTAL	2	1	2	0	0	0	0	0
CAL ST. FULLERTON								
Bob Dye (Idaho St. '62) 78RR	1	2	1	0	0	0	0	1
TOTAL	1	2	1	0	0	0	0	1
CAL ST. LOS ANGELES								
Bob Miller (Occidental '53) 74	1	0	1	0	0	0	0	0
TOTAL	1	0	1	0	0	0	0	0
CAMPBELL								
Billy Lee (Barton '71) 92	1	0	1	0	0	0	0	0
TOTAL	1	0	1	0	0	0	0	0
CANISIUS								
Joseph Curran (Canisius '43) 55RR, 56RR, 57	3	6	3	0	0	0	0	2
TOTAL	3	6	3	0	0	0	0	2
CATHOLIC								
John Long (Catholic '28) 44RR	1	0	2	0	0	0	0	1
TOTAL	1	0	2	0	0	0	0	1
CENTRAL MICH.								
Dick Parfitt (Central Mich. '53) 75, 77	2	2	2	0	0	0	0	0
Charlie Coles [Miami (Ohio) '65] 87	1	0	1	0	0	0	0	0
TOTAL	3	2	3	0	0	0	0	0

	Yrs.	Won	Lost	CH	2d	3d%	4th	RR
CINCINNATI								
George Smith (Cincinnati '35) 58, 59-3d, 60-3d.........	3	7	3	0	0	2	0	0
Ed Jucker (Cincinnati '40) 61-CH, 62-CH, 63-2d......	3	11	1	2	1	0	0	0
Tay Baker (Cincinnati '50) 66...........................	1	0	2	0	0	0	0	0
Gale Catlett (West Va. '63) 75, 76, 77..................	3	2	3	0	0	0	0	0
Bob Huggins (West Va. '77) 92-tie 3d.................	1	4	1	0	0	1	0	0
TOTAL	11	24	10	2	1	3	0	0
CCNY								
Nat Holman (Savage School of Phys. Ed. '17) 47-4th, 50-CH...	2	4	2	1	0	0	1	0
TOTAL	2	4	2	1	0	0	1	0
CLEMSON								
William C. "Bill" Foster (Carson-Newman '58) 80RR....	1	3	1	0	0	0	0	1
Cliff Ellis (Florida St. '68) 87, 89, 90..................	3	3	3	0	0	0	0	0
TOTAL	4	6	4	0	0	0	0	1
CLEVELAND ST.								
Kevin Mackey (St. Anselm '67) 86.....................	1	2	1	0	0	0	0	0
TOTAL	1	2	1	0	0	0	0	0
COASTAL CARO.								
Russ Bergman (Louisiana St. '70) 91..................	1	0	1	0	0	0	0	0
TOTAL	1	0	1	0	0	0	0	0
COLORADO								
Forrest "Frosty" Cox (Kansas '30) 40RR, 42-tie 3d, 46RR...	3	2	4	0	0	1	0	2
Horace "Bebe" Lee (Stanford '38) 54, 55-3d...........	2	3	3	0	0	1	0	0
Russell "Sox" Walseth (Colorado '48) 62RR, 63RR, 69..	3	3	3	0	0	0	0	2
TOTAL	8	8	10	0	0	2	0	4
COLORADO ST.								
Bill Strannigan (Wyoming '41) 54.....................	1	0	2	0	0	0	0	0
Jim Williams (Utah St. '47) 63, 65, 66, 69RR...........	4	2	4	0	0	0	0	1
Boyd Grant (Colorado St. '57) 89, 90..................	2	1	2	0	0	0	0	0
TOTAL	7	3	8	0	0	0	0	1
COLUMBIA								
Gordon Ridings (Oregon '29) 48RR....................	1	0	2	0	0	0	0	1
Lou Rossini (Columbia '48) 51.........................	1	0	1	0	0	0	0	0
John "Jack" Rohan (Columbia '53) 68.................	1	2	1	0	0	0	0	0
TOTAL	3	2	4	0	0	0	0	1
CONNECTICUT								
Hugh Greer (Connecticut '26) 51, 54, 56, 57, 58, 59, 60.	7	1	8	0	0	0	0	0
George Wigton (Ohio St. '56) 63.......................	1	0	1	0	0	0	0	0
Fred Shabel (Duke '54) 64RR, 65, 67..................	3	2	3	0	0	0	0	1
Donald "Dee" Rowe (Middlebury '52) 76...............	1	1	1	0	0	0	0	0
Dom Perno (Connecticut '64) 79.......................	1	0	1	0	0	0	0	0
Jim Calhoun (American Int'l '68) 90RR, 91, 92.........	3	6	3	0	0	0	0	1
TOTAL	16	10	17	0	0	0	0	2
COPPIN ST.								
Ron Mitchell (Edison '84) 90...........................	1	0	1	0	0	0	0	0
TOTAL	1	0	1	0	0	0	0	0
CORNELL								
Royner Greene (Illinois '29) 54........................	1	0	2	0	0	0	0	0
Mike Dement (East Caro. '76) 88......................	1	0	1	0	0	0	0	0
TOTAL	2	0	3	0	0	0	0	0
CREIGHTON								
Eddie Hickey (Creighton '27) 41RR....................	1	1	1	0	0	0	0	1
John "Red" McManus (St. Ambrose '49) 62, 64........	2	3	3	0	0	0	0	0
Eddie Sutton (Oklahoma St. '59) 74....................	1	2	1	0	0	0	0	0
Tom Apke (Creighton '65) 75, 78, 81..................	3	0	3	0	0	0	0	0
Tony Barone (Duke '68) 89, 91........................	2	1	2	0	0	0	0	0
TOTAL	9	7	10	0	0	0	0	1
DARTMOUTH								
Osborne "Ozzie" Cowles (Carleton '22) 41RR, 42-2d, 43RR..	3	4	3	0	1	0	0	2
Earl Brown (Notre Dame '39) 44-2d....................	1	2	1	0	1	0	0	0
Alvin "Doggie" Julian (Bucknell '23) 56, 58RR, 59......	3	4	3	0	0	0	0	1
TOTAL	7	10	7	0	2	0	0	3
DAVIDSON								
Charles "Lefty" Driesell (Duke '54) 66, 68RR, 69RR.....	3	5	4	0	0	0	0	2
Terry Holland (Davidson '64) 70.......................	1	0	1	0	0	0	0	0
Bobby Hussey (Appalachian St. '62) 86................	1	0	1	0	0	0	0	0
TOTAL	5	5	6	0	0	0	0	2

	Yrs.	Won	Lost	CH	2d	3d%	4th	RR
DAYTON								
Tom Blackburn [Wilmington (Ohio) '31] 52............	1	1	1	0	0	0	0	0
Don Donoher (Dayton '54) 65, 66, 67-2d, 69, 70, 74, 84RR, 85..	8	11	10	0	1	0	0	1
Jim O'Brien [St. Joseph's (Pa.) '74] 90.................	1	1	1	0	0	0	0	0
TOTAL	10	13	12	0	1	0	0	1
DELAWARE								
Steve Steinwedel (Mississippi St. '75) 92...............	1	0	1	0	0	0	0	0
TOTAL	1	0	1	0	0	0	0	0
DePAUL								
Ray Meyer (Notre Dame '38) 43-tie 3d, 53, 56, 59, 60, 65, 76, 78RR, 79-3d, 80, 81, 82, 84...................	13	14	16	0	0	2	0	1
Joey Meyer (DePaul '71) 85, 86, 87, 88, 89, 91, 92......	7	6	7	0	0	0	0	0
TOTAL	20	20	23	0	0	2	0	1
DETROIT MERCY								
Robert Calihan (Detroit Mercy '40) 62..................	1	0	1	0	0	0	0	0
Dick Vitale (Seton Hall '62) 77...........................	1	1	1	0	0	0	0	0
Dave "Smokey" Gaines (LeMoyne-Owen '63) 79......	1	0	1	0	0	0	0	0
TOTAL	3	1	3	0	0	0	0	0
DRAKE								
Maurice John (Central Mo. St. '41) 69-3d, 70RR, 71RR.	3	5	3	0	0	1	0	2
TOTAL	3	5	3	0	0	1	0	2
DREXEL								
Eddie Burke (La Salle '67) 86..........................	1	0	1	0	0	0	0	0
TOTAL	1	0	1	0	0	0	0	0
DUKE								
Harold Bradley (Hartwick '34) 55.......................	1	0	1	0	0	0	0	0
Vic Bubas (North Caro. St. '51) 60RR, 63-3d, 64-2d, 66-3d..	4	11	4	0	1	2	0	1
William E. "Bill" Foster (Elizabethtown '54) 78-2d, 79, 80RR..	3	6	3	0	1	0	0	1
Mike Krzyzewski (Army '69) 84, 85, 86-2d, 87, 88-tie 3d, 89-tie 3d, 90-2nd, 91-CH, 92-CH....................	9	33	7	2	2	2	0	0
TOTAL	17	50	15	2	4	4	0	2
DUQUESNE								
Charles "Chick" Davies (Duquesne '34) 40-tie 3d.......	1	1	1	0	0	1	0	0
Donald "Dudey" Moore (Duquesne '34) 52RR..........	1	1	1	0	0	0	0	1
John "Red" Manning (Duquesne '51) 69, 71............	2	2	2	0	0	0	0	0
John Cinicola (Duquesne '55) 77......................	1	0	1	0	0	0	0	0
TOTAL	5	4	5	0	0	1	0	1
EAST CARO.								
Tom Quinn (Marshall '54) 72...........................	1	0	1	0	0	0	0	0
TOTAL	1	0	1	0	0	0	0	0
EAST TENN. ST.								
J. Madison Brooks (Louisiana Tech '37) 68............	1	1	2	0	0	0	0	0
Les Robinson (North Caro. St. '64) 89, 90..............	2	0	2	0	0	0	0	0
Alan LeForce (Cumberland '57) 91, 92.................	2	1	2	0	0	0	0	0
TOTAL	5	2	6	0	0	0	0	0
EASTERN ILL.								
Rick Samuels (Chadron St. '71) 92.....................	1	0	1	0	0	0	0	0
TOTAL	1	0	1	0	0	0	0	0
EASTERN KY.								
Paul McBrayer (Kentucky '30) 53, 59..................	2	0	2	0	0	0	0	0
Jim Baechtold (Eastern Ky. '52) 65....................	1	0	1	0	0	0	0	0
Guy Strong (Eastern Ky. '55) 72.......................	1	0	1	0	0	0	0	0
Ed Byhre [Augustana (S.D.) '66] 79...................	1	0	1	0	0	0	0	0
TOTAL	5	0	5	0	0	0	0	0
EASTERN MICH.								
Ben Braun (Wisconsin '75) 88, 91.....................	2	2	2	0	0	0	0	0
TOTAL	2	2	2	0	0	0	0	0
EVANSVILLE								
Dick Walters (Illinois St. '69) 82......................	1	0	1	0	0	0	0	0
Jim Crews (Indiana '76) 89, 92........................	2	1	2	0	0	0	0	0
TOTAL	3	1	3	0	0	0	0	0
FAIRFIELD								
Mitch Buonaguro (Boston College '75) 86, 87..........	2	0	2	0	0	0	0	0
TOTAL	2	0	2	0	0	0	0	0
FDU-TEANECK								
Tom Green (Syracuse '71) 85, 88......................	2	0	2	0	0	0	0	0
TOTAL	2	0	2	0	0	0	0	0

	Yrs.	Won	Lost	CH	2d	3d%	4th	RR
FLORIDA*								
Norm Sloan (North Caro. St. '51) 87, 88, 89............	3	3	3	0	0	0	0	0
TOTAL	3	3	3	0	0	0	0	0
FLORIDA ST.								
Hugh Durham (Florida St. '59) 68, 72-2d, 78...........	3	4	3	0	1	0	0	0
Joe Williams (Southern Methodist '56) 80..............	1	1	1	0	0	0	0	0
Pat Kennedy [King's (Pa.) '76] 88, 89, 91, 92............	4	3	4	0	0	0	0	0
TOTAL	8	8	8	0	1	0	0	0
FORDHAM								
John Bach (Fordham '48) 53, 54.......................	2	0	2	0	0	0	0	0
Richard "Digger" Phelps (Rider '63) 71................	1	2	1	0	0	0	0	0
Nick Macarchuk (Fairfield '63) 92.....................	1	0	1	0	0	0	0	0
TOTAL	4	2	4	0	0	0	0	0
FRESNO ST.								
Boyd Grant (Colorado St. '61) 81, 82, 84..............	3	1	3	0	0	0	0	0
TOTAL	3	1	3	0	0	0	0	0
FURMAN								
Joe Williams (Southern Methodist '56) 71, 73, 74, 75, 78..	5	1	6	0	0	0	0	0
Eddie Holbrook (Lenoir-Rhyne '62) 80................	1	0	1	0	0	0	0	0
TOTAL	6	1	7	0	0	0	0	0
GEORGE MASON								
Ernie Nestor (Alderson-Broaddus '68) 89.............	1	0	1	0	0	0	0	0
TOTAL	1	0	1	0	0	0	0	0
GEO. WASHINGTON								
Bill Reinhart (Oregon '23) 54, 61.....................	2	0	2	0	0	0	0	0
TOTAL	2	0	2	0	0	0	0	0
GEORGETOWN								
Elmer Ripley (No college) 43-2d.....................	1	2	1	0	1	0	0	0
John Thompson (Providence '64) 75, 76, 79, 80RR, 81, 82-2d, 83, 84-CH, 85-2d, 86, 87RR, 88, 89RR, 90, 91, 92..	16	28	15	1	2	0	0	3
TOTAL	17	30	16	1	3	0	0	3
GEORGIA*								
Hugh Durham (Florida St. '59) 83-tie 3d, 85, 87, 90, 91..	5	4	5	0	0	1	0	0
TOTAL	5	4	5	0	0	1	0	0
GA. SOUTHERN								
Frank Kerns (Alabama '57) 83, 87, 92.................	3	0	3	0	0	0	0	0
TOTAL	3	0	3	0	0	0	0	0
GEORGIA ST.								
Bob Reinhart (Indiana '61) 91........................	1	0	1	0	0	0	0	0
TOTAL	1	0	1	0	0	0	0	0
GEORGIA TECH								
John "Whack" Hyder (Georgia Tech '37) 60RR........	1	1	1	0	0	0	0	1
Bobby Cremins (South Caro. '70) 85RR, 86, 87, 88, 89, 90-tie 3d, 91, 92....................................	8	13	8	0	0	1	0	1
TOTAL	9	14	9	0	0	1	0	2
HARDIN-SIMMONS								
Bill Scott (Hardin-Simmons '47) 53, 57................	2	0	2	0	0	0	0	0
TOTAL	2	0	2	0	0	0	0	0
HARVARD								
Floyd Stahl (Illinois '26) 46RR........................	1	0	2	0	0	0	0	1
TOTAL	1	0	2	0	0	0	0	1
HAWAII								
Ephraim "Red" Rocha (Oregon St. '50) 72.............	1	0	1	0	0	0	0	0
TOTAL	1	0	1	0	0	0	0	0
HOFSTRA								
Roger Gaeckler (Gettysburg '65) 76, 77...............	2	0	2	0	0	0	0	0
TOTAL	2	0	2	0	0	0	0	0
HOLY CROSS								
Alvin "Doggie" Julian (Bucknell '23) 47-CH, 48-3d......	2	5	1	1	0	1	0	0
Lester "Buster" Sheary (Catholic '33) 50RR, 53RR......	2	2	3	0	0	0	0	2
Roy Leenig [Trinity (Conn.) '42] 56...................	1	0	1	0	0	0	0	0
George Blaney (Holy Cross '61) 77, 80................	2	0	2	0	0	0	0	0
TOTAL	7	7	7	1	0	1	0	2
HOUSTON								
Alden Pasche (Rice '32) 56............................	1	0	2	0	0	0	0	0
Guy Lewis (Houston '47) 61, 65, 66, 67-3d, 68-4th, 70, 71, 72, 73, 78, 81, 82-tie 3d, 83-2d, 84-2d............	14	26	18	0	2	2	1	0
Pat Foster (Arkansas '61) 87, 90, 92..................	3	0	3	0	0	0	0	0
TOTAL	18	26	23	0	2	2	1	0

	Yrs.	Won	Lost	CH	2d	3d%	4th	RR
HOUSTON BAPTIST								
Gene Iba (Tulsa '63) 84...............................	1	0	1	0	0	0	0	0
TOTAL	1	0	1	0	0	0	0	0
HOWARD								
A. B. Williamson (North Caro. A&T '68) 81............	1	0	1	0	0	0	0	0
Alfred "Butch" Beard (Louisville '72) 92................	1	0	1	0	0	0	0	0
TOTAL	2	0	2	0	0	0	0	0
IDAHO								
Don Monson (Idaho '55) 81, 82........................	2	1	2	0	0	0	0	0
Kermit Davis Jr. (Mississippi St. '82) 89, 90.............	2	0	2	0	0	0	0	0
TOTAL	4	1	4	0	0	0	0	0
IDAHO ST.								
Steve Belko (Idaho '39) 53, 54, 55, 56.................	4	2	4	0	0	0	0	0
John Grayson (Oklahoma '38) 57, 58, 59...............	3	4	5	0	0	0	0	0
John Evans (Idaho '48) 60.............................	1	0	1	0	0	0	0	0
Jim Killingsworth (Northeastern Okla. St. '48) 74, 77RR..	2	2	2	0	0	0	0	1
Jim Boutin (Lewis & Clark '64) 87.....................	1	0	1	0	0	0	0	0
TOTAL	11	8	13	0	0	0	0	1
ILLINOIS								
Doug Mills (Illinois '30) 42RR..........................	1	0	2	0	0	0	0	1
Harry Combes (Illinois '37) 49-3d, 51-3d, 52-3d, 63RR..	4	9	4	0	0	3	0	1
Lou Henson (New Mexico St. '55) 81, 83, 84RR, 85, 86, 87, 88, 89-tie 3d, 90.................................	9	11	9	0	0	1	0	1
TOTAL	14	20	15	0	0	4	0	3
ILLINOIS ST.								
Bob Donewald (Hanover '64) 83, 84, 85...............	3	2	3	0	0	0	0	0
Bob Bender (Duke '80) 90.............................	1	0	1	0	0	0	0	0
TOTAL	4	2	4	0	0	0	0	0
INDIANA								
Branch McCracken (Indiana '30) 40-CH, 53-CH, 54, 58	4	9	2	2	0	0	0	0
Lou Watson (Indiana '50) 67...........................	1	1	1	0	0	0	0	0
Bob Knight (Ohio St. '62) 73-3d, 75RR, 76-CH, 78, 80, 81-CH, 82, 83, 84RR, 86, 87-CH, 88, 89, 90, 91, 92-tie 3d..	16	35	13	3	0	2	0	2
TOTAL	21	45	16	5	0	2	0	2
INDIANA ST.								
Bill Hodges (Marian '70) 79-2d........................	1	4	1	0	1	0	0	0
TOTAL	1	4	1	0	1	0	0	0
IONA*								
Jim Valvano (Rutgers '67) 79, 80......................	2	1	2	0	0	0	0	0
Pat Kennedy [King's (Pa.) '76] 84, 85..................	2	0	2	0	0	0	0	0
TOTAL	4	1	4	0	0	0	0	0
IOWA								
Frank "Bucky" O'Connor (Drake '38) 55-4th, 56-2d.....	2	5	3	0	1	0	1	0
Ralph Miller (Kansas '42) 70..........................	1	1	1	0	0	0	0	0
Luther "Lute" Olson (Augsburg '57) 79, 80-4th, 81, 82, 83	5	7	6	0	0	0	1	0
George Raveling (Villanova '60) 85, 86.................	2	0	2	0	0	0	0	0
Tom Davis (Wis.-Platteville '60) 87RR, 88, 89, 91, 92....	5	8	5	0	0	0	0	1
TOTAL	15	21	17	0	1	0	2	1
IOWA ST.								
Louis Menze (Central Mo. St. '28) 44-tie 3d...........	1	1	1	0	0	1	0	0
Johnny Orr (Beloit '49) 85, 86, 88, 89, 92...............	5	3	5	0	0	0	0	0
TOTAL	6	4	6	0	0	1	0	0
JACKSONVILLE								
Joe Williams (Southern Methodist '56) 70-2d...........	1	4	1	0	1	0	0	0
Tom Wasdin (Florida '57) 71, 73.......................	2	0	2	0	0	0	0	0
Tates Locke (Ohio Wesleyan '59) 79....................	1	0	1	0	0	0	0	0
Bob Wenzel (Rutgers '71) 86...........................	1	0	1	0	0	0	0	0
TOTAL	5	4	5	0	1	0	0	0
JAMES MADISON								
Lou Campanelli (Montclair St. '60) 81, 82, 83...........	3	3	3	0	0	0	0	0
TOTAL	3	3	3	0	0	0	0	0
KANSAS								
Forrest C. "Phog" Allen (Kansas '06) 40-2d, 42RR, 52-CH, 53-2d..	4	10	3	1	2	0	0	1
Dick Harp (Kansas '40) 57-2d, 60RR...................	2	4	2	0	1	0	0	1
Ted Owens (Oklahoma '51) 66RR, 67, 71-4th, 74-4th, 75, 78, 81.......................................	7	8	9	0	0	0	2	1
Larry Brown (North Caro. '63) 84, 85, 86-tie 3d, 87, 88-CH...	5	14	4	1	0	1	0	0
Roy Williams (North Caro. '72) 90, 91-2d, 92...........	3	7	3	0	1	0	0	0
TOTAL	21	43	21	2	4	1	2	3

	Yrs.	Won	Lost	CH	2d	3d%	4th	RR
KANSAS ST.								
Jack Gardner (Southern Cal '32) 48-4th, 51-2d	2	4	3	0	1	0	1	0
Fred "Tex" Winter (Southern Cal '47) 56, 58-4th, 59RR, 61RR, 64-4th, 68	6	7	9	0	0	0	2	2
Lowell "Cotton" Fitzsimmons (Midwestern St. '55) 70...	1	1	1	0	0	0	0	0
Jack Hartman (Oklahoma St. '49) 72RR, 73RR, 75RR, 77, 80, 81RR, 82	7	11	7	0	0	0	0	4
Lon Kruger (Kansas St. '74) 87, 88, 89, 90	4	4	4	0	0	0	0	1
TOTAL	20	27	24	0	1	0	3	7
KENTUCKY*								
Adolph Rupp (Kansas '23) 42-tie 3d, 45RR, 48-CH, 49-CH, 51-CH, 52RR, 55, 56RR, 57RR, 58-CH, 59, 61RR, 62RR, 64, 66-2d, 68RR, 69, 70RR, 71, 72RR....	20	30	18	4	1	1	0	9
Joe Hall (Sewanee '51) 73RR, 75-2d, 77RR, 78-CH, 80, 81, 82, 83RR, 84-tie 3d, 85..........................	10	20	9	1	1	1	0	3
Eddie Sutton (Oklahoma St. '59) 86RR, 87, 88.........	3	5	3	0	0	0	0	1
Rick Pitino (Massachusetts '74) 92RR..................	1	3	1	0	0	0	0	1
TOTAL	34	58	31	5	2	2	0	14
LA SALLE								
Ken Loeffler (Penn St. '24) 54-CH, 55-2d..............	2	9	1	1	1	0	0	0
Jim Harding (Iowa '49) 68...............................	1	0	1	0	0	0	0	0
Paul Westhead [St. Joseph's (Pa.) '61] 75, 78...........	2	0	2	0	0	0	0	0
Dave "Lefty" Ervin (La Salle '68) 80, 83................	2	1	2	0	0	0	0	0
Bill "Speedy" Morris [St. Joseph's (Pa.) '73] 88, 89, 90, 92..	4	1	4	0	0	0	0	0
TOTAL	11	11	10	1	1	0	0	0
LAFAYETTE								
George Davidson (Lafayette '51) 57....................	1	0	2	0	0	0	0	0
TOTAL	1	0	2	0	0	0	0	0
LAMAR								
Billy Tubbs (Lamar '58) 79, 80.........................	2	3	2	0	0	0	0	0
Pat Foster (Arkansas '61) 81, 83.......................	2	2	2	0	0	0	0	0
TOTAL	4	5	4	0	0	0	0	0
LEBANON VALLEY								
George "Rinso" Marquette (Lebanon Valley '48) 53.....	1	1	2	0	0	0	0	0
TOTAL	1	1	2	0	0	0	0	0
LEHIGH								
Tom Schneider (Bucknell '69) 85.......................	1	0	1	0	0	0	0	0
Fran McCaffery (Pennsylvania '82) 88..................	1	0	1	0	0	0	0	0
TOTAL	2	0	2	0	0	0	0	0
LONG BEACH ST.*								
Jerry Tarkanian (Fresno St. '56) 70, 71RR, 72RR, 73....	4	7	5	0	0	0	0	2
Dwight Jones (Pepperdine '65) 77......................	1	0	1	0	0	0	0	0
TOTAL	5	7	6	0	0	0	0	2
LIU-BROOKLYN								
Paul Lizzo (Northwest Mo. St. '63) 81, 84...............	2	0	2	0	0	0	0	0
TOTAL	2	0	2	0	0	0	0	0
LOUISIANA ST.								
Harry Rabenhorst (Wake Forest '21) 53-4th, 54.........	2	2	4	0	0	0	1	0
Dale Brown (Minot St. '57) 79, 80RR, 81-4th, 84, 85, 86-tie 3d, 87RR, 88, 89, 90, 91, 92..................	12	15	13	0	0	1	1	2
TOTAL	14	17	17	0	0	1	2	2
LOUISIANA TECH								
Andy Russo (Lake Forest '70) 84, 85....................	2	3	2	0	0	0	0	0
Tommy Joe Eagles (Louisiana Tech '71) 87, 89.........	2	1	2	0	0	0	0	0
Jerry Loyd (LeTourneau '76) 91.......................	1	0	1	0	0	0	0	0
TOTAL	5	4	5	0	0	0	0	0
LOUISVILLE								
Bernard "Peck" Hickman (Western Ky. '35) 51, 59-4th, 61, 64, 67...	5	5	7	0	0	0	1	0
John Dromo (John Carroll '39) 68.....................	1	1	1	0	0	0	0	0
Denny Crum (UCLA '59) 72-4th, 74, 75-3d, 77, 78, 79, 80-CH, 81, 82-tie 3d, 83-tie 3d, 84, 86-CH, 88, 89, 90, 92...	16	33	16	2	0	3	1	0
TOTAL	22	39	24	2	0	3	2	0
LOYOLA (CAL.)*								
John Arndt [Loyola (Cal.) '50] 61......................	1	1	1	0	0	0	0	0
Ron Jacobs (Southern Cal '64) 80.....................	1	0	1	0	0	0	0	0
Paul Westhead [St. Joseph's (Pa.) '61] 88, 89, 90RR....	3	4	3	0	0	0	0	1
TOTAL	5	5	5	0	0	0	0	1

	Yrs.	Won	Lost	CH	2d	3d%	4th	RR
LOYOLA (ILL.)								
George Ireland (Notre Dame '36) 63–CH, 64, 66, 68.....	4	7	3	1	0	0	0	0
Gene Sullivan (Notre Dame '53) 85...................	1	2	1	0	0	0	0	0
TOTAL	5	9	4	1	0	0	0	0
LOYOLA (LA.)								
Jim McCafferty [Loyola (La.) '42] 54, 57...............	2	0	2	0	0	0	0	0
Jim Harding (Iowa '49) 58............................	1	0	1	0	0	0	0	0
TOTAL	3	0	3	0	0	0	0	0
MANHATTAN								
Ken Norton (LIU-Brooklyn '39) 56, 58..................	2	1	3	0	0	0	0	0
TOTAL	2	1	3	0	0	0	0	0
MARIST								
Matt Furjanic (Point Park '73) 86.......................	1	0	1	0	0	0	0	0
Dave Magarity [St. Francis (Pa.) '74] 87...............	1	0	1	0	0	0	0	0
TOTAL	2	0	2	0	0	0	0	0
MARQUETTE								
Jack Nagle (Marquette '40) 55RR......................	1	2	1	0	0	0	0	1
Eddie Hickey (Creighton '27) 59, 61....................	2	1	3	0	0	0	0	0
Al McGuire [St. John's (N.Y.) '51] 68, 69RR, 71, 72, 73, 74-2d, 75, 76RR, 77–CH...........................	9	20	9	1	1	0	0	2
Hank Raymonds (St. Louis '48) 78, 79, 80, 82, 83.......	5	2	5	0	0	0	0	0
TOTAL	17	25	18	1	1	0	0	3
MARSHALL*								
Jule Rivlin (Marshall '40) 56...........................	1	0	1	0	0	0	0	0
Carl Tacy (Davis & Elkins '56) 72.......................	1	0	1	0	0	0	0	0
Ricky Huckabay (Louisiana Tech '67) 84, 85, 87........	3	0	3	0	0	0	0	0
TOTAL	5	0	5	0	0	0	0	0
MARYLAND*								
H. A. "Bud" Millikan (Oklahoma St. '42) 58.............	1	2	1	0	0	0	0	0
Charles "Lefty" Driesell (Duke '54) 73RR, 75RR, 80, 81, 83, 84, 85, 86...............................	8	10	8	0	0	0	0	2
Bob Wade (Morgan St. '67) 88.........................	1	1	1	0	0	0	0	0
TOTAL	10	13	10	0	0	0	0	2
MASSACHUSETTS								
Matt Zunic (Geo. Washington '42) 62..................	1	0	1	0	0	0	0	0
John Calipari (Clarion St. '82) 92.....................	1	2	1	0	0	0	0	0
TOTAL	2	2	2	0	0	0	0	0
McNEESE ST.								
Steve Welch (Southeastern La. '71) 89................	1	0	1	0	0	0	0	0
TOTAL	1	0	1	0	0	0	0	0
MEMPHIS ST.*								
Eugene Lambert (Arkansas '29) 55, 56.................	2	0	2	0	0	0	0	0
Bob Vanatta (Central Methodist '45) 62...............	1	0	1	0	0	0	0	0
Gene Bartow (Northeast Mo. St. '53) 73-2d...........	1	3	1	0	1	0	0	0
Wayne Yates (Memphis St. '61) 76....................	1	0	1	0	0	0	0	0
Dana Kirk (Marshall '60) 82, 83, 84, 85-tie 3d, 86.......	5	9	5	0	0	1	0	0
Larry Finch (Memphis St. '73) 88, 89, 92RR...........	3	4	3	0	0	0	0	1
TOTAL	13	16	13	0	1	1	0	1
MERCER								
Bill Bibb (Ky. Wesleyan '57) 81, 85....................	2	0	2	0	0	0	0	0
TOTAL	2	0	2	0	0	0	0	0
MIAMI (FLA.)								
Bruce Hale (Santa Clara '41) 60......................	1	0	1	0	0	0	0	0
TOTAL	1	0	1	0	0	0	0	0
MIAMI (OHIO)								
Bill Rohr (Ohio Wesleyan '40) 53, 55, 57...............	3	0	3	0	0	0	0	0
Dick Shrider (Ohio '48) 58, 66........................	2	1	3	0	0	0	0	0
Tates Locke (Ohio Wesleyan '59) 69..................	1	1	2	0	0	0	0	0
Darrell Hedric [Miami (Ohio) '55] 71, 73, 78, 84........	4	1	4	0	0	0	0	0
Jerry Peirson [Miami (Ohio) '66] 85, 86................	2	0	2	0	0	0	0	0
Joby Wright (Indiana '72) 92..........................	1	0	1	0	0	0	0	0
TOTAL	13	3	15	0	0	0	0	0
MICHIGAN#								
Osborne "Ozzie" Cowles (Carleton '22) 48RR.........	1	1	1	0	0	0	0	1
Dave Strack (Michigan '46) 64-3d, 65-2d, 66RR........	3	7	3	0	1	1	0	1
Johnny Orr (Beloit '49) 74RR, 75, 76-2d, 77RR........	4	7	4	0	1	0	0	2
Bill Frieder (Michigan '64) 85, 86, 87, 88..............	4	5	4	0	0	0	0	0
Steve Fisher (Illinois St. '67) 89–CH, 90, 92-2d.........	3	12	2	1	1	0	0	0
TOTAL	15	32	14	1	3	1	0	4

	Yrs.	Won	Lost	CH	2d	3d%	4th	RR
MICHIGAN ST.								
Forrest "Forddy" Anderson (Stanford '42) 57–4th, 59RR	2	3	3	0	0	0	1	1
George "Jud" Heathcote (Washington St. '50) 78RR, 79–CH, 85, 86, 90, 91, 92	7	13	6	1	0	0	0	1
TOTAL	9	16	9	1	0	0	1	2
MIDDLE TENN. ST.								
Jimmy Earle (Middle Tenn. St. '59) 75, 77	2	0	2	0	0	0	0	0
Stan Simpson (Ga. Southern '61) 82	1	1	1	0	0	0	0	0
Bruce Stewart (Jacksonville St. '75) 85, 87, 89	3	1	3	0	0	0	0	0
TOTAL	6	2	6	0	0	0	0	0
MINNESOTA*								
Bill Musselman (Wittenberg '61) 72	1	1	1	0	0	0	0	0
Jim Dutcher (Michigan '55) 82	1	1	1	0	0	0	0	0
Clem Haskins (Western Ky. '67) 89, 90RR	2	5	2	0	0	0	0	1
TOTAL	4	7	4	0	0	0	0	1
MISSISSIPPI								
Bob Weltlich (Ohio St. '67) 81	1	0	1	0	0	0	0	0
TOTAL	1	0	1	0	0	0	0	0
MISSISSIPPI ST.								
James "Babe" McCarthy (Mississippi St. '49) 63	1	1	1	0	0	0	0	0
Richard Williams (Mississippi St. '67) 91	1	0	1	0	0	0	0	0
TOTAL	2	1	2	0	0	0	0	0
MISSISSIPPI VAL.								
Lafayette Stribling (Mississippi Industrial '57) 86, 92	2	0	2	0	0	0	0	0
TOTAL	2	0	2	0	0	0	0	0
MISSOURI#								
George Edwards (Missouri '13) 44RR	1	1	1	0	0	0	0	1
Norm Stewart (Missouri '56) 76RR, 78, 80, 81, 82, 83, 86, 87, 88, 89, 90, 92	12	8	12	0	0	0	0	1
TOTAL	13	9	13	0	0	0	0	2
MONTANA								
George "Jud" Heathcote (Washington St. '50) 75	1	1	2	0	0	0	0	0
Stew Morrill (Gonzaga '74) 91	1	0	1	0	0	0	0	0
Blaine Taylor (Montana '82) 92	1	0	1	0	0	0	0	0
TOTAL	3	1	4	0	0	0	0	0
MONTANA ST.								
John Breeden (Montana St. '29) 51	1	0	1	0	0	0	0	0
Stu Starner (Minn.-Morris '65) 86	1	0	1	0	0	0	0	0
TOTAL	2	0	2	0	0	0	0	0
MOREHEAD ST.								
Robert Laughlin (Morehead St. '37) 56, 57, 61	3	3	4	0	0	0	0	0
Wayne Martin (Morehead St. '68) 83, 84	2	1	2	0	0	0	0	0
TOTAL	5	4	6	0	0	0	0	0
MURRAY ST.								
Cal Luther (Valparaiso '51) 64, 69	2	0	2	0	0	0	0	0
Steve Newton (Indiana St. '63) 88, 90, 91	3	1	3	0	0	0	0	0
Edgar Scott (Pitt.-Johnstown '78) 92	1	0	1	0	0	0	0	0
TOTAL	6	1	6	0	0	0	0	0
NAVY								
Ben Carnevale (New York U. '38) 47RR, 53, 54RR, 59, 60	5	4	6	0	0	0	0	2
Paul Evans (Ithaca '67) 85, 86RR	2	4	2	0	0	0	0	1
Pete Herrmann (Geneseo St. '70) 87	1	0	1	0	0	0	0	0
TOTAL	8	8	9	0	0	0	0	3
NEBRASKA								
Moe Iba (Oklahoma St. '62) 86	1	0	1	0	0	0	0	0
Danny Nee (St. Mary of the Plains '71) 91, 92	2	0	2	0	0	0	0	0
TOTAL	3	0	3	0	0	0	0	0
NEVADA-LAS VEGAS								
Jerry Tarkanian (Fresno St. '56) 75, 76, 77–3d, 83, 84, 85, 86, 87–tie 3d, 88, 89RR, 90–CH, 91–tie 3d	12	30	11	1	0	3	0	1
TOTAL	12	30	11	1	0	3	0	1
NEVADA								
Sonny Allen (Marshall '59) 84, 85	2	0	2	0	0	0	0	0
TOTAL	2	0	2	0	0	0	0	0
NEW MEXICO								
Bob King (Iowa '47) 68	1	0	2	0	0	0	0	0
Norm Ellenberger (Butler '55) 74, 78	2	2	2	0	0	0	0	0
Dave Bliss (Cornell '65) 91	1	0	1	0	0	0	0	0
TOTAL	4	2	5	0	0	0	0	0

	Yrs.	Won	Lost	CH	2d	3d%	4th	RR
NEW MEXICO ST.								
George McCarty (New Mexico St. '50) 52	1	0	2	0	0	0	0	0
Presley Askew (Southeastern Okla. St. '30) 59, 60	2	0	2	0	0	0	0	0
Lou Henson (New Mexico St. '55) 67, 68, 69, 70-3d, 71, 75	6	7	7	0	0	1	0	0
Ken Hayes (Northeastern Okla. St. '56) 79	1	0	1	0	0	0	0	0
Neil McCarthy (Cal St. Sacramento '65) 90, 91, 92	3	2	3	0	0	0	0	0
TOTAL	13	9	15	0	0	1	0	0
NEW ORLEANS								
Benny Dees (Wyoming '58) 87	1	1	1	0	0	0	0	0
Tim Floyd (Louisiana Tech '77) 91	1	0	1	0	0	0	0	0
TOTAL	2	1	2	0	0	0	0	0
NEW YORK U.								
Howard Cann (New York U. '20) 43RR, 45-2d, 46RR	3	3	4	0	1	0	0	2
Lou Rossini (Columbia '48) 60-4th, 62, 63	3	6	5	0	0	0	1	0
TOTAL	6	9	9	0	1	0	1	2
NIAGARA								
Frank Layden (Niagara '55) 70	1	1	2	0	0	0	0	0
TOTAL	1	1	2	0	0	0	0	0
NORTH CARO.								
Bill Lange (Wittenberg '21) 41RR	1	0	2	0	0	0	0	1
Ben Carnevale (New York U. '38) 46-2d	1	2	1	0	1	0	0	0
Frank McGuire [St. John's (N.Y.) '36] 57-CH, 59	2	5	1	1	0	0	0	0
Dean Smith (Kansas '53) 67-4th, 68-2d, 69-4th, 72-3d, 75, 76, 77-2d, 78, 79, 80, 81-2d, 82-CH, 83RR, 84, 85RR, 86, 87RR, 88RR, 89, 90, 91-tie 3d, 92	22	49	23	1	3	2	2	4
TOTAL	26	56	27	2	4	2	2	5
NORTH CARO. A&T								
Don Corbett [Lincoln (Mo.) '65] 82, 83, 84, 85, 86, 87, 88	7	0	7	0	0	0	0	0
TOTAL	7	0	7	0	0	0	0	0
N.C.-CHARLOTTE								
Lee Rose (Transylvania '58) 77-4th	1	3	2	0	0	0	1	0
Jeff Mullins (Duke '64) 88, 92	2	0	2	0	0	0	0	0
TOTAL	3	3	4	0	0	0	1	0
NORTH CARO. ST.*								
Everett Case (Wisconsin '23) 50-3d, 51RR, 52, 54, 56	5	6	6	0	0	1	0	1
Press Maravich (Davis & Elkins '41) 65	1	1	1	0	0	0	0	0
Norm Sloan (North Caro. St. '51) 70, 74-CH, 80	3	5	2	1	0	0	0	0
Jim Valvano (Rutgers '67) 82, 83-CH, 85RR, 86RR, 87, 88, 89	7	14	6	1	0	0	0	2
Les Robinson (North Caro. St. '64) 91	1	1	1	0	0	0	0	0
TOTAL	17	27	16	2	0	1	0	3
NORTH TEXAS								
Jimmy Gales (Alcorn St. '63) 88	1	0	1	0	0	0	0	0
TOTAL	1	0	1	0	0	0	0	0
NORTHEAST LA.								
Mike Vining (Northeast La. '67) 82, 86, 90, 91, 92	5	0	5	0	0	0	0	0
TOTAL	5	0	5	0	0	0	0	0
NORTHEASTERN								
Jim Calhoun (American Int'l '66) 81, 82, 84, 85, 86	5	3	5	0	0	0	0	0
Karl Fogel (Colby '68) 87, 91	2	0	2	0	0	0	0	0
TOTAL	7	3	7	0	0	0	0	0
NORTHERN ILL.								
John McDougal (Evansville '50) 82	1	0	1	0	0	0	0	0
Jim Molinari (Ill. Wesleyan '77) 91	1	0	1	0	0	0	0	0
TOTAL	2	0	2	0	0	0	0	0
NORTHERN IOWA								
Eldon Miller (Wittenberg '61) 90	1	1	1	0	0	0	0	0
TOTAL	1	1	1	0	0	0	0	0
NOTRE DAME								
John Jordan (Notre Dame '35) 53RR, 54RR, 57, 58RR, 60, 63	6	8	6	0	0	0	0	3
Johnny Dee (Notre Dame '46) 65, 69, 70, 71	4	2	6	0	0	0	0	0
Richard "Digger" Phelps (Rider '63) 74, 75, 76, 77, 78-4th, 79RR, 80, 81, 85, 86, 87, 88, 89, 90	14	15	16	0	0	0	1	1
TOTAL	24	25	28	0	0	0	1	4
OHIO								
James Snyder (Ohio '41) 60, 61, 64RR, 65, 70, 72, 74	7	3	8	0	0	0	0	1
Danny Nee (St. Mary of the Plains '71) 83, 85	2	1	2	0	0	0	0	0
TOTAL	9	4	10	0	0	0	0	1

	Yrs.	Won	Lost	CH	2d	3d%	4th	RR
OHIO ST.								
Harold Olsen (Wisconsin '17) 39-2d, 44-tie 3d, 45-tie 3d, 46-3d..	4	6	4	0	1	3	0	0
William H. H. "Tippy" Dye (Ohio St. '37) 50RR.........	1	1	1	0	0	0	0	1
Fred Taylor (Ohio St. '50) 60-CH, 61-2d, 62-2d, 68-3d, 71RR...	5	14	4	1	2	1	0	1
Eldon Miller (Wittenberg '61) 80, 82, 83, 85.............	4	3	4	0	0	0	0	0
Gary Williams (Maryland '67) 87......................	1	1	1	0	0	0	0	0
Randy Ayers [Miami (Ohio) '78] 90, 91, 92RR..........	3	6	3	0	0	0	0	1
TOTAL	18	31	17	1	3	4	0	3
OKLAHOMA								
Bruce Drake (Oklahoma '29) 39-tie 3d, 43RR, 47-2d....	3	4	3	0	1	1	0	1
Dave Bliss (Cornell '65) 79......................	1	1	1	0	0	0	0	0
Billy Tubbs (Lamar '58) 83, 84, 85RR, 86, 87, 88-2d, 89, 90, 92...	9	15	9	0	1	0	0	1
TOTAL	13	20	13	0	2	1	0	2
OKLAHOMA CITY								
Doyle Parrack (Oklahoma St. '45) 52, 53, 54, 55........	4	1	5	0	0	0	0	0
A. E. "Abe" Lemons (Oklahoma City '49) 56RR, 57RR 63, 64, 65, 66, 73...................................	7	7	8	0	0	0	0	2
TOTAL	11	8	13	0	0	0	0	2
OKLAHOMA ST.								
Henry Iba [Westminster (Mo.) '28] 45-CH, 46-CH, 49-2d, 51-4th, 53RR, 54RR, 58RR, 65RR......	8	15	7	2	1	0	1	4
Paul Hansen (Oklahoma City '50) 83...................	1	0	1	0	0	0	0	0
Eddie Sutton (Oklahoma St. '59) 91, 92...............	2	4	2	0	0	0	0	0
TOTAL	11	19	10	2	1	0	1	4
OLD DOMINION								
Paul Webb (William & Mary '51) 80, 82, 85.............	3	0	3	0	0	0	0	0
Tom Young (Maryland '58) 86..........................	1	1	1	0	0	0	0	0
Oliver Purnell (Old Dominion '75) 92...................	1	0	1	0	0	0	0	0
TOTAL	5	1	5	0	0	0	0	0
ORAL ROBERTS								
Ken Trickey (Middle Tenn. St. '54) 74RR...............	1	2	1	0	0	0	0	1
Dick Acres (UC Santa Barb.) 84......................	1	0	1	0	0	0	0	0
TOTAL	2	2	2	0	0	0	0	1
OREGON								
Howard Hobson (Oregon '26) 39-CH..................	1	3	0	1	0	0	0	0
John Warren (Oregon '28) 45RR.......................	1	1	1	0	0	0	0	1
Steve Belko (Idaho '39) 60RR, 61.....................	2	2	2	0	0	0	0	1
TOTAL	4	6	3	1	0	0	0	2
OREGON ST.*								
Amory "Slats" Gill (Oregon St. '25) 47RR, 49-4th, 55RR, 62RR, 63-4th, 64.............................	6	8	8	0	0	0	2	3
Paul Valenti (Oregon St. '42) 66RR....................	1	1	1	0	0	0	0	1
Ralph Miller (Kansas '42) 75, 80, 81, 82RR, 84, 85, 88, 89...	8	3	9	0	0	0	0	1
Jim Anderson (Oregon St. '59) 90.....................	1	0	1	0	0	0	0	0
TOTAL	16	12	19	0	0	0	2	5
PACIFIC (CAL.)								
Dick Edwards (Culver-Stockton '52) 66, 67RR, 71......	3	2	4	0	0	0	0	1
Stan Morrison (California '62) 79......................	1	0	1	0	0	0	0	0
TOTAL	4	2	5	0	0	0	0	1
PENN ST.								
John Lawther [Westminster (Pa.) '19] 42RR.............	1	1	1	0	0	0	0	1
Elmer Gross (Penn St. '42) 52, 54-3d..................	2	4	3	0	0	1	0	0
John Egli (Penn St. '47) 55, 65.......................	2	1	3	0	0	0	0	0
Bruce Parkhill (Lock Haven '71) 91....................	1	1	1	0	0	0	0	0
TOTAL	6	7	8	0	0	1	0	1
PENNSYLVANIA								
Howie Dallmar (Stanford '48) 53.......................	1	1	1	0	0	0	0	0
Dick Harter (Pennsylvania '53) 70, 71RR..............	2	2	2	0	0	0	0	1
Chuck Daly (Bloomsburg '53) 72RR, 73, 74, 75.........	4	3	5	0	0	0	0	1
Bob Weinhauer (Cortland St. '61) 78, 79-4th, 80, 82.....	4	6	5	0	0	0	1	0
Craig Littlepage (Pennsylvania '73) 85.................	1	0	1	0	0	0	0	0
Tom Schneider (Bucknell '69) 87......................	1	0	1	0	0	0	0	0
TOTAL	13	12	15	0	0	0	1	2
PEPPERDINE								
Al Duer (Emporia St. '29) 44RR.......................	1	0	2	0	0	0	0	1
R. L. "Duck" Dowell (Northwest Mo. St. '33) 62.........	1	1	1	0	0	0	0	0
Gary Colson (David Lipscomb '56) 76, 79..............	2	2	2	0	0	0	0	0
Jim Harrick [Charleston (W. Va.) '60] 82, 83, 85, 86.....	4	1	4	0	0	0	0	0
Tom Asbury (Wyoming '67) 91, 92.....................	2	0	2	0	0	0	0	0
TOTAL	10	4	11	0	0	0	0	1

	Yrs.	Won	Lost	CH	2d	3d%	4th	RR
PITTSBURGH								
Henry Carlson (Pittsburgh '17) 41-tie 3d.............	1	1	1	0	0	1	0	0
Bob Timmons (Pittsburgh '33) 57, 58, 63..............	3	1	4	0	0	0	0	0
Charles "Buzz" Ridl [Westminster (Pa.) '42] 74RR......	1	2	1	0	0	0	0	1
Roy Chipman (Maine '61) 81, 82, 85...................	3	1	3	0	0	0	0	0
Paul Evans (Ithaca '67) 87, 88, 89, 91.................	4	3	4	0	0	0	0	0
TOTAL	12	8	13	0	0	1	0	1
PORTLAND								
Al Negratti (Seton Hall '43) 59.........................	1	0	1	0	0	0	0	0
TOTAL	1	0	1	0	0	0	0	0
PRINCETON#								
Franklin Cappon (Michigan '24) 52, 55, 60.............	3	0	5	0	0	0	0	0
J. L. "Jake" McCandless (Princeton '51) 61............	1	1	2	0	0	0	0	0
Bill van Breda Kolff (Princeton '47) 63, 64, 65-3d, 67....	4	7	5	0	0	1	0	0
Pete Carril (Lafayette '52) 69, 76, 77, 81, 83, 84, 89, 90, 91, 92...	10	3	10	0	0	0	0	0
TOTAL	18	11	22	0	0	1	0	0
PROVIDENCE								
Joe Mullaney (Holy Cross '49) 64, 65RR, 66...........	3	2	3	0	0	0	0	1
Dave Gavitt (Dartmouth '59) 72, 73-4th, 74, 77, 78......	5	5	6	0	0	0	1	0
Rick Pitino (Massachusetts '74) 87 tie-3d.............	1	4	1	0	0	1	0	0
Rick Barnes (Lenoir-Rhyne '77) 89, 90................	2	0	2	0	0	0	0	0
TOTAL	11	11	12	0	0	1	1	1
PURDUE								
George King [Charleston (W. Va.) '50] 69-2d...........	1	3	1	0	1	0	0	0
Fred Schaus (West Va. '49) 77.......................	1	0	1	0	0	0	0	0
Lee Rose (Transylvania '58) 80-3d....................	1	5	1	0	0	1	0	0
Gene Keady (Kansas St. '58) 83, 84, 85, 86, 87, 88, 90, 91..	8	5	8	0	0	0	0	0
TOTAL	11	13	11	0	1	1	0	0
RHODE ISLAND								
Ernie Calverley (Rhode Island '46) 61, 66..............	2	0	2	0	0	0	0	0
Jack Kraft [St. Joseph's (Pa.) '42] 78....................	1	0	1	0	0	0	0	0
Tom Penders (Connecticut '67) 88....................	1	2	1	0	0	0	0	0
TOTAL	4	2	4	0	0	0	0	0
RICE								
Byron "Buster" Brannon (Texas Christian '33) 40RR, 42RR...	2	1	3	0	0	0	0	2
Don Suman (Rice '44) 54..............................	1	1	1	0	0	0	0	0
Don Knodel [Miami (Ohio) '53] 70....................	1	0	1	0	0	0	0	0
TOTAL	4	2	5	0	0	0	0	2
RICHMOND								
Dick Tarrant (Fordham '51) 84, 86, 88, 90, 91...........	5	5	5	0	0	0	0	0
TOTAL	5	5	5	0	0	0	0	0
RIDER								
John Carpenter (Penn St. '58) 84......................	1	0	1	0	0	0	0	0
TOTAL	1	0	1	0	0	0	0	0
ROBERT MORRIS								
Matt Furjanic (Point Park '73) 82, 83..................	2	1	2	0	0	0	0	0
Jarrett Durham (Duquesne '71) 89, 90, 92..............	3	0	3	0	0	0	0	0
TOTAL	5	1	5	0	0	0	0	0
RUTGERS								
Tom Young (Maryland '58) 75, 76-4th, 79, 83..........	4	5	5	0	0	0	1	0
Bob Wenzel (Rutgers '71) 89, 91......................	2	0	2	0	0	0	0	0
TOTAL	6	5	7	0	0	0	1	0
ST. BONAVENTURE								
Eddie Donovan (St. Bonaventure '50) 61...............	1	2	1	0	0	0	0	0
Larry Weise (St. Bonaventure '58) 68, 70-4th..........	2	4	4	0	0	0	1	0
Jim Satalin (St. Bonaventure '69) 78..................	1	0	1	0	0	0	0	0
TOTAL	4	6	6	0	0	0	1	0
ST. FRANCIS (PA.)								
Jim Baron (St. Bonaventure '77) 91....................	1	0	1	0	0	0	0	0
TOTAL	1	0	1	0	0	0	0	0
ST. JOHN'S (N.Y.)								
Frank McGuire [St. John's (N.Y.) '36] 51RR, 52-2d......	2	5	2	0	1	0	0	1
Joe Lapchick (No college) 61..........................	1	0	1	0	0	0	0	0
Frank Mulzoff [St. John's (N.Y.) '51] 73..............	1	0	1	0	0	0	0	0
Lou Carnesecca [St. John's (N.Y.) '46] 67, 68, 69, 76, 77, 78, 79RR, 80, 82, 83, 84, 85-tie 3rd, 86, 87, 88, 90, 91RR, 92...	18	17	20	0	0	1	0	2
TOTAL	22	22	24	0	1	1	0	3

	Yrs.	Won	Lost	CH	2d	3d%	4th	RR
ST. JOSEPH'S (PA.)*								
John "Jack" Ramsay [St. Joseph's (Pa.) '49] 59, 60, 61-3d, 62, 63RR, 65, 66	7	8	11	0	0	1	0	1
John "Jack" McKinney [St. Joseph's (Pa.) '57] 69, 71, 73, 74	4	0	4	0	0	0	0	0
Jim Lynam [St. Joseph's (Pa.) '64] 81RR	1	3	1	0	0	0	0	1
Jim Boyle [St. Joseph's (Pa.) '64] 82, 86	2	1	2	0	0	0	0	0
TOTAL	14	12	18	0	0	1	0	2
ST. LOUIS								
Eddie Hickey (Creighton '27) 52RR, 57	2	1	3	0	0	0	0	1
TOTAL	2	1	3	0	0	0	0	1
ST. MARY'S (CAL.)								
James Weaver (DePaul '47) 59RR	1	1	1	0	0	0	0	1
Lynn Nance (Washington '65) 89	1	0	1	0	0	0	0	0
TOTAL	2	1	2	0	0	0	0	1
ST. PETER'S								
Ted Fiore (Seton Hall '62) 91	1	0	1	0	0	0	0	0
TOTAL	1	0	1	0	0	0	0	0
SAN DIEGO								
Jim Brovelli (San Francisco '64) 84	1	0	1	0	0	0	0	0
Hank Egan (Navy '60) 87	1	0	1	0	0	0	0	0
TOTAL	2	0	2	0	0	0	0	0
SAN DIEGO ST.								
Tim Vezie (Denver '67) 75, 76	2	0	2	0	0	0	0	0
Dave "Smokey" Gaines (LeMoyne-Owen '63) 85	1	0	1	0	0	0	0	0
TOTAL	3	0	3	0	0	0	0	0
SAN FRANCISCO								
Phil Woolpert [Loyola (Cal.) '40] 55-CH, 56-CH, 57-3d, 58	4	13	2	2	0	1	0	0
Peter Peletta (Cal St. Sacramento '50) 63, 64RR, 65RR	3	3	3	0	0	0	0	2
Bob Gaillard (San Francisco '62) 72, 73RR, 74RR, 77, 78	5	4	5	0	0	0	0	2
Dan Belluomini (San Francisco '64) 79	1	1	1	0	0	0	0	0
Peter Barry (San Francisco '70) 81, 82	2	0	2	0	0	0	0	0
TOTAL	15	21	13	2	0	1	0	4
SAN JOSE ST.								
Walter McPherson (San Jose St. '40) 51	1	0	1	0	0	0	0	0
Bill Berry (Michigan St. '65) 80	1	0	1	0	0	0	0	0
TOTAL	2	0	2	0	0	0	0	0
SANTA CLARA								
Bob Feerick (Santa Clara '41) 52-4th, 53RR, 54RR, 60	4	6	6	0	0	0	1	2
Dick Garibaldi (Santa Clara '57) 68RR, 69RR, 70	3	3	3	0	0	0	0	2
Carroll Williams (San Jose St. '55) 87	1	0	1	0	0	0	0	0
TOTAL	8	9	10	0	0	0	1	4
SEATTLE#								
Al Brightman [Charleston (W. Va.)] 53, 54, 55, 56	4	4	6	0	0	0	0	0
John Castellani (Notre Dame '52) 58-2d	1	4	1	0	1	0	0	0
Vince Cazzetta (Arnold '50) 61, 62	2	0	2	0	0	0	0	0
Clair Markey (Seattle '63) 63	1	0	1	0	0	0	0	0
Bob Boyd (Southern Cal '53) 64	1	2	1	0	0	0	0	0
Lionel Purcell (UC Santa Barb. '52) 67	1	0	1	0	0	0	0	0
Morris Buckwalter (Utah '56) 69	1	0	1	0	0	0	0	0
TOTAL	11	10	13	0	1	0	0	0
SETON HALL								
P. J. Carlesimo (Fordham '71) 88, 89-2d, 91RR, 92	4	11	4	0	1	0	0	1
TOTAL	4	11	4	0	1	0	0	1
SIENA								
Mike Deane (Potsdam St. '74) 89	1	1	1	0	0	0	0	0
TOTAL	1	1	1	0	0	0	0	0
SOUTH ALA.								
Cliff Ellis (Florida St. '68) 79, 80	2	0	2	0	0	0	0	0
Ronnie Arrow (Southwest Tex. St. '69) 89, 91	2	1	2	0	0	0	0	0
TOTAL	4	1	4	0	0	0	0	0
SOUTH CARO.								
Frank McGuire [St. John's (N.Y.) '36] 71, 72, 73, 74	4	4	5	0	0	0	0	0
George Felton (South Caro. '75) 89	1	0	1	0	0	0	0	0
TOTAL	5	4	6	0	0	0	0	0
SOUTH CARO. ST.								
Cy Alexander (Catawba '75) 89	1	0	1	0	0	0	0	0
TOTAL	1	0	1	0	0	0	0	0

	Yrs.	Won	Lost	CH	2d	3d%	4th	RR
SOUTH FLA.								
Bobby Paschal (Stetson '64) 90, 92	2	0	2	0	0	0	0	0
TOTAL	2	0	2	0	0	0	0	0
SOUTHERN-B.R.								
Carl Stewart (Grambling '54) 81	1	0	1	0	0	0	0	0
Robert Hopkins (Grambling '56) 85	1	0	1	0	0	0	0	0
Ben Jobe (Fisk '56) 87, 88, 89	3	0	3	0	0	0	0	0
TOTAL	5	0	5	0	0	0	0	0
SOUTHERN CAL								
Justin "Sam" Barry (Wisconsin '16) 40-tie 3d	1	1	1	0	0	1	0	0
Forrest Twogood (Iowa '29) 54-4th, 60, 61	3	3	5	0	0	0	1	0
Bob Boyd (Southern Cal '53) 79	1	1	1	0	0	0	0	0
Stan Morrison (California '62) 82, 85	2	0	2	0	0	0	0	0
George Raveling (Villanova '60) 91, 92	2	1	2	0	0	0	0	0
TOTAL	9	6	11	0	0	1	1	0
SOUTHERN ILL.								
Paul Lambert (William Jewell '56) 77	1	1	1	0	0	0	0	0
TOTAL	1	1	1	0	0	0	0	0
SOUTHERN METHODIST								
E. O. "Doc" Hayes (North Texas '27) 55, 56-4th, 57, 65, 66, 67RR	6	7	8	0	0	0	1	1
Dave Bliss (Cornell '65) 84, 85, 88	3	3	3	0	0	0	0	0
TOTAL	9	10	11	0	0	0	1	1
SOUTHERN MISS.								
M. K. Turk (Livingston '64) 90, 91	2	0	2	0	0	0	0	0
TOTAL	2	0	2	0	0	0	0	0
SOUTHWEST MO. ST.								
Charlie Spoonhour (School of Ozarks '61) 87, 88, 89, 90, 92	5	1	5	0	0	0	0	0
TOTAL	5	1	5	0	0	0	0	0
SOUTHWESTERN LA.*								
Beryl Shipley (Delta St. '51) 72, 73	2	3	3	0	0	0	0	0
Bobby Paschal (Stetson '64) 82, 83	2	0	2	0	0	0	0	0
Marty Fletcher (Maryland '73) 92	1	1	1	0	0	0	0	0
TOTAL	5	4	6	0	0	0	0	0
SPRINGFIELD								
Ed Hickox (Ohio Wesleyan '05) 40RR	1	0	1	0	0	0	0	1
TOTAL	1	0	1	0	0	0	0	1
STANFORD								
Everett Dean (Indiana '21) 42-CH	1	3	0	1	0	0	0	0
Mike Montgomery (Long Beach St. '68) 89, 92	2	0	2	0	0	0	0	0
TOTAL	3	3	2	1	0	0	0	0
SYRACUSE								
Marc Guley (Syracuse '36) 57RR	1	2	1	0	0	0	0	1
Fred Lewis (Eastern Ky. '46) 66RR	1	1	1	0	0	0	0	1
Roy Danforth (Southern Miss. '62) 73, 74, 75-4th, 76	4	5	5	0	0	0	1	0
Jim Boeheim (Syracuse '66) 77, 78, 79, 80, 83, 84, 85, 86, 87-2d, 88, 89RR, 90, 91, 92	14	19	14	0	1	0	0	1
TOTAL	20	27	21	0	1	0	1	3
TEMPLE								
Josh Cody (Vanderbilt '20) 44RR	1	1	1	0	0	0	0	1
Harry Litwack (Temple '30) 56-3d, 58-3d, 64, 67, 70, 72	6	7	6	0	0	2	0	0
Don Casey (Temple '70) 79	1	0	1	0	0	0	0	0
John Chaney (Bethune-Cookman '55) 84, 85, 86, 87, 88RR, 90, 91RR, 92	8	10	8	0	0	0	0	2
TOTAL	16	18	16	0	0	2	0	3
TENNESSEE								
Ramon "Ray" Mears [Miami (Ohio) '49] 67, 76, 77	3	0	4	0	0	0	0	0
Don DeVoe (Ohio St. '64) 79, 80, 81, 82, 83, 89	6	5	6	0	0	0	0	0
TOTAL	9	5	10	0	0	0	0	0
TENN.-CHATT.								
Murray Arnold (American '60) 81, 82, 83	3	1	3	0	0	0	0	0
Mack McCarthy (Virginia Tech '74) 88	1	0	1	0	0	0	0	0
TOTAL	4	1	4	0	0	0	0	0
TENNESSEE TECH								
Johnny Oldham (Western Ky. '48) 58, 63	2	0	2	0	0	0	0	0
TOTAL	2	0	2	0	0	0	0	0

	Yrs.	Won	Lost	CH	2d	3d%	4th	RR
TEXAS								
H. C. "Bully" Gilstrap (Texas '22) 43-tie 3d.............	1	1	1	0	0	1	0	0
Jack Gray (Texas '35) 39RR, 47-3d....................	2	2	3	0	0	1	0	1
Harold Bradley (Hartwick '34) 60, 63..................	2	2	3	0	0	0	0	0
Leon Black (Texas '53) 72, 74.........................	2	1	3	0	0	0	0	0
A. E. "Abe" Lemons (Oklahoma City '49) 79..........	1	0	1	0	0	0	0	0
Tom Penders (Connecticut '67) 89, 90RR, 91, 92......	4	5	4	0	0	0	0	1
TOTAL	12	11	15	0	0	2	0	2
TEXAS A&M								
John Floyd (Oklahoma St. '41) 51......................	1	0	1	0	0	0	0	0
Shelby Metcalf (East Tex. St. '53) 64, 69, 75, 80, 87.....	5	3	6	0	0	0	0	0
TOTAL	6	3	7	0	0	0	0	0
TEXAS CHRISTIAN								
Byron "Buster" Brannon (Texas Christian '33) 52, 53, 59.........	3	3	3	0	0	0	0	0
Johnny Swaim (Texas Christian '53) 68RR, 71........	2	1	2	0	0	0	0	1
Jim Killingsworth (Northeastern Okla. St. '48) 87.......	1	1	1	0	0	0	0	0
TOTAL	6	5	6	0	0	0	0	1
TEXAS-SAN ANTONIO								
Ken Burmeister [St. Mary's (Tex.) '71] 88..............	1	0	1	0	0	0	0	0
TOTAL	1	0	1	0	0	0	0	0
TEXAS SOUTHERN								
Robert Moreland (Tougaloo '62) 90...................	1	0	1	0	0	0	0	0
TOTAL	1	0	1	0	0	0	0	0
TEXAS TECH								
Polk Robison (Texas Tech '35) 54, 56, 61..............	3	1	3	0	0	0	0	0
Gene Gibson (Texas Tech '50) 62......................	1	1	2	0	0	0	0	0
Gerald Myers (Texas Tech '59) 73, 76, 85, 86..........	4	1	4	0	0	0	0	0
TOTAL	8	3	9	0	0	0	0	0
TOLEDO								
Jerry Bush [St. John's (N.Y.) '38] 54...................	1	0	1	0	0	0	0	0
Bob Nichols (Toledo '53) 67, 79, 80...................	3	1	3	0	0	0	0	0
TOTAL	4	1	4	0	0	0	0	0
TOWSON ST.								
Terry Truax (Maryland '68) 90, 91.....................	2	0	2	0	0	0	0	0
TOTAL	2	0	2	0	0	0	0	0
TRINITY (TEX.)								
Bob Polk (Evansville '39) 69..........................	1	0	1	0	0	0	0	0
TOTAL	1	0	1	0	0	0	0	0
TUFTS								
Richard Cochran (Tufts '34) 45RR.....................	1	0	2	0	0	0	0	1
TOTAL	1	0	2	0	0	0	0	1
TULANE								
Perry Clark (Gettysburg '74) 92.......................	1	1	1	0	0	0	0	0
TOTAL	1	1	1	0	0	0	0	0
TULSA								
Clarence Iba (Panhandle St. '36) 55...................	1	1	1	0	0	0	0	0
Nolan Richardson (UTEP '65) 82, 84, 85..............	3	0	3	0	0	0	0	0
J. D. Barnett (Winona St. '66) 86, 87..................	2	0	2	0	0	0	0	0
TOTAL	6	1	6	0	0	0	0	0
UCLA*								
John Wooden (Purdue '32) 50RR, 52, 56, 62-4th, 63, 64-CH, 65-CH, 67-CH, 68-CH, 69-CH, 70-CH, 71-CH, 72-CH, 73-CH, 74-3d, 75-CH...............	16	47	10	10	0	1	1	1
Gene Bartow (Northeast Mo. St. '53) 76-3d, 77........	2	5	2	0	0	1	0	0
Gary Cunningham (UCLA '62) 78, 79RR..............	2	3	2	0	0	0	0	1
Larry Brown (North Caro. '63) 80-2d, 81..............	2	5	2	0	1	0	0	0
Larry Farmer (UCLA '73) 83..........................	1	0	1	0	0	0	0	0
Walt Hazzard (UCLA '64) 87..........................	1	1	1	0	0	0	0	0
Jim Harrick [Charleston (W. Va.) '60] 89, 90, 91, 92RR..	4	6	4	0	0	0	0	1
TOTAL	28	67	22	10	1	2	1	3
UTAH								
Vadal Peterson (Utah '20) 44-CH, 45RR..............	2	3	2	1	0	0	0	1
Jack Gardner (Southern Cal '32) 55, 56RR, 59, 60, 61-4th, 66-4th...	6	8	9	0	0	0	2	1
Jerry Pimm (Southern Cal '60) 77, 78, 79, 81, 83.......	5	5	5	0	0	0	0	0
Lynn Archibald (Fresno St. '68) 86....................	1	0	1	0	0	0	0	0
Rick Majerus (Marquette '70) 91......................	1	2	1	0	0	0	0	0
TOTAL	15	18	18	1	0	0	2	2

	Yrs.	Won	Lost	CH	2d	3d%	4th	RR
UTAH ST.								
E. L. "Dick" Romney (Utah '17) 39RR..............	1	1	1	0	0	0	0	1
Ladell Andersen (Utah St. '51) 62, 63, 64, 70RR, 71.....	5	4	7	0	0	0	0	1
Gordon "Dutch" Belnap (Utah St. '58) 75, 79..........	2	0	2	0	0	0	0	0
Rod Tueller (Utah St. '59) 80, 83, 88....................	3	0	3	0	0	0	0	0
TOTAL	11	5	13	0	0	0	0	2
UTEP								
Don Haskins (Oklahoma St. '53) 63, 64, 66-CH, 67, 70, 75, 84, 85, 86, 87, 88, 89, 90, 92.....................	14	14	13	1	0	0	0	0
TOTAL	14	14	13	1	0	0	0	0
VANDERBILT								
Roy Skinner (Presbyterian '52) 65RR, 74..............	2	1	3	0	0	0	0	1
C. M. Newton (Kentucky '52) 88, 89....................	2	2	2	0	0	0	0	0
Eddie Fogler (North Caro. '70) 91......................	1	0	1	0	0	0	0	0
TOTAL	5	3	6	0	0	0	0	1
VILLANOVA*								
Alex Severance (Villanova '29) 39-tie 3d, 49RR, 51, 55..	4	4	4	0	0	1	0	1
Jack Kraft [St. Joseph's (Pa.) '42] 62RR, 64, 69, 70RR, 71-2d, 72...	6	11	7	0	1	0	0	2
Rollie Massimino (Vermont '56) 78RR, 80, 81, 82RR, 83RR, 84, 85-CH, 86, 88, 90, 91....................	11	20	10	1	0	0	0	4
TOTAL	21	35	21	1	1	1	0	7
VIRGINIA								
Terry Holland (Davidson '64) 76, 81-3d, 82, 83RR, 84-tie 3d, 86, 87, 89RR, 90....................	9	15	9	0	0	2	0	2
Jeff Jones, (Virginia '82) 91...........................	1	0	1	0	0	0	0	0
TOTAL	10	15	10	0	0	2	0	2
VA. COMMONWEALTH								
J. D. Barnett (Winona St. '66) 80, 81, 83, 84, 85.........	5	4	5	0	0	0	0	0
TOTAL	5	4	5	0	0	0	0	0
VA. MILITARY								
Louis "Weenie" Miller (Richmond '47) 64..............	1	0	1	0	0	0	0	0
Bill Blair (Va. Military '64) 76RR......................	1	2	1	0	0	0	0	1
Charlie Schmaus (Va. Military '66) 77..................	1	1	1	0	0	0	0	0
TOTAL	3	3	3	0	0	0	0	1
VIRGINIA TECH								
Howard Shannon (Kansas St. '48) 67RR..............	1	2	1	0	0	0	0	1
Don DeVoe (Ohio St. '64) 76..........................	1	0	1	0	0	0	0	0
Charles Moir (Appalachian St. '52) 79, 80, 85, 86.......	4	2	4	0	0	0	0	0
TOTAL	6	4	6	0	0	0	0	1
WAKE FOREST								
Murray Greason (Wake Forest '26) 39RR, 53...........	2	1	2	0	0	0	0	1
Horace "Bones" McKinney (North Caro. '46) 61RR, 62-3d..	2	6	2	0	0	1	0	1
Carl Tacy (Davis & Elkins '56) 77RR, 81, 82, 84RR......	4	5	4	0	0	0	0	2
Dave Odom (Guilford '65) 91, 92......................	2	1	2	0	0	0	0	0
TOTAL	10	13	10	0	0	1	0	4
WASHINGTON								
Clarence "Hec" Edmundson (Idaho '09) 43RR.........	1	0	2	0	0	0	0	1
Art McLarney (Washington St. '32) 48RR..............	1	1	1	0	0	0	0	1
William H. H. "Tippy" Dye (Ohio St. '37) 51RR, 53-3d...	2	5	2	0	0	1	0	1
Marv Harshman (Pacific Lutheran '42) 76, 84, 85.......	3	2	3	0	0	0	0	0
Andy Russo (Lake Forest '70) 86......................	1	0	1	0	0	0	0	0
TOTAL	8	8	9	0	0	1	0	3
WASHINGTON ST.								
Jack Friel (Washington St. '23) 41-2d..................	1	2	1	0	1	0	0	0
George Raveling (Villanova '60) 80, 83.................	2	1	2	0	0	0	0	0
TOTAL	3	3	3	0	1	0	0	0
WAYNE ST. (MICH.)								
Joel Mason (Western Mich. '36) 56....................	1	1	2	0	0	0	0	0
TOTAL	1	1	2	0	0	0	0	0
WEBER ST.								
Dick Motta (Utah St. '53) 68..........................	1	0	1	0	0	0	0	0
Phil Johnson (Utah St. '53) 69, 70, 71.................	3	2	3	0	0	0	0	0
Gene Visscher (Weber St. '66) 72, 73..................	2	1	3	0	0	0	0	0
Neil McCarthy (Cal St. Sacramento '65) 78, 79, 80, 83..	4	1	4	0	0	0	0	0
TOTAL	10	4	11	0	0	0	0	0
WEST TEX. ST.								
W. A. "Gus" Miller (West Tex. St. '27) 55..............	1	0	1	0	0	0	0	0
TOTAL	1	0	1	0	0	0	0	0

	Yrs.	Won	Lost	CH	2d	3d%	4th	RR
WEST VA.								
Fred Schaus (West Va. '49) 55, 56, 57, 58, 59-2d, 60.....	6	6	6	0	1	0	0	0
George King [Charleston (W. Va.) '50] 62, 63, 65.......	3	2	3	0	0	0	0	0
Raymond "Bucky" Waters (North Caro. St. '57) 67......	1	0	1	0	0	0	0	0
Gale Catlett (West Va. '63) 82, 83, 84, 86, 87, 89, 92.....	7	3	7	0	0	0	0	0
TOTAL	17	11	17	0	1	0	0	0
WESTERN KY.*								
Ed Diddle (Centre '21) 40RR, 60, 62....................	3	3	4	0	0	0	0	1
Johnny Oldham (Western Ky. '48) 66, 67, 70, 71-3d....	4	6	4	0	0	1	0	0
Jim Richards (Western Ky. '59) 76, 78.................	2	1	2	0	0	0	0	0
Gene Keady (Kansas St. '58) 80.......................	1	0	1	0	0	0	0	0
Clem Haskins (Western Ky. '67) 81, 86...............	2	1	2	0	0	0	0	0
Murray Arnold (American '60) 87.....................	1	1	1	0	0	0	0	0
TOTAL	13	12	14	0	0	1	0	1
WESTERN MICH.								
Eldon Miller (Wittenberg '61) 76......................	1	1	1	0	0	0	0	0
TOTAL	1	1	1	0	0	0	0	0
WICHITA ST.								
Ralph Miller (Kansas '42) 64RR......................	1	1	1	0	0	0	0	1
Gary Thompson (Wichita St. '54) 65-4th..............	1	2	2	0	0	0	1	0
Harry Miller (Eastern N. Mex. '51) 76................	1	0	1	0	0	0	0	0
Gene Smithson (North Central '61) 81RR, 85..........	2	3	2	0	0	0	0	1
Eddie Fogler (North Caro. '70) 87, 88................	2	0	2	0	0	0	0	0
TOTAL	7	6	8	0	0	0	1	2
WILLIAMS								
Alex Shaw (Michigan '32) 55..........................	1	0	1	0	0	0	0	0
TOTAL	1	0	1	0	0	0	0	0
WISCONSIN								
Harold "Bud" Foster (Wisconsin '30) 41-CH, 47RR.....	2	4	1	1	0	0	0	1
TOTAL	2	4	1	1	0	0	0	1
WIS.-GREEN BAY								
Dick Bennett (Ripon '65) 91...........................	1	0	1	0	0	0	0	0
TOTAL	1	0	1	0	0	0	0	0
WYOMING								
Everett Shelton (Phillips '23) 41RR, 43-CH, 47RR, 48RR, 49RR, 52RR, 53, 58........................	8	4	12	1	0	0	0	5
Bill Strannigan (Wyoming '41) 67.....................	1	0	2	0	0	0	0	0
Jim Brandenburg (Colorado St. '58) 81, 82, 87.........	3	4	3	0	0	0	0	0
Benny Dees (Wyoming '58) 88.........................	1	0	1	0	0	0	0	0
TOTAL	13	8	18	1	0	0	0	5
XAVIER (OHIO)								
Jim McCafferty [Loyola (La.) '42] 61....................	1	0	1	0	0	0	0	0
Bob Staak (Connecticut '71) 83.......................	1	0	1	0	0	0	0	0
Pete Gillen (Fairfield '68) 86, 87, 88, 89, 90, 91.........	6	4	6	0	0	0	0	0
TOTAL	8	4	8	0	0	0	0	0
YALE								
Howard Hobson (Oregon '26) 49RR....................	1	0	2	0	0	0	0	1
Joe Vancisin (Dartmouth '44) 57, 62...................	2	0	2	0	0	0	0	0
TOTAL	3	0	4	0	0	0	0	1

% National third-place games did not start until 1946 and ended in 1981; in other years, two teams tied for third and both listed this column.   RR Regional runner-up, or one victory from Final Four, thus in top eight.

NOTES ON TEAMS AND COACHES:

MICHIGAN: Steve Fisher coached Michigan in the 1989 tournament; Bill Frieder was the coach during the regular season.

MISSOURI: Rich Daly coached Missouri in the 1989 tournament due to Norm Stewart's illness; Missouri credits the entire 1989 season to Stewart.

PRINCETON: J. L. McCandless coached Princeton in the 1961 tournament; Franklin Cappon suffered a heart attack 11 games into the season; Princeton credits the 1961 regular season to Cappon and the postseason to McCandless.

SEATTLE: Clair Markey coached Seattle in the 1963 tournament due to Vince Cazetta's resignation.

TOURNAMENT TRIVIA QUESTION...
What school has made five Final Four appearances without winning it all? Answer: Houston.

*TEAMS WITH VACATED NCAA TOURNAMENT ACTION, YEARS AND RECORDS

Teams	Years	Rec.	Place	Conference
Alabama	1987	2-1		Southeastern
Austin Peay	1973	1-2		Ohio Valley
Florida	1987-88	3-2		Southeastern
Georgia	1985	1-1		Southeastern
Iona	1980	1-1		Metro Atlantic
Kentucky	1988	2-1		Southeastern
Long Beach St.	1971-72-73	6-3	2RR	Big West
Loyola (Cal.)	1980	0-1		West Coast
Marshall	1987	0-1		Southern
Maryland	1988	1-1		Atlantic Coast
Memphis St.	1982-83-84-85-86	9-5	3rd	Metro
Minnesota	1972	1-1		Big Ten
North Caro. St.	1987-88	0-2		Atlantic Coast
Oregon St.	1980-81-82	2-3		Pacific-10
St. Joseph's (Pa.)	1961	3-1	3rd	Atlantic 10
Southwestern La.	1972-73	3-3		Independent
UCLA	1980	5-1	2nd	Pacific-10
Villanova	1971	4-1	2nd	Big East
Western Ky.	1971	4-1	3rd	Sun Belt
19 teams	30 years	48-32	2 2nd, 3 3rd, 2RR	

Official NCAA Records:	Yrs.	Won	Lost	CH	2d	3d	4th	RR
Alabama	11	11	11	0	0	0	0	0
Austin Peay	2	1	2	0	0	0	0	0
Florida	1	0	1	0	0	0	0	0
Georgia	4	3	4	0	0	1	0	0
Iona	3	0	3	0	0	0	0	0
Kentucky	33	56	30	5	2	2	0	13
Long Beach St.	2	1	3	0	0	0	0	0
Loyola (Cal.)	4	5	4	0	0	0	0	0
Marshall	4	0	4	0	0	0	0	0
Maryland	9	12	9	0	0	0	0	2
Memphis St.	8	7	8	0	1	0	0	1
Minnesota	3	6	3	0	0	0	0	1
North Caro. St.	15	27	14	2	0	1	0	2
Oregon St.	13	10	16	0	0	0	2	3
St. Joseph's (Pa.)	13	9	17	0	0	0	0	2
Southwestern La.	3	1	3	0	0	0	0	0
UCLA	27	62	21	10	0	2	1	2
Villanova	20	31	20	1	0	1	0	6
Western Ky.	12	8	13	0	0	0	0	0

TOURNAMENT TRIVIA QUESTION...
Who was the last player to be named the tournament's most outstanding player and not come from the championship team? Answer: Akeem Olajuwon in 1983 from Houston, which finished second.

THE
COACHES

Twenty years ago, John Wooden and the UCLA Bruins won their record seventh consecutive NCAA championship. Wooden's 10 championships, 12 Final Four appearances and 21 Final Four wins are tournament records. The Bruins won 10 titles in 12 years between 1964 and 1975.

COACHES AND FINAL SEASON
WON-LOST RECORDS OF CHAMPIONS

Year	Champion	Coach	W-L	Pct.
1939	Oregon	Howard Hobson	29- 5	.853
1940	Indiana	Branch McCracken	21- 3	.875
1941	Wisconsin	Harold Foster	20- 3	.870
1942	Stanford	Everett Dean	27- 4	.871
1943	Wyoming	Everett Shelton	31- 2	.939
1944	Utah	Vadal Peterson	22- 4	.846
1945	Oklahoma St.	Henry Iba	27- 4	.871
1946	Oklahoma St.	Henry Iba	31- 2	.939
1947	Holy Cross	Doggie Julian	27- 3	.900
1948	Kentucky	Adolph Rupp	36- 3	.923
1949	Kentucky	Adolph Rupp	32- 2	.941
1950	CCNY	Nat Holman	24- 5	.828
1951	Kentucky	Adolph Rupp	32- 2	.941
1952	Kansas	Phog Allen	26- 2	.929
1953	Indiana	Branch McCracken	23- 3	.885
1954	La Salle	Ken Loeffler	26- 4	.867
1955	San Francisco	Phil Woolpert	28- 1	.966
1956	San Francisco	Phil Woolpert	29- 0	1.000
1957	North Caro.	Frank McGuire	32- 0	1.000
1958	Kentucky	Adolph Rupp	23- 6	.793
1959	California	Pete Newell	25- 4	.862
1960	Ohio St.	Fred Taylor	25- 3	.893
1961	Cincinnati	Ed Jucker	27- 3	.900
1962	Cincinnati	Ed Jucker	29- 2	.935
1963	Loyola (Ill.)	George Ireland	29- 2	.935
1964	UCLA	John Wooden	30- 0	1.000
1965	UCLA	John Wooden	28- 2	.933
1966	UTEP	Don Haskins	28- 1	.966
1967	UCLA	John Wooden	30- 0	1.000
1968	UCLA	John Wooden	29- 1	.967
1969	UCLA	John Wooden	29- 1	.967
1970	UCLA	John Wooden	28- 1	.966
1971	UCLA	John Wooden	29- 1	.967
1972	UCLA	John Wooden	30- 0	1.000
1973	UCLA	John Wooden	30- 0	1.000
1974	North Caro. St.	Norm Sloan	30- 1	.968
1975	UCLA	John Wooden	28- 3	.903
1976	Indiana	Bob Knight	32- 0	1.000
1977	Marquette	Al McGuire	25- 7	.781
1978	Kentucky	Joe Hall	30- 2	.938
1979	Michigan St.	Jud Heathcote	26- 6	.813
1980	Louisville	Denny Crum	33- 3	.917
1981	Indiana	Bob Knight	26- 9	.743
1982	North Caro.	Dean Smith	32- 2	.941
1983	North Caro. St.	Jim Valvano	26-10	.722
1984	Georgetown	John Thompson	34- 3	.919
1985	Villanova	Rollie Massimino	25-10	.714
1986	Louisville	Denny Crum	32- 7	.821
1987	Indiana	Bob Knight	30- 4	.882
1988	Kansas	Larry Brown	27-11	.711
1989	Michigan	Steve Fisher	30- 7	.811
1990	Nevada-Las Vegas	Jerry Tarkanian	35- 5	.875
1991	Duke	Mike Krzyzewski	32- 7	.821
1992	Duke	Mike Krzyzewski	35- 2	.946

TOURNAMENT TRIVIA QUESTION...
Name the only three active coaches who have won more than one NCAA championship? Answer: Bob Knight, Indiana (three); Denny Crum, Louisville (two), and Mike Krzyzewski, Duke (two).

FINAL FOUR RECORDS FOR COACHES

Most NCAA Championships
10, John Wooden, UCLA, 1962-75
4, Adolph Rupp, Kentucky, 1942-66
3, Bob Knight, Indiana, 1973-87
2, Denny Crum, Louisville, 1972-86
2, Henry Iba, Oklahoma St., 1945-51
2, Ed Jucker, Cincinnati, 1961-63
2, Mike Krzyzewski, Duke, 1991-92
2, Branch McCracken, Indiana, 1940-53
2, Phil Woolpert, San Francisco, 1955-57
1, 25 tied

Most Final Four Appearances
12, John Wooden, UCLA, 1962-75
8, Dean Smith, North Caro., 1967-91
6, Denny Crum, Louisville, 1972-86
6, Mike Krzyzewski, Duke, 1986-92
6, Adolph Rupp, Kentucky, 1942-66
5, Bob Knight, Indiana, 1973-92
5, Guy Lewis, Houston, 1967-84
4, Jack Gardner, Kansas St. and Utah, 1948-66
4, Henry Iba, Oklahoma St., 1945-51
4, Harold Olsen, Ohio St., 1939-46
4, Jerry Tarkanian, Nevada-Las Vegas, 1977-91
4, Fred Taylor, Ohio St., 1960-68

Most Consecutive Final Four Appearances
9, John Wooden, UCLA, 1967-75
5, Mike Krzyzewski, Duke, 1988-92
3, Ed Jucker, Cincinnati, 1961-63
3, Guy Lewis, Houston, 1982-84
3, Harold Olsen, Ohio St., 1944-46
3, Dean Smith, North Caro., 1967-69
3, Fred Taylor, Ohio St., 1960-62

3, Phil Woolpert, San Francisco, 1955-57
2, 16 tied

Most Final Four Wins
21, John Wooden, UCLA, 1962-75
9, Adolph Rupp, Kentucky, 1942-66
7, Bob Knight, Indiana, 1973-87
6, Mike Krzyzewski, Duke, 1988-92
6, Dean Smith, North Caro., 1967-91
5, Denny Crum, Louisville, 1972-91
5, Henry Iba, Oklahoma St., 1945-51
5, Ed Jucker, Cincinnati, 1961-63
5, Fred Taylor, Ohio St., 1960-68
5, Phil Woolpert, San Francisco, 1955-57
4, Phog Allen, Kansas, 1940-53
4, Branch McCracken, Indiana, 1940-53
4, John Thompson, Georgetown, 1982-85

**Highest Final Four Winning Percentage
(minimum 3 games)**
100.0% (4-0), Branch McCracken, Indiana, 1940-53
87.5% (21-3), John Wooden, UCLA, 1962-75
83.3% (5-1), Ed Jucker, Cincinnati, 1961-63
83.3% (5-1), Phil Woolpert, San Francisco, 1955-57
81.8% (9-2), Adolph Rupp, Kentucky, 1942-66
77.8% (7-2), Bob Knight, Indiana, 1973-92
75.0% (3-1), Doggie Julian, Holy Cross, 1947-48
75.0% (3-1), Ken Loeffler, La Salle, 1954-55
75.0% (3-1), Al McGuire, Marquette, 1974-77
75.0% (3-1), Frank McGuire, St. John's (N.Y.) and North Caro., 1952-57
75.0% (3-1), Pete Newell, California, 1959-60

TOURNAMENT RECORDS FOR COACHES

Most Tournament Appearances
22, Dean Smith, North Caro., 1967-92
20, Adolph Rupp, Kentucky, 1942-72
18, Lou Carnesecca, St. John's (N.Y.), 1967-92
16, Denny Crum, Louisville, 1972-92
16, Bob Knight, Indiana, 1973-92
16, John Thompson, Georgetown, 1975-92
16, John Wooden, UCLA, 1950-75
15, Lou Henson, New Mexico St. and Illinois, 1967-90
15, Digger Phelps, Fordham and Notre Dame, 1971-90
15, Eddie Sutton, Creighton, Arkansas, Kentucky and Oklahoma St., 1974-92

Most Consecutive Tournament Appearances
18, Dean Smith, North Caro., 1975-92
14, John Thompson, Georgetown, 1979-92
12, Eddie Sutton, Arkansas and Kentucky, 1977-88
10, Jim Boeheim, Syracuse, 1983-92
9, Dale Brown, Louisiana St., 1984-92
9, Mike Krzyzewski, Duke, 1984-92
9, Jerry Tarkanian, Nevada-Las Vegas, 1983-91
9, John Wooden, UCLA, 1967-75
8, Bobby Cremins, Georgia Tech, 1985-92
8, Denny Crum, Louisville, 1977-84
8, Lou Henson, Illinois, 1983-90
8, Lute Olson, Arizona, 1985-92
8, Digger Phelps, Notre Dame, 1974-81
8, Billy Tubbs, Oklahoma, 1983-90

Most Tournament Wins
49, Dean Smith, North Caro., 1967-92
47, John Wooden, UCLA, 1950-75
35, Bob Knight, Indiana, 1973-92
33, Denny Crum, Louisville, 1972-92
33, Mike Krzyzewski, Duke, 1984-92
31, Jerry Tarkanian, Long Beach St. and Nevada-Las Vegas, 1970-91
30, Adolph Rupp, Kentucky, 1942-72
28, John Thompson, Georgetown, 1975-92
26, Guy Lewis, Houston, 1961-84
21, Eddie Sutton, Creighton, Arkansas, Kentucky and Oklahoma St., 1974-92
20, Joe Hall, Kentucky, 1973-85
20, Rollie Massimino, Villanova, 1978-91
20, Al McGuire, Marquette, 1968-77

**Highest Tournament Winning Percentage
(minimum 10 games)**
91.7% (11-1), Ed Jucker, Cincinnati, 1961-63
90.0% (9-1), Ken Loeffler, La Salle, 1954-55
86.7% (13-2), Phil Woolpert, San Francisco, 1955-57
85.7% (12-2), Steve Fisher, Michigan, 1989-92
82.5% (33-7), Mike Krzyzewski, Duke, 1984-92
82.5% (47-10), John Wooden, UCLA, 1950-75
81.8% (9-2), Branch McCracken, Indiana, 1940-58
77.8% (14-4), Fred Taylor, Ohio St., 1960-71
76.9% (10-3), Phog Allen, Kansas, 1940-53
76.9% (10-3), Pete Newell, California, 1957-60

TOURNAMENT RECORDS FOR ACTIVE COACHES

Most Tournament Appearances
22, Dean Smith, North Caro., 1967-92
16, Denny Crum, Louisville, 1972-92
16, Bob Knight, Indiana, 1973-92
16, John Thompson, Georgetown, 1975-92
15, Lou Henson, New Mexico St. and Illinois, 1967-90
15, Eddie Sutton, Creighton, Arkansas, Kentucky and Oklahoma St., 1974-92
14, Jim Boeheim, Syracuse, 1977-92
14, Don Haskins, UTEP, 1963-92
13, Lute Olson, Iowa and Arizona, 1980-92
12, Dale Brown, Louisiana St., 1979-92
12, Norm Stewart, Missouri, 1976-92

Most Consecutive Tournament Appearances
18, Dean Smith, North Caro., 1975-92
14, John Thompson, Georgetown, 1979-92
12, Eddie Sutton, Arkansas and Kentucky, 1977-88
10, Jim Boeheim, Syracuse, 1983-92
9, Dale Brown, Louisiana St., 1984-92
9, Mike Krzyzewski, Duke, 1984-92
8, Bobby Cremins, Georgia Tech, 1985-92
8, Denny Crum, Louisville, 1977-84
8, Lou Henson, Illinois, 1983-90
8, Lute Olson, Arizona, 1985-92
8, Billy Tubbs, Oklahoma, 1983-90

Current Most Consecutive Tournament Appearances
18, Dean Smith, North Caro., 1975-92
14, John Thompson, Georgetown, 1979-92
10, Jim Boeheim, Syracuse, 1983-92
9, Dale Brown, Louisiana St., 1984-92
9, Mike Krzyzewski, Duke, 1984-92
8, Bobby Cremins, Georgia Tech, 1985-92
8, Lute Olson, Arizona, 1985-92

7, Bob Knight, Indiana, 1986-92
5, Tom Penders, Rhode Island and Texas, 1988-92
5, Nolan Richardson, Arkansas, 1988-92

Most Tournament Wins
49, Dean Smith, North Caro., 1967-92
35, Bob Knight, Indiana, 1973-92
33, Denny Crum, Louisville, 1972-92
33, Mike Krzyzewski, Duke, 1984-92
28, John Thompson, Georgetown, 1975-92
21, Eddie Sutton, Creighton, Arkansas, Kentucky and Oklahoma St., 1974-92
20, Rollie Massimino, Villanova, 1978-91
19, Jim Boeheim, Syracuse, 1976-92
18, Lou Henson, New Mexico St. and Illinois, 1967-90
18, Billy Tubbs, Lamar and Oklahoma, 1979-92

Highest Tournament Winning Percentage (minimum 10 games)
85.7% (12-2), Steve Fisher, Michigan, 1989-92
82.5% (33-7), Mike Krzyzewski, Duke, 1984-92
73.3% (11-4), P. J. Carlesimo, Seton Hall, 1988-92
72.9% (35-13), Bob Knight, Indiana, 1973-92
70.0% (7-3), Rick Pitino, Boston U., Providence and Kentucky, 1983-92
68.1% (49-23), Dean Smith, North Caro., 1967-92
67.3% (33-16), Denny Crum, Louisville, 1972-92
66.7% (20-10), Rollie Massimino, Villanova, 1978-91
65.0% (13-7), Tom Davis, Boston College and Iowa, 1981-92
65.1% (28-15), John Thompson, Georgetown, 1975-92

COACHES WHO HAVE TAKEN TWO DIFFERENT SCHOOLS TO THE NCAA FINAL FOUR (NINE)

Coach	First School	Second School
Forddy Anderson	Bradley	Michigan St.
†Gene Bartow	Memphis St.	UCLA
Larry Brown	UCLA	Kansas
†Hugh Durham	Florida St.	Georgia
Jack Gardner	Kansas St.	Utah
†Lou Henson	New Mexico St.	Illinois
Frank McGuire	St. John's (N.Y.)	North Caro.
†Lute Olson	Iowa	Arizona
Lee Rose	N.C.-Charlotte	Purdue

COACHES WHO HAVE TAKEN FOUR DIFFERENT SCHOOLS TO THE NCAA TOURNAMENT (ONE)

Coach	First School	Second School	Third School	Fourth School
†Eddie Sutton	Creighton	Arkansas	Kentucky	Oklahoma St.

COACHES WHO HAVE TAKEN THREE DIFFERENT SCHOOLS TO THE NCAA TOURNAMENT (NINE)

Coach	First School	Second School	Third School
†Gene Bartow	Memphis St.	UCLA	Ala.-Birmingham
†Dave Bliss	Oklahoma	Southern Methodist	New Mexico
Eddie Hickey	Creighton	St. Louis	Marquette
Frank McGuire	St. John's (N.Y.)	North Caro.	South Caro.
†Eldon Miller	Western Mich.	Ohio St.	Northern Iowa
Ralph Miller	Wichita St.	Iowa	Oregon St.
†Rick Pitino	Boston U.	Providence	Kentucky
†George Raveling	Washington St.	Iowa	Southern Cal
Joe Williams	Jacksonville	Furman	Florida St.

COACHES WHO HAVE TAKEN TWO DIFFERENT
SCHOOLS TO THE NCAA TOURNAMENT (81)

Coach	First School	Second School
Ladell Andersen	Utah St.	Brigham Young
Forddy Anderson	Bradley	Michigan St.
Murray Arnold	Tenn.-Chatt.	Western Ky.
†J. D. Barnett	Va. Commonwealth	Tulsa
Steve Belko	Idaho St.	Oregon
Bob Boyd	Seattle	Southern Cal
Harold Bradley	Duke	Texas
Buster Brannon	Rice	Texas Christian
Larry Brown	UCLA	Kansas
†Jim Calhoun	Northeastern	Connecticut
†Lou Campanelli	James Madison	California
Ben Carnevale	North Caro.	Navy
†Gale Catlett	Cincinnati	West Va.
Ozzie Cowles	Dartmouth	Michigan
†Bobby Cremins	Appalachian St.	Georgia Tech
†Tom Davis	Boston College	Iowa
†Benny Dees	New Orleans	Wyoming
†Don DeVoe	Virginia Tech	Tennessee
†Lefty Driesell	Davidson	Maryland
†Hugh Durham	Florida St.	Georgia
†Bob Dye	Cal St. Fullerton	Boise St.
Tippy Dye	Ohio St.	Washington
†Cliff Ellis	South Ala.	Clemson
†Paul Evans	Navy	Pittsburgh
†Eddie Fogler	Wichita St.	Vanderbilt
†Pat Foster	Lamar	Houston
†Bill Frieder	Michigan	Arizona St.
Matt Furjanic	Robert Morris	Marist
Smokey Gaines	Detroit Mercy	San Diego St.
Jack Gardner	Kansas St.	Utah
Boyd Grant	Fresno St.	Colorado St.
Jim Harding	Loyola (La.)	La Salle
†Jim Harrick	Pepperdine	UCLA
†Clem Haskins	Western Ky.	Minnesota
†Jud Heathcote	Montana	Michigan St.
†Lou Henson	New Mexico St.	Illinois
Howard Hobson	Oregon	Yale
Terry Holland	Davidson	Virginia
†Bob Huggins	Akron	Cincinnati
†Gene Iba	Houston Baptist	Baylor
Doggie Julian	Holy Cross	Dartmouth
†Gene Keady	Western Ky.	Purdue
†Pat Kennedy	Iona	Florida St.
Jim Killingsworth	Idaho St.	Texas Christian
George King	West Va.	Purdue
Jack Kraft	Villanova	Rhode Island
Eugene Lambert	Arkansas	Memphis St.
Abe Lemons	Oklahoma City	Texas
†Tates Locke	Miami (Ohio)	Jacksonville
†Rick Majerus	Ball St.	Utah
Jim McCafferty	Loyola (La.)	Xavier (Ohio)
†Neil McCarthy	Weber St.	New Mexico St.
†Stan Morrison	Pacific (Cal.)	Southern Cal
†Danny Nee	Ohio	Nebraska
C. M. Newton	Alabama	Vanderbilt
Johnny Oldham	Tennessee Tech	Western Ky.
†Lute Olson	Iowa	Arizona
†Johnny Orr	Michigan	Iowa St.
†Bobby Paschal	Southwestern La.	South Fla.
†Tom Penders	Rhode Island	Texas
Digger Phelps	Fordham	Notre Dame
†Jerry Pimm	Utah	UC Santa Barb.
†Nolan Richardson	Tulsa	Arkansas
†Les Robinson	East Tenn. St.	North Caro. St.
Lee Rose	N.C.-Charlotte	Purdue
Lou Rossini	Columbia	New York U.
Andy Russo	Louisiana Tech	Washington
Fred Schaus	West Va.	Purdue

Coach	First School	Second School
†Tom Schneider	Lehigh	Pennsylvania
Norm Sloan	North Caro. St.	Florida
Bill Strannigan	Colorado St.	Wyoming
Carl Tacy	Marshall	Wake Forest
Jerry Tarkanian	Long Beach St.	Nevada-Las Vegas
†Billy Tubbs	Lamar	Oklahoma
Jim Valvano	Iona	North Caro. St.
Bob Vanatta	Bradley	Memphis St.
†Bob Wenzel	Jacksonville	Rutgers
Paul Westhead	La Salle	Loyola (Cal.)
†Gary Williams	Boston College	Ohio St.
Tom Young	Rutgers	Old Dominion
Matt Zunic	Boston U.	Massachusetts

† Active.

BOTH PLAYED AND COACHED IN FINAL FOUR (FIVE)

	Player—Final Four Appearances	Coach
Vic Bubas	North Caro. St.: 50-3d	Duke: 63-3d, 64-2d, 66-3d
Dick Harp	Kansas: 40-2d	Kansas: 57-2d
Bob Knight	Ohio St.: 60-CH, 61-2d, 62-2d	Indiana: 73-3d, 76-CH, 81-CH, 87-CH
Bones McKinney	North Caro.: 46-2d	Wake Forest: 62-3d
Dean Smith	Kansas: 52-CH, 53-2d	North Caro.: 67-4th, 68-2d, 69-4th, 72-3d, 77-2d, 81-2d, 82-CH, 91-tie 3d

BOTH PLAYED AND COACHED IN TOURNAMENT (78)

NCAA Coach	Played in NCAA Team-Years	G	FG-FGA	FT-FTA	RB	Pts.	Team W-L+	Finish
Stan Albeck	Bradley 55	3	13	15		41	2-1	55-RR
Tom Apke	Creighton 64	3	0- 6	0- 1	9	0	1-2	
Frank Arnold	Idaho St. 55	1	0	0	0	0	0-1	
Tom Asbury	Wyoming 67	2	11- 28	4- 7	16	26	0-2	
Randy Ayers	Miami (Ohio) 78	2	16- 24	6- 7	18	38	1-1	
Tony Barone	Duke 66	2	1- 2	0- 0	1	2	1-1	66-3d
Butch Beard	Louisville 67, 68	4	31- 68	11-20	27	73	1-3	
Dan Belluomini	San Francisco 64	1	0- 0	0- 0	1	0	0-1	
Bob Bender	Indiana 76, Duke 78, 80	10	9- 22	17-24	12	35	8-2	76-CH, 78-2d, 80-RR
Bill Blair	Va. Military 64	1	6- 20	8-12	4	20	0-1	
Jim Boeheim	Syracuse 66	2	13- 19	3- 4	4	29	1-1	66-RR
Jim Boyle	St. Joseph's (Pa.) 62, 63	5	26- 60	16-19	35	68	2-3	63-RR
Jim Brovelli	San Francisco 63, 64	4	16- 30	7- 8	9	39	2-2	64-RR
Vic Bubas	North Caro. St. 50	3	4- 12	6- 8		14	2-1	50-3d
Morris Buckwalter	Utah 55, 56	4	8	19		35	2-2	56-RR
Mitch Buonaguro	Boston College 75	1	2- 2	0- 1	1	4	0-1	
P. J. Carlesimo	Fordham 71	3	0- 0	0- 0	0	0	2-1	
Gale Catlett	West Va. 62, 63	4	11- 29	4- 5	11	26	2-2	
Bus Connor	Idaho St. 53, 54, 55	5	15	20		50	2-3	
Bob Cousy	Holy Cross 47, 48	6	17	12		46	5-1	47-CH, 48-3d
Jim Crews	Indiana 73, 75, 76	8	13- 30	4- 6	15	30	7-1	73-3d, 75-RR, 76-CH
Gary Cunningham	UCLA 62	4	26- 58	17-19	38	69	2-2	62-4th
Howie Dallmar	Stanford 42	3	11	4- 6		26	3-0	42-CH
Don Donoher	Dayton 52	2	2	1		5	1-1	
Jarrett Durham	Duquesne 69, 71	4	29- 49	16-21	22	74	2-2	
Hank Egan	Navy 59, 60	3	4- 9	2- 4	3	10	1-2	
John Egli	Penn St. 42	2	6	4- 6		16	1-1	
Lefty Ervin	La Salle 68	1	1- 2	0- 0	0	2	0-1	
Larry Farmer	UCLA 71, 72, 73	11	36- 84	11-20	43	83	11-0	71, 72 & 73-CH
Larry Finch	Memphis St. 73	4	34- 64	39-44	10	107	3-1	73-2d
Eddie Fogler	North Caro. 68, 69	8	15- 41	7-11	9	37	5-3	68-2d, 69-4th
Dave Gavitt	Dartmouth 58, 59	4	5- 19	1- 2	12	11	2-2	58-RR
Elmer Gross	Penn St. 42	2	3	7- 9		13	1-1	
Dick Harp	Kansas 40	3	11	5- 8		27	2-1	40-2d
Clem Haskins	Western Ky. 66, 67	4	26- 65	16-23	45	68	2-2	
Don Haskins	Oklahoma St. 53	1	0	0		0	1-1	53-RR
Walt Hazzard	UCLA 62, 63, 64	10	57-123	48-61	57	162	6-4	62-4th, 64-CH
Darrell Hedric	Miami (Ohio) 53, 55	2	2	0		4	0-2	
Jeff Jones	Virginia 81, 82	7	27- 46	15-19	16	69	5-2	81-3d
Bob Knight	Ohio St. 60, 61, 62	11	14- 36	2- 3	14	30	9-2	60-CH, 61 & 62-2d
Don Knodell	Miami (Ohio) 53	1	4	1		9	0-1	
Lon Kruger	Kansas St. 72, 73	4	19- 40	18-22	21	56	2-2	

NCAA Coach	Played in NCAA Team-Years	G	FG-FGA	FT-FTA	RB	Pts.	Team W-L+	Finish
Craig Littlepage	Pennsylvania 71, 72, 73	9	10- 24	12-21	26	32	5-4	71-RR, 72-RR
Jim Lynam	St. Joseph's (Pa.) 62, 63	5	25- 44	13-20	13	63	2-3	63-RR
Fran McCaffery	Pennsylvania 82	1	1- 4	0- 1	0	2	0-1	
Al McGuire	St. John's (N.Y.) 51	3	6- 15	9-17	12	21	2-1	51-RR
Bones McKinney	North Caro. 46	3	10	5-10		25	2-1	46-2d
Ralph Miller	Kansas 40, 42	5	11	12-23		34	3-2	40-2d
Stan Morrison	California 60	3	2	1		5	2-1	60-2d
Joe Mullaney	Holy Cross 47, 48	6	14	4		32	5-1	47-CH, 48-3d
Jeff Mullins	Duke 63, 64	8	84-156	32-40	63	200	6-2	63-3d, 64-2d
Frank Mulzoff	St. John's (N.Y.) 51	3	2- 15	2- 2	9	6	2-1	51-RR
C. M. Newton	Kentucky 51	2	0- 0	0- 0	0	0	2-0	51-CH
Jim O'Brien	St. Joseph's (Pa.) 73, 74	2	4- 15	2- 3	3	10	0-2	
Doyle Parrack	Oklahoma St. 45	3	12	2		26	3-0	45-CH
Jerry Peirson	Miami (Ohio) 66	1	4- 7	1- 2	4	9	0-1	
Tom Penders	Connecticut 65, 67	2	4- 9	3- 6	4	11	0-2	
Dom Perno	Connecticut 63, 64	4	10- 44	13-19	11	33	2-2	64-RR
Jerry Pimm	Southern Cal 60	1	6- 20	4- 5	7	16	0-1	
Roger Reid	Weber St. 68	1	2- 4	0- 0	1	4	0-1	
Nolan Richardson	UTEP 63	1	2- 7	0- 1	2	4	0-1	
Red Rocha	Oregon St. 47	2	8	5		21	1-1	
Jack Rohan	Columbia 51	1	0- 1	0- 0	0	0	0-1	
Jim Satalin	St. Bonaventure 68	3	9- 35	6- 7	11	24	1-2	
Charlie Schmaus	Va. Military 64	1	2- 7	1- 1	5	5	0-1	
Howard Shannon	Kansas St. 48	3	11	15		37	1-2	48-4th
Dean Smith	Kansas 52, 53	7	1	2		4	6-1	52-CH, 53-2d
Bill Strannigan	Wyoming 41	2	11	2- 5		24	0-2	
Gene Sullivan	Notre Dame 53	3	3	2		8	2-1	53-RR
Eddie Sutton	Oklahoma St. 58	3	8- 13	4- 4	11	20	2-1	58-RR
Johnny Swaim	Texas Christian 52, 53	4	8	3		19	2-2	
Fred Taylor	Ohio St. 50	2	9- 26	0- 3		18	1-1	
John Thompson	Providence 64	1	7- 13	4- 8	3	18	0-1	
Joe Vancisin	Dartmouth 44	3	5	0- 0		10	2-1	44-2d
Sox Walseth	Colorado 46	2	7	4- 4		18	1-1	
Paul Westhead	St. Joseph's (Pa.) 60, 61	5	3- 15	4- 6	11	10	2-3	61-3d*
Richard Williams	Mississippi St. 63	1	0- 5	1- 2	6	1	1-0	
Tom Young	Maryland 58	3	9	20		38	2-1	

+ W-L for games he played in only (blanks above mean those figures were not listed in available box scores).
* Record later vacated.

TOURNAMENT TRIVIA QUESTION...
Name the six coaches to earn a trip to the Final Four in their first season? Answer: Ray Meyer (DePaul 1943), Gary Thompson (Wichita State 1965), Denny Crum (Louisville 1972), Bill Hodges (Indiana State 1979), Larry Brown (UCLA 1980) and Steve Fisher (Michigan 1989).

FINAL FOUR COACHES OF ALL TIME (117)

Coach	Tournament Team: Year-Finish	W-L	Pct.
12 Times			
John Wooden	UCLA: 62-4th, 64-CH, 65-CH, 67-CH, 68-CH, 69-CH, 70-CH, 71-CH, 72-CH, 73-CH, 74-3d, 75-CH	21-3	.875
8 Times			
+Dean Smith	North Caro.: 67-4th, 68-2d, 69-4th, 72-3d, 77-2d, 81-2d, 82-CH, 91-T3d	6-9	.400
6 Times			
+Denny Crum	Louisville: 72-4th, 75-3d, 80-CH, 82-T3d, 83-T3d, 86-CH	5-5	.500
+Mike Krzyzewski	Duke: 86-2d, 88-T3d, 89-T3d, 90-2d, 91-CH, 92-CH	6-4	.600
Adolph Rupp	Kentucky: 42-T3d, 48-CH, 49-CH, 51-CH, 58-CH, 66-2d	9-2	.818
5 Times			
+Bob Knight	Indiana: 73-3d, 76-CH, 81-CH, 87-CH, 92-T3d	7-2	.778
Guy Lewis	Houston: 67-3d, 68-4th, 82-T3d, 83-2d, 84-2d	3-6	.333
4 Times			
Jack Gardner	Kansas St.: 48-4th, 51-2d; Utah: 61-4th, 66-4th	1-7	.125
Henry Iba	Oklahoma St.: 45-CH, 46-CH, 49-2d, 51-4th	5-3	.625
Harold Olsen	Ohio St.: 39-2d, 44-T3d, 45-T3d, 46-3d	2-4	.333
Jerry Tarkanian	Nevada-Las Vegas: 77-3d, 87-T3d, 90-CH, 91-T3d	3-3	.500
Fred Taylor	Ohio St.: 60-CH, 61-2d, 62-2d, 68-3d	5-3	.625
3 Times			
Phog Allen	Kansas: 40-2d, 52-CH, 53-2d	4-3	.571
Forddy Anderson	Bradley: 50-2d, 54-2d; Michigan St.: 57-4th	2-4	.333
Larry Brown	*UCLA: 80-2d; Kansas: 86-T3d, 88-CH	3-2	.600
Vic Bubas	Duke: 63-3d, 64-2d, 66-3d	3-3	.500
Harry Combes	Illinois: 49-3d, 51-3d, 52-3d	3-3	.500
Joe Hall	Kentucky: 75-2d, 78-CH, 84-T3d	3-2	.600
Ed Jucker	Cincinnati: 61-CH, 62-CH, 63-2d	5-1	.833
+John Thompson	Georgetown: 82-2d, 84-CH, 85-2d	4-2	.667
Phil Woolpert	San Francisco: 55-CH, 56-CH, 57-3d	5-1	.833
2 Times			
+Gene Bartow	Memphis St.: 73-2d; UCLA: 76-3d	2-2	.500
+Dale Brown	Louisiana St.: 81-4th, 86-T3d	0-3	.000
Bruce Drake	Oklahoma: 39-T3d, 47-2d	1-2	.333
+Hugh Durham	Florida St.: 72-2d; Georgia: 83-T3d	1-2	.333
+Steve Fisher	Michigan: 89-CH, 92-2d	3-1	.750
Slats Gill	Oregon St.: 49-4th, 63-4th	0-4	.000
Bill Henderson	Baylor: 48-2d, 50-4th	1-3	.250
+Lou Henson	New Mexico St.: 70-3d; Illinois: 89-T3d	1-2	.333
Terry Holland	Virginia: 81-3d, 84-T3d	1-2	.333
Nat Holman	CCNY: 47-4th, 50-CH	2-2	.500
Doggie Julian	Holy Cross: 47-CH, 48-3d	3-2	.600
Harry Litwack	Temple: 56-3d, 58-3d	2-2	.500
Ken Loeffler	La Salle: 54-CH, 55-2d	3-1	.750
Branch McCracken	Indiana: 40-CH, 53-CH	4-0	1.000
Al McGuire	Marquette: 74-2d, 77-CH	3-2	.600
Frank McGuire	St. John's (N.Y.): 52-2d; North Caro.: 57-CH	3-1	.750
Ray Meyer	DePaul: 43-T3d, 79-3d	1-2	.333
Pete Newell	California: 59-CH, 60-2d	3-1	.750
Bucky O'Connor	Iowa: 55-4th, 56-2d	1-3	.250
+Lute Olson	Iowa: 80-4th; Arizona: 88-T3d	0-3	.000
Ted Owens	Kansas: 71-4th, 74-4th	0-4	.000
Lee Rose	N.C.-Charlotte: 77-4th; Purdue: 80-3d	1-3	.250
George Smith	Cincinnati: 59-3d, 60-3d	2-2	.500
Dave Strack	Michigan: 64-3d, 65-2d	2-2	.500
Tex Winter	Kansas St.: 58-4th, 64-4th	0-4	.000
1 Time			
Sam Barry	Southern Cal: 40-T3d	0-1	.000
+Jim Boeheim	Syracuse: 87-2d	1-1	.500
Earl Brown	Dartmouth: 44-2d	1-1	.500
Howard Cann	New York U.: 45-2d	1-1	.500
+P. J. Carlesimo	Seton Hall: 89-2d	1-1	.500
Harold Carlson	Pittsburgh: 41-T3d	0-1	.000
Lou Carnesecca	St. John's (N.Y.): 85-T3d	0-1	.000
Ben Carnevale	North Caro.: 46-2d	1-1	.500
Everett Case	North Caro. St.: 50-3d	1-1	.500
John Castellani	Seattle: 58-2d	1-1	.500
Ozzie Cowles	Dartmouth: 42-2d	1-1	.500
Frosty Cox	Colorado: 42-T3d	0-1	.000
+Bobby Cremins	Georgia Tech: 90-T3d	0-1	.000
Roy Danforth	Syracuse: 75-4th	0-2	.000
Chick Davies	Duquesne: 40-T3d	0-1	.000
Everett Dean	Stanford: 42-CH	2-0	1.000

Coach 1 Time	Tournament Team: Year-Finish	W-L	Pct.
Don Donoher	Dayton: 67-2d	1-1	.500
Tippy Dye	Washington: 53-3d	1-1	.500
Bob Feerick	Santa Clara: 52-4th	0-2	.000
+Bill E. Foster	Duke: 78-2d	1-1	.500
Bud Foster	Wisconsin: 41-CH	2-0	1.000
Jack Friel	Washington St.: 41-2d	1-1	.500
Dave Gavitt	Providence: 73-4th	0-2	.000
Bully Gilstrap	Texas: 43-T3d	0-1	.000
Jack Gray	Texas: 47-3d	1-1	.500
Elmer Gross	Penn St.: 54-3d	1-1	.500
Dick Harp	Kansas: 57-2d	1-1	.500
+Don Haskins	UTEP: 66-CH	2-0	1.000
Doc Hayes	Southern Methodist: 56-4th	0-2	.000
+Jud Heathcote	Michigan St.: 79-CH	2-0	1.000
Peck Hickman	Louisville: 59-4th	0-2	.000
Howard Hobson	Oregon: 39-CH	2-0	1.000
Bill Hodges	Indiana St.: 79-2d	1-1	.500
+Bob Huggins	Cincinnati: 92-T3d	0-1	.000
George Ireland	Loyola (Ill.): 63-CH	2-0	1.000
Maurice John	Drake: 69-3d	1-1	.500
George King	Purdue: 69-2d	1-1	.500
Dana Kirk	*Memphis St.: 85-T3d	0-1	.000
Jack Kraft	*Villanova: 71-2d	1-1	.500
Eugene Lambert	Arkansas: 45-T3d	0-1	.000
Bebe Lee	Colorado: 55-3d	1-1	.500
+Rollie Massimino	Villanova: 85-CH	2-0	1.000
Bones McKinney	Wake Forest: 62-3d	1-1	.500
Louis Menze	Iowa St.: 44-T3d	0-1	.000
Johnny Oldham	*Western Ky.: 71-3d	1-1	.500
+Johnny Orr	Michigan: 76-2d	1-1	.500
Vadal Peterson	Utah: 44-CH	2-0	1.000
Digger Phelps	Notre Dame: 78-4th	0-2	.000
+Rick Pitino	Providence: 87-T3d	0-1	.000
Nibs Price	California: 46-4th	0-2	.000
Harry Rabenhorst	Louisiana St.: 53-4th	0-2	.000
Jack Ramsay	*St. Joseph's (Pa.): 61-3d	1-1	.500
+Nolan Richardson	Arkansas: 90-T3d	0-1	.000
Elmer Ripley	Georgetown: 43-2d	1-1	.500
Glen Rose	Arkansas: 41-T3d	0-1	.000
Lou Rossini	New York U.: 60-4th	0-2	.000
Fred Schaus	West Va.: 59-2d	1-1	.500
Alex Severance	Villanova: 39-T3d	0-1	.000
Everett Shelton	Wyoming: 43-CH	2-0	1.000
Norm Sloan	North Caro. St.: 74-CH	2-0	1.000
+Eddie Sutton	Arkansas: 78-3d	1-1	.500
Gary Thompson	Wichita St.: 65-4th	0-2	.000
+Billy Tubbs	Oklahoma: 88-2d	1-1	.500
Forrest Twogood	Southern Cal: 54-4th	0-2	.000
Jim Valvano	North Caro. St.: 83-CH	2-0	1.000
+Bill van Breda Kolff	Princeton: 65-3d	1-1	.500
Bob Weinhauer	Pennsylvania: 79-4th	0-2	.000
Larry Weise	St. Bonaventure: 70-4th	0-2	.000
Joe Williams	Jacksonville: 70-2d	1-1	.500
+Roy Williams	Kansas: 91-2d	1-1	.500
Tom Young	Rutgers: 76-4th	0-2	.000

+ Active.
* Final Four records later vacated.

TOURNAMENT TRIVIA QUESTION...
Who are the only two coaches to take two different schools to the NCAA championship game? Answer:
Frank McGuire, St. John's (second in 1952) and North Carolina (champions in 1957); and Larry Brown,
UCLA (second in 1980) and Kansas (champions in 1988).

NCAA MEN'S DIVISION I TOURNAMENT
COACHES OF ALL TIME
1939-1992 (490)

Coach (Alma Mater)	Seasons, Career Record, Tourney Teams and Years in Tourney	Yrs.	W	L	Pct.	Last Year of Career
DICK ACRES (UC Santa Barb.) 3: 47-34; Oral Roberts: 84		1	0	1	.000	1985
STAN ALBECK (Bradley '55) 19: 284-188; Bradley: 88		1	0	1	.000	1991
CY ALEXANDER (Catawba '75) 5: 81-67; South Caro. St.: 89		1	0	1	.000	Active
PHOG ALLEN (Kansas '06) 46: 746-264; Kansas: 40-2d, 42RR, 52-CH, 53-2d		4	10	3	.769	1956
GEORGE ALLEN (West Va. '35) 3: 39-20; Brown: 39		1	0	1	.000	1941
SONNY ALLEN (Marshall '59) 22: 356-260; Nevada: 84, 85		2	0	2	.000	1987
LADELL ANDERSEN (Utah St. '51) 16: 286-168; 5 at Utah St.: 62, 63, 64, 70RR, 71; 3 at Brigham Young: 84, 87, 88		8	6	10	.375	1989
FORDDY ANDERSON (Stanford '42) 24: 368-234; 2 at Bradley: 50-2d, 54-2d; 2 at Michigan St.: 57-4th, 59RR		4	9	5	.643	1970
HAROLD ANDERSON (Otterbein '24) 29: 504-226; Bowling Green: 59, 62, 63		3	1	4	.200	1963
JIM ANDERSON (Oregon St. '59) 3: 51-37; Oregon St.: 90		1	0	1	.000	Active
TOM APKE (Creighton '65) 18: 282-226; Creighton: 75, 78, 81		3	0	3	.000	Active
LYNN ARCHIBALD (Fresno St. '68) 11: 163-152; Utah: 86		1	0	1	.000	1989
JOHN ARNDT [Loyola (Cal.) '50] 7: 91-90; Loyola (Cal.): 61		1	1	1	.500	1968
FRANK ARNOLD (Idaho St. '56) 10: 148-139; Brigham Young: 79, 80, 81RR		3	3	3	.500	1987
MURRAY ARNOLD (American '60) 18: 365-174; 3 at Tenn.-Chatt.: 81, 82, 83; 1 at Western Ky.: 87		4	2	4	.333	1990
RONNIE ARROW (Southwest Tex. St. '69) 5: 85-63; South Ala.: 89, 91		2	1	2	.333	Active
TOM ASBURY (Wyoming '67) 4: 83-40; Pepperdine: 91, 92		2	0	2	.000	Active
PRESLEY ASKEW (Southeastern Okla. St. '30) 15: 179-181; New Mexico St.: 59, 60		2	0	2	.000	1965
RANDY AYERS [Miami (Ohio) '78] 3: 70-23; Ohio St.: 90, 91, 92RR		3	6	3	.667	Active
JOHN BACH (Fordham '48) 28: 384-314; Fordham: 53, 54		2	0	2	.000	1978
JIM BAECHTOLD (Eastern Ky. '52) 6: 70-57; Eastern Ky.: 65		1	0	1	.000	1967
TAY BAKER (Cincinnati '50) 13: 195-149; Cincinnati: 66		1	0	2	.000	1979
RICK BARNES (Lenoir-Rhyne '77) 5: 83-63; Providence: 89, 90		2	0	2	.000	Active
J. D. BARNETT (Winona St. '66) 16: 290-175; 5 at Va. Common-wealth: 80, 81, 83, 84, 85; 2 at Tulsa: 86, 87		7	4	7	.364	1991
JIM BARON (St. Bonaventure '77) 5: 74-71; St. Francis (Pa.): 91		1	0	1	.000	Active
TONY BARONE (Duke '68) 7: 108-104; Creighton: 89, 91		2	1	2	.333	Active
PETER BARRY (San Francisco '70) 2: 49-13; San Francisco: 81, 82		2	0	2	.000	1982
SAM BARRY (Wisconsin '16) 28: 365-217; Southern Cal: 40-T3d		1	1	1	.500	1950
GENE BARTOW (Northeast Mo. St. '53) 30: 574-301; 1 at Memphis St.: 73-2d; 2 at UCLA: 76-3d, 77; 8 at Ala.-Birmingham: 81, 82RR, 83, 84, 85, 86, 87, 90		11	14	11	.560	Active
BUTCH BEARD (Louisville '72) 2: 25-34; Howard: 92		1	0	1	.000	Active
STEVE BELKO (Idaho '39) 26: 287-263; 4 at Idaho St.: 53, 54, 55, 56; 2 at Oregon: 60RR, 61		6	4	6	.400	1971
DAN BELLUOMINI (San Francisco '64) 2: 44-14; San Francisco: 79		1	1	1	.500	1980
DUTCH BELNAP (Utah St. '58) 6: 108-56; Utah St.: 75, 79		2	0	2	.000	1979
BOB BENDER (Duke '80) 3: 41-47; Illinois St.: 90		1	0	1	.000	Active
DICK BENNETT (Ripon '65) 16: 299-159; Wis.-Green Bay: 91		1	0	1	.000	Active
RUSS BERGMAN (Louisiana St. '70) 17: 269-225; Coastal Caro.: 91		1	0	1	.000	Active
BILL BERRY (Michigan St. '65) 10: 142-144; San Jose St.: 80		1	0	1	.000	1989
BILL BIBB (Ky. Wesleyan '57) 15: 222-194; Mercer: 81, 85		2	0	2	.000	1989
LEON BLACK (Texas '53) 9: 106-121; Texas: 72, 74		2	1	3	.250	1976
TOM BLACKBURN [Wilmington (Ohio) '31] 17: 352-141; Dayton: 52		1	1	1	.500	1964
BILL BLAIR (Va. Military '64) 9: 114-130; Va. Military: 76RR		1	2	1	.667	1981
GEORGE BLANEY (Holy Cross '61) 25: 384-313; Holy Cross: 77, 80		2	0	2	.000	Active
DAVE BLISS (Cornell '65) 17: 301-211; 1 at Oklahoma: 79; 3 at Southern Methodist: 84, 85, 88; 1 at New Mexico: 91		5	4	5	.444	Active
JIM BOEHEIM (Syracuse '66) 16: 391-124; Syracuse: 77, 78, 79, 80, 83, 84, 85, 86, 87-2d, 88, 89RR, 90, 91, 92		14	19	14	.576	Active
JIM BOUTIN (Lewis & Clark '64) 23: 397-253; Idaho St.: 87		1	0	1	.000	1990
BOB BOYD (Southern Cal '53) 20: 312-231; 1 at Seattle: 64; 1 at Southern Cal: 79		2	3	2	.600	1986
JIM BOYLE [St. Joseph's (Pa.) '64] 9: 151-114; St. Joseph's (Pa.): 82, 86		2	1	2	.333	1990
HAROLD BRADLEY (Hartwick '34) 20: 337-169; 1 at Duke: 55; 2 at Texas: 60, 63		3	2	4	.333	1967
JIM BRANDENBURG (Colorado St. '58) 16: 267-199; Wyoming: 81, 82, 87		3	4	3	.571	1992
BUSTER BRANNON (Texas Christian '33) 24: 285-290; 2 at Rice: 40, 42; 3 at Texas Christian: 52, 53, 59		5	4	6	.400	1967
BEN BRAUN (Wisconsin '75) 15: 260-190; Eastern Mich.: 88, 91		2	2	2	.500	Active

Coach (Alma Mater)	Seasons, Career Record, Tourney Teams and Years in Tourney	Yrs.	W	L	Pct.	Last Year of Career
JOHN BREEDEN (Montana St. '29) 17: 283-198; Montana St.: 51		1	0	1	.000	1954
AL BRIGHTMAN [Charleston (W. Va.)] 8: 174-67; Seattle: 53, 54, 55, 56		4	4	6	.400	1956
J. MADISON BROOKS (Louisiana Tech '37) 25: 370-267; East Tenn. St.: 68		1	1	2	.333	1973
JIM BROVELLI (San Francisco '64) 18: 242-247; San Diego: 84		1	0	1	.000	Active
AL BROWN (Purdue '64) 5: 68-75; Ball St.: 86		1	0	1	.000	1987
DALE BROWN (Minot St. '57) 20: 381-222; Louisiana St.: 79, 80RR, 81-4th, 84, 85, 86-T3d, 87RR, 88, 89, 90, 91, 92		12	15	13	.536	Active
EARL BROWN (Notre Dame '39) 1: 19-2; Dartmouth: 44-2d		1	2	1	.667	1944
LARRY BROWN* (North Caro. '63) 7: 172-60; 2 at UCLA: 80-2d, 81; 5 at Kansas: 84, 85, 86-T3d, 87, 88-CH		7	19	6	.760	1988
VIC BUBAS (North Caro. St. '51) 10: 213-67; Duke: 60RR, 63-3d, 64-2d, 66-3d		4	11	4	.733	1969
MORRIS BUCKWALTER (Utah '56) 5: 78-54; Seattle: 69		1	0	1	.000	1972
MITCH BUONAGURO (Boston College '75) 6: 72-103; Fairfield: 86, 87		2	0	2	.000	1991
EDDIE BURKE (La Salle '67) 14: 205-189; Drexel: 86		1	0	1	.000	1991
KEN BURMEISTER [St. Mary's (Tex.) '71] 4: 72-44; Texas-San Antonio: 88		1	0	1	.000	1990
JERRY BUSH [St. John's (N.Y.) '38] 16: 209-190; Toledo: 54		1	0	1	.000	1963
ED BYHRE [Augustana (S.D.) '66] 5: 69-63; Eastern Ky.: 79		1	0	1	.000	1981
JIM CALHOUN (American Int'l '66) 20: 366-210; 5 at Northeastern: 81, 82, 84, 85, 86; 3 at Connecticut: 90RR, 91, 92		8	9	8	.529	Active
ROBERT CALIHAN (Detroit Mercy '40) 21: 299-242; Detroit Mercy: 62		1	0	1	.000	1969
JOHN CALIPARI (Clarion St. '82) 4: 77-50; Massachusetts: 92		1	2	1	.667	Active
ERNIE CALVERLEY (Rhode Island '46) 11: 154-125; Rhode Island: 61, 66		2	0	2	.000	1968
LOU CAMPANELLI (Montclair St. '60) 20: 351-219; 3 at James Madison: 81, 82, 83; 1 at California: 90		4	4	4	.500	Active
HOWARD CANN (New York U. '20) 35: 409-232; New York U.: 43, 45-2d, 46		3	3	4	.429	1958
FRANKLIN CAPPON# (Michigan '24) 28: 361-257; Princeton: 52, 55, 60		3	0	5	.000	1961
P. J. CARLESIMO (Fordham '71) 17: 246-252; Seton Hall: 88, 89-2d, 91RR, 92		4	11	4	.733	Active
HENRY CARLSON (Pittsburgh '17) 31: 367-248; Pittsburgh: 41-T3d		1	1	1	.500	1953
LOU CARNESECCA [St. John's (N.Y.) '46] 24: 526-200; St. John's (N.Y.): 67, 68, 69, 76, 77, 78, 79RR, 80, 82, 83, 84, 85-T3d, 86, 87, 88, 90, 91RR, 92		18	17	20	.459	1992
BEN CARNEVALE (New York U. '38) 22: 309-171; 1 at North Caro.: 46-2d; 5 at Navy: 47, 53, 54RR, 59, 60		6	6	7	.462	1966
JOHN CARPENTER (Penn St. '58) 23: 292-328; Rider: 84		1	0	1	.000	1989
PETE CARRIL (Lafayette '52) 26: 454-237; Princeton: 69, 76, 77, 81, 83, 84, 89, 90, 91, 92		10	3	10	.231	Active
EVERETT CASE (Wisconsin '23) 18: 377-134; North Caro. St.: 50-3d, 51RR, 52, 54, 56		5	6	6	.500	1964
DON CASEY (Temple '70) 9: 151-94; Temple: 79		1	0	1	.000	1982
JOHN CASTELLANI (Notre Dame '52) 2: 45-9; Seattle: 58-2d		1	4	1	.800	1958
GALE CATLETT (West Va. '63) 20: 412-189; 3 at Cincinnati: 75, 76, 77; 7 at West Va.: 82, 83, 84, 86, 87, 89, 92		10	5	10	.333	Active
VINCE CAZZETTA# (Arnold '50) 5: 94-39; Seattle: 61, 62		2	0	2	.000	1963
JOHN CHANEY (Bethune-Cookman '55) 20: 458-143; Temple: 84, 85, 86, 87, 88RR, 90, 91RR, 92		8	10	8	.556	Active
ROY CHIPMAN (Maine '61) 18: 326-160; Pittsburgh: 81, 82, 85		3	1	3	.250	1986
MIKE CINGISER (Brown '62) 10: 93-170; Brown: 86		1	0	1	.000	1991
JOHN CINICOLA (Duquesne '55) 4: 52-56; Duquesne: 77		1	0	1	.000	1978
PERRY CLARK (Gettysburg '74) 3: 41-46; Tulane: 92		1	1	1	.500	Active
RICHARD COCHRAN (Tufts '34) 2: 17-17; Tufts: 45		1	0	2	.000	1946
JOSH CODY (Vanderbilt '20) 24: 259-243; Temple: 44		1	1	1	.500	1952
CHARLIE COLES [Miami (Ohio) '65] 6: 92-84; Central Mich.: 87		1	0	1	.000	1991
GARY COLSON (David Lipscomb '56) 31: 516-344; Pepperdine: 76, 79		2	2	2	.500	Active
HARRY COMBES (Illinois '37) 20: 316-150; Illinois: 49-3d, 51-3d, 52-3d, 63RR		4	9	4	.692	1967
BUS CONNOR (Idaho St. '55) 8: 93-106; Boise St.: 76		1	0	1	.000	1980
DON CORBETT [Lincoln (Mo.) '65] 21: 399-191; North Caro. A&T: 82, 83, 84, 85, 86, 87, 88		7	0	7	.000	Active
BOB COUSEY (Holy Cross '48) 6: 114-38; Boston College: 67RR, 68		2	2	2	.500	1969
OZZIE COWLES (Carleton '22) 31: 421-198; 3 at Dartmouth: 41, 42-2d, 43RR; 1 at Michigan: 48		4	5	4	.556	1959
FROSTY COX (Kansas '30) 18: 203-151; Colorado: 40, 41-T3d, 46		3	2	4	.333	1960

Coach (Alma Mater) / Seasons, Career Record, Tourney Teams and Years in Tourney	Yrs.	W	L	Pct.	Last Year of Career
BOBBY CREMINS (South Caro. '70) 17: 321-194; 1 at Appalachian St.: 79; 8 at Georgia Tech: 85RR, 86, 87, 88, 89, 90-T3d, 91, 92	9	13	9	.591	Active
JIM CREWS (Indiana '76) 7: 125-80; Evansville: 89, 92	2	1	2	.333	Active
DENNY CRUM (UCLA '59) 21: 496-183; Louisville: 72-4th, 74, 75-3d, 77, 78, 79, 80-CH, 81, 82-T3d, 83-T3d, 84, 86-CH, 88, 89, 90, 92	16	33	16	.673	Active
GARY CUNNINGHAM (UCLA '62) 2: 50-8; UCLA: 78, 79RR	2	3	2	.600	1979
JOSEPH CURRAN (Canisius '43) 6: 76-66; Canisius: 55RR, 56RR, 57	3	6	3	.667	1959
HOWIE DALLMAR (Stanford '48) 27: 363-315; Pennsylvania: 53	1	1	1	.500	1975
CHUCK DALY (Bloomsburg '53) 8: 151-62; Pennsylvania: 72RR, 73, 74, 75	4	3	5	.375	1977
ROY DANFORTH (Southern Miss. '62) 13: 193-161; Syracuse: 73, 74, 75-4th, 76	4	5	5	.500	1981
GEORGE DAVIDSON (Lafayette '51) 12: 170-116; Lafayette: 57	1	0	2	.000	1967
CHICK DAVIES (Duquesne '34) 21: 314-106; Duquesne: 40-T3d	1	1	1	.500	1948
KERMIT DAVIS JR. (Mississippi St. '82) 3: 58-33; Idaho: 89, 90	2	0	2	.000	1991
TOM DAVIS (Wis.-Platteville '60) 21: 403-213; 2 at Boston College: 81, 82RR; 5 at Iowa: 87RR, 88, 89, 91, 92	7	12	7	.632	Active
EVERETT DEAN (Indiana '21) 28: 374-215; Stanford: 42-CH	1	3	0	1.000	1951
MIKE DEANE (Potsdam St. '74) 8: 149-82; Siena: 89	1	1	1	.500	Active
JOHNNY DEE (Notre Dame '46) 11: 184-105; Notre Dame: 65, 69, 70, 71	4	2	6	.250	1971
BENNY DEES (Wyoming '58) 9: 158-99; 1 at New Orleans: 87; 1 at Wyoming: 88	2	1	2	.333	Active
MIKE DEMENT (East Caro. '76) 6: 74-88; Cornell: 88	1	0	1	.000	Active
DON DeVOE (Ohio St. '64) 19: 328-228; 1 at Virginia Tech: 76; 6 at Tennessee: 79, 80, 81, 82, 83, 89	7	5	7	.417	Active
ED DIDDLE (Centre '21) 42: 759-302; Western Ky.: 40, 60, 62	3	3	4	.429	1964
BOB DONEWALD (Hanover '64) 14: 242-171; Illinois St.: 83, 84, 85	3	2	3	.400	Active
DON DONOHER (Dayton '54) 25: 437-275; Dayton: 65, 66, 67-2d, 69, 70, 74, 84RR, 85	8	11	10	.524	1989
EDDIE DONOVAN (St. Bonaventure '50) 8: 139-57; St. Bonaventure: 61	1	2	1	.667	1961
DUCK DOWELL (Northwest Mo. St. '33) 20: 263-263; Pepperdine: 62	1	1	1	.500	1968
BRUCE DRAKE (Oklahoma '29) 17: 200-181; Oklahoma: 39-T3d, 43, 47-2d	3	4	3	.571	1955
LEFTY DRIESELL (Duke '54) 30: 600-270; 3 at Davidson: 66, 68RR, 69RR; 8 at Maryland: 73RR, 75RR, 80, 81, 83, 84, 85, 86	11	15	12	.556	Active
JOHN DROMO (John Carroll '39) 4: 80-31; Louisville: 68	1	1	1	.500	1971
AL DUER (Emporia St. '29) 19: 176-95; Pepperdine: 44	1	0	2	.000	1948
HUGH DURHAM* (Florida St. '59) 26: 480-270; 3 at Florida St.: 68, 72-2d, 78; 5 at Georgia: 83-T3d, 85, 87, 90, 91	8	8	8	.500	Active
JARRETT DURHAM (Duquesne '71) 8: 125-105; Robert Morris: 89, 90, 92	3	0	3	.000	Active
JIM DUTCHER (Michigan '55) 17: 290-196; Minnesota: 82	1	1	1	.500	1986
BOB DYE (Idaho St. '62) 18: 318-190; 1 at Cal St. Fullerton: 78RR; 1 at Boise St.: 88	2	2	2	.500	Active
TIPPY DYE (Ohio St. '37) 14: 225-132; 1 at Ohio St.: 50; 2 at Washington: 51RR, 53-3d	3	6	3	.667	1959
TOMMY JOE EAGLES (Louisiana Tech '71) 7: 125-89; Louisiana Tech: 87, 89	2	1	2	.333	Active
JIMMY EARLE (Middle Tenn. St. '59) 10: 164-103; Middle Tenn. St.: 75, 77	2	0	2	.000	1979
HEC EDMUNDSON (Idaho '09) 29: 497-201; Washington: 43	1	0	2	.000	1947
DICK EDWARDS (Culver-Stockton '52) 15: 241-157; Pacific (Cal.): 66, 67RR, 71	3	2	4	.333	1978
GEORGE EDWARDS (Missouri '13) 20: 181-172; Missouri: 44	1	1	1	.500	1946
HANK EGAN (Navy '60) 21: 272-287; San Diego: 87	1	0	1	.000	Active
JOHN EGLI (Penn St. '47) 14: 187-135; Penn St.: 55, 65	2	1	3	.250	1968
NORM ELLENBERGER (Butler '55) 10: 164-98; New Mexico: 74, 78	2	2	2	.500	1979
CLIFF ELLIS (Florida St. '68) 17: 315-184; 2 at South Ala.: 79, 80; 3 at Clemson: 87, 89, 90	5	3	5	.375	Active
FRED ENKE (Minnesota '21) 38: 522-344; Arizona: 51	1	0	1	.000	1961
LEFTY ERVIN (La Salle '68) 7: 119-87; La Salle: 80, 83	2	1	2	.333	1986
JOHN EVANS (Idaho '48) 4: 60-41; Idaho St.: 60	1	0	1	.000	1963
PAUL EVANS (Ithaca '67) 19: 362-183; 2 at Navy: 85, 86RR; 4 at Pittsburgh: 87, 88, 89, 91	6	7	6	.538	Active
LARRY FARMER (UCLA '73) 6: 95-77; UCLA: 83	1	0	1	.000	1988
BOB FEERICK (Santa Clara '41) 12: 186-120; Santa Clara: 52-4th, 53RR, 54RR, 60	4	6	6	.500	1962
GEORGE FELTON (South Caro. '75) 5: 87-62; South Caro.: 89	1	0	1	.000	1991
LARRY FINCH (Memphis St. '73) 6: 125-69; Memphis St.: 88, 89, 92RR	3	4	3	.571	Active
TED FIORE (Seton Hall '62) 6: 109-68; St. Peter's: 91	1	0	1	.000	Active

Coach (Alma Mater)	Seasons, Career Record, Tourney Teams and Years in Tourney	Tournament Yrs.	W	L	Pct.	Last Year of Career
STEVE FISHER# (Illinois St. '57) 4: 68-32; Michigan: 89-CH, 90, 92-2d		3	12	2	.857	Active
BILL FITCH (Coe '54) 12: 185-114; Bowling Green: 68		1	0	1	.000	1970
COTTON FITZSIMMONS (Midwestern St. '55) 2: 34-20; Kansas St.: 70		1	1	1	.500	1970
MARTY FLETCHER (Maryland '73) 10: 139-150; Southwestern La.: 92		1	1	1	.500	Active
JOHN FLOYD (Oklahoma St. '41) 5: 38-82; Texas A&M: 51		1	0	1	.000	1955
TIM FLOYD (Louisiana Tech '77) 6: 116-99; New Orleans: 91		1	0	1	.000	Active
KARL FOGEL (Colby '68) 9: 139-113; Northeastern: 87, 91		2	0	2	.000	Active
EDDIE FOGLER (North Caro. '70) 6: 114-74; 2 at Wichita St.: 87, 88; 1 at Vanderbilt: 91		3	0	3	.000	Active
BILL C. FOSTER (Carson-Newman '58) 25: 441-265; Clemson: 80RR		1	3	1	.750	Active
BILL E. FOSTER (Elizabethtown '54) 32: 459-390; Duke: 78-2d, 79, 80RR		3	6	3	.667	Active
BUD FOSTER (Wisconsin '30) 25: 265-267; Wisconsin: 41-CH, 47		2	4	1	.800	1959
PAT FOSTER (Arkansas '61) 12: 255-113; 2 at Lamar: 81, 83; 3 at Houston: 87, 90, 92		5	2	5	.286	Active
BILL FRIEDER# (Michigan '64) 12: 242-130; 4 at Michigan: 85, 86, 87, 88; 1 at Arizona St.: 91		5	6	5	.545	Active
JACK FRIEL (Washington St. '23) 30: 494-377; Washington St.: 41-2d		1	2	1	.667	1958
MATT FURJANIC (Point Park '73) 7: 109-95; 2 at Robert Morris: 82, 83; 1 at Marist: 86		3	1	3	.250	1986
ROGER GAECKLER (Gettysburg '65) 10: 131-124; Hofstra: 76, 77		2	0	2	.000	1979
BOB GAILLARD (San Francisco '62) 8: 165-57; San Francisco: 72, 73RR, 74RR, 77, 78		5	4	5	.444	1978
SMOKEY GAINES (LeMoyne-Owen '63) 10: 159-127; 1 at Detroit Mercy: 79; 1 at San Diego St.: 85		2	0	2	.000	1987
JIMMY GALES (Alcorn St. '63) 6: 79-95; North Texas: 88		1	0	1	.000	Active
JACK GARDNER (Southern Cal '32) 28: 486-235; 2 at Kansas St.: 48-4th, 51-2d; 6 at Utah: 55, 56RR, 59, 60, 61-4th, 66-4th		8	12	12	.500	1971
DICK GARIBALDI (Santa Clara '57) 8: 137-79; Santa Clara: 68RR, 69RR, 70		3	3	3	.500	1970
DAVE GAVITT (Dartmouth '59) 12: 227-117; Providence: 72, 73-4th, 74, 77, 78		5	5	6	.455	1979
GENE GIBSON (Texas Tech '50) 8: 100-92; Texas Tech: 62		1	1	2	.333	1969
SLATS GILL (Oregon St. '25) 36: 599-392; Oregon St.: 47RR, 49-4th, 55RR, 62RR, 63-4th, 64		6	8	8	.500	1964
PETE GILLEN (Fairfield '68) 7: 156-61; Xavier (Ohio): 86, 87, 88, 89, 90, 91		6	4	6	.400	Active
BULLY GILSTRAP (Texas '22) 3: 43-28; Texas: 43-T3d		1	1	1	.500	1945
BOYD GRANT (Colorado St. '61) 13: 275-120; 3 at Fresno St.: 81, 82, 84; 2 at Colorado St.: 89, 90		5	2	5	.286	1991
JACK GRAY (Texas '35) 12: 194-97; Texas: 39, 47-3d		2	2	3	.400	1951
JOHN GRAYSON (Oklahoma '38) 9: 165-82; Idaho St.: 57, 58, 59		3	4	5	.444	1963
MURRAY GREASON (Wake Forest '26) 23: 285-244; Wake Forest: 39, 53		2	1	2	.333	1957
TOM GREEN (Syracuse '71) 9: 171-95; FDU-Teaneck: 85, 88		2	0	2	.000	Active
ROYNER GREENE (Illinois '29) 20: 236-216; Cornell: 54		1	0	1	.000	1967
HUGH GREER (Connecticut '26) 17: 286-112; Connecticut: 51, 54, 56, 57, 58, 59, 60		7	1	8	.111	1963
ELMER GROSS (Penn St. '42) 5: 80-40; Penn St.: 52, 54-3d		2	4	3	.571	1954
MARC GULEY (Syracuse '36) 12: 136-129; Syracuse: 57RR		1	2	1	.667	1962
BRUCE HALE (Santa Clara '41) 16: 246-164; Miami (Fla.): 60		1	0	1	.000	1973
JOE HALL (Sewanee '51) 19: 373-156; Kentucky: 73RR, 75-2d, 77RR, 78-CH, 80, 81, 82, 83RR, 84-T3d, 85		10	20	9	.690	1985
PAUL HANSEN (Oklahoma City '50) 13: 139-168; Oklahoma St.: 83		1	0	1	.000	1986
JIM HARDING (Iowa '49) 9: 147-71; 1 at Loyola (La.): 58; 1 at La Salle: 68		2	0	2	.000	1973
DICK HARP (Kansas '40) 10: 141-105; Kansas: 57-2d, 60RR		2	4	2	.667	1964
JIM HARRICK [Charleston (W. Va.) '60] 13: 261-132; 4 at Pepperdine: 82, 83, 85, 86; 4 at UCLA: 89, 90, 91, 92RR		8	7	8	.467	Active
MARV HARSHMAN (Pacific Lutheran '42) 40: 642-448; Washington: 76, 84, 85		3	2	3	.400	1986
DICK HARTER (Pennsylvania '53) 18: 296-195; Pennsylvania: 70, 71RR		2	2	2	.500	1983
JACK HARTMAN (Oklahoma St. '49) 24: 439-233; Kansas St.: 72RR, 73RR, 75RR, 77, 80, 81RR, 82		7	11	7	.611	1986
CLEM HASKINS (Western Ky. '67) 12: 190-163; 2 at Western Ky.: 81, 86; 2 at Minnesota: 89, 90RR		4	6	4	.600	Active
DON HASKINS (Oklahoma St. '53) 31: 606-263; UTEP: 63, 64, 66-CH, 67, 70, 75, 84, 85, 86, 87, 88, 89, 90, 92		14	14	13	.519	Active

Coach (Alma Mater)	Seasons, Career Record, Tourney Teams and Years in Tourney	Yrs.	W	L	Pct.	Last Year of Career
DOC HAYES (North Texas '27) 20: 298-191; Southern Methodist: 55, 56-4th, 57, 65, 66, 67RR		6	7	8	.467	1967
KEN HAYES (Northeastern Okla. St. '56) 15: 236-158; New Mexico St.: 79		1	0	1	.000	1983
WALT HAZZARD (UCLA '64) 6: 120-61; UCLA: 87		1	1	1	.500	1988
JUD HEATHCOTE (Washington St. '50) 21: 360-244; 1 at Montana: 75; 7 at Michigan St.: 78RR, 79-CH, 85, 86, 90, 91, 92		8	14	8	.636	Active
DARRELL HEDRIC [Miami (Ohio) '55] 14: 216-157; Miami (Ohio): 71, 73, 78, 84		4	1	4	.200	1984
BILL HENDERSON (Howard Payne '25) 18: 201-232; Baylor: 46, 48-2d, 50-4th		3	3	5	.375	1961
LOU HENSON (New Mexico St. '55) 30: 590-282; 6 at New Mexico St.: 67, 68, 69, 70-3d, 71, 75; 9 at Illinois: 81, 83, 84RR, 85, 86, 87, 88, 89-T3d, 90		15	18	16	.529	Active
PETE HERRMANN (Geneseo St. '70) 6: 63-110; Navy: 87		1	0	1	.000	1992
EDDIE HICKEY (Creighton '27) 26: 435-231; 1 at Creighton: 41; 2 at St. Louis: 52RR, 57; 2 at Marquette: 59, 61		5	3	7	.300	1964
PECK HICKMAN (Western Ky. '35) 23: 443-183; Louisville: 51, 59-4th, 61, 64, 67		5	5	7	.417	1967
ED HICKOX (Ohio Wesleyan '05) 18: 241-100; Springfield: 40		1	0	1	.000	1947
TONY HINKLE (Chicago '21) 41: 560-392; Butler: 62		1	2	1	.667	1970
HOWARD HOBSON (Oregon '26) 23: 400-257; 1 at Oregon: 39-CH, 1 at Yale: 49		2	3	2	.600	1956
BILL HODGES (Marian '70) 10: 188-119; Indiana St.: 79-2d		1	4	1	.800	Active
EDDIE HOLBROOK (Lenoir-Rhyne '62) 13: 283-89; Furman: 80		1	0	1	.000	1982
TERRY HOLLAND (Davidson '64) 21: 418-216; 1 at Davidson: 70; 9 at Virginia: 76, 81-3d, 82, 83RR, 84-T3d, 86, 87, 89RR, 90		10	15	10	.600	1990
NAT HOLMAN (Savage School of Phys. Ed. '17) 37: 423-190; CCNY: 47-4th, 50-CH		2	4	2	.667	1960
ROBERT HOPKINS (Grambling '56) 16: 256-166; Southern-B.R.: 85		1	0	1	.000	1992
RICKY HUCKABAY* (Louisiana Tech '67) 6: 129-59; Marshall: 84, 85, 87		3	0	3	.000	1989
BOB HUGGINS (West Va. '77) 11: 235-103; 1 at Akron: 86; 1 at Cincinnati: 92-T3d		2	4	2	.667	Active
DICK HUNSAKER (Weber St. '77) 3: 71-26; Ball St.: 90		1	2	1	.667	Active
BOBBY HUSSEY (Appalachian St. '62) 18: 287-238; Davidson: 86		1	0	1	.000	1989
WHACK HYDER (Georgia Tech '37) 22: 292-271; Georgia Tech: 60RR		1	1	1	.500	1973
CLARENCE IBA (Panhandle St. '36) 11: 137-147; Tulsa: 55		1	1	1	.500	1960
GENE IBA (Tulsa '63) 15: 226-202; 1 at Houston Baptist: 84; 1 at Baylor: 88		2	0	2	.000	1992
HENRY IBA (Northwest Mo. St. '31) 41: 767-338; Oklahoma St.: 45-CH, 46-CH, 49-2d, 51-4th, 53RR, 54RR, 58RR, 65RR		8	15	7	.682	1970
MOE IBA (Oklahoma St. '62) 15: 226-202; Nebraska: 86		1	0	1	.000	Active
GEORGE IRELAND (Notre Dame '36) 24: 318-255; Loyola (Ill.): 63-CH, 64, 66, 68		4	7	3	.700	1975
MIKE JARVIS (Northeastern '68) 7: 136-75; Boston U.: 88, 90		2	0	2	.000	Active
BEN JOBE (Fisk '56) 21: 401-183; Southern-B.R.: 87, 88, 89		3	0	3	.000	Active
RON JACOBS* (Southern Cal '64) 1: 14-13; Loyola (Cal.): 80		1	0	1	.000	1980
MAURICE JOHN (Central Mo. St. '41) 16: 243-156; Drake: 69-3d, 70RR, 71RR		3	5	3	.625	1974
PHIL JOHNSON (Utah St. '53) 3: 68-16; Weber St.: 69, 70, 71		3	2	3	.400	1971
DWIGHT JONES (Pepperdine '65) 4: 70-40; Long Beach St.: 77		1	0	1	.000	1978
JEFF JONES (Virginia '82) 2: 41-25; Virginia: 91		1	0	1	.000	Active
JOHN JORDAN (Notre Dame '35) 14: 214-145; Notre Dame: 53RR, 54RR, 57, 58RR, 60, 63		6	8	6	.571	1964
ED JUCKER (Cincinnati '40) 17: 266-109; Cincinnati: 61-CH, 62-CH, 63-2d		3	11	1	.917	1977
DOGGIE JULIAN (Bucknell '23) 32: 388-358; 2 at Holy Cross: 47-CH, 48-3d; 3 at Dartmouth: 56, 58RR, 59		5	9	4	.692	1967
GENE KEADY (Kansas St. '58) 14: 288-139; 1 at Western Ky.: 80; 8 at Purdue: 83, 84, 85, 86, 87, 88, 90, 91		9	5	9	.357	Active
LAKE KELLY* (Georgia Tech '56) 13: 218-144; Austin Peay: 73, 74, 87		3	2	4	.333	1990
PAT KENNEDY (King's '76) 12: 243-126; 2 at Iona: 84, 85; 4 at Florida St.: 88, 89, 91, 92		6	3	6	.333	Active
FRANK KERNS (Alabama '57) 19: 347-187; Ga. Southern: 83, 87, 92		3	0	3	.000	Active
JIM KILLINGSWORTH (Northeastern Okla. St. '48) 16: 261-191; 2 at Idaho St.: 74, 77RR; 1 at Texas Christian: 87		3	3	3	.500	1987
BOB KING (Iowa '47) 13: 236-113; New Mexico: 68		1	0	2	.000	1978
GEORGE KING [Charleston (W. Va.) '50] 13: 223-119; 3 at West Va.: 62, 63, 65; 1 at Purdue: 69-2d		4	5	4	.556	1972
DANA KIRK* (Marshall '60) 15: 281-131; Memphis St.: 82, 83, 84, 85-T3d, 86		5	9	5	.643	1986

Coach (Alma Mater)	Seasons, Career Record, Tourney Teams and Years in Tourney	Yrs.	W	L	Pct.	Last Year of Career
BOB KNIGHT (Ohio St. '62) 27: 588-210; Indiana: 73-3d, 75RR, 76-CH, 78, 80, 81-CH, 82, 83, 84RR, 86, 87-CH, 88, 89, 90, 91 92-T3d		16	35	13	.729	Active
DON KNODEL [Miami (Ohio) '53] 8: 77-126; Rice: 70		1	0	1	.000	1974
JACK KRAFT* [St. Joseph's (Pa.) '42] 20: 361-191; 6 at Villanova: 62RR, 64, 69, 70RR, 71-2d, 72; 1 at Rhode Island: 78		7	11	8	.579	1981
LON KRUGER (Kansas St. '74) 10: 163-136; Kansas St.: 87, 88RR, 89		3	4	3	.571	Active
MIKE KRZYZEWSKI (Army '69) 17: 370-169; Duke: 84, 85, 86-2d, 87, 88-T3d, 89-T3d, 90-2d, 91-CH, 92-CH		9	33	7	.825	Active
EUGENE LAMBERT (Arkansas '29) 18: 264-190; 2 at Arkansas: 45-T3d, 49; 2 at Memphis St.: 55, 56		4	2	4	.333	1960
PAUL LAMBERT (William Jewell '56) 15: 227-160; Southern Ill.: 77		1	1	1	.500	1978
BILL LANGE (Wittenberg '21) 18: 219-134; North Caro.: 41		1	0	2	.000	1944
JOE LAPCHICK (No college) 20: 334-130; St. John's (N.Y.): 61		1	0	1	.000	1965
ROBERT LAUGHLIN (Morehead St. '37) 12: 166-119; Morehead St.: 56, 57, 61		3	3	4	.429	1965
JOHN LAWTHER [Westminster (Pa.) '19] 13: 153-93; Penn St.: 42		1	1	1	.500	1949
FRANK LAYDEN (Niagara '55) 10: 135-121; Niagara: 70		1	1	2	.333	1976
BEBE LEE (Stanford '38) 9: 92-119; Colorado: 54, 55-3d		2	3	3	.500	1956
BILLY LEE (Barton '71) 14: 218-192; Campbell: 92		1	0	1	.000	Active
ROY LEENIG [Trinity (Conn.) '42] 6: 104-48; Holy Cross: 56		1	0	1	.000	1961
ALAN LeFORCE (Cumberland '57) 11: 182-102; East Tenn. St.: 91, 92		2	1	2	.333	Active
ABE LEMONS (Oklahoma City '49) 34: 597-344; 7 at Oklahoma City: 56RR, 57RR, 63, 64, 65, 66, 73; 1 at Texas: 79		8	7	9	.438	1990
FRED LEWIS (Eastern Ky. '46) 13: 208-125; Syracuse: 66RR		1	1	1	.500	1985
GUY LEWIS (Houston '47) 30: 592-279; Houston: 61, 65, 66, 67-3d, 68-4th, 70, 71, 72, 73, 78, 81, 82-T3d, 83-2d, 84-2d		14	26	18	.591	1986
CRAIG LITTLEPAGE (Pennsylvania '73) 6: 63-102; Pennsylvania: 85		1	0	1	.000	1988
HARRY LITWACK (Temple '30) 21: 373-193; Temple: 56-3d, 58-3d, 64, 67, 70, 72		6	7	6	.538	1973
PAUL LIZZO (Northwest Mo. St. '63) 21: 271-295; LIU-Brooklyn: 81, 84		2	0	2	.000	Active
TATES LOCKE (Ohio Wesleyan '59) 17: 240-215; 1 at Miami (Ohio): 69; 1 at Jacksonville: 79		2	1	3	.250	Active
KEN LOEFFLER (Penn St. '24) 22: 310-198; La Salle: 54-CH, 55-2d		2	9	1	.900	1957
JOHN LONG (Catholic '28) 1: 17-7; Catholic: 44		1	0	2	.000	1944
JERRY LOYD (LeTourneau '76) 3: 63-27; Louisiana Tech: 91		1	0	1	.000	Active
CAL LUTHER (Valparaiso '51) 20: 286-194; Murray St.: 64, 69		2	0	2	.000	1974
JIM LYNAM [St. Joseph's (Pa.) '64] 10: 158-118; St. Joseph's (Pa.): 81RR		1	3	1	.750	1981
NICK MACARCHUK (Fairfield '63) 15: 244-192; Fordham: 92		1	0	1	.000	Active
KEVIN MACKEY (St. Anselm '67) 7: 144-67; Cleveland St.: 86RR		1	2	1	.667	1990
DAVE MAGARITY [St. Francis (Pa.) '74] 11: 144-163; Marist: 87		1	0	1	.000	Active
RICK MAJERUS (Marquette '70) 8: 157-69; 1 at Ball St.: 89; 1 at Utah: 91		2	3	2	.600	Active
RED MANNING (Duquesne '51) 16: 247-138; Duquesne: 69, 71		2	2	2	.500	1974
PRESS MARAVICH (Davis & Elkins '41) 20: 232-279; North Caro. St.: 65		1	1	1	.500	1975
CLAIR MARKEY# (Seattle '63) 1: 0-1; Seattle: 63		1	0	1	.000	1963
RINSO MARQUETTE (Lebanon Valley '48) 8: 98-74; Lebanon Valley: 53		1	1	2	.333	1960
DONALD MARTIN (Georgetown '41) 9: 109-102; Boston College: 58		1	0	1	.000	1962
WAYNE MARTIN (Morehead St. '68) 13: 216-153; Morehead St.: 83, 84		2	1	2	.333	1987
JOEL MASON (Western Mich. '36) 18: 186-173; Wayne St. (Mich.): 56		1	1	2	.333	1966
ROLLIE MASSIMINO (Vermont '56) 21: 389-252; Villanova: 78RR, 80, 81, 82RR, 83RR, 84, 85-CH, 86, 88RR, 90, 91		11	20	10	.667	Active
PAUL McBRAYER (Kentucky '30) 16: 212-141; Eastern Ky.: 53, 59		2	0	2	.000	1962
JIM McCAFFERTY [Loyola (La.) '42] 10: 132-117; 2 at Loyola (La.): 54, 57; 1 at Xavier (Ohio): 61		3	0	3	.000	1962
FRAN McCAFFERY (Pennsylvania '82) 3: 49-39; Lehigh: 88		1	0	1	.000	1988
JAKE McCANDLESS# (Princeton '51) 1: 13-10; Princeton: 61		1	1	2	.333	1962
BABE McCARTHY (Mississippi St. '49) 11: 175-103; Mississippi St.: 63		1	1	1	.500	1967
MACK McCARTHY (Virginia Tech '74) 7: 136-74; Tenn.-Chatt.: 88		1	0	1	.000	Active
NEIL McCARTHY (Cal St. Sacramento '65) 17: 344-171; 4 at Weber St.: 78, 79, 80, 83; 3 at New Mexico St.: 90, 91, 92		7	3	7	.300	Active
GEORGE McCARTY (New Mexico St. '50) 4: 60-51; New Mexico St.: 52		1	0	2	.000	1953
BRANCH McCRACKEN (Indiana '30) 32: 450-231; Indiana: 40-CH, 53-CH, 54, 58		4	9	2	.818	1965
JOHN McDOUGAL (Evansville '50) 10: 136-141; Northern Ill.: 82		1	0	1	.000	1986
AL McGUIRE [St. John's (N.Y.) '51] 20: 405-143; Marquette: 68, 69RR, 71, 72, 73, 74-2d, 75, 76RR, 77-CH		9	20	9	.690	1977

Coach (Alma Mater)	Seasons, Career Record, Tourney Teams and Years in Tourney	Tournament Yrs.	W	L	Pct.	Last Year of Career
FRANK McGUIRE [St. John's (N.Y.) '36] 30: 550-235; 2 at St. John's (N.Y.): 51RR, 52-2d; 2 at North Caro.: 57-CH, 59; 4 at South Caro.: 71, 72, 73, 74		8	14	8	.636	1980
BONES McKINNEY (North Caro. '46) 8: 122-94; Wake Forest: 61RR, 62-3d		2	6	2	.750	1965
JACK McKINNEY [St. Joseph's (Pa.) '57] 9: 164-83; St. Joseph's (Pa.): 69, 71, 73, 74		4	0	4	.000	1974
ART McLARNEY (Washington St. '32) 3: 53-36; Washington: 48		1	1	1	.500	1950
RED McMANUS (St. Ambrose '49) 10: 138-118; Creighton: 62, 64		2	3	3	.500	1969
WALTER McPHERSON (San Jose St. '40) 17: 252-197; San Jose St.: 51		1	0	1	.000	1960
RAY MEARS [Miami (Ohio) '49] 21: 399-135; Tennessee: 67, 76, 77		3	0	4	.000	1977
LOUIS MENZE (Central Mo. St. '28) 19: 166-153; Iowa St.: 44-T3d		1	1	1	.500	1947
SHELBY METCALF (East Tex. St. '53) 27: 443-313; Texas A&M: 64, 69, 75, 80, 87		5	3	6	.333	1990
JOEY MEYER (DePaul '71) 8: 168-79; DePaul: 85, 86, 87, 88, 89, 91, 92		7	6	7	.462	Active
RAY MEYER (Notre Dame '38) 42: 724-354; DePaul: 43-T3d, 53, 56, 59, 60, 65, 76, 78RR, 79-3d, 80, 81, 82, 84		13	14	16	.467	1984
BOB MILLER (Occidental '53) 9: 124-112; Cal St. Los Angeles: 74		1	0	1	.000	1978
ELDON MILLER (Wittenberg '61) 30: 492-329; 1 at Western Mich.: 76; 4 at Ohio St.: 80, 82, 83, 85; 1 at Northern Iowa: 90		6	5	6	.455	Active
HARRY MILLER (Eastern N. Mex. '51) 34: 534-374; Wichita St.: 76		1	0	1	.000	1988
WEENIE MILLER (Richmond '47) 9: 79-123; Va. Military: 64		1	0	1	.000	1964
RALPH MILLER* (Kansas '42) 38: 657-382; 1 at Wichita St.: 64RR; 1 at Iowa: 70; 8 at Oregon St.: 75, 80, 81, 82RR, 84, 85, 88, 89		10	5	11	.313	1989
GUS MILLER (West Tex. St. '27) 22: 377-168; West Tex. St.: 55		1	0	1	.000	1957
BUD MILLIKAN (Oklahoma St. '42) 17: 243-182; Maryland: 58		1	2	1	.667	1967
DOUG MILLS (Illinois '30) 11: 151-66; Illinois: 42		1	0	2	.000	1947
RON MITCHELL (Edison '84) 6: 99-75; Coppin St.: 90		1	0	1	.000	Active
CHARLES MOIR (Appalachian St. '52) 20: 392-196; Virginia Tech: 79, 80, 85, 86		4	2	4	.333	1987
JIM MOLINARI (Ill. Wesleyan '77) 3: 49-40; Northern Ill.: 91		1	0	1	.000	Active
DON MONSON (Idaho '55) 14: 216-186; Idaho: 81, 82		2	1	2	.333	1992
MIKE MONTGOMERY (Long Beach St. '68) 14: 272-145; Stanford: 89, 92		2	0	2	.000	Active
DUDEY MOORE (Duquesne '34) 15: 270-107; Duquesne: 52RR		1	1	1	.500	1963
ROBERT MORELAND (Tougaloo '62) 17: 276-218; Texas Southern: 90		1	0	1	.000	Active
STEW MORRILL (Gonzaga '74) 6: 111-69; Montana: 91		1	0	1	.000	Active
SPEEDY MORRIS [St. Joseph's (Pa.) '73] 6: 139-52; La Salle: 88, 89, 90, 92		4	1	4	.200	Active
STAN MORRISON (California '62) 17: 220-247; 1 at Pacific (Cal.): 79; 2 at Southern Cal: 82, 85		3	0	3	.000	Active
DICK MOTTA (Utah St. '53) 6: 120-33; Weber St.: 68		1	0	1	.000	1968
JOE MULLANEY (Holy Cross '49) 22: 366-218; Providence: 64, 65RR, 66		3	2	3	.400	1985
JEFF MULLINS (Duke '64) 7: 118-92; N.C.-Charlotte: 88, 92		2	0	2	.000	Active
FRANK MULZOFF [St. John's (N.Y.) '51] 3: 56-27; St. John's (N.Y.): 73		1	0	1	.000	1986
BILL MUSSELMAN* (Wittenberg '61) 10: 197-63; Minnesota: 72		1	1	1	.500	1975
GERALD MYERS (Texas Tech '59) 24: 357-305; Texas Tech: 73, 76, 85, 86		4	1	4	.200	1991
JACK NAGLE (Marquette '40) 8: 108-70; Marquette: 55RR		1	2	1	.667	1958
LYNN NANCE (Washington '65) 15: 256-174; St. Mary's (Cal.): 89		1	0	1	.000	Active
DANNY NEE (St. Mary of the Plains '71) 12: 213-149; 2 at Ohio: 83, 85; 2 at Nebraska: 91, 92		4	1	4	.200	Active
AL NEGRATTI (Seton Hall '43) 12: 163-156; Portland: 59		1	0	1	.000	1967
ERNIE NESTOR (Alderson-Broaddus '68) 4: 61-60; George Mason: 89		1	0	1	.000	Active
MIKE NEWELL (Sam Houston St. '73) 8: 160-92; Ark.-Lit. Rock: 86, 89, 90		3	1	3	.250	Active
PETE NEWELL [Loyola (Cal.) '40] 14: 234-123; California: 57RR, 58RR, 59-CH, 60-2d		4	10	3	.769	1960
C. M. NEWTON (Kentucky '52) 32: 509-375; 2 at Alabama: 75, 76; 2 at Vanderbilt: 88, 89		4	3	4	.429	1989
STEVE NEWTON (Indiana St. '63) 7: 127-82; Murray St.: 88, 90, 91		3	1	3	.250	Active
BOB NICHOLS (Toledo '53) 22: 377-211; Toledo: 67, 79, 80		3	1	3	.250	1987
KEN NORTON (LIU-Brooklyn '39) 22: 310-205; Manhattan: 56, 58		2	1	3	.250	1968
JIM O'BRIEN [St. Joseph's (Pa.) '74] 8: 125-109; Dayton: 90		1	1	1	.500	Active
BUCKY O'CONNOR (Drake '38) 7: 108-54; Iowa: 55-4th, 56-2d		2	5	3	.625	1958
DAVE ODOM (Guilford '65) 6: 86-81; Wake Forest: 91, 92		2	1	2	.333	Active
JOHNNY OLDHAM* (Western Ky. '48) 16: 260-123; 2 at Tennessee Tech: 58, 63; 4 at Western Ky.: 66, 67, 70, 71-3d		6	6	6	.500	1971

Coach (Alma Mater)	Seasons, Career Record, Tourney Teams and Years in Tourney	Tournament Yrs.	W	L	Pct.	Last Year of Career
PURNELL OLIVER (Old Dominion '75) 4: 59-57; Old Dominion: 92...		1	0	1	.000	Active
HAROLD OLSEN (Wisconsin '17) 30: 306-234; Ohio St.: 39-2d, 44-T3d, 45-T3d, 46-3d............		4	6	4	.600	1952
LUTE OLSON (Augsburg '57) 19: 405-169; 5 at Iowa: 79, 80-4th, 81, 82, 83; 8 at Arizona: 85, 86, 87, 88-T3d, 89, 90, 91, 92............		13	16	14	.533	Active
JOHNNY ORR (Beloit '49) 27: 432-322; 4 at Michigan: 74RR, 75, 76-2d, 77RR; 5 at Iowa St.: 85, 86, 88, 89, 92.................		9	10	9	.526	Active
TED OWENS (Oklahoma '51) 21: 369-217; Kansas: 66RR, 67, 71-4th, 74-4th, 75, 78, 81............		7	8	9	.471	1987
DICK PARFITT (Central Mich. '53) 14: 193-179; Central Mich.: 75, 77..		2	2	2	.500	1985
BRUCE PARKHILL (Lock Haven '71) 15: 229-199; Penn St.: 91........		1	1	1	.500	Active
DOYLE PARRACK (Oklahoma St. '45) 15: 208-178; Oklahoma City: 52, 53, 54, 55............		4	1	5	.167	1962
BOBBY PASCHAL (Stetson '64) 14: 232-180; 2 at Southwestern La.: 82, 83; 2 at South Fla.: 90, 92............		4	0	4	.000	Active
ALDEN PASCHE (Rice '32) 11: 135-116; Houston: 56............		1	0	2	.000	1956
JERRY PEIRSON [Miami (Ohio) '66] 6: 94-80; Miami (Ohio): 85, 86...		2	0	2	.000	1990
PETER PELETTA (Cal St. Sacramento '50) 6: 114-51; San Francisco: 63, 64RR, 65RR............		3	3	3	.500	1966
TOM PENDERS (Connecticut '67) 21: 365-248; 1 at Rhode Island: 88; 4 at Texas: 89, 90RR, 91, 92............		5	7	5	.583	Active
DOM PERNO (Connecticut '64) 9: 139-114; Connecticut: 79.........		1	0	1	.000	1986
VADAL PETERSON (Utah '20) 26: 384-224; Utah: 44-CH, 45.........		2	3	2	.600	1953
DIGGER PHELPS (Rider '63) 21: 419-200; 1 at Fordham: 71; 14 at Notre Dame: 74, 75, 76, 77, 78-4th, 79RR, 80, 81, 85, 86, 87 88, 89, 90............		15	17	17	.500	1991
JERRY PIMM (Southern Cal '60) 18: 321-197; 5 at Utah: 77, 78, 79, 81, 83; 2 at UC Santa Barb.: 88, 90............		7	6	7	.462	Active
RICK PITINO (Massachusetts '74) 10: 198-101; 1 at Boston U.: 83; 1 at Providence: 87-T3d; 1 at Kentucky: 92RR............		3	7	3	.700	Active
BOB POLK (Evansville '39) 25: 355-257; Trinity (Tex.): 69............		1	0	1	.000	1977
NIBS PRICE (California '14) 31: 463-298; California: 46-4th...........		1	1	2	.333	1954
LIONEL PURCELL (UC Santa Barb. '52) 2: 24-18; Seattle: 67.........		1	0	1	.000	1967
TOM QUINN (Marshall '54) 16: 258-175; East Caro.: 72............		1	0	1	.000	1974
HARRY RABENHORST (Wake Forest '21) 29: 340-264; Louisiana St.: 53-4th, 54............		2	2	4	.333	1957
JACK RAMSAY* [St. Joseph's (Pa.) '49] 11: 231-71; St. Joseph's (Pa.): 59, 60, 61-3d, 62, 63RR, 65, 66............		7	8	11	.421	1966
GEORGE RAVELING (Villanova '60) 20: 302-268; 2 at Washington St.: 80, 83; 2 at Iowa: 85, 86; 2 at Southern Cal: 91, 92............		6	2	6	.250	Active
HANK RAYMONDS (St. Louis '48) 12: 237-97; Marquette: 78, 79, 80, 82, 83............		5	2	5	.286	1983
ROGER REID (Weber St. '67) 3: 67-29; Brigham Young: 90, 91, 92....		3	1	3	.250	Active
BOB REINHART (Indiana '61) 7: 81-120; Georgia St.: 91..............		1	0	1	.000	Active
BILL REINHART (Oregon '23) 36: 464-331; Geo. Washington: 54, 61..		2	0	2	.000	1966
JIM RICHARDS (Western Ky. '59) 7: 102-84; Western Ky.: 76, 78....		2	1	2	.333	1978
NOLAN RICHARDSON (UTEP '65) 12: 286-100; 3 at Tulsa: 82, 84, 85; 5 at Arkansas: 88, 89, 90-T3d, 91RR, 92............		8	9	8	.529	Active
GORDON RIDINGS (Oregon '29) 4: 70-21; Columbia: 48............		1	0	2	.000	1950
BUZZ RIDL [Westminster (Pa.) '42] 19: 312-174; Pittsburgh: 74RR....		1	2	1	.667	1975
ELMER RIPLEY (No college) 10: 133-82; Georgetown: 43-2d.........		1	2	1	.667	1949
JULE RIVLIN (Marshall '40) 8: 120-88; Marshall: 56............		1	0	1	.000	1963
LES ROBINSON (North Caro. St. '64) 18: 245-261; 2 at East Tenn. St.: 89, 90; 1 at North Caro. St.: 91............		3	1	3	.250	Active
POLK ROBISON (Texas Tech '35) 18: 253-196; Texas Tech: 54, 56, 61............		3	1	3	.250	1961
RED ROCHA (Oregon St. '50) 10: 110-135; Hawaii: 72................		1	0	1	.000	1973
JACK ROHAN (Columbia '53) 15: 171-196; Columbia: 68............		1	2	1	.667	Active
BILL ROHR (Ohio Wesleyan '40) 12: 157-117; Miami (Ohio): 53, 55, 57............		3	0	3	.000	1963
DICK ROMNEY (Utah '17) 22: 224-160; Utah St.: 39............		1	1	1	.500	1941
GLEN ROSE (Arkansas '28) 27: 383-233; Arkansas: 41-T3d, 58.......		2	1	3	.250	1966
LEE ROSE (Transylvania '58) 19: 388-162; 1 at N.C.-Charlotte: 77-4th; 1 at Purdue: 80-3d............		2	8	3	.727	1986
LOU ROSSINI (Columbia '48) 25: 359-256; 1 at Columbia: 51; 3 at New York U.: 60-4th, 62, 63............		4	6	6	.500	1979
DEE ROWE (Middlebury '52) 8: 120-88; Connecticut: 76............		1	1	1	.500	1977
ADOLPH RUPP (Kansas '23) 41: 875-190; Kentucky: 42-T3d, 45, 48-CH, 49-CH, 51-CH, 52RR, 55, 56RR, 57RR, 58-CH, 59, 61RR, 62RR, 64, 66-2d, 68RR, 69, 70RR, 71, 72RR............		20	30	18	.625	1972
ANDY RUSSO (Lake Forest '70) 10: 183-117; 2 at Louisiana Tech: 84, 85; 1 at Washington: 86............		3	3	3	.500	1989
RICK SAMUELS (Chadron St. '71) 12: 183-168; Eastern Ill.: 92........		1	0	1	.000	Active

Coach (Alma Mater)	Seasons, Career Record, Tourney Teams and Years in Tourney	Tournament Yrs.	W	L	Pct.	Last Year of Career
WIMP SANDERSON* (North Ala. '59) 12: 265-118; Alabama: 82, 83, 84, 85, 86, 87, 89, 90, 91, 92.		10	12	10	.545	1992
JIM SATALIN (St. Bonaventure '69) 16: 240-213; St. Bonaventure: 78..		1	0	1	.000	1989
FRED SCHAUS (West Va. '49) 12: 251-96; 6 at West Va.: 55, 56, 57, 58, 59-2d, 60; 1 at Purdue: 77.		7	6	7	.462	1978
CHARLIE SCHMAUS (Va. Military '66) 6: 75-90; Va. Military: 77.		1	1	1	.500	1982
TOM SCHNEIDER (Bucknell '69) 9: 97-150; 1 at Lehigh: 85; 1 at Pennsylvania: 87.		2	0	2	.000	Active
BILL SCOTT (Hardin-Simmons '47) 11: 129-161; Hardin-Simmons: 53, 57.		2	0	2	.000	1962
EDGAR SCOTT (Pitt.-Johnstown '78) 1: 17-13; Murray St.: 92.		1	0	1	.000	Active
ALEX SEVERANCE (Villanova '29) 25: 413-201; Villanova: 39-T3d, 49, 51, 55.		4	4	4	.500	1961
FRED SHABEL (Duke '54) 4: 72-29; Connecticut: 64RR, 65, 67.		3	2	3	.400	1967
HOWARD SHANNON (Kansas St. '48) 7: 104-68; Virginia Tech: 67RR.		1	2	1	.667	1971
ALEX SHAW (Michigan '32) 24: 299-169; Williams: 55.		1	0	1	.000	1973
BUSTER SHEARY (Catholic '33) 7: 155-36; Holy Cross: 50, 53RR.		2	2	3	.400	1955
EVERETT SHELTON (Phillips '23) 31: 494-347; Wyoming: 41, 43-CH, 47, 48, 49, 52RR, 53, 58.		8	4	12	.250	1968
BERYL SHIPLEY* (Delta St. '51) 16: 293-126; Southwestern La.: 72, 73.		2	3	3	.500	1973
DICK SHRIDER (Ohio '48) 9: 126-96; Miami (Ohio): 58, 66.		2	1	3	.250	1966
STAN SIMPSON (Ga. Southern '61) 5: 71-66; Middle Tenn. St.: 82.		1	1	1	.500	1984
ROY SKINNER (Presbyterian '52) 16: 278-135; Vanderbilt: 65RR, 74.		2	1	3	.250	1976
NORM SLOAN* (North Caro. St. '51) 37: 627-395; 3 at North Caro. St.: 70, 74-CH, 80; 3 at Florida: 87, 88, 89.		6	8	5	.615	1989
DEAN SMITH (Kansas '53) 31: 740-219; North Caro.: 67-4th, 68-2d, 69-4th, 72-3d, 75, 76, 77-2d, 78, 79, 80, 81-2d, 82-CH, 83RR, 84, 85RR, 86, 87RR, 88RR, 89, 90, 91-T3d, 92.		22	49	23	.681	Active
GEORGE SMITH (Cincinnati '35) 8: 154-56; Cincinnati: 58, 59-3d, 60-3d.		3	7	3	.700	1960
SONNY SMITH (Milligan '58) 16: 242-226; Auburn: 84, 85, 86RR, 87, 88.		5	7	5	.583	Active
GENE SMITHSON (North Central '61) 11: 221-99; Wichita St.: 81RR, 85.		2	3	2	.600	1986
FRED SNOWDEN (Wayne St. '58) 10: 167-108; Arizona: 76RR, 77.		2	2	2	.500	1982
JAMES SNYDER (Ohio '41) 25: 354-245; Ohio: 60, 61, 64RR, 65, 70, 72, 74.		7	3	8	.273	1974
BOB SPEAR (DePauw '41) 15: 177-176; Air Force: 60, 62.		2	0	2	.000	1971
CHARLES SPOONHOUR (School of Ozarks '61) 9: 197-81; Southwest Mo. St.: 87, 88, 89, 90, 92.		5	1	5	.167	Active
BOB STAAK (Connecticut '71) 10: 133-155; Xavier (Ohio): 83.		1	0	1	.000	1989
FLOYD STAHL (Illinois '26) 11: 107-120; Harvard: 46.		1	0	2	.000	1958
STU STARNER (Minn.-Morris '65) 9: 152-111; Montana St.: 86.		1	0	1	.000	Active
STEVE STEINWEDEL (Mississippi St. '75) 7: 115-85; Delaware: 92.		1	0	1	.000	Active
BRUCE STEWART (Jacksonville St. '75) 9: 205-84; Middle Tenn. St.: 85, 87, 89.		3	1	3	.250	1991
CARL STEWART (Grambling '54) 10: 153-119; Southern-B.R.: 81.		1	0	1	.000	1982
NORM STEWART# (Missouri '56) 31: 593-292; Missouri: 76RR, 78, 80, 81, 82, 83, 86, 87, 88, 89, 90, 92.		12	8	12	.400	Active
DAVE STRACK (Michigan '46) 9: 124-104; Michigan: 64-3d, 65-2d, 66RR.		3	7	3	.700	1968
BILL STRANNIGAN (Wyoming '41) 23: 308-289; 1 at Colorado St.: 54; 1 at Wyoming: 67.		2	0	4	.000	1973
LAFAYETTE STRIBLING (Mississippi Industrial '57) 9: 118-141; Mississippi Val.: 86, 92.		2	0	2	.000	Active
GUY STRONG (Eastern Ky. '55) 14: 191-161; Eastern Ky.: 72.		1	0	1	.000	1977
GENE SULLIVAN (Notre Dame '53) 9: 149-114; Loyola (Ill.): 85.		1	2	1	.667	1989
DON SUMAN (Rice '44) 10: 132-105; Rice: 54.		1	1	1	.500	1959
EDDIE SUTTON* (Oklahoma St. '59) 22: 482-180; 1 at Creighton: 74; 9 at Arkansas: 77, 78-3d, 79RR, 80, 81, 82, 83, 84, 85; 3 at Kentucky: 86RR, 87, 88; 2 at Oklahoma St.: 91, 92.		15	21	15	.583	Active
JOHNNY SWAIM (Texas Christian '53) 10: 102-151; Texas Christian: 68RR, 71.		2	1	2	.333	1977
CARL TACY (Davis & Elkins '56) 14: 245-153; 1 at Marshall: 72; 4 at Wake Forest: 77RR, 81, 82, 84RR.		5	5	5	.500	1985
JERRY TARKANIAN* (Fresno St. '56) 24: 625-122; 4 at Long Beach St.: 70, 71RR, 72, 73; 12 at Nevada-Las Vegas: 75, 76, 77-3d, 83, 84, 85, 86, 87-T3d, 88, 89RR, 90-CH, 91-T3d.		16	37	16	.698	1992
DICK TARRANT (Fordham '51) 11: 224-114; Richmond: 84, 86, 88, 90, 91.		5	5	5	.500	Active
BLAINE TAYLOR (Montana '82) 1: 27-4; Montana: 92.		1	0	1	.000	Active

Coach (Alma Mater)	Seasons, Career Record, Tourney Teams and Years in Tourney	Yrs.	W	L	Pct.	Last Year of Career
FRED TAYLOR (Ohio St. '50) 18: 297-158; Ohio St.: 60-CH, 61-2d, 62-2d, 68-3d, 71RR		5	14	4	.778	1976
GARY THOMPSON (Wichita St. '54) 7: 93-94; Wichita St.: 65-4th		1	2	2	.500	1971
JOHN THOMPSON (Providence '64) 20: 464-165; Georgetown: 75, 76, 79, 80RR, 81, 82-2d, 83, 84-CH, 85-2d, 86, 87RR, 88, 89RR, 90, 91, 92		16	28	15	.651	Active
BOB TIMMONS (Pittsburgh '33) 15: 174-189; Pittsburgh: 57, 58, 63		3	1	4	.200	1968
KEN TRICKEY (Middle Tenn. St. '54) 15: 217-173; Oral Roberts: 74RR		1	2	1	.667	1989
TERRY TRUAX (Maryland '68) 9: 126-139; Towson St.: 90, 91		2	0	2	.000	Active
BILLY TUBBS (Lamar '58) 18: 404-177; 2 at Lamar: 79, 80; 9 at Oklahoma: 83, 84, 85RR, 86, 87, 88-2d, 89, 90, 92		11	18	11	.621	Active
ROD TUELLER (Utah St. '59) 9: 139-120; Utah St.: 80, 83, 88		3	0	3	.000	1988
M. K. TURK (Livingston '64) 16: 246-207; Southern Miss.: 90, 91		2	0	2	.000	Active
FORREST TWOGOOD (Iowa '29) 21: 321-256; Southern Cal: 54-4th, 60, 61		3	3	5	.375	1966
PAUL VALENTI (Oregon St. '42) 7: 91-82; Oregon St.: 66RR		1	1	1	.500	1970
JIM VALVANO* (Rutgers '67) 19: 345-211; 2 at Iona: 79, 80; 7 at North Caro. St.: 82, 83-CH, 85RR, 86RR, 87, 88, 89		9	15	8	.652	1990
BOB VANATTA (Central Methodist '45) 22: 349-199; 1 at Bradley: 55RR; 1 at Memphis St.: 62		2	2	2	.500	1973
BILL van BREDA KOLFF (Princeton '47) 26: 464-234; Princeton: 63, 64, 65-3d, 67		4	7	5	.583	Active
JOE VANCISIN (Dartmouth '44) 19: 206-242; Yale: 57, 62		2	0	2	.000	1975
DICK VERSACE (Wisconsin '64) 8: 156-88; Bradley: 80, 86		2	1	2	.333	1986
TIM VEZIE (Denver '67) 7: 103-86; San Diego St.: 75, 76		2	0	2	.000	1979
MIKE VINING (Northeast La. '67) 11: 204-121; Northeast La.: 82, 86, 90, 91, 92		5	0	5	.000	Active
GENE VISSCHER (Weber St. '66) 6: 74-74; Weber St.: 72, 73		2	1	3	.250	1983
DICK VITALE (Seton Hall '62) 4: 78-30; Detroit Mercy: 77		1	1	1	.500	1977
BOB WADE* (Morgan St. '67) 3: 36-50; Maryland: 88		1	1	1	.500	1989
SOX WALSETH (Colorado '48) 22: 292-263; Colorado: 62RR, 63RR, 69		3	3	3	.500	1976
DICK WALTERS (Illinois St. '69) 7: 114-87; Evansville: 82		1	0	1	.000	1985
JOHN WARREN (Oregon '28) 5: 87-74; Oregon: 45RR		1	1	1	.500	1951
TOM WASDIN (Florida '57) 3: 63-18; Jacksonville: 71, 73		2	0	2	.000	1973
BUCKY WATERS (North Caro. St. '57) 8: 132-86; West Va.: 67		1	0	1	.000	1973
LOU WATSON (Indiana '50) 5: 62-60; Indiana: 67		1	1	1	.500	1971
STAN WATTS (Brigham Young '38) 23: 371-254; Brigham Young: 50, 51RR, 57, 65, 69, 71, 72		7	4	10	.286	1972
JAMES WEAVER (DePaul '47) 7: 110-69; St. Mary's (Cal.): 59RR		1	1	1	.500	1962
PAUL WEBB (William & Mary '51) 29: 511-257; Old Dominion: 80, 82, 85		3	0	3	.000	1985
BOB WEINHAUER (Cortland St. '61) 8: 143-90; Pennsylvania: 78, 79-4th, 80, 82		4	6	5	.545	1985
LARRY WEISE (St. Bonaventure '58) 12: 202-90; St. Bonaventure: 68, 70-4th		2	4	4	.500	1973
STEVE WELCH (Southeastern La. '71) 5: 52-90; McNeese St.: 89		1	0	1	.000	Active
BOB WELTLICH (Ohio St. '67) 14: 177-225; Mississippi: 81		1	0	1	.000	Active
BOB WENZEL (Rutgers '71) 10: 159-141; 1 at Jacksonville: 86; 2 at Rutgers: 89, 91		3	0	3	.000	Active
PAUL WESTHEAD [St. Joseph's (Pa.) '61] 14: 247-153; 2 at La Salle: 75, 78; 3 at Loyola (Cal.): 88, 89, 90RR		5	4	5	.444	1990
DAVEY WHITNEY (Kentucky St. '53) 25: 450-263; Alcorn St.: 80, 82, 83, 84		4	3	4	.429	1989
GEORGE WIGTON (Ohio St. '56) 21: 175-275; Connecticut: 63		1	0	1	.000	1986
CARROLL WILLIAMS (San Jose St. '55) 22: 341-277; Santa Clara: 87		1	0	1	.000	Active
GARY WILLIAMS (Maryland '67) 14: 256-169; 2 at Boston College: 83, 85; 1 at Ohio St.: 87		3	4	3	.571	Active
JIM WILLIAMS (Utah St. '47) 26: 352-293; Colorado St.: 63, 65, 66, 69RR		4	2	4	.333	1980
JOE WILLIAMS (Southern Methodist '56) 22: 363-253; 1 at Jacksonville: 70-2d; 5 at Furman: 71, 73, 74, 75, 78; 1 at Florida St.: 80		7	6	8	.429	1986
RICHARD WILLIAMS (Mississippi St. '67) 6: 85-87; Mississippi St.: 91		1	0	1	.000	Active
ROY WILLIAMS (North Caro. '72) 4: 103-30; Kansas: 90, 91-2d, 92		3	7	3	.700	Active
A. B. WILLIAMSON (North Caro. A&T '68) 15: 241-182; Howard: 81		1	0	1	.000	1990
TEX WINTER (Southern Cal '47) 30: 454-333; Kansas St.: 56, 58-4th, 59RR, 61RR, 64-4th, 68		6	7	9	.438	1983
JOHN WOODEN (Purdue '32) 29: 667-161; UCLA: 50, 52, 56, 62-4th, 63, 64-CH, 65-CH, 67-CH, 68-CH, 69-CH, 70-CH, 71-CH, 72-CH, 73-CH, 74-3d, 75-CH		16	47	10	.825	1975

Coach (Alma Mater)	Seasons, Career Record, Tourney Teams and Years in Tourney	Tournament Yrs.	W	L	Pct.	Last Year of Career
CHARLES WOOLLUM (William & Mary '62) 17: 285-198; Bucknell: 87, 89...		2	0	2	.000	Active
PHIL WOOLPERT [Loyola (Cal.) '40] 16: 239-164; San Francisco: 55-CH, 56-CH, 57-3d, 58..		4	13	2	.867	1969
NED WULK (Wis.-La Crosse '42) 31: 495-342; Arizona St.: 58, 61RR, 62, 63RR, 64, 73, 75RR, 80, 81....................................		9	8	10	.444	1982
WAYNE YATES (Memphis St. '61) 10: 141-141; Memphis St.: 76.......		1	0	1	.000	1985
STEVE YODER (Ill. Wesleyan '62) 15: 205-227; Ball St.: 81...........		1	0	1	.000	1992
TOM YOUNG (Maryland '58) 31: 524-328; 4 at Rutgers: 75, 76-4th, 79, 83; 1 at Old Dominion: 86...		5	6	6	.500	1991
BOB ZUFFELATO (Central Conn. St. '59) 10: 154-121; Boston College: 75..		1	1	2	.333	1983
MATT ZUNIC (Geo. Washington '42) 15: 213-135; 1 at Boston U.: 59RR; 1 at Massachusetts: 62....................................		2	2	2	.500	1976

NOTES ON COACHES
JAKE McCANDLESS coached Princeton in the 1961 tournament; FRANKLIN CAPPON suffered a heart attack 11 games into the season; Princeton credits the 1961 regular season to Cappon and the postseason to McCandless.
CLAIR MARKEY coached Seattle in the 1963 tournament due to VINCE CAZETTA's resignation.
STEVE FISHER coached Michigan in the 1989 tournament; BILL FRIEDER was the coach during the regular season.
Rick Daly coached Missouri in the 1989 tournament due to NORM STEWART's illness; Missouri credits the entire 1989 season to Stewart.

*Official NCAA Tournament Records	Yrs.	Won	Lost	Pct.
Larry Brown..	6	14	5	.737
Hugh Durham..	7	7	7	.500
Ricky Huckabay..	2	0	2	.000
Ron Jacobs..	0	0	0	.000
Lake Kelly...	2	1	2	.333
Dana Kirk..	0	0	0	.000
Jack Kraft...	6	7	7	.500
Ralph Miller..	7	3	8	.273
Bill Musselman...	0	0	0	.000
Johnny Oldham..	5	2	5	.286
Jack Ramsay...	6	5	10	.333
Wimp Sanderson...	9	10	9	.529
Beryl Shipley..	0	0	0	.000
Norm Sloan...	4	5	3	.625
Eddie Sutton..	14	19	14	.567
Jerry Tarkanian..	13	31	13	.705
Jim Valvano..	6	14	5	.737
Bob Wade...	0	0	0	.000

TOURNAMENT TRIVIA QUESTION...
Before first-year coach Steve Fisher led Michigan to the NCAA championship in 1989, when was the last time a coach won the title in his first tournament appearance? Answer: In 1963, George Ireland coached Loyola (Illinois) to the national title in his first tournament appearance.

ATTENDANCE
AND
SITES

Ten years ago, the Syracuse Carrier Dome was the site for the East regional, hosting St. John's (New York), Georgia, Ohio State and North Carolina. The semifinal session drew 23,286 fans, an East region attendance record.

ATTENDANCE HISTORY BY TOURNAMENT

Year	Final Date	Final Crowd	*Total Atten.	Ses.	Avg. Atten.	Final Site	Final Facility	No. of Teams
1939	3-27	5,500	15,025	5	3,005	Evanston, IL	Patten Gymnasium	8
1940	3-30	10,000	36,880	5	7,376	Kansas City, MO	Municipal Auditorium	8
1941	3-29	7,219	48,055	5	9,611	Kansas City, MO	Municipal Auditorium	8
1942	3-28	6,500	24,372	5	4,874	Kansas City, MO	Municipal Auditorium	8
1943	3-30	13,300	56,876	5	11,375	New York City, NY	Madison Sq. Garden	8
1944	3-28	15,000	59,369	5	11,874	New York City, NY	Madison Sq. Garden	8
1945	3-27	18,035	67,780	5	13,556	New York City, NY	Madison Sq. Garden	8
1946	3-26	18,479	73,116	5	14,623	New York City, NY	Madison Sq. Garden	8
1947	3-25	18,445	72,959	5	14,592	New York City, NY	Madison Sq. Garden	8
1948	3-23	16,174	72,523	5	14,505	New York City, NY	Madison Sq. Garden	8
1949	3-26	10,600	66,077	5	13,215	Seattle, WA	Edmundson Pavilion	8
1950	3-28	18,142	75,464	5	15,093	New York City, NY	Madison Sq. Garden	8
1951	3-27	15,348	110,645	9	12,294	Minneapolis, MN	Williams Arena	16
1952	3-26	10,700	115,712	10	11,571	Seattle, WA	U. of W. Pavilion	16
1953	3-18	10,500	127,149	14	9,082	Kansas City, MO	Municipal Auditorium	22
1954	3-20	10,500	115,391	15	7,693	Kansas City, MO	Municipal Auditorium	24
1955	3-19	10,500	116,983	15	7,799	Kansas City, MO	Municipal Auditorium	24
1956	3-24	10,600	132,513	15	8,834	Evanston, IL	McGaw Hall	25
1957	3-23	10,500	108,891	14	7,778	Kansas City, MO	Municipal Auditorium	23
1958	3-22	18,803	176,878	14	12,634	Louisville, KY	Freedom Hall	24
1959	3-21	18,498	161,809	14	11,558	Louisville, KY	Freedom Hall	23
1960	3-19	14,500	155,491	16	9,718	San Francisco, CA	Cow Palace	25
1961	3-25	10,700	169,520	14	12,109	Kansas City, MO	Municipal Auditorium	24
1962	3-24	18,469	177,469	14	12,676	Louisville, KY	Freedom Hall	25
1963	3-23	19,153	153,065	14	10,933	Louisville, KY	Freedom Hall	25
1964	3-21	10,864	140,790	14	10,056	Kansas City, MO	Municipal Auditorium	25
1965	3-20	13,204	140,673	13	10,821	Portland, OR	Memorial Coliseum	23
1966	3-19	14,253	140,925	13	10,840	College Park, MD	Cole Fieldhouse	22
1967	3-25	18,892	159,570	14	11,398	Louisville, KY	Freedom Hall	23
1968	3-23	14,438	160,888	14	11,492	Los Angeles, CA	Sports Arena	23
1969	3-22	18,669	165,712	15	11,047	Louisville, KY	Freedom Hall	25
1970	3-21	14,380	146,794	16	9,175	College Park, MD	Cole Fieldhouse	25
1971	3-27	31,765	207,200	16	12,950	Houston, TX	Astrodome	25
1972	3-25	15,063	147,304	16	9,207	Los Angeles, CA	Sports Arena	25
1973	3-26	19,301	163,160	16	10,198	St. Louis, MO	St. Louis Arena	25
1974	3-25	15,742	154,112	16	9,632	Greensboro, NC	Greensboro Coliseum	25
1975	3-31	15,151	183,857	18	10,214	San Diego, CA	Sports Arena	32
1976	3-29	17,540	202,502	18	11,250	Philadelphia, PA	Spectrum	32
1977	3-28	16,086	241,610	18	13,423	Atlanta, GA	Omni	32
1978	3-27	18,721	227,149	18	12,619	St. Louis, MO	Checkerdome	32
1979	3-26	15,410	262,101	22	11,914	Salt Lake City, UT	Special Events Center	40
1980	3-24	16,637	321,260	26	12,356	Indianapolis, IN	Market Square Arena	48
1981	3-30	18,276	347,414	26	13,362	Philadelphia, PA	Spectrum	48
1982	3-29	61,612	427,251	26	16,433	New Orleans, LA	Louisiana Superdome	48
1983	4-4	17,327	364,356	28	13,013	Albuquerque, NM	U. of New Mexico Pit	52
1984	4-2	38,471	397,481	28	14,196	Seattle, WA	Kingdome	53
1985	4-1	23,124	422,519	34	12,427	Lexington, KY	Rupp Arena	64
1986	3-31	16,493	499,704	34	14,697	Dallas, TX	Reunion Arena	64
1987	3-30	64,959	654,744	34	19,257	New Orleans, LA	Louisiana Superdome	64
1988	4-4	16,392	558,998	34	16,441	Kansas City, MO	Kemper Arena	64
1989	4-3	39,187	613,242	34	18,037	Seattle, WA	Kingdome	64
1990	4-2	17,675	537,138	34	15,798	Denver, CO	McNichols Arena	64
1991	4-1	47,100	665,707	34	19,580	Indianapolis, IN	Hoosier Dome	64
1992	4-6	50,379	573,175	34	16,858	Minneapolis, MN	Humphrey Metrodome	
1993	4-5					New Orleans, LA	Louisiana Superdome	
1994	4-4					Charlotte, NC	Charlotte Coliseum	
1995	4-3					Seattle, WA	Kingdome	
1996	4-1					East Rutherford, NJ	Meadowlands Arena	
1997	3-31					Indianapolis, IN	Hoosier Dome	

TOURNAMENT TRIVIA QUESTIONS...

What state has produced the most NCAA Division I basketball champions? Answer: California with 14. What states make up the rest of this list? Answer: Kentucky with 7, North Carolina 6, Indiana 5, Ohio 3, and Kansas, Michigan, Oklahoma, Pennsylvania and Wisconsin all with 2 apiece. With one each are the District of Columbia, Illinois, Massachusetts, Nevada, New York, Oregon, Texas, Utah and Wyoming.

	Championship Game...				Entire Tournament History...		
Years	Final Ses.	*Total Atten.	Avg. Atten.		All Sessions	*Total Atten.	*Avg. Atten.
1939-49	11	139,252	12,659		55	593,032	10,782
1950-59	10	134,091	13,409		125	1,241,435	9,931
1960-69	10	153,142	15,314		141	1,564,103	11,093
1970-79	10	179,159	17,916		174	1,935,789	11,125
1980-89	10	312,478	31,248		304	4,606,969	15,155
1990-92	3	115,154	38,385		102	1,776,020	17,412
All Time	54	1,033,276	19,135		901	11,717,348	13,005

*Total attendance: 1939-69; paid attendance: 1970-present.

ATTENDANCE RECORDS

Highest Total for Tournament
665,707, 1991 (34 sessions)
654,744, 1987 (34)
613,242, 1989 (34)
573,175, 1992 (34)
558,998, 1988 (34)
537,138, 1990 (34)
499,704, 1986 (34)
427,251, 1982 (26)
422,519, 1985 (34)
397,481, 1984 (28)

Highest Average per Game or Session for Tournament
19,580, 1991 (665,707 in 34 sessions)
19,257, 1987 (654,744 in 34 sessions)
18,037, 1989 (613,242 in 34)
16,858, 1992 (573,175 in 34)
16,441, 1988 (558,998 in 34)
16,433, 1982 (427,251 in 26)
15,798, 1990 (537,138 in 34)
15,093, 1950 (75,464 in 5)
14,697, 1986 (499,704 in 34)
14,623, 1946 (73,116 in 5)

Highest Game or Session for Tournament
64,959, Louisiana Superdome, New Orleans, La., CH, 1987, Indiana (74) vs. Syracuse (73); NSF, 1987, Indiana (97) vs. Nevada-Las Vegas (93) and Syracuse (77) vs. Providence (63)
61,612, Louisiana Superdome, New Orleans, La., CH, 1982, North Caro. (63) vs. Georgetown (62); NSF, 1982, North Caro., (68) vs. Houston (63) and Georgetown (50) vs. Louisville (46)
50,379, Hubert H. Humphrey Metrodome, Minneapolis, Minn., CH, 1992, Duke (71) vs. Michigan (51); NSF, 1992, Duke (81) vs. Indiana (78) and Michigan (76) vs. Cincinnati (72)
47,100, Hoosier Dome, Indianapolis, Ind., CH, 1991, Duke (72) vs. Kansas (65); NSF, 1991, Duke (79) vs. Nevada-Las Vegas (77) and Kansas (79) vs. North Caro. (73)
39,940, Hoosier Dome, Indianapolis, Ind., MW 1st (2nd session), 1990, Texas (100) vs. Georgia (88) and Purdue (75) vs. Northeast La. (63)
39,417, Hoosier Dome, Indianapolis, Ind., MW 1st (1st session), 1990, Georgetown (70) vs. Texas Southern (52) and Xavier (Ohio) (87) vs. Kansas St. (79)
39,187, Kingdome, Seattle, Wash., CH, 1989, Michigan (80) vs. Seton Hall (79) (ot); NSF, 1989, Michigan (83) vs. Illinois (81) and Seton Hall (95) vs. Duke (78)
38,471, Kingdome, Seattle, Wash., CH, 1984, Georgetown (84) vs. Houston (75); NSF, 1984, Georgetown (53) vs. Kentucky (40) and Houston (49) vs. Virginia (47) (ot)
37,842, Hoosier Dome, Indianapolis, Ind., MW 2nd, 1990, Texas (73) vs. Purdue (72) and Xavier (Ohio) (74) vs. Georgetown (71)
37,444, Hoosier Dome, Indianapolis, Ind., MW 2nd, 1989, Illinois (72) vs. Ball St. (60) and Louisville (93) vs. Arkansas (84)

[Note: Figures are paid attendance. For Final Four games, media also is included.]

Highest Single Game or Session—Final Four
64,959, Louisiana Superdome, New Orleans, La., CH, 1987, Indiana (74) vs. Syracuse (73); NSF, 1987, Indiana (97) vs. Nevada-Las Vegas (93) and Syracuse (77) vs. Providence (63)
61,612, Louisiana Superdome, New Orleans, La., CH, 1982, North Caro. (63) vs. Georgetown (62); NSF, 1982, North Caro. (68) vs. Houston (63) and Georgetown (50) vs. Louisville (46)
50,379, Hubert H. Humphrey Metrodome, Minneapolis, Minn., CH, 1992, Duke (71) vs. Michigan (51); NSF, 1992, Duke (81) vs. Indiana (78) and Michigan (76) vs. Cincinnati (72)
47,100, Hoosier Dome, Indianapolis, Ind., CH, 1991, Duke (72) vs. Kansas (65); NSF, 1991, Duke (79) vs. Nevada-Las Vegas (77) and Kansas (79) vs. North Caro. (73)
39,187, Kingdome, Seattle, Wash., CH, 1989, Michigan (80) vs. Seton Hall (79) (ot); NSF, 1989, Michigan (83) vs. Illinois (81) and Seton Hall (95) vs. Duke (78)
38,471, Kingdome, Seattle, Wash., CH, 1984, Georgetown (84) vs. Houston (75); NSF, 1984, Georgetown (53) vs. Kentucky (40) and Houston (49) vs. Virginia (47) (ot)
31,765, Astrodome, Houston, Tex., CH, 1971, UCLA (68) vs. Villanova (62)
31,428, Astrodome, Houston, Tex., NSF, 1971, Villanova (92) vs. Western Ky. (89) (2 ot) and UCLA (68) vs. Kansas (60)
23,124, Rupp Arena, Lexington, Ky., CH, 1985, Villanova (66) vs. Georgetown (64); NSF, 1985, Villanova (52) vs. Memphis St. (45) and Georgetown (77) vs. St. John's (N.Y.) (59)
19,301, St. Louis Arena, St. Louis, Mo., CH, 1973, UCLA (87) vs. Memphis St. (66); N3d, 1973, Indiana (97) vs. Providence (79)

[Note: Figures are paid attendance. For Final Four games, media also is included.]

Highest Single Game—National Championship Game
64,959, Louisiana Superdome, New Orleans, La., 1987, Indiana (74) vs. Syracuse (73)
61,612, Louisiana Superdome, New Orleans, La., 1982, North Caro. (63) vs. Georgetown (62)
50,379, Hubert H. Humphrey Metrodome, Minneapolis, Minn., 1992, Duke (71) vs. Michigan (51)
47,100, Hoosier Dome, Indianapolis, Ind., CH, 1991, Duke (72) vs. Kansas (65)
39,187, Kingdome, Seattle, Wash., 1989, Michigan (80) vs. Seton Hall (79) (ot)

Highest Single Game—Regionals Final Game
33,560, Hubert H. Humphrey Metrodome, Minneapolis, Minn., MW, 1989, Illinois (89) vs. Syracuse (86)
32,747, Louisiana Superdome, New Orleans, La., MW, 1981, Louisiana St. (96) vs. Wichita St. (85)
31,632, Silverdome, Pontiac, Mich., MW, 1988, Kansas (71) vs. Kansas St. (58)
25,634, Silverdome, Pontiac, Mich., MW, 1991, Duke (78) vs. St. John's (N.Y.) (61)
23,666, Kingdome, Seattle, Wash., West, 1991, Nevada-Las Vegas (77) vs. Seton Hall (65)

Highest Single Session—Regionals Semifinal Games
34,036, Louisiana Superdome, New Orleans, La., MW, 1981, Wichita St. (66) vs. Kansas (65) and Louisiana St. (72) vs. Arkansas (56)
33,560, Hubert H. Humphrey Metrodome, Minneapolis, Minn., MW, 1989, Illinois (83) vs. Louisville (69) and Syracuse (83) vs. Missouri (80)
31,309, Silverdome, Pontiac, Mich., MW, 1988, Kansas (77) vs. Vanderbilt (64) and Kansas St. (73) vs. Purdue (70)
30,461, Silverdome, Pontiac, Mich., MW, 1991, Duke (81) vs. Connecticut (67) and St. John's (N.Y.) (91) vs. Ohio St. (74)
23,525, Rupp Arena, Lexington, Ky., SE, 1984, Illinois (72) vs. Maryland (70) and Kentucky (72) vs. Louisville (67)

Highest Single Session—Second Round
37,842, Hoosier Dome, Indianapolis, Ind., MW 2nd, 1990, Texas (73) vs. Purdue (72) and Xavier (Ohio) (74) vs. Georgetown (71)
37,444, Hoosier Dome, Indianapolis, Ind., MW, 1989, Illinois (72) vs. Ball St. (60) and Louisville (93) vs. Arkansas (84)
34,576, Hoosier Dome, Indianapolis, Ind., MW, 1987, Duke (65) vs. Xavier (Ohio) (60) and Indiana (107) vs. Auburn (90)
28,114, Hubert H. Humphrey Metrodome, Minneapolis, Minn., MW, 1991, Connecticut (66) vs. Xavier (Ohio) (50) and Duke (85) vs. Iowa (70)
25,543, Hubert H. Humphrey Metrodome, Minneapolis, Minn., MW, 1986, North Caro. St. (80) vs. Ark.-Lit. Rock (66) (2 ot) and Iowa St. (72) vs. Michigan (69)

Highest Single Session—First Round
39,940, Hoosier Dome, Indianapolis, Ind., MW 1st (2nd session), 1990, Texas (100) vs. Georgia (88) and Purdue (75) vs. Northeast La. (63)
39,417, Hoosier Dome, Indianapolis, Ind., MW 1st (1st session), 1990, Georgetown (70) vs. Texas Southern (52) and Xavier (Ohio) (87) vs. Kansas St. (79)
36,823, Hoosier Dome, Indianapolis, Ind., MW 1st (2nd session), 1989, Illinois (77) vs. McNeese St. (71) and Ball St. (68) vs. Pittsburgh (64)
36,705, Hoosier Dome, Indianapolis, Ind., MW 1st (1st session), 1989, Arkansas (120) vs.

Loyola (Cal.) (101) and Louisville (76) vs. Ark.-Lit. Rock (71)
29,610, Hoosier Dome, Indianapolis, Ind., MW 1st (2nd session), 1987, Auburn (62) vs. San Diego (61) and Indiana (92) vs. Fairfield (58)

Highest Single Game or Session—East
23,286, Carrier Dome, Syracuse, N.Y., RSF, 1983, North Caro. (64) vs. Ohio St. (51) and Georgia (70) vs. St. John's (N.Y.) (67)
22,984, Carrier Dome, Syracuse, N.Y., RF, 1983, Georgia (82) vs. North Caro. (77)
21,713, Carrier Dome, Syracuse, N.Y., 2nd, 1986, Cleveland St. (75) vs. St. Joseph's (Pa.) (69) and Navy (97) vs. Syracuse (85)
20,505, Smith Center, Chapel Hill, N.C., 2nd, 1988, Rhode Island (97) vs. Syracuse (94) and Duke (94) vs. Southern Methodist (79)
19,633, Meadowlands Arena, East Rutherford, N.J., RF, 1988, Duke (63) vs. Temple (53)

Highest Single Game or Session—Southeast
23,525, Rupp Arena, Lexington, Ky., RF, 1984, Kentucky (54) vs. Illinois (51)
23,525, Rupp Arena, Lexington, Ky., RSF, 1984, Illinois (72) vs. Maryland (70) and Kentucky (72) vs. Louisville (67)
23,287, Charlotte Coliseum, Charlotte, N.C., RSF, 1991, Arkansas (93) vs. Alabama (70) and Kansas (83) vs. Indiana (65)
23,124, Rupp Arena, Lexington, Ky., RSF, 1992, Michigan (75) vs. Oklahoma St. (72) and Ohio St. (80) vs. North Caro. (73)
23,047, Rupp Arena, Lexington, Ky., RF, 1992, Michigan (75) vs. Ohio St. (71) (ot)

Highest Single Game or Session—Midwest
39,940, Hoosier Dome, Indianapolis, Ind., 1st (2nd session), 1990, Texas (100) vs. Georgia (88) and Purdue (75) vs. Northeast La. (63)
39,417, Hoosier Dome, Indianapolis, Ind., 1st (1st session), 1990, Georgetown (70) vs. Texas Southern (52) and Xavier (Ohio) (87) vs. Kansas St. (79)
37,842, Hoosier Dome, Indianapolis, Ind., 2nd, 1990, Texas (73) vs. Purdue (72) and Xavier (Ohio) (74) vs. Georgetown (71)
37,444, Hoosier Dome, Indianapolis, Ind., 2nd, 1989, Illinois (72) vs. Ball St. (60) and Louisville (93) vs. Arkansas (84)
36,823, Hoosier Dome, Indianapolis, Ind., 1st (2nd session), 1989, Illinois (77) vs. McNeese St. (71) and Ball St. (68) vs. Pittsburgh (64)

Highest Single Game or Session—West
23,666, Kingdome, Seattle, Wash., RF, 1991, Nevada-Las Vegas (77) vs. Seton Hall (65)
23,229, Kingdome, Seattle, Wash., RSF, 1988, Arizona (99) vs. Iowa (79) and North Caro. (78) vs. Michigan (69)
23,035, Kingdome, Seattle, Wash., RSF, 1987, Iowa (93) vs. Oklahoma (91) (ot) and Nevada-Las Vegas (92) vs. Wyoming (78)
22,914, Kingdome, Seattle, Wash., RF, 1987, Nevada-Las Vegas (84) vs. Iowa (81)
22,628, Kingdome, Seattle, Wash., RSF, 1991, Nevada-Las Vegas (83) vs. Utah (66) and Seton Hall (81) vs. Arizona (77)

ALL-TIME SITE AND ARENA HISTORY

Most Tournament Games by Arena
83, Municipal Auditorium, Kansas City, Mo., 1940-64
71, Madison Square Garden III, New York, N.Y., 1943-61
55, Omni, Atlanta, Ga., 1977-92
51, Palestra, Philadelphia, Pa., 1939-84
50, Charlotte Coliseum I, Charlotte, N.C., 1958-87
50, Freedom Hall, Louisville, Ky., 1958-91
49, University of Dayton Arena, Dayton, Ohio, 1970-92
45, Jon W. Huntsman Center, Salt Lake City, Utah, 1971-91
41, Gill Coliseum, Corvallis, Ore., 1952-83
41, William Neal Reynolds Coliseum, Raleigh, N.C., 1951-82

Most Regional Championship Games by Arena
13, Municipal Auditorium, Kansas City, Mo., 1940-52
9, Madison Square Garden III, New York, N.Y., 1943-51
8, Allen Field House, Lawrence, Kan., 1956-78
8, Gill Coliseum, Corvallis, Ore., 1952-67
8, William Neal Reynolds Coliseum, Raleigh, N.C., 1952-82
6, Ahearn Field House, Manhattan, Kan., 1953-69
6, Cole Field House, College Park, Md., 1962-77
6, Meadowlands Arena, East Rutherford, N.J., 1984-91
6, Palestra, Philadelphia, Pa., 1939-80
5, Charlotte Coliseum I, Charlotte, N.C., 1958-73
5, Pauley Pavilion, Los Angeles, Calif., 1966-84
5, Rupp Arena, Lexington, Ky., 1977-92

Most National Championship Games by Arena
9, Municipal Auditorium, Kansas City, Mo., 1940-64
7, Madison Square Garden III, New York, N.Y., 1943-50
6, Freedom Hall, Louisville, Ky., 1958-69
2, St. Louis Arena, St. Louis, Mo., 1973-78
2, Cole Field House, College Park, Md., 1966-70
2, Kingdome, Seattle, Wash., 1984-89
2, L.A. Sports Arena, Los Angeles, Calif., 1968-72
2, Louisiana Superdome, New Orleans, La., 1982-87
2, Spectrum, Philadelphia, Pa., 1976-81
1, 19 tied

Most Tournament Games by City
95, Kansas City, Mo., 1940-92
76, New York, N.Y., 1943-74
62, Philadelphia, Pa., 1939-92
55, Atlanta, Ga., 1977-92
53, Charlotte, N.C., 1958-91
50, Louisville, Ky., 1958-91
49, Dayton, Ohio, 1970-92
47, Salt Lake City, Utah, 1968-91
46, Lexington, Ky., 1955-92
41, Corvallis, Ore., 1952-83
41, Raleigh, N.C., 1951-82

Most Regional Championships by City
16, Kansas City, Mo., 1940-92
9, Lexington, Ky., 1957-92
9, New York, N.Y., 1943-51
8, Corvallis, Ore., 1952-67
8, Lawrence, Kan., 1956-78
8, Raleigh, N.C., 1951-82
7, Provo, Utah, 1962-82
6, Charlotte, N.C., 1958-91

6, College Park, Md., 1962-77
6, East Rutherford, N.J.,1986-91
6, Manhattan, Kan., 1953-69
6, New Orleans, La., 1972-90
6, Philadelphia, Pa., 1939-92

Most National Championship Games by City
10, Kansas City, Mo., 1940-88
7, New York, N.Y., 1943-50
6, Louisville, Ky., 1958-69
4, Seattle, Wash., 1949-89
2, College Park, Md., 1966-70
2, Evanston, Ill., 1939-56
2, Indianapolis, Ind., 1980-91
2, Los Angeles, Calif., 1968-72
2, Minneapolis, Minn., 1951-92
2, New Orleans, La., 1982-87
2, Philadelphia, Pa., 1976-81
2, St. Louis, Mo., 1973-78

Most Tournament Games by State
137, North Carolina, 1951-92
109, Missouri, 1940-92
103, New York, 1943-91
102, Kentucky, 1955-92
96, Utah, 1960-91
92, Texas, 1957-90
85, Kansas, 1953-81
81, California, 1939-90
77, Ohio, 1957-92
76, Indiana, 1940-91

Most Regional Championships by State
18, Missouri, 1940-92
17, Kansas, 1953-78
16, North Carolina , 1952-91
13, Kentucky , 1957-92
10, Oregon, 1952-75
10, Utah, 1962-83
10, New York, 1943-83
9, California, 1939-90
7, Texas, 1957-90
6, Ohio, 1970-87
6, Pennsylvania, 1939-92
6, Maryland, 1962-77
6, New Jersey, 1986-91

Most National Championship Games by State
12, Missouri, 1940-88
7, Kentucky, 1958-85
7, New York, 1943-50
4, California, 1960-75
4, Washington, 1949-89
2, Illinois, 1939-56
2, Indiana, 1980-91
2, Louisiana, 1982-87
2, Maryland, 1966-70
2, Minnesota, 1951-92
2, Pennsylvania, 1976-81
2, Texas, 1971-86

TOURNAMENT GAME ARENAS BY SITE

G	S	Yr.	Round	City	Facility	Built	Capacity
ALABAMA							
3	2	82	ME Rgnl	Birmingham	#Birmingham-Jefferson Civic Center	1976	17,500
4	2	84	E 1st-2d	"	"		"
3	2	85	SE Rgnl	"	"		"
6	3	87	SE 1st-2nd	"	"		"
3	2	88	SE Rgnl	"	"		"
4	2	74	ME Rgnl	Tuscaloosa	Memorial Coliseum	1968	15,043
2	1	75	ME lst	"	"		"
4	2	81	ME lst-2nd	"	"		"
					(now named Coleman Coliseum)		
ARIZONA							
2	1	75	W 1st	Tempe	University Activity Center	1974	14,287
2	1	76	W 1st	"	"		"
2	1	78	W 1st	"	"		"

G	S	Yr.	Round	City	Facility	Built	Capacity
4	2	80	W 1st-2nd	"	"		"
6	3	92	W 1st-2nd	"	"		"
4	2	74	W Rgnl	Tucson	McKale Center	1973	14,214
2	1	77	W 1st	"	"		"
2	1	79	W 2nd	"	"		
3	2	80	W Rgnl	"	"		
6	3	87	W 1st-2nd	"	"		13,124
6	3	89	W 1st-2nd	"	"		13,477
6	3	91	W 1st-2nd	"	"		"
CALIFORNIA							
2	1	58	W 1st	Berkeley	Harmon Arena	1933	6,450
6	3	86	W 1st-2nd	Long Beach	#Long Beach Arena	1965	12,000
6	3	90	W 1st-2nd	"	"		
4	2	68	Final Four	Los Angeles	#L.A. Sports Arena	1959	15,509
4	2	72	Final Four	"	"		"
4	2	66	W Rgnl	"	Pauley Pavilion	1965	12,543
4	2	69	W Rgnl	"	"		"
4	2	73	W Rgnl	"	"		"
3	2	76	W Rgnl	"	"		"
4	2	79	W 1st-2nd	"	"		"
4	2	81	W 1st-2nd	"	"		"
3	2	84	W Rgnl	"	"		"
6	3	88	W 1st-2nd	"	"		"
3	2	90	W Rgnl	Oakland	#Oakland Coliseum	1966	15,000
1	1	53	W-2 1st	Palo Alto	Old Pavilion	1922	3,000
4	2	75	Final Four	San Diego	#San Diego Sports Arena	1967	13,741
4	2	39	Wn Rgnl	San Francisco	#California Coliseum	1938	9,476
2	1	55	W-2 1st	"	#Cow Palace	1941	14,500
4	2	58	W Rgnl	"	"		
4	2	59	W Rgnl	"	"		"
1	1	60	W 1st	"	"		"
4	2	60	Final Four	"	"		"
COLORADO							
3	2	85	W Rgnl	Denver	#McNichols Sports Arena	1974	17,022
3	2	89	W Rgnl	"	"		"
3	2	90	Final Four	"	"		"
2	1	67	MW, W 1st	Fort Collins	Moby Arena	1966	9,001
CONNECTICUT							
4	2	83	E 1st-2nd	Hartford	#Hartford Civic Center	1975	16,016
6	3	85	E 1st-2nd	"	"		"
6	3	88	E 1st-2nd	"	"		"
6	3	90	E 1st-2nd	"	"		"
FLORIDA							
4	2	83	ME 1st-2nd	Tampa	USF Sun Dome	1980	10,347
GEORGIA							
4	2	71	ME Rgnl	Athens	Georgia Coliseum	1964	11,200
4	2	77	Final Four	Atlanta	#Omni	1972	16,271
3	2	81	E Rgnl	"	"		"
3	2	84	E Rgnl	"	"		"
6	3	85	E 1st-2nd	"	"		"
3	2	86	SE Rgnl	"	"		"
6	3	87	SE 1st-2nd	"	"		"
6	3	88	SE 1st-2nd	"	"		"
6	3	89	SE 1st-2nd	"	"		"
6	3	90	E 1st-2nd	"	"		"
6	3	91	SE 1st-2nd	"	"		"
6	3	92	SE 1st-2nd	"	"		"
IDAHO							
4	2	83	W 1st-2nd	Boise	BSU Pavilion	1982	12,200
6	3	89	W 1st-2nd	"	"		"
6	3	92	W 1st-2nd	"	"		"
1	1	57	W 1st	Pocatello	ISU Gymnasium (now named Reed Gym)	1948	3,500
2	1	72	W 1st	"	ISU Minidome	1969	12,000
2	1	74	W 1st	"	"		"
2	1	77	W 1st	"	(now named Holt Arena)		"
ILLINOIS							
2	1	69	ME 1st	Carbondale	SIU Arena	1964	10,014
1	1	60	MW 1st	Chicago	Alumni Arena	1956	5,308
4	2	52	E-2 Rgnl	"	#Chicago Stadium	1929	17,458
4	2	53	E-2 Rgnl	"	"		"
4	2	55	E-2 Rgnl	Evanston	McGaw Hall	1952	10,500

G	S	Yr.	Round	City	Facility	Built	Capacity
4	2	56	Final Four	"	"		"
2	1	58	ME 1st	"	"		"
4	2	59	ME Rgnl	"	"		"
2	1	63	ME 1st	"	"		"
2	1	64	ME 1st	"	"		"
4	2	67	ME Rgnl	"	"		"
					(now named Welsh-Ryan Arena/McGaw Hall)		
1	1	39	CH	"	Patten Gym	1910	6,000
1	1	54	W-1 1st	Peoria	Robertson Memorial Field House	1949	7,300
6	3	87	MW 1st-2nd	Rosemont	#Rosemont Horizon	1980	17,500
INDIANA							
2	1	77	ME 1st	Bloomington	Assembly Hall	1971	17,357
2	1	79	ME 2nd	"	"	"	"
3	2	81	ME Rgnl	"	"	"	"
4	2	83	ME 1st-2nd	Evansville	#Roberts Municipal Stadium	1956	11,096
2	1	53	E-2 1st	Fort Wayne	#Allen County Coliseum	1952	9,500
2	1	54	E-2 1st	"	"	"	"
2	1	56	ME 1st	"	"	"	"
3	2	40	En Rgnl	Indianapolis	Butler Field House	1928	15,000
					(now named Hinkle Field House)		
6	3	87	MW 1st-2nd	"	#Hoosier Dome	1984	47,100
6	3	89	MW 1st-2nd	"	"	"	"
6	3	90	MW 1st-2nd	"	"	"	"
3	2	91	Final Four	"	"	"	"
2	1	78	ME 1st	"	#Market Square Arena	1974	17,000
3	2	79	ME Rgnl	"	"	"	"
4	2	80	Final Four	"	"	"	"
4	2	82	ME 1st-2nd	"	"	"	"
2	1	71	ME 1st	South Bend	Athletic & Convocation Center	1968	11,350
2	1	76	ME 1st	"	"	"	"
6	3	85	SE 1st-2nd	"	"	"	"
6	3	88	MW 1st-2nd	"	"	"	"
2	1	74	ME 1st	Terre Haute	Hulman Center	1973	10,200
4	2	80	ME 1st-2nd	West Lafayette	Mackey Arena	1967	14,123
IOWA							
4	2	72	MW Rgnl	Ames	James Hilton Coliseum	1971	14,020
4	2	54	E-2 Rgnl	Iowa City	Iowa Field House	1927	13,500
4	2	56	MW Rgnl	"	"	"	"
4	2	62	ME Rgnl	"	"	"	"
4	2	66	ME Rgnl	"	"	"	"
KANSAS							
4	2	56	MW Rgnl	Lawrence	Allen Field House	1955	15,200
4	2	58	MW Rgnl	"	"	"	"
4	2	59	MW Rgnl	"	"	"	"
4	2	61	MW Rgnl	"	"	"	"
4	2	63	MW Rgnl	"	"	"	"
4	2	67	MW Rgnl	"	"	"	"
4	2	70	MW Rgnl	"	"	"	"
2	1	76	MW 1st	"	"	"	"
3	2	78	MW Rgnl	"	"	"	"
4	2	79	MW 1st-2nd	"	"	"	"
4	2	53	W-1 Rgnl	Manhattan	Ahearn Field House	1951	12,500
4	2	55	W-1 Rgnl	"	"	"	"
4	2	60	MW Rgnl	"	"	"	"
4	2	62	MW Rgnl	"	"	"	"
4	2	65	MW Rgnl	"	"	"	"
4	2	69	MW Rgnl	"	"	"	"
2	1	56	MW 1st	Wichita	Levitt Arena	1955	10,716
4	2	64	MW Rgnl	"	"	"	10,666
2	1	66	MW, W 1st	"	"	"	"
4	2	68	MW Rgnl	"	"	"	"
4	2	71	MW Rgnl	"	"	"	"
2	1	73	MW 1st	"	"	"	"
2	1	78	MW 1st	"	"	"	"
4	2	81	MW 1st-2nd	"	"	"	"
KENTUCKY							
2	1	65	ME 1st	Bowling Green	E.A. Diddle Arena	1963	8,500
4	2	80	ME 1st-2nd	"	"		12,370
2	1	55	E-2 1st	Lexington	Memorial Coliseum	1950	11,500
4	2	57	ME Rgnl	"	"	"	"
4	2	58	ME Rgnl	"	"	"	"
2	1	59	ME 1st	"	"	"	"
2	1	60	ME 1st	"	"	"	"

G	S	Yr.	Round	City	Facility	Built	Capacity
2	1	62	ME 1st	"	"		"
4	2	65	ME Rgnl	"	"		"
2	1	67	ME 1st	"	"		"
4	2	68	ME Rgnl	"	"		"
2	1	75	ME 1st	"	"		"
3	2	77	ME Rgnl	"	#Rupp Arena	1976	23,000
3	2	80	ME Rgnl	"	"		"
3	2	84	ME Rgnl	"	"		"
3	2	85	Final Four	"	"		"
3	2	89	SE Rgnl	"	"		"
3	2	92	SE Rgnl	"	"		"
4	2	58	Final Four	Louisville	#Freedom Hall	1956	17,865
4	2	59	Final Four	"	"		18,750
4	2	60	ME Rgnl	"	"		"
6	3	61	ME 1st-Rgnl	"	"		18,000
4	2	62	Final Four	"	"		"
4	2	63	Final Four	"	"		"
4	2	67	Final Four	"	"		18,800
4	2	69	Final Four	"	"		"
3	2	76	MW Rgnl	"	"		16,433
4	2	83	MW 1st-2nd	"	"		16,613
3	2	87	SE Rgnl	"	"		19,865
6	3	91	SE 1st-2nd	"	"		18,946

LOUISIANA

G	S	Yr.	Round	City	Facility	Built	Capacity
3	2	76	ME Rgnl	Baton Rouge	Assembly Center	1971	14,327
2	1	77	ME 1st	"	"		14,327
6	3	86	ME 1st-2nd	"	"		14,236
4	2	42	En Rgnl	New Orleans	Tulane Gym (now named Fogelman Arena)	1933	3,000
3	2	81	MW Rgnl	"	#Louisiana Superdome	1975	64,959
3	2	82	Final Four	"	"		"
3	2	87	Final Four	"	"		"
3	2	90	SE Rgnl	"	"		"

MARYLAND

G	S	Yr.	Round	City	Facility	Built	Capacity
4	2	62	E Rgnl	College Park	Cole Field House	1955	14,500
4	2	63	E Rgnl	"	"		"
4	2	65	E Rgnl	"	"		"
4	2	66	Final Four	"	"		"
4	2	67	E Rgnl	"	"		"
2	1	68	E 1st	"	"		"
4	2	69	E Rgnl	"	"		"
4	2	70	Final Four	"	"		"
3	2	77	E Rgnl	"	"		"
6	3	91	E 1st-2nd	"	"		"

MASSACHUSETTS

G	S	Yr.	Round	City	Facility	Built	Capacity
6	3	92	E 1st-2nd	Worcester	#Centrum	1983	13,452

MICHIGAN

G	S	Yr.	Round	City	Facility	Built	Capacity
4	2	63	ME Rgnl	East Lansing	Jenison Field House	1940	12,500
3	2	88	MW Rgnl	Pontiac	#Pontiac Silverdome	1975	36,000
3	2	91	MW Rgnl	"	"		"

MINNESOTA

G	S	Yr.	Round	City	Facility	Built	Capacity
6	3	86	MW 1st-2nd	Minneapolis	#Hubert H. Humphrey Metrodome	1982	35,000
3	2	89	MW Rgnl	"	"		"
6	3	91	MW 1st-2nd	"	"		"
3	2	92	Final Four	"	"		"
2	1	51	CH-3d	"	Williams Arena	1928	18,052
4	2	64	ME Rgnl	"	"		"

MISSOURI

G	S	Yr.	Round	City	Facility	Built	Capacity
3	2	83	MW Rgnl	Kansas City	#Kemper Arena	1975	17,153
3	2	86	MW Rgnl	"	"		"
3	2	88	Final Four	"	"		"
3	2	92	MW Rgnl	"	"		"
5	3	40	Wn Rgnl-CH	"	#Municipal Auditorium	1935	10,500
5	3	41	Wn Rgnl-CH	"	"		"
5	3	42	Wn Rgnl-CH	"	"		"
4	2	43	Wn Rgnl	"	"		"
4	2	44	Wn Rgnl	"	"		"
4	2	45	Wn Rgnl	"	"		"
4	2	46	Wn Rgnl	"	"		"
4	2	47	Wn Rgnl	"	"		"
4	2	48	Wn Rgnl	"	"		"
4	2	49	Wn Rgnl	"	"		"
4	2	50	Wn Rgnl	"	"		"
8	4	51	W 1st-Rgnl	"	"		"

G	S	Yr.	Round	City	Facility	Built	Capacity
4	2	52	W-1 Rgnl	"	"		"
4	2	53	Final Four	"	"		"
4	2	54	Final Four	"	"		"
4	2	55	Final Four	"	"		"
4	2	57	Final Four	"	"		"
4	2	61	Final Four	"	"		"
4	2	64	Final Four	"	"		"
4	2	73	Final Four	St. Louis	#The Arena	1929	18,500
4	2	78	Final Four	"	#Checkerdome (name change)		"
3	2	82	MW Rgnl	"			"
3	2	84	MW Rgnl	"	#The Arena (name changed back)		"
NEBRASKA							
4	2	80	MW 1st-2nd	Lincoln	Bob Devaney Sports Center	1976	14,478
4	2	84	MW 1st-2nd	"	"		"
6	3	88	MW 1st-2nd	"	"		"
2	1	77	MW 1st	Omaha	#Omaha Civic Auditorium	1954	9,373
NEW JERSEY							
4	2	84	E 1st-2nd	East Rutherford	#Meadowlands Arena	1981	20,149
3	2	86	E Rgnl	"	"		"
3	2	87	E Rgnl	"	"		"
3	2	88	E Rgnl	"	"		"
3	2	89	E Rgnl	"	"		"
3	2	90	E Rgnl	"	"		"
3	2	91	E Rgnl	"	"		"
1	1	70	E 1st	Princeton	Jadwin Gymnasium	1969	7,550
1	1	72	E 1st	"			"
NEW MEXICO							
4	2	68	W Rgnl	Albuquerque	University Arena	1966	14,831
3	2	78	W Rgnl	"	"		17,126
3	2	83	Final Four	"	"		"
6	3	85	W 1st-2nd	"	"		"
3	2	92	W Rgnl	"	"		"
1	1	59	W 1st	Las Cruces	Las Cruces HS Gymnasium	1958	5,000
2	1	69	W 1st	"	Pan American Center	1968	13,222
2	1	72	W 1st	"	"		"
4	2	75	W Rgnl	"	"		"
NEW YORK							
2	1	54	E-1 1st	Buffalo	#Buffalo Memorial Auditorium	1936	13,900
1	1	70	E 1st	Jamaica	Alumni Hall	1962	6,000
1	1	71	E 1st	"	"		"
1	1	72	E 1st	"	"		"
1	1	73	E 1st	"	"		"
1	1	74	E 1st	"	"		"
5	3	43	En Rgnl-CH	New York City	#Madison Square Garden III	1925	18,479
5	3	44	En Rgnl-CH	"	"		"
5	3	45	En Rgnl-CH	"	"		"
6	3	46	En Rgnl-CH-3d	"	"		
6	3	47	En Rgnl-CH-3d	"	"		"
6	3	48	En Rgnl-CH-3d	"	"		"
4	2	49	En Rgnl	"	"		"
6	3	50	En Rgnl-CH-3d	"	"		"
6	3	51	E 1st-Rgnl	"	"		"
3	1	55	E-1 1st TH	"	"		"
4	2	56	E 1st	"	"		"
3	1	57	E 1st TH	"	"		"
3	1	58	E 1st TH	"	"		"
3	1	59	E 1st TH	"	"		"
3	1	60	E 1st TH	"	"		"
3	1	61	E 1st TH	"	"		"
3	2	83	E Rgnl	Syracuse	Carrier Dome	1980	33,000
6	3	86	E 1st-2nd	"	"		"
6	3	87	E 1st-2nd	"	"		"
6	3	91	E 1st-2nd	"	"		"
4	2	82	E 1st-2nd	Uniondale	#Nassau Coliseum	1972	16,547
NORTH CAROLINA							
6	3	88	E 1st-2nd	Chapel Hill	Dean E. Smith Center	1986	21,444
4	2	58	E Rgnl	Charlotte	#Charlotte Coliseum I	1951	11,666
4	2	59	E Rgnl	"	"		"
4	2	60	E Rgnl	"	"		"
4	2	61	E Rgnl	"	"		"
4	2	73	E Rgnl	"	"		"

G	S	Yr.	Round	City	Facility	Built	Capacity
2	1	75	E 1st	"	"		"
2	1	76	E 1st	"	"		"
2	1	78	E 1st	"	"		"
4	2	81	E 1st-2nd	"	"		"
4	2	82	E 1st-2nd	"	"		"
4	2	84	E 1st-2nd	"	"		"
6	3	86	SE 1st-2nd	"	"		"
6	3	87	E 1st-2nd	"	"		"
3	2	91	SE Rgnl	"	#Charlotte Coliseum II	1988	23,339
1	1	54	E-1 1st	Durham	Cameron Indoor Stadium	1939	8,564
4	2	74	Final Four	Greensboro	#Greensboro Coliseum	1959	16,000
3	2	76	E Rgnl	"	"		"
3	2	79	E Rgnl	"	"		"
4	2	80	E 1st-2nd	"	"		"
4	2	83	E 1st-2nd	"	"		"
6	3	86	E 1st-2nd	"	"		"
6	3	89	E 1st-2nd	"	"		"
6	3	92	E 1st-2nd	"	"		"
2	1	51	E 1st	Raleigh	William Neal Reynolds Coliseum	1949	12,400
4	2	52	E-1 Rgnl	"	"		"
4	2	53	E-1 Rgnl	"	"		"
4	2	64	E Rgnl	"	"		"
4	2	66	E Rgnl	"	"		"
4	2	68	E Rgnl	"	"		"
2	1	69	E 1st	"	"		"
4	2	71	E Rgnl	"	"		"
4	2	74	E Rgnl	"	"		"
2	1	77	E 1st	"	"		"
4	2	79	E 1st-2nd	"	"		"
3	2	82	E Rgnl	"	"		"

OHIO

G	S	Yr.	Round	City	Facility	Built	Capacity
3	2	79	MW Rgnl	Cincinnati	#Riverfront Coliseum	1975	16,562
3	2	87	MW Rgnl	"	"		"
6	3	88	SE 1st-2nd	"	"		"
6	3	92	SE 1st-2nd	"	"		"
2	1	57	ME 1st	Columbus	St. John Arena	1956	13,489
4	2	70	ME Rgnl	"	"		"
2	1	70	ME 1st	Dayton	University of Dayton Arena	1969	13,455
4	2	72	ME Rgnl	"	"		"
2	1	73	ME 1st	"	"		"
4	2	75	ME Rgnl	"	"		"
2	1	76	ME 1st	"	"		"
3	2	78	ME Rgnl	"	"		"
4	2	81	ME 1st-2nd	"	"		"
2	1	83	OR	"	"		"
2	1	84	OR	"	"		"
6	3	85	SE 1st-2nd	"	"		"
6	3	86	MW 1st-2nd	"	"		"
6	3	91	MW 1st-2nd	"	"		"
6	3	92	MW 1st-2nd	"	"		"
2	1	66	ME 1st	Kent	Memorial Gymnasium	1950	6,034
2	1	68	ME 1st	"	"		"

OKLAHOMA

G	S	Yr.	Round	City	Facility	Built	Capacity
1	1	55	W-1 1st	El Reno	Thunderbird Coliseum	1954	4,000
2	1	77	MW 1st	Norman	Lloyd Noble Center	1975	10,871
1	1	57	MW 1st	Oklahoma City	Capitol Hill HS Arena	1953	4,000
3	2	77	MW Rgnl	"	#Myriad Convention Center	1974	15,200
4	2	54	W-1 Rgnl	Stillwater	Gallagher Hall	1938	7,400
1	1	58	MW 1st	"	"		"
4	2	74	MW Rgnl	Tulsa	Mabee Center	1972	10,575
2	1	75	MW 1st	"	"		"
2	1	78	MW 1st	"	"		"
4	2	82	MW 1st-2nd	"	"		"
6	3	85	MW 1st-2nd	"	"		"

OREGON

G	S	Yr.	Round	City	Facility	Built	Capacity
4	2	52	W-2 Rgnl	Corvallis	Gill Coliseum	1949	10,000
4	2	53	W-2 Rgnl	"	"		"
6	3	54	W -2 1st-Rgnl	"	"		"
4	2	55	W-2 Rgnl	"	"		"
4	2	56	FW Rgnl	"	"		"
4	2	57	W Rgnl	"	"		"
1	1	60	W 1st	"	"		"
2	1	62	W 1st	"	"		"
4	2	64	W Rgnl	"	"		"
4	2	67	W Rgnl	"	"		"

G	S	Yr.	Round	City	Facility	Built	Capacity
				"	"		"
4	2	83	W 1st-2nd	"	"		
2	1	63	W 1st	Eugene	McArthur Court	1926	10,099
2	1	64	W 1st	"	"		
2	1	76	W 1st	"	"		"
2	1	78	W 1st	"	"		"
6	3	61	W 1st-Rgnl	Portland	#Memorial Coliseum	1960	12,666
4	2	65	Final Four	"	"		"
4	2	75	W Rgnl	"	"		"
1	1	59	W 1st	"	#Pacific International Livestock Pavilion (now named Pacific Exposition Center)	1919	4,200

PENNSYLVANIA

G	S	Yr.	Round	City	Facility	Built	Capacity
3	2	39	En Rgnl	Philadelphia	Palestra	1927	9,200
2	1	53	E-1 1st	"	"		"
4	2	54	E-1 Rgnl	"	"		"
4	2	55	E-1 Rgnl	"	"		"
4	2	56	E Rgnl	"	"		"
4	2	57	E Rgnl	"	"		"
3	1	62	E 1st TH	"	"		"
3	1	63	E 1st TH	"	"		"
3	1	64	E 1st TH	"	"		"
3	1	65	E 1st TH	"	"		"
1	1	70	E 1st	"	"		"
1	1	71	E 1st	"	"		"
1	1	73	E 1st	"	"		"
1	1	74	E 1st	"	"		"
2	1	75	E 1st	"	"		"
2	1	77	E 1st	"	"		"
2	1	78	E 1st	"	"		"
3	2	80	E Rgnl	"	"		"
2	1	83	OR	"	"		"
3	1	84	OR TH	"	"		"
4	2	76	Final Four	"	#Spectrum	1967	17,937
4	2	81	Final Four	"	"		"
3	2	92	E Rgnl	"	"		"

RHODE ISLAND

G	S	Yr.	Round	City	Facility	Built	Capacity
1	1	67	E 1st	Kingston	Keaney Gymnasium	1953	5,000
1	1	68	E 1st	"	"		"
1	1	69	E 1st	"	"		"
4	2	75	E Rgnl	Providence	#Providence Civic Center	1972	12,155
2	1	76	E 1st	"	"		"
3	2	78	E Rgnl	"	"		"
2	1	79	E 2nd	"	"		"
4	2	80	E 1st-2nd	"	"		"
4	2	81	E 1st-2nd	"	"		"
3	2	85	E Rgnl	"	"		"
6	3	89	E 1st-2nd	"	"		13,100

SOUTH CAROLINA

G	S	Yr.	Round	City	Facility	Built	Capacity
4	2	70	E Rgnl	Columbia	Carolina Coliseum	1968	12,401

TENNESSEE

G	S	Yr.	Round	City	Facility	Built	Capacity
2	1	72	ME 1st	Knoxville	Stokley Athletics Center	1966	12,700
2	1	78	ME 1st	"	"		"
3	2	83	ME Rgnl	"	"		"
6	3	83	SE 1st-2nd	"	Thompson-Boling Arena	1987	24,535
4	2	84	MW 1st-2nd	Memphis	#Mid-South Coliseum	1975	11,200
4	2	79	ME 1st-2nd	Murfreesboro	Murphy Athletic Center	1972	11,520
4	2	73	ME Rgnl	Nashville	Memorial Gymnasium	1952	15,626
4	2	82	ME 1st-2nd	"	"		"
6	3	89	SE 1st-2nd	"	"		"

TEXAS

G	S	Yr.	Round	City	Facility	Built	Capacity
4	2	81	MW 1st-2nd	Austin	Frank Erwin Center	1977	16,231
6	3	90	MW 1st-2nd	"	"		"
4	2	57	MW Rgnl	Dallas	Moody Coliseum	1956	9,007
2	1	62	MW 1st	"	"		"
2	1	64	MW 1st	"	"		"
2	1	79	MW 2nd	"	"		"
4	2	82	MW 1st-2nd	"	#Reunion Arena	1980	17,000
3	2	85	MW Rgnl	"	"		"
3	2	86	Final Four	"	"		"
6	3	89	MW 1st-2nd	"	"		"
3	2	90	MW Rgnl	"	"		"
2	1	74	MW 1st	Denton	North Texas Coliseum	1973	10,000
2	1	76	MW 1st	"	"		"
4	2	80	MW 1st-2nd	"	"		"
4	2	81	W 1st-2nd	El Paso	Special Events Center	1977	12,000

G	S	Yr.	Round	City	Facility	Built	Capacity
2	1	69	MW 1st	Fort Worth	Daniel-Meyer Coliseum	1961	7,166
2	1	70	MW 1st	"	"		"
4	2	71	Final Four	Houston	#Astrodome	1965	31,765
1	1	61	MW 1st	"	Delmar Field House	1960	5,300
2	1	71	MW 1st	"	Hofheinz Pavilion	1969	10,066
4	2	73	MW Rgnl	"	"		"
6	3	85	MW 1st-2nd	"	"		"
3	2	80	MW Rgnl	"	#The Summit	1975	16,016
4	2	83	MW 1st-2nd	"	"		"
3	2	86	W Rgnl	"	"		"
2	1	63	MW 1st	Lubbock	Lubbock Memorial Coliseum	1956	8,174
2	1	65	MW 1st	"	"		"
4	2	66	MW Rgnl	"	"		"
2	1	75	MW 1st	"	"		"
UTAH
2	1	71	W 1st	Logan	Dee Glen Smith Spectrum	1970	10,270
2	1	73	W 1st	"	"		"
4	2	82	W 1st-2nd	"	"		"
4	2	80	W 1st-2nd	Ogden	Dee Event Center	1977	11,592
3	2	83	W Rgnl	"	"		"
6	3	86	W 1st-2nd	"	"		"
1	1	60	W 1st	Provo	George Albert Smith Field House	1951	10,500
4	2	62	W Rgnl	"	"		"
4	2	63	W Rgnl	"	"		"
4	2	65	W Rgnl	"	"		"
2	1	70	W 1st	"	"		"
4	2	72	W Rgnl	"	Marriott Center	1971	22,700
3	2	77	W Rgnl	"	"		"
3	2	79	W Rgnl	"	"		"
3	2	82	W Rgnl	"	"		"
2	1	68	MW,W 1st	Salt Lake City	Nielsen Field House	1940	5,000
4	2	71	W Rgnl	"	Special Events Center	1969	15,000
4	2	79	Final Four	"	"		"
3	2	81	W Rgnl	"	"		"
4	2	84	W 1st-2nd	"	"		"
6	3	85	W 1st-2nd	"	"		"
6	3	87	W 1st-2nd	"	"		"
6	3	88	W 1st-2nd	"	Jon W. Huntsman Center (name change)		"
6	3	90	W 1st-2nd	"	"		"
6	3	91	W 1st-2nd	"	"		"
VIRGINIA
2	1	66	E 1st	Blacksburg	Cassell Coliseum	1964	10,000
2	1	67	W 1st	"	"		"
6	3	90	SE 1st-2nd	Richmond	#Richmond Coliseum	1971	11,051
1	1	72	E 1st	Williamsburg	William and Mary Hall	1970	10,070
1	1	73	E 1st	"	"		"
WASHINGTON
2	1	75	W 1st	Pullman	Wallis Beasley Performing Arts Coliseum	1973	12,058
4	2	82	W 1st-2nd	"	"		"
4	2	84	W 1st-2nd	"	"		"
2	1	49	CH-3d	Seattle	Edmundson Pavilion	1927	9,000
4	2	52	Final Four	"	"		"
1	1	53	W-2 1st	"	"		"
1	1	56	FW 1st	"	"		"
4	2	60	W Rgnl	"	"		"
4	2	70	W Rgnl	"	"		"
3	2	84	Final Four	"	#Kingdome	1976	38,471
3	2	87	W Rgnl	"	"		"
3	2	88	W Rgnl	"	"		"
3	2	89	Final Four	"	"		"
3	2	91	W Rgnl	"	"		"
WEST VIRGINIA
1	1	71	E 1st	Morgantown	WVU Coliseum	1970	14,000
4	2	72	E Rgnl	"	"		"
1	1	74	E 1st	"	"		"
WISCONSIN
4	2	41	En Rgnl	Madison	Wisconsin Field House	1927	14,000
4	2	69	ME Rgnl	"	"		13,000
4	2	84	ME 1st-2nd	Milwaukee	#Milwaukee Exposition & Convention Center	1950	11,052
6	3	92	MW 1st-2nd	"	Bradley Center	1988	18,600

G—Number of games.
S—Number of sessions.
Yr.—Year.
CH—National championship game.
3d—National third-place game.
Rgnl—Regional.
2nd—Second round.
1st—First round.
OR—Opening round.
East—East region.
SE—Southeast region.
ME—Mideast region.
MW—Midwest region.
W—West region.
FW—Far West region.
En—Eastern region.
Wn—Western region.
E-1—East-1 region.
E-2—East-2 region.
W-1—West-1 region.
W-2—West-2 region.
TH—Triple-header.
#Noncampus arena.

TOURNAMENT FACTS...

TOURNAMENT TICKET PRICES

Year	Ticket Sales	Avg. Per Ticket	Year	Ticket Sales	Avg. Per Ticket
1977	$1,880,190	$ 7.78	1985	5,864,704	13.84
1978	1,805,399	7.95	1986	7.382,986	14.77
1979	2,482,528	9.47	1987	10,623,809	16.23
1980	3,113,214	9.69	1988	9,157,202	16.38
1981	3,769,732	10.85	1989	10,916,138	17.80
1982	4,987,948	11.67	1990	9,845,904	18.33
1983	4,482,242	12.30	1991	$14,402,237	$21.63
1984	5,666,841	14.26	1992	$12,367,201	$21.32

THE
BRACKETS

en years ago, North Carolina State shocked the college basketball world by
upsetting Houston, 54-52, in the championship game. The Wolfpack, led by
coach Jim Valvano, was seeded sixth in the West region and defeated two No.
seeds on its way to the national title.

1939 Championship Bracket

Regional Semifinals	Regional Finals	National Championship

WESTERN REGIONALS

Oregon
March 20 — Oregon 56-41
Texas
San Francisco, CA
March 21
Oklahoma
March 20 — Oklahoma 50-39
Utah St.

Oregon 55-37

EASTERN REGIONALS
Evanston, IL
March 27

Oregon 46-33
NATIONAL CHAMPION

Villanova
March 17 — Villanova 42-30
Brown
Philadelphia, PA
March 18
Wake Forest
March 17 — Ohio St. 64-52
Ohio St.

Ohio St. 53-36

Regional Third Place
March 21
at San Francisco, CA
Utah St. 51, Texas 49

1940 Championship Bracket

Regional Semifinals	Regional Finals	National Championship

EASTERN REGIONALS

Indiana
March 20 — Indiana 48-24
Springfield
Indianapolis, IN
March 21
Duquesne
March 20 — Duquesne 30-29
Western Ky.

Indiana 39-30

Kansas City, MO
March 30

Indiana 60-42
NATIONAL CHAMPION

WESTERN REGIONALS
Southern Cal
March 20 — Southern Cal 38-32
Colorado
Kansas City, MO
March 21
Rice
March 20 — Kansas 50-44
Kansas

Kansas 43-42

Regional Third Place
March 21
at Kansas City, MO
Rice 60, Colorado 56 (ot)

1941 Championship Bracket

Regional Semifinals	Regional Finals	National Championship

EASTERN REGIONALS

Wisconsin
March 21 — Wisconsin 51-50
Dartmouth
Madison, WI
March 22
Pittsburgh
March 21 — Pittsburgh 26-20
North Caro.

Wisconsin 36-30

Kansas City, MO
March 29

Wisconsin 39-34
NATIONAL CHAMPION

WESTERN REGIONALS
Arkansas
March 21 — Arkansas 52-40
Wyoming
Kansas City, MO
March 22
Creighton
March 21 — Washington St. 48-39
Washington St.

Washington St. 64-53

Regional Third Place
March 22
at Madison, WI
Dartmouth 60, North Caro. 59
at Kansas City, MO
Creighton 45, Wyoming 44

1942 Championship Bracket

Regional Semifinals | Regional Finals | National Championship

EASTERN REGIONALS

Dartmouth
March 20 — Dartmouth 44-39
Penn St.
                          New Orleans, LA — Dartmouth 47-28
                          March 21
Kentucky
March 20 — Kentucky 46-44
Illinois

                                                    Kansas City, MO — Stanford 53-38
                                                    March 28 — NATIONAL CHAMPION

WESTERN REGIONALS
Stanford
March 20 — Stanford 53-47
Rice
                          Kansas City, MO — Stanford 46-35
                          March 21
Colorado
March 20 — Colorado 46-44
Kansas

                          Regional Third Place
                          March 21
                          at New Orleans, LA
                          Penn St. 41, Illinois 34
                          at Kansas City, MO
                          Kansas 55, Rice 53

1943 Championship Bracket

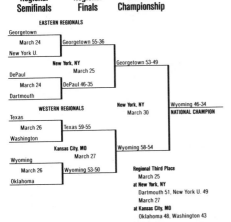

Regional Semifinals | Regional Finals | National Championship

EASTERN REGIONALS

Georgetown
March 24 — Georgetown 55-36
New York U.
                          New York, NY — Georgetown 53-49
                          March 25
DePaul
March 24 — DePaul 46-35
Dartmouth

                                                    New York, NY — Wyoming 46-34
                                                    March 30 — NATIONAL CHAMPION

WESTERN REGIONALS
Texas
March 26 — Texas 59-55
Washington
                          Kansas City, MO — Wyoming 58-54
                          March 27
Wyoming
March 26 — Wyoming 53-50
Oklahoma

                          Regional Third Place
                          March 25
                          at New York, NY
                          Dartmouth 51, New York U. 49
                          March 27
                          at Kansas City, MO
                          Oklahoma 48, Washington 43

1944 Championship Bracket

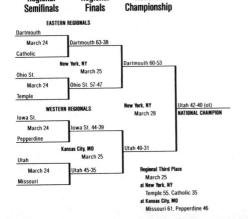

Regional Semifinals | Regional Finals | National Championship

EASTERN REGIONALS

Dartmouth
March 24 — Dartmouth 63-38
Catholic
                          New York, NY — Dartmouth 60-53
                          March 25
Ohio St.
March 24 — Ohio St. 57-47
Temple

                                                    New York, NY — Utah 42-40 (ot)
                                                    March 28 — NATIONAL CHAMPION

WESTERN REGIONALS
Iowa St.
March 24 — Iowa St. 44-39
Pepperdine
                          Kansas City, MO — Utah 40-31
                          March 25
Utah
March 24 — Utah 45-35
Missouri

                          Regional Third Place
                          March 25
                          at New York, NY
                          Temple 55, Catholic 35
                          at Kansas City, MO
                          Missouri 61, Pepperdine 46

1945 Championship Bracket

Regional Semifinals   Regional Finals   National Championship

EASTERN REGIONALS

New York U.
March 22
Tufts
New York U. 59-44

New York, NY
March 24
Ohio St.
March 22
Kentucky
Ohio St. 45-37

New York U. 70-65 (ot)

WESTERN REGIONALS
Arkansas
March 23
Oregon
Arkansas 79-76

Kansas City, MO
March 24
Oklahoma St.
March 23
Utah
Oklahoma St. 62-37

Oklahoma St. 68-41

New York, NY
March 27

Oklahoma St. 49-45
NATIONAL CHAMPION

Regional Third Place
March 24
at New York, NY
Kentucky 66, Tufts 56
at Kansas City, MO
Oregon 69, Utah 66

1946 Championship Bracket

Regional Semifinals   Regional Finals   National Championship

EASTERN REGIONALS

Ohio St.
March 21
Harvard
Ohio St. 46-38

New York, NY
March 23
North Caro.
March 21
New York U.
North Caro. 57-49

North Caro. 60-57 (ot)

WESTERN REGIONALS
Oklahoma St.
March 22
Baylor
Oklahoma St. 44-29

Kansas City, MO
March 23
California
March 22
Colorado
California 50-44

Oklahoma St. 52-35

New York, NY
March 26

Oklahoma St. 43-40
NATIONAL CHAMPION

Ohio St.
California
Ohio St. 63-45
NATIONAL 3rd PLACE

Regional Third Place
March 23
at New York, NY
New York U. 67, Harvard 61
at Kansas City, MO
Colorado 59, Baylor 44

1947 Championship Bracket

Regional Semifinals   Regional Finals   National Championship

EASTERN REGIONALS

Holy Cross
March 20
Navy
Holy Cross 55-47

New York, NY
March 22
CCNY
March 20
Wisconsin
CCNY 70-56

Holy Cross 60-45

WESTERN REGIONALS
Texas
March 19
Wyoming
Texas 42-40

Kansas City, MO
March 22
Oklahoma
March 21
Oregon St.
Oklahoma 56-54

Oklahoma 55-54

New York, NY
March 25

Holy Cross 58-47
NATIONAL CHAMPION

Texas
CCNY
Texas 54-50
NATIONAL 3rd PLACE

Regional Third Place
March 22
at New York, NY
Wisconsin 50, Navy 49
at Kansas City, MO
Oregon St. 63, Wyoming 46

1948 Championship Bracket

Regional Semifinals	Regional Finals	National Championship

EASTERN REGIONALS

Holy Cross

Kansas St.

Holy Cross 60-54
NATIONAL 3rd PLACE

Kentucky
March 19
Columbia
Kentucky 76-53

New York, NY
March 20
Kentucky 60-52

Holy Cross
March 19
Michigan
Holy Cross 63-45

Regional Third Place
March 20
at New York, NY
Michigan 66, Columbia 49
at Kansas City, MO
Washington 57, Wyoming 47

New York, NY
March 23
Kentucky 58-42
NATIONAL CHAMPION

WESTERN REGIONALS

Kansas St.
March 19
Wyoming
Kansas St. 58-48

Kansas City, MO
March 20
Baylor 60-52

Baylor
March 19
Washington
Baylor 64-62

1949 Championship Bracket

Regional Semifinals	Regional Finals	National Championship

EASTERN REGIONALS

Illinois

Oregon St.

Illinois 57-53
NATIONAL 3rd PLACE

Illinois
March 21
Yale
Illinois 71-67

New York, NY
March 22
Kentucky 76-47

Kentucky
March 21
Villanova
Kentucky 85-72

Regional Third Place
March 22
at New York, NY
Villanova 78, Yale 67
March 19
at Kansas City, MO
Arkansas 61, Wyoming 48

Seattle, WA
March 26
Kentucky 46-36
NATIONAL CHAMPION

WESTERN REGIONALS

Oklahoma St.
March 18
Wyoming
Oklahoma St. 40-39

Kansas City, MO
March 19
Oklahoma St. 55-30

Oregon St.
March 18
Arkansas
Oregon St. 56-38

1950 Championship Bracket

Regional Semifinals	Regional Finals	National Championship

EASTERN REGIONALS

North Caro. St.

Baylor

North Caro. St. 53-41
NATIONAL 3rd PLACE

CCNY
March 23
Ohio St.
CCNY 56-55

New York, NY
March 25
CCNY 78-73

North Caro. St.
March 24
Holy Cross
North Caro. St. 87-74

Regional Third Place
March 25
at New York, NY
Ohio St. 72, Holy Cross 52
at Kansas City, MO
Brigham Young 83, UCLA 62

New York, NY
March 28
CCNY 71-68
NATIONAL CHAMPION

WESTERN REGIONALS

Baylor
March 23
Brigham Young
Baylor 56-55

Kansas City, MO
March 25
Bradley 68-66

Bradley
March 24
UCLA
Bradley 73-59

1951 Championship Bracket

| 1st Round | Regional Semifinals | Regional Finals | National Championship |

WEST

Kansas St.
March 21 — Kansas St. 61-59
Arizona

Kansas City, MO
March 23 — Kansas St. 64-54
Brigham Young
March 21 — Brigham Young 68-61
San Jose St.

Kansas City, MO
March 24 — Kansas St. 68-44

Oklahoma St.
March 22 — Oklahoma St. 50-46
Montana St.

Kansas City, MO
March 23 — Oklahoma St. 61-57
Washington
March 22 — Washington 62-40
Texas A&M

EAST

Columbia
March 20 — Illinois 79-71
Illinois

New York, NY
March 22 — Illinois 84-70
New York, NY
North Caro. St.
March 20 — North Caro. St. 67-62
Villanova

New York, NY
March 24 — Kentucky 76-74

Raleigh, NC
Kentucky
March 20 — Kentucky 79-68
Louisville

New York, NY
March 22 — Kentucky 59-43
Raleigh, NC
St. John's (N.Y.)
March 20 — St. John's (N.Y.) 63-52
Connecticut
New York, NY

Minneapolis, MN
March 27 — Kentucky 68-58
NATIONAL CHAMPION

Oklahoma St.

Illinois 61-46
NATIONAL 3rd PLACE

Illinois

Regional Third Place
March 24
at Kansas City, MO
Washington 80, Brigham Young 67
at New York, NY
St. John's (N.Y.) 71, North Caro. St. 59

TOURNAMENT TRIVIA QUESTION...

Many teams show big improvement from one year to the next, but only seven teams since 1978 have gone from not appearing in the NCAA tournament to being a No. 1 seed the next year. Can you name them? Answer: Indiana State in 1979, Kentucky in 1980, Virginia in 1981, DePaul in 1984, Michigan in 1985, and Connecticut and Michigan State in 1990.

1952 Championship Bracket

Regional Semifinals	Regional Finals	National Semifinals	National Championship

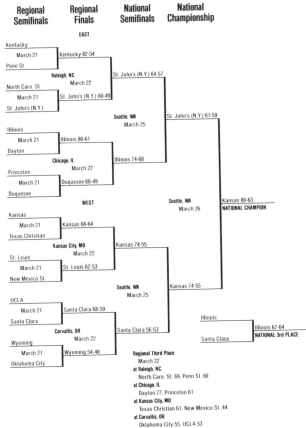

EAST

Kentucky
March 21
Penn St.
   Kentucky 82-54
Raleigh, NC
March 22
North Caro. St.
March 21
St. John's (N.Y.)
   St. John's (N.Y.) 60-49
   St. John's (N.Y.) 64-57

Seattle, WA
March 25
   St. John's (N.Y.) 61-59

Illinois
March 21
Dayton
   Illinois 80-61
Chicago, IL
March 22
Princeton
March 21
Duquesne
   Duquesne 60-49
   Illinois 74-68

WEST

Seattle, WA
March 26
   Kansas 80-63
   NATIONAL CHAMPION

Kansas
March 21
Texas Christian
   Kansas 68-64
Kansas City, MO
March 22
St. Louis
March 21
New Mexico St.
   St. Louis 62-53
   Kansas 74-55

Seattle, WA
March 25
   Kansas 74-55

UCLA
March 21
Santa Clara
   Santa Clara 68-59
Corvallis, OR
March 22
Wyoming
March 21
Oklahoma City
   Wyoming 54-48
   Santa Clara 56-53

Illinois
   Illinois 67-64
   NATIONAL 3rd PLACE
Santa Clara

Regional Third Place
March 22
at Raleigh, NC
North Caro. St. 69, Penn St. 60
at Chicago, IL
Dayton 77, Princeton 61
at Kansas City, MO
Texas Christian 61, New Mexico St. 44
at Corvallis, OR
Oklahoma City 55, UCLA 53

TOURNAMENT TRIVIA QUESTION...
Since 1956, when the Final Four competitors came from four regionals, what region has produced the most national champions? Answer: The West/Far West with 16, next are the Southeast/Mideast with nine, the Midwest with eight and the East with four. Remember, though, that any team can play in any region to best balance the bracket in the committee's judgment.

1953 Championship Bracket

1st Round	Regional Semifinals	Regional Finals	National Semifinals	National Championship

EAST

Lebanon Valley
March 10
Fordham
Philadelphia, PA

Lebanon Valley 80-67
March 13

Louisiana St.

Louisiana St. 89-76

Raleigh, NC
March 14

Holy Cross
March 10
Navy
Philadelphia, PA

Holy Cross 87-74
March 13

Wake Forest

Holy Cross 79-71

Louisiana St. 81-73

Kansas City, MO
March 17

Notre Dame
March 10
Eastern Ky.
Fort Wayne, IN

Notre Dame 72-57
March 13

Pennsylvania

Notre Dame 69-57

Chicago, IL
March 14

DePaul
March 10
Miami (Ohio)
Fort Wayne, IN

DePaul 74-72
March 13

Indiana

Indiana 82-80

Indiana 79-66

Indiana 80-67

WEST

Seattle
March 10
Idaho St.
Seattle, WA

Seattle 88-77
March 13

Washington

Washington 92-70

Corvallis, OR
March 14

Santa Clara
March 10
Hardin-Simmons
Palo Alto, CA

Santa Clara 81-56
March 13

Wyoming

Santa Clara 67-52

Washington 74-62

Kansas City, MO
March 18

Indiana 69-68
NATIONAL CHAMPION

Kansas City, MO
March 17

Texas Christian
March 13

Oklahoma St.

Oklahoma St. 71-54

Manhattan, KS
March 14

Kansas
March 13

Oklahoma City

Kansas 73-65

Kansas 61-55

Kansas 79-53

Louisiana St.

Washington

Washington 88-69
NATIONAL 3rd PLACE

Regional Third Place
March 14
at Raleigh, NC
  Wake Forest 91, Lebanon Valley 71
at Chicago, IL
  Pennsylvania 90, DePaul 70
at Corvallis, OR
  Seattle 80, Wyoming 64
at Manhattan, KS
  Texas Christian 58, Oklahoma City 56

1954 Championship Bracket

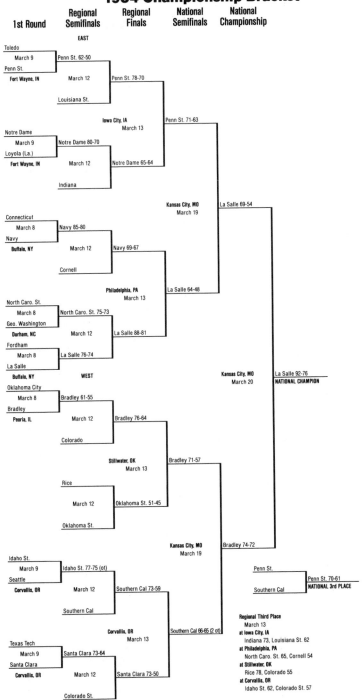

1st Round	Regional Semifinals	Regional Finals	National Semifinals	National Championship

EAST

Toledo
March 9
Penn St.
Fort Wayne, IN — Penn St. 62-50
March 12 — Penn St. 78-70

Louisiana St.

Iowa City, IA
March 13 — Penn St. 71-63

Notre Dame
March 9
Loyola (La.)
Fort Wayne, IN — Notre Dame 80-70
March 12 — Notre Dame 65-64

Indiana

Kansas City, MO
March 19 — La Salle 69-54

Connecticut
March 8
Navy
Buffalo, NY — Navy 85-80
March 12 — Navy 69-67

Cornell

Philadelphia, PA
March 13 — La Salle 64-48

North Caro. St.
March 8
Geo. Washington
Durham, NC — North Caro. St. 75-73
March 12 — La Salle 88-81

Fordham
March 8
La Salle
Buffalo, NY — La Salle 76-74

WEST

Kansas City, MO
March 20 — La Salle 92-76
NATIONAL CHAMPION

Oklahoma City
March 8
Bradley
Peoria, IL — Bradley 61-55
March 12 — Bradley 76-64

Colorado

Stillwater, OK
March 13 — Bradley 71-57

Rice
March 12 — Oklahoma St. 51-45

Oklahoma St.

Kansas City, MO
March 19 — Bradley 74-72

Idaho St.
March 9
Seattle
Corvallis, OR — Idaho St. 77-75 (ot)
March 12 — Southern Cal 73-59

Southern Cal

Penn St.
Southern Cal — Penn St. 70-61
NATIONAL 3rd PLACE

Corvallis, OR
March 13 — Southern Cal 66-65 (2 ot)

Texas Tech
March 9
Santa Clara
Corvallis, OR — Santa Clara 73-64
March 12 — Santa Clara 73-50

Colorado St.

Regional Third Place
March 13
at Iowa City, IA
Indiana 73, Louisiana St. 62
at Philadelphia, PA
North Caro. St. 65, Cornell 54
at Stillwater, OK
Rice 78, Colorado 55
at Corvallis, OR
Idaho St. 62, Colorado St. 57

1955 Championship Bracket

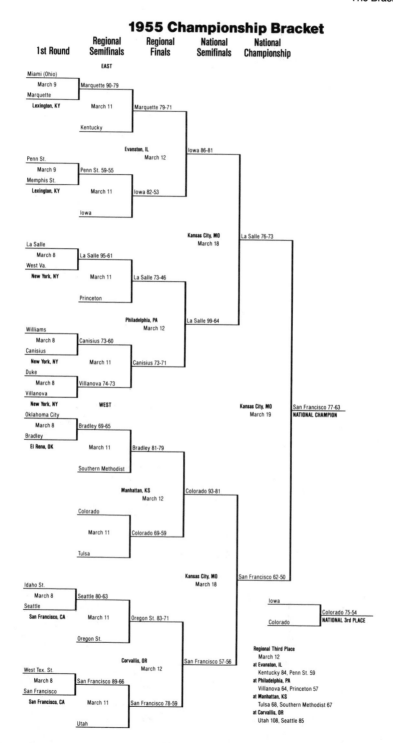

	Regional	Regional	National	National
1st Round	Semifinals	Finals	Semifinals	Championship

EAST

Miami (Ohio)
March 9
Marquette
Lexington, KY

Marquette 90-79
March 11

Marquette 79-71

Kentucky

Evanston, IL
March 12

Iowa 86-81

Penn St.
March 9
Memphis St.
Lexington, KY

Penn St. 59-55
March 11

Iowa 82-53

Iowa

Kansas City, MO
March 18

La Salle 76-73

La Salle
March 8
West Va.
New York, NY

La Salle 95-61
March 11

La Salle 73-46

Princeton

Philadelphia, PA
March 12

La Salle 99-64

Williams
March 8
Canisius
New York, NY

Canisius 73-60
March 11

Canisius 73-71

Duke
March 8
Villanova
New York, NY

Villanova 74-73

WEST

Kansas City, MO
March 19

San Francisco 77-63
NATIONAL CHAMPION

Oklahoma City
March 8
Bradley
El Reno, OK

Bradley 69-65
March 11

Bradley 81-79

Southern Methodist

Manhattan, KS
March 12

Colorado 93-81

Colorado
March 11

Colorado 69-59

Tulsa

Kansas City, MO
March 18

San Francisco 62-50

Idaho St.
March 8
Seattle
San Francisco, CA

Seattle 80-63
March 11

Oregon St. 83-71

Oregon St.

Iowa

Colorado

Colorado 75-54
NATIONAL 3rd PLACE

Corvallis, OR
March 12

San Francisco 57-56

West Tex. St.
March 8
San Francisco
San Francisco, CA

San Francisco 89-66
March 11

San Francisco 78-59

Utah

Regional Third Place
March 12
at Evanston, IL
    Kentucky 84, Penn St. 59
at Philadelphia, PA
    Villanova 64, Princeton 57
at Manhattan, KS
    Tulsa 68, Southern Methodist 67
at Corvallis, OR
    Utah 108, Seattle 85

1956 Championship Bracket

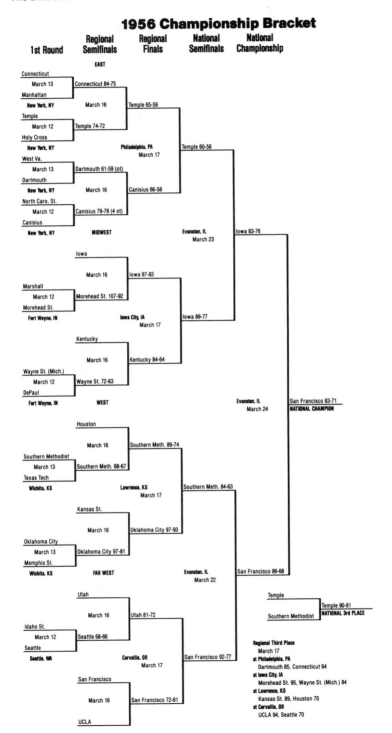

1st Round	Regional Semifinals	Regional Finals	National Semifinals	National Championship

EAST

Connecticut
March 13
Manhattan
New York, NY — Connecticut 84-75
March 16 — Temple 65-59

Temple
March 12
Holy Cross
New York, NY — Temple 74-72

Philadelphia, PA
March 17 — Temple 60-58

West Va.
March 13
Dartmouth
New York, NY — Dartmouth 61-59 (ot)
March 16 — Canisius 66-58

North Caro. St.
March 12
Canisius
New York, NY — Canisius 79-78 (4 ot)

Evanston, IL
March 23 — Iowa 83-76

MIDWEST

Iowa
March 16 — Iowa 97-83

Marshall
March 12
Morehead St.
Fort Wayne, IN — Morehead St. 107-92

Iowa City, IA
March 17 — Iowa 89-77

Kentucky
March 16 — Kentucky 84-64

Wayne St. (Mich.)
March 12
DePaul
Fort Wayne, IN — Wayne St. 72-63

Evanston, IL
March 24

San Francisco 83-71
NATIONAL CHAMPION

WEST

Houston
March 16 — Southern Meth. 89-74

Southern Methodist
March 13
Texas Tech
Wichita, KS — Southern Meth. 68-67

Lawrence, KS
March 17 — Southern Meth. 84-63

Kansas St.
March 16 — Oklahoma City 97-93

Oklahoma City
March 13
Memphis St.
Wichita, KS — Oklahoma City 97-81

Evanston, IL
March 22 — San Francisco 86-68

FAR WEST

Utah
March 16 — Utah 81-72

Idaho St.
March 12
Seattle
Seattle, WA — Seattle 68-66

Carvallis, OR
March 17 — San Francisco 92-77

San Francisco
March 16 — San Francisco 72-61

UCLA

Temple
Southern Methodist — Temple 90-81
NATIONAL 3rd PLACE

Regional Third Place
March 17
at Philadelphia, PA
Dartmouth 85, Connecticut 64
at Iowa City, IA
Morehead St. 95, Wayne St. (Mich.) 84
at Lawrence, KS
Kansas St. 89, Houston 70
at Carvallis, OR
UCLA 94, Seattle 70

1957 Championship Bracket

1st Round	Regional Semifinals	Regional Finals	National Semifinals	National Championship

EAST

Lafayette

March 15 — Syracuse 75-71

Connecticut

March 12 — Syracuse 82-76

Syracuse

New York, NY

West Va.

March 12 — Canisius 64-56

Canisius

New York, NY — Philadelphia, PA / March 16 — North Caro. 67-58

North Caro.

March 15 — North Caro. 87-75

March 12 — North Caro. 90-74

Yale

New York, NY

MIDEAST

Kansas City, MO / March 22 — North Caro. 74-70 (3 ot)

Kentucky

March 15 — Kentucky 98-92

Morehead St.

March 11 — Pittsburgh 86-85

Pittsburgh

Columbus, OH — Lexington, KY / March 16 — Michigan St. 80-68

Miami (Ohio)

March 11 — Notre Dame 89-77

Notre Dame

Columbus, OH

March 15 — Michigan St. 85-83

Michigan St.

MIDWEST

Kansas City, MO / March 23 — North Caro. 54-53 (3 ot) / **NATIONAL CHAMPION**

St. Louis

March 15 — Oklahoma City 75-66

Oklahoma City

March 12 — Oklahoma City 76-55

Loyola (La.)

Oklahoma City, OK — Dallas, TX / March 16 — Kansas 81-61

Kansas

March 15 — Kansas 73-65 (ot)

Southern Methodist

WEST

Kansas City, MO / March 22 — Kansas 80-56

Brigham Young

March 15 — California 86-59

California

Corvallis, OR / March 16 — San Francisco 50-46

Idaho St.

March 11 — Idaho St. 68-57

Hardin-Simmons

Pocatello, ID

March 15 — San Francisco 66-51

San Francisco

Michigan St.

San Francisco 67-60 — **NATIONAL 3rd PLACE**

San Francisco

Regional Third Place
March 16
at Philadelphia, PA
Canisius 82, Lafayette 76
at Lexington, KY
Notre Dame 86, Pittsburgh 85
at Dallas, TX
Southern Methodist 78, St. Louis 68
at Corvallis, OR
Brigham Young 65, Idaho St. 54

1958 Championship Bracket

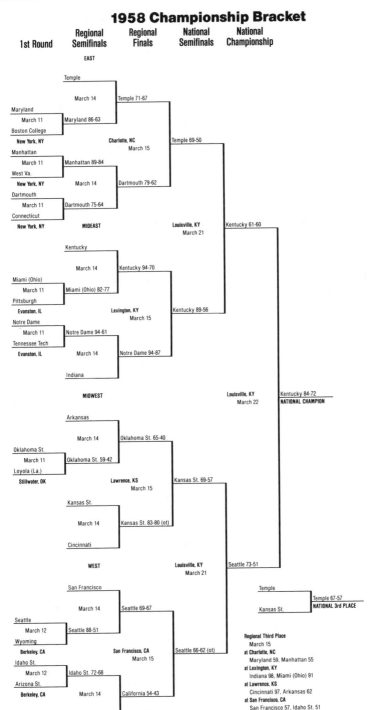

1st Round	Regional Semifinals	Regional Finals	National Semifinals	National Championship

EAST

Temple

March 14 — Temple 71-67

Maryland
March 11 — Maryland 86-63
Boston College
New York, NY

Charlotte, NC — Temple 69-50
March 15

Manhattan
March 11 — Manhattan 89-84
West Va.
New York, NY

March 14 — Dartmouth 79-62

Dartmouth
March 11 — Dartmouth 75-64
Connecticut
New York, NY

MIDEAST   Louisville, KY — Kentucky 61-60
                           March 21

Kentucky

March 14 — Kentucky 94-70

Miami (Ohio)
March 11 — Miami (Ohio) 82-77
Pittsburgh
Evanston, IL

Lexington, KY — Kentucky 89-56
March 15

Notre Dame
March 11 — Notre Dame 94-61
Tennessee Tech
Evanston, IL

March 14 — Notre Dame 94-87

Indiana

MIDWEST   Louisville, KY — Kentucky 84-72
                           March 22   NATIONAL CHAMPION

Arkansas

March 14 — Oklahoma St. 65-40

Oklahoma St.
March 11 — Oklahoma St. 59-42
Loyola (La.)
Stillwater, OK

Lawrence, KS — Kansas St. 69-57
March 15

Kansas St.

March 14 — Kansas St. 83-80 (ot)

Cincinnati

WEST   Louisville, KY — Seattle 73-51
                           March 21

San Francisco

March 14 — Seattle 69-67

Seattle
March 12 — Seattle 88-51
Wyoming
Berkeley, CA

San Francisco, CA — Seattle 66-62 (ot)
March 15

Idaho St.
March 12 — Idaho St. 72-68
Arizona St.
Berkeley, CA

March 14 — California 54-43

California

Temple

Temple 67-57
NATIONAL 3rd PLACE

Kansas St.

Regional Third Place
March 15
at Charlotte, NC
Maryland 59, Manhattan 55
at Lexington, KY
Indiana 98, Miami (Ohio) 91
at Lawrence, KS
Cincinnati 97, Arkansas 62
at San Francisco, CA
San Francisco 57, Idaho St. 51

1959 Championship Bracket

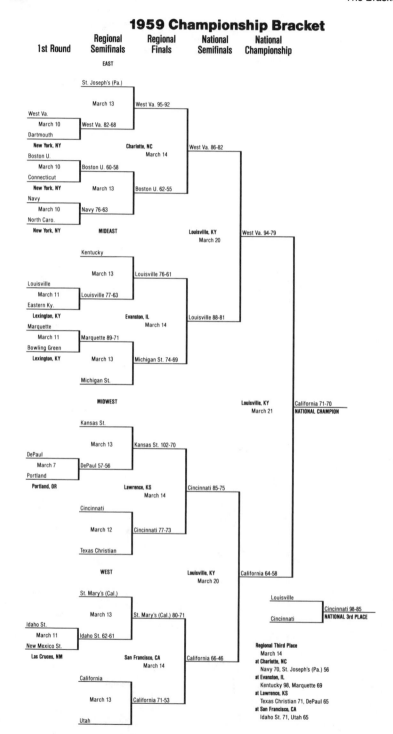

1st Round	Regional Semifinals	Regional Finals	National Semifinals	National Championship

EAST

St. Joseph's (Pa.)

March 13 — West Va. 95-92

West Va.
March 10 — West Va. 82-68

Dartmouth

New York, NY

Charlotte, NC — West Va. 86-82
March 14

Boston U.
March 10 — Boston U. 60-58

Connecticut

New York, NY   March 13 — Boston U. 62-55

Navy
March 10 — Navy 76-63

North Caro.

New York, NY

MIDEAST

Louisville, KY — West Va. 94-79
March 20

Kentucky

March 13 — Louisville 76-61

Louisville
March 11 — Louisville 77-63

Eastern Ky.

Lexington, KY

Evanston, IL — Louisville 88-81
March 14

Marquette
March 11 — Marquette 89-71

Bowling Green

Lexington, KY   March 13 — Michigan St. 74-69

Michigan St.

MIDWEST

Louisville, KY — California 71-70
March 21 — **NATIONAL CHAMPION**

Kansas St.

March 13 — Kansas St. 102-70

DePaul
March 7 — DePaul 57-56

Portland

Portland, OR

Lawrence, KS — Cincinnati 85-75
March 14

Cincinnati

March 12 — Cincinnati 77-73

Texas Christian

WEST

Louisville, KY — California 64-58
March 20

St. Mary's (Cal.)

March 13 — St. Mary's (Cal.) 80-71

Idaho St.
March 11 — Idaho St. 62-61

New Mexico St.

Las Cruces, NM

San Francisco, CA — California 66-46
March 14

California

March 13 — California 71-53

Utah

Louisville
                          Cincinnati 98-85
Cincinnati   **NATIONAL 3rd PLACE**

Regional Third Place
March 14
at Charlotte, NC
 Navy 70, St. Joseph's (Pa.) 56
at Evanston, IL
 Kentucky 98, Marquette 69
at Lawrence, KS
 Texas Christian 71, DePaul 65
at San Francisco, CA
 Idaho St. 71, Utah 65

1960 Championship Bracket

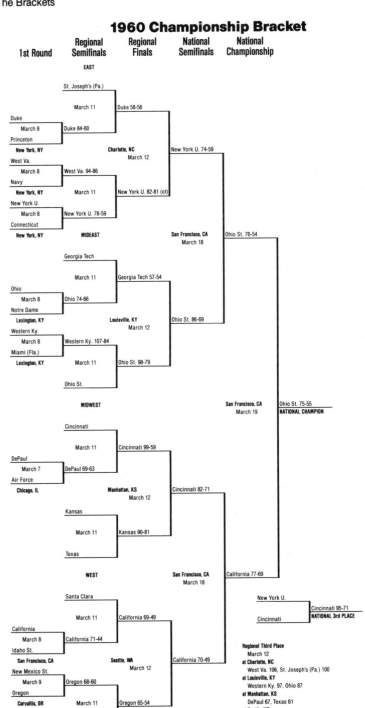

1st Round	Regional Semifinals	Regional Finals	National Semifinals	National Championship

EAST

St. Joseph's (Pa.)

March 11 — Duke 58-56

Duke
March 8 — Duke 84-60
Princeton
New York, NY

West Va.
March 8 — West Va. 94-86
Navy
New York, NY

Charlotte, NC
March 12

New York U. 74-59

New York U. 82-81 (ot)

New York U.
March 8 — New York U. 78-59
Connecticut
New York, NY

MIDEAST

San Francisco, CA
March 18

Ohio St. 76-54

Georgia Tech

March 11 — Georgia Tech 57-54

Ohio
March 8 — Ohio 74-66
Notre Dame
Lexington, KY

Western Ky.
March 8 — Western Ky. 107-84
Miami (Fla.)
Lexington, KY

Louisville, KY
March 12

Ohio St. 86-69

March 11 — Ohio St. 98-79

Ohio St.

MIDWEST

San Francisco, CA
March 19

Ohio St. 75-55
NATIONAL CHAMPION

Cincinnati

March 11 — Cincinnati 99-59

DePaul
March 7 — DePaul 69-63
Air Force
Chicago, IL

Manhattan, KS
March 12

Cincinnati 82-71

Kansas

March 11 — Kansas 90-81

Texas

WEST

San Francisco, CA
March 18

California 77-69

New York U.

Cincinnati

Cincinnati 95-71
NATIONAL 3rd PLACE

Santa Clara

March 11 — California 69-49

California
March 8 — California 71-44
Idaho St.
San Francisco, CA

New Mexico St.
March 9 — Oregon 68-60
Oregon
Corvallis, OR

Southern Cal
March 7 — Utah 80-73
Utah
Provo, UT

Seattle, WA
March 12

California 70-49

Oregon 65-54

Regional Third Place
March 12
at Charlotte, NC
West Va. 106, St. Joseph's (Pa.) 100
at Louisville, KY
Western Ky. 97, Ohio 87
at Manhattan, KS
DePaul 67, Texas 61
at Seattle, WA
Utah 89, Santa Clara 81

1961 Championship Bracket

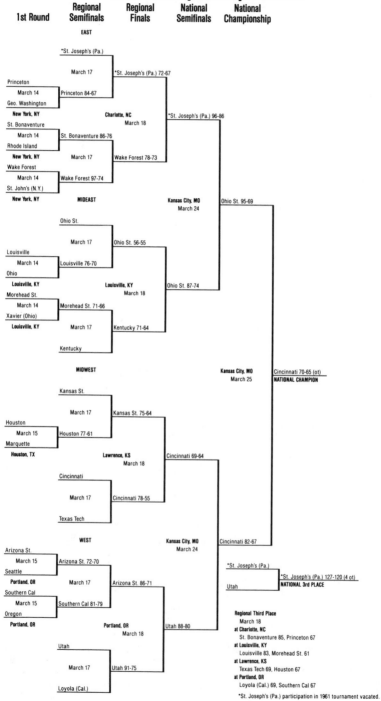

| 1st Round | Regional Semifinals | Regional Finals | National Semifinals | National Championship |

EAST

*St. Joseph's (Pa.)

March 17
*St. Joseph's (Pa.) 72-67

Princeton
March 14
Geo. Washington
Princeton 84-67

New York, NY
St. Bonaventure
March 14
Rhode Island
St. Bonaventure 86-76

Charlotte, NC
March 18
*St. Joseph's (Pa.) 96-86

New York, NY
Wake Forest
March 14
St. John's (N.Y.)
Wake Forest 97-74

Wake Forest 78-73

New York, NY

MIDEAST

Ohio St.

March 17
Ohio St. 56-55

Louisville
March 14
Ohio
Louisville 76-70

Louisville, KY
Morehead St.
March 14
Xavier (Ohio)
Morehead St. 71-66

Louisville, KY

Louisville, KY
March 18
Ohio St. 87-74

Kentucky 71-64

Kentucky

Kansas City, MO
March 24
Ohio St. 95-69

MIDWEST

Kansas St.

March 17
Kansas St. 75-64

Houston
March 15
Marquette
Houston 77-61

Houston, TX

Lawrence, KS
March 18
Cincinnati 69-64

Cincinnati
March 17
Cincinnati 78-55

Texas Tech

Kansas City, MO
March 25
Cincinnati 70-65 (ot)
NATIONAL CHAMPION

Kansas City, MO
March 25
Cincinnati 69-64

WEST

Arizona St.
March 15
Seattle
Arizona St. 72-70

Portland, OR
March 17
Arizona St. 86-71

Southern Cal
March 15
Oregon
Southern Cal 81-79

Portland, OR

Portland, OR
March 18
Utah 88-80

Utah
March 17
Utah 91-75

Loyola (Cal.)

Kansas City, MO
March 24
Cincinnati 82-67

*St. Joseph's (Pa.)

Utah

*St. Joseph's (Pa.) 127-120 (4 ot)
NATIONAL 3rd PLACE

Regional Third Place
March 18
at Charlotte, NC
St. Bonaventure 85, Princeton 67
at Louisville, KY
Louisville 83, Morehead St. 61
at Lawrence, KS
Texas Tech 69, Houston 67
at Portland, OR
Loyola (Cal.) 69, Southern Cal 67

*St. Joseph's (Pa.) participation in 1961 tournament vacated.

1962 Championship Bracket

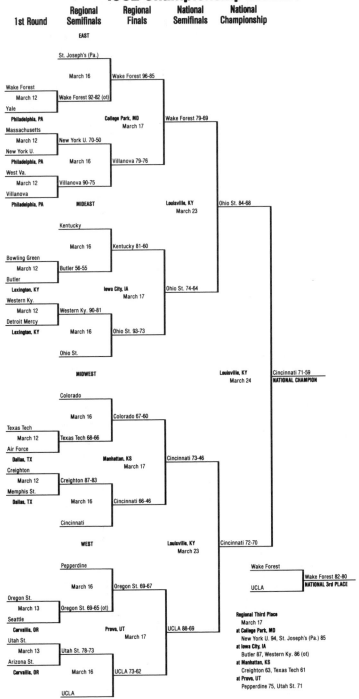

	Regional	Regional	National	National
1st Round	Semifinals	Finals	Semifinals	Championship

EAST

St. Joseph's (Pa.)

March 16 — Wake Forest 96-85

Wake Forest
March 12 — Wake Forest 92-82 (ot)
Yale
Philadelphia, PA   **College Park, MD** — Wake Forest 79-69
Massachusetts   March 17
March 12 — New York U. 70-50
New York U.
Philadelphia, PA   March 16 — Villanova 79-76
West Va.
March 12 — Villanova 90-75
Villanova
Philadelphia, PA   **MIDEAST**   **Louisville, KY** — Ohio St. 84-68
                                              March 23

Kentucky

March 16 — Kentucky 81-60

Bowling Green
March 12 — Butler 56-55
Butler
Lexington, KY   **Iowa City, IA** — Ohio St. 74-64
Western Ky.   March 17
March 12 — Western Ky. 90-81
Detroit Mercy
Lexington, KY   March 16 — Ohio St. 93-73

Ohio St.

MIDWEST   **Louisville, KY**   Cincinnati 71-59
                                     March 24   **NATIONAL CHAMPION**

Colorado

March 16 — Colorado 67-60

Texas Tech
March 12 — Texas Tech 68-66
Air Force
Dallas, TX   **Manhattan, KS** — Cincinnati 73-46
Creighton   March 17
March 12 — Creighton 87-83
Memphis St.
Dallas, TX   March 16 — Cincinnati 66-46

Cincinnati

WEST   **Louisville, KY**   Cincinnati 72-70
                                  March 23

Pepperdine

March 16 — Oregon St. 69-67   Wake Forest
                                                        Wake Forest 82-80
Oregon St.   UCLA   **NATIONAL 3rd PLACE**
March 13 — Oregon St. 69-65 (ot)
Seattle
Corvallis, OR   **Provo, UT** — UCLA 88-69
Utah St.   March 17
March 13 — Utah St. 78-73
Arizona St.
Corvallis, OR   March 16 — UCLA 73-62

UCLA

Regional Third Place
March 17
at College Park, MD
   New York U. 94, St. Joseph's (Pa.) 85
at Iowa City, IA
   Butler 87, Western Ky. 86 (ot)
at Manhattan, KS
   Creighton 63, Texas Tech 61
at Provo, UT
   Pepperdine 75, Utah St. 71

1963 Championship Bracket

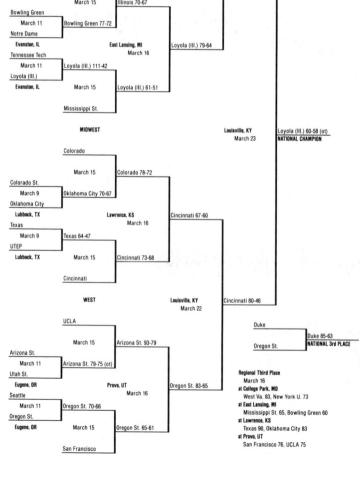

1st Round	Regional Semifinals	Regional Finals	National Semifinals	National Championship

EAST

Duke

March 15 — Duke 81-76

New York U.
March 11 — New York U. 93-83
Pittsburgh
Philadelphia, PA

College Park, MD
March 16 — Duke 73-59

West Va.
March 11 — West Va. 77-71
Connecticut
Philadelphia, PA

March 15 — St. Joseph's 97-88

St. Joseph's (Pa.)
March 11 — St. Joseph's 82-81
Princeton
Philadelphia, PA

Louisville, KY
March 22 — Loyola (Ill.) 94-75

MIDEAST

Illinois

March 15 — Illinois 70-67

Bowling Green
March 11 — Bowling Green 77-72
Notre Dame
Evanston, IL

East Lansing, MI
March 16 — Loyola (Ill.) 79-64

Tennessee Tech
March 11 — Loyola (Ill.) 111-42
Loyola (Ill.)
Evanston, IL

March 15 — Loyola (Ill.) 61-51

Mississippi St.

Louisville, KY
March 23 — Loyola (Ill.) 60-58 (ot)
NATIONAL CHAMPION

MIDWEST

Colorado

March 15 — Colorado 78-72

Colorado St.
March 9 — Oklahoma City 70-67
Oklahoma City
Lubbock, TX

Lawrence, KS
March 16 — Cincinnati 67-60

Texas
March 9 — Texas 64-47
UTEP
Lubbock, TX

March 15 — Cincinnati 73-68

Cincinnati

Louisville, KY
March 22 — Cincinnati 80-46

WEST

UCLA

March 15 — Arizona St. 93-79

Arizona St.
March 11 — Arizona St. 79-75 (ot)
Utah St.
Eugene, OR

Provo, UT
March 16 — Oregon St. 83-65

Seattle
March 11 — Oregon St. 70-66
Oregon St.
Eugene, OR

March 15 — Oregon St. 65-61

San Francisco

Duke

Duke 85-63
NATIONAL 3rd PLACE

Oregon St.

Regional Third Place
March 16
at College Park, MD
   West Va. 83, New York U. 73
at East Lansing, MI
   Mississippi St. 65, Bowling Green 60
at Lawrence, KS
   Texas 90, Oklahoma City 83
at Provo, UT
   San Francisco 76, UCLA 75

1964 Championship Bracket

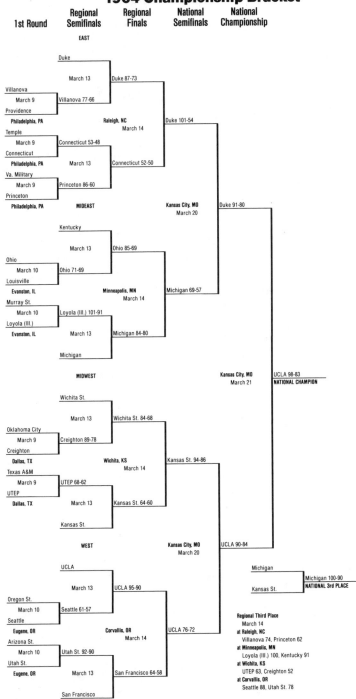

1st Round	Regional Semifinals	Regional Finals	National Semifinals	National Championship

EAST

Duke
March 13 — Duke 87-73
Villanova
March 9 — Villanova 77-66
Providence
Philadelphia, PA
Raleigh, NC — March 14
Duke 101-54
Temple
March 9 — Connecticut 53-48
Connecticut
Philadelphia, PA — March 13 — Connecticut 52-50
Va. Military
March 9 — Princeton 86-60
Princeton
Philadelphia, PA

Kansas City, MO — March 20 — Duke 91-80

MIDEAST

Kentucky
March 13 — Ohio 85-69
Ohio
March 10 — Ohio 71-69
Louisville
Evanston, IL
Minneapolis, MN — March 14
Michigan 69-57
Murray St.
March 10 — Loyola (Ill.) 101-91
Loyola (Ill.)
Evanston, IL — March 13 — Michigan 84-80
Michigan

MIDWEST

Kansas City, MO — March 21 — UCLA 98-83 — NATIONAL CHAMPION

Wichita St.
March 13 — Wichita St. 84-68
Oklahoma City
March 9 — Creighton 89-78
Creighton
Dallas, TX
Wichita, KS — March 14
Kansas St. 94-86
Texas A&M
March 9 — UTEP 68-62
UTEP
Dallas, TX — March 13 — Kansas St. 64-60
Kansas St.

Kansas City, MO — March 20 — UCLA 90-84

WEST

UCLA
March 13 — UCLA 95-90
Oregon St.
March 10 — Seattle 61-57
Seattle
Eugene, OR
Corvallis, OR — March 14
UCLA 76-72
Arizona St.
March 10 — Utah St. 92-90
Utah St.
Eugene, OR — March 13 — San Francisco 64-58
San Francisco

Michigan
Kansas St.
Michigan 100-90 — NATIONAL 3rd PLACE

Regional Third Place
March 14
at Raleigh, NC
Villanova 74, Princeton 62
at Minneapolis, MN
Loyola (Ill.) 100, Kentucky 91
at Wichita, KS
UTEP 63, Creighton 52
at Corvallis, OR
Seattle 88, Utah St. 78

1965 Championship Bracket

1st Round	Regional Semifinals	Regional Finals	National Semifinals	National Championship

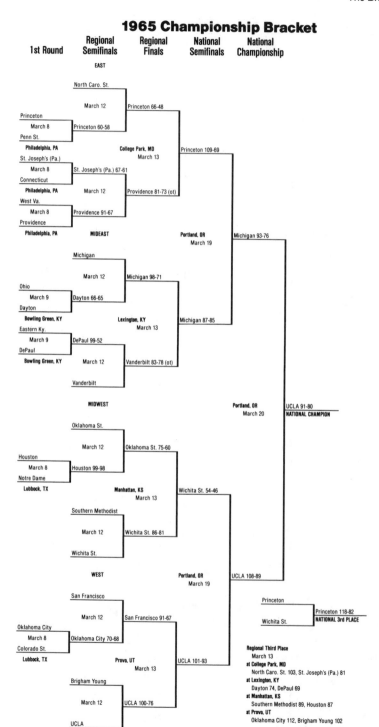

EAST

North Caro. St.

March 12 — Princeton 66-48

Princeton
March 8 — Princeton 60-58
Penn St.

Philadelphia, PA

St. Joseph's (Pa.)
March 8 — St. Joseph's (Pa.) 67-61
Connecticut

Philadelphia, PA — March 12 — Providence 81-73 (ot)

West Va.
March 8 — Providence 91-67
Providence

Philadelphia, PA

College Park, MD — March 13 — Princeton 109-69

MIDEAST

Michigan

March 12 — Michigan 98-71

Ohio
March 9 — Dayton 66-65
Dayton

Bowling Green, KY

Eastern Ky.
March 9 — DePaul 99-52
DePaul

Bowling Green, KY — March 12 — Vanderbilt 83-78 (ot)

Vanderbilt

Lexington, KY — March 13 — Michigan 87-85

Portland, OR — March 19 — Michigan 93-76

MIDWEST

Oklahoma St.

March 12 — Oklahoma St. 75-60

Houston
March 8 — Houston 99-98
Notre Dame

Lubbock, TX

Southern Methodist

March 12 — Wichita St. 86-81

Wichita St.

Manhattan, KS — March 13 — Wichita St. 54-46

WEST

San Francisco

March 12 — San Francisco 91-67

Oklahoma City
March 8 — Oklahoma City 70-68
Colorado St.

Lubbock, TX

Brigham Young

March 12 — UCLA 100-76

UCLA

Provo, UT — March 13 — UCLA 101-93

Portland, OR — March 19 — UCLA 108-89

Portland, OR — March 20 — UCLA 91-80 **NATIONAL CHAMPION**

Princeton

Wichita St.

Princeton 118-82 **NATIONAL 3rd PLACE**

Regional Third Place
March 13
at **College Park, MD**
    North Caro. St. 103, St. Joseph's (Pa.) 81
at **Lexington, KY**
    Dayton 74, DePaul 69
at **Manhattan, KS**
    Southern Methodist 89, Houston 87
at **Provo, UT**
    Oklahoma City 112, Brigham Young 102

1966 Championship Bracket

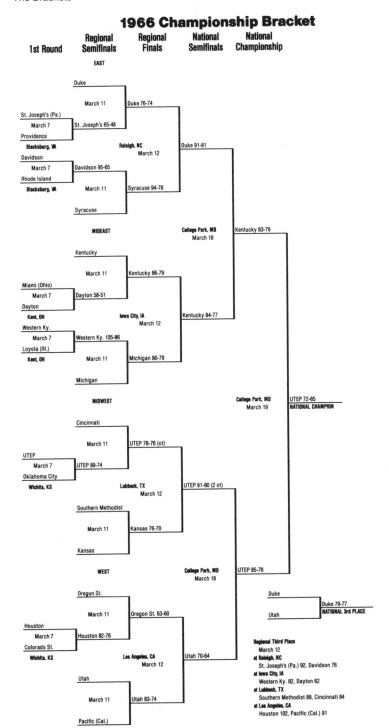

1st Round	Regional Semifinals	Regional Finals	National Semifinals	National Championship

EAST

Duke

March 11 — Duke 76-74

St. Joseph's (Pa.)
March 7 — St. Joseph's 65-48
Providence
Blacksburg, VA

Raleigh, NC
March 12 — Duke 91-81

Davidson
March 7 — Davidson 95-65
Rhode Island
Blacksburg, VA

March 11 — Syracuse 94-78

Syracuse

MIDEAST

College Park, MD
March 18 — Kentucky 83-79

Kentucky

March 11 — Kentucky 86-79

Miami (Ohio)
March 7 — Dayton 58-51
Dayton
Kent, OH

Iowa City, IA
March 12 — Kentucky 84-77

Western Ky.
March 7 — Western Ky. 105-86
Loyola (Ill.)
Kent, OH

March 11 — Michigan 80-79

Michigan

MIDWEST

College Park, MD
March 19 — UTEP 72-65
NATIONAL CHAMPION

Cincinnati

March 11 — UTEP 78-76 (ot)

UTEP
March 7 — UTEP 89-74
Oklahoma City
Wichita, KS

Lubbock, TX
March 12 — UTEP 81-80 (2 ot)

Southern Methodist

March 11 — Kansas 76-70

Kansas

WEST

College Park, MD
March 18 — UTEP 85-78

Oregon St.

March 11 — Oregon St. 63-60

Houston
March 7 — Houston 82-76
Colorado St.
Wichita, KS

Los Angeles, CA
March 12 — Utah 70-64

Utah

March 11 — Utah 83-74

Pacific (Cal.)

Duke

Duke 79-77
NATIONAL 3rd PLACE

Utah

Regional Third Place
March 12
at Raleigh, NC
 St. Joseph's (Pa.) 92, Davidson 76
at Iowa City, IA
 Western Ky. 82, Dayton 62
at Lubbock, TX
 Southern Methodist 89, Cincinnati 84
at Los Angeles, CA
 Houston 102, Pacific (Cal.) 91

1967 Championship Bracket

1st Round	Regional Semifinals	Regional Finals	National Semifinals	National Championship

EAST

North Caro.

March 17 — North Caro. 78-70 (ot)

Princeton

March 11 — Princeton 68-57

West Va.

Blacksburg, VA — **College Park, MD** — North Caro. 96-80
March 18

St. John's (N.Y.)

March 11 — St. John's (N.Y.) 57-53

Temple

Blacksburg, VA — March 17 — Boston College 63-62

Boston College

March 11 — Boston College 48-42

Connecticut

Kingston, RI — **MIDEAST** — **Louisville, KY** — Dayton 76-62
March 24

Tennessee

March 17 — Dayton 53-52

Dayton

March 11 — Dayton 69-67 (ot)

Western Ky.

Lexington, KY — **Evanston, IL** — Dayton 71-66 (ot)
March 18

Virginia Tech

March 11 — Virginia Tech 82-76

Toledo

Lexington, KY — March 17 — Virginia Tech 79-70

Indiana

MIDWEST — **Louisville, KY** — UCLA 79-64
March 25 — **NATIONAL CHAMPION**

Kansas

March 17 — Houston 66-53

Houston

March 11 — Houston 59-58

New Mexico St.

Ft. Collins, CO — **Lawrence, KS** — Houston 83-75
March 18

Southern Methodist

March 17 — Southern Meth. 83-81

Louisville

WEST — **Louisville, KY** — UCLA 73-58
March 24

Pacific (Cal.)

North Caro.

March 17 — Pacific (Cal.) 72-63 — Houston 84-62

UTEP — Houston — **NATIONAL 3rd PLACE**

March 11 — UTEP 62-54

Seattle

Ft. Collins, CO — **Corvallis, OR** — UCLA 80-64
March 18

UCLA

March 17 — UCLA 109-60

Wyoming

Regional Third Place
March 18
at College Park, MD
 Princeton 78, St. John's (N.Y.) 58
at Evanston, IL
 Indiana 51, Tennessee 44
at Lawrence, KS
 Kansas 70, Louisville 68
at Corvallis, OR
 UTEP 69, Wyoming 67

1968 Championship Bracket

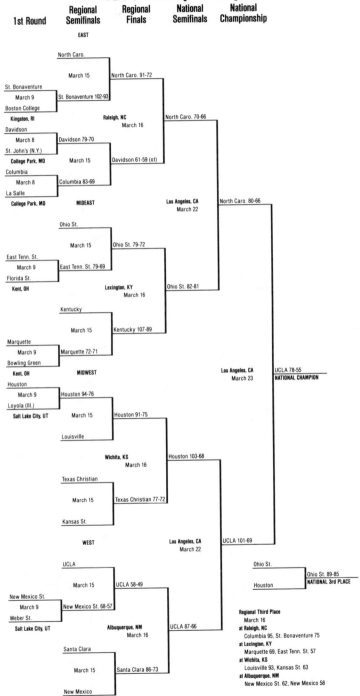

1st Round	Regional Semifinals	Regional Finals	National Semifinals	National Championship

EAST

North Caro.

March 15 — North Caro. 91-72

St. Bonaventure
March 9 — St. Bonaventure 102-93
Boston College
Kingston, RI

Raleigh, NC
March 16 — North Caro. 70-66

Davidson
March 8 — Davidson 79-70
St. John's (N.Y.)
College Park, MD — March 15 — Davidson 61-59 (ot)

Columbia
March 8 — Columbia 83-69
La Salle
College Park, MD

Los Angeles, CA
March 22 — North Caro. 80-66

MIDEAST

Ohio St.

March 15 — Ohio St. 79-72

East Tenn. St.
March 9 — East Tenn. St. 79-69
Florida St.
Kent, OH

Lexington, KY
March 16 — Ohio St. 82-81

Kentucky

March 15 — Kentucky 107-89

Marquette
March 9 — Marquette 72-71
Bowling Green
Kent, OH

MIDWEST

Los Angeles, CA
March 23 — UCLA 78-55 **NATIONAL CHAMPION**

Houston
March 9 — Houston 94-76
Loyola (Ill.)
Salt Lake City, UT — March 15 — Houston 91-75

Louisville

Wichita, KS
March 16 — Houston 103-68

Texas Christian

March 15 — Texas Christian 77-72

Kansas St.

Los Angeles, CA
March 22 — UCLA 101-69

WEST

UCLA

March 15 — UCLA 58-49

New Mexico St.
March 9 — New Mexico St. 68-57
Weber St.
Salt Lake City, UT

Albuquerque, NM
March 16 — UCLA 87-66

Santa Clara

March 15 — Santa Clara 86-73

New Mexico

Ohio St.

Ohio St. 89-85 **NATIONAL 3rd PLACE**

Houston

Regional Third Place
March 16
at Raleigh, NC
Columbia 95, St. Bonaventure 75
at Lexington, KY
Marquette 69, East Tenn. St. 57
at Wichita, KS
Louisville 93, Kansas St. 63
at Albuquerque, NM
New Mexico St. 62, New Mexico 58

1969 Championship Bracket

1st Round | Regional Semifinals | Regional Finals | National Semifinals | National Championship

EAST

1st Round

- Duquesne vs. St. Joseph's (Pa.) — March 8, **Kingston, RI**
- Davidson vs. Villanova — March 8, **Raleigh, NC**
- St. John's (N.Y.) vs. Princeton — March 8, **Raleigh, NC**

Regional Semifinals — March 13

- North Caro. vs. Duquesne 74-52
- Davidson 75-61 vs. St. John's (N.Y.) 72-63

Regional Finals — **College Park, MD**, March 15

- North Caro. 79-78 vs. Davidson 79-69

Winner: North Caro. 87-85

MIDEAST

1st Round

- Miami (Ohio) vs. Notre Dame — March 8, **Carbondale, IL**
- Marquette vs. Murray St. — March 8, **Carbondale, IL**

Regional Semifinals — March 13

- Purdue vs. Miami (Ohio) 63-60
- Marquette 82-62 vs. Kentucky

Regional Finals — **Madison, WI**, March 15

- Purdue 91-71 vs. Marquette 81-74

Winner: Purdue 75-73 (ot)

National Semifinal — **Louisville, KY**, March 20

- North Caro. 87-85 vs. Purdue 75-73 (ot) — Purdue 92-65

MIDWEST

1st Round

- Texas A&M vs. Trinity (Tex.) — March 8, **Fort Worth, TX**
- Colorado St. vs. Dayton — March 8, **Fort Worth, TX**

Regional Semifinals — March 13

- Drake vs. Texas A&M 81-66
- Colorado St. 52-50 vs. Colorado

Regional Finals — **Manhattan, KS**, March 15

- Drake 81-63 vs. Colorado St. 64-56

Winner: Drake 84-77

WEST

1st Round

- New Mexico St. vs. Brigham Young — March 8, **Las Cruces, NM**
- Weber St. vs. Seattle — March 8, **Las Cruces, NM**

Regional Semifinals — March 13

- UCLA vs. New Mexico St. 74-62
- Santa Clara vs. Weber St. 75-73

Regional Finals — **Los Angeles, CA**, March 15

- UCLA 53-38 vs. Santa Clara 63-59

Winner: UCLA 90-52

National Semifinal — **Louisville, KY**, March 20

- Drake 84-77 vs. UCLA 90-52 — UCLA 85-82

National Championship

Louisville, KY, March 22

Purdue 92-65 vs. UCLA 85-82 — UCLA 92-72

NATIONAL CHAMPION

National Third Place

Drake vs. North Caro. — Drake 104-84

NATIONAL 3rd PLACE

Regional Third Place

March 15

at College Park, MD

Duquesne 75, St. John's (N.Y.) 72

at Madison, WI

Kentucky 72, Miami (Ohio) 71

at Manhattan, KS

Colorado 97, Texas A&M 82

at Los Angeles, CA

Weber St. 58, New Mexico St. 56

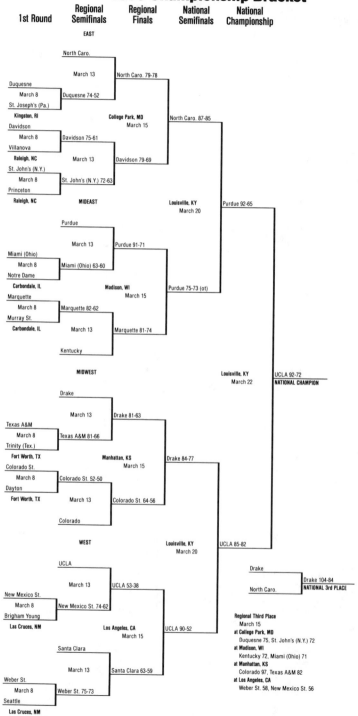

1970 Championship Bracket

1st Round	Regional Semifinals	Regional Finals	National Semifinals	National Championship

EAST

St. Bonaventure
March 7
Davidson
Jamaica, NY

St. Bonaventure 85-72
March 13

St. Bonaventure 80-68

North Caro. St.

Columbia, SC
March 14

St. Bonaventure 97-74

Villanova
March 7
Temple
Philadelphia, PA

Villanova 77-69
March 12

Villanova 98-73

Niagara
March 7
Pennsylvania
Princeton, NJ

Niagara 79-69

MIDEAST

College Park, MD
March 19

Jacksonville 91-83

Jacksonville
March 7
Western Ky.
Dayton, OH

Jacksonville 109-96
March 12

Jacksonville 104-103

Iowa

Columbus, OH
March 14

Jacksonville 106-100

Kentucky
March 12

Kentucky 109-99

Notre Dame
March 7
Ohio
Dayton, OH

Notre Dame 112-82

MIDWEST

College Park, MD
March 21

UCLA 80-69
NATIONAL CHAMPION

New Mexico St.
March 7
Rice
Fort Worth, TX

New Mexico St. 101-77
March 12

New Mexico St. 70-66

Kansas St.

Lawrence, KS
March 14

New Mexico St. 87-78

Drake
March 12

Drake 92-87

Houston
March 7
Dayton
Fort Worth, TX

Houston 71-64

WEST

College Park, MD
March 19

UCLA 93-77

UCLA
March 12

UCLA 88-65

New Mexico St.

New Mexico St. 79-73
NATIONAL 3rd PLACE

St. Bonaventure

Long Beach St.
March 7
Weber St.
Provo, UT

Long Beach St. 92-73

Utah St.

Seattle, WA
March 14

UCLA 101-79

Regional Third Place
March 14
at Columbia, SC
North Caro. St. 108, Niagara 88
at Columbus, OH
Iowa 121, Notre Dame 106
at Lawrence, KS
Kansas St. 107, Houston 98
at Seattle, WA
Santa Clara 89, Long Beach St. 86

Utah St.
March 7
UTEP
Provo, UT

Utah St. 91-81
March 12

Utah St. 69-68

Santa Clara

1971 Championship Bracket

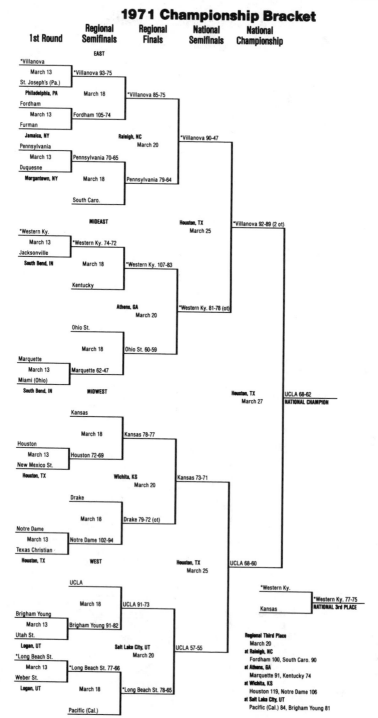

1st Round	Regional Semifinals	Regional Finals	National Semifinals	National Championship

EAST

*Villanova
March 13
St. Joseph's (Pa.)
Philadelphia, PA

*Villanova 93-75
March 18

*Villanova 85-75

Fordham
March 13
Furman
Jamaica, NY

Fordham 105-74

*Villanova 90-47
Raleigh, NC
March 20

Pennsylvania
March 13
Duquesne
Morgantown, NY

Pennsylvania 70-65
March 18

Pennsylvania 79-64

South Caro.

*Villanova 92-89 (2 ot)

MIDEAST
Houston, TX
March 25

*Western Ky.
March 13
Jacksonville
South Bend, IN

*Western Ky. 74-72
March 18

*Western Ky. 107-83

Kentucky

*Western Ky. 81-78 (ot)
Athens, GA
March 20

Ohio St.
March 18

Ohio St. 60-59

Marquette
March 13
Miami (Ohio)
South Bend, IN

Marquette 62-47

Houston, TX
March 27

UCLA 68-62
NATIONAL CHAMPION

MIDWEST

Kansas
March 18

Kansas 78-77

Houston
March 13
New Mexico St.
Houston, TX

Houston 72-69

Kansas 73-71
Wichita, KS
March 20

Drake
March 18

Drake 79-72 (ot)

Notre Dame
March 13
Texas Christian
Houston, TX

Notre Dame 102-94

UCLA 68-60

Houston, TX
March 25

WEST

UCLA
March 18

UCLA 91-73

Brigham Young
March 13
Utah St.
Logan, UT

Brigham Young 91-82

UCLA 57-55
Salt Lake City, UT
March 20

*Long Beach St.
March 13
Weber St.
Logan, UT

*Long Beach St. 77-66
March 18

*Long Beach St. 78-65

Pacific (Cal.)

*Western Ky.

*Western Ky. 77-75
NATIONAL 3rd PLACE

Kansas

Regional Third Place
March 20
at Raleigh, NC
Fordham 100, South Caro. 90
at Athens, GA
Marquette 91, Kentucky 74
at Wichita, KS
Houston 119, Notre Dame 106
at Salt Lake City, UT
Pacific (Cal.) 84, Brigham Young 81

*Villanova's, Western Kentucky's and Long Beach State's participation in 1971 tournament vacated.

1972 Championship Bracket

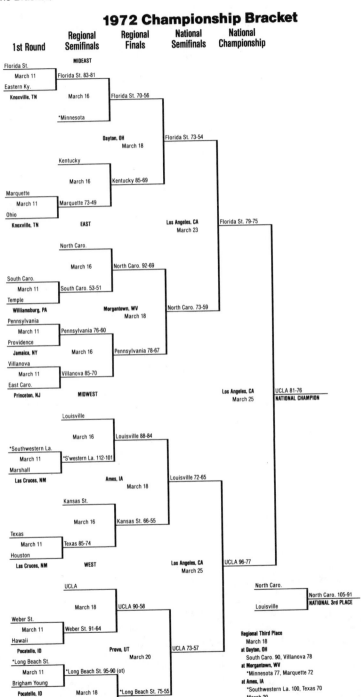

1st Round	Regional Semifinals	Regional Finals	National Semifinals	National Championship

MIDEAST

Florida St.
March 11
Eastern Ky.
Knoxville, TN

Florida St. 83-81
March 16

*Minnesota

Florida St. 70-56

Dayton, OH
March 18

Florida St. 73-54

Kentucky
March 16

Kentucky 85-69

Marquette
March 11
Ohio
Knoxville, TN

Marquette 73-49

EAST

Los Angeles, CA
March 23

Florida St. 79-75

North Caro.
March 16

North Caro. 92-69

South Caro.
March 11
Temple
Williamsburg, PA

South Caro. 53-51

Morgantown, WV
March 18

North Caro. 73-59

Pennsylvania
March 11
Providence
Jamaica, NY

Pennsylvania 76-60

Pennsylvania 78-67

Villanova
March 11
East Caro.
Princeton, NJ

Villanova 85-70

MIDWEST

Los Angeles, CA
March 25

UCLA 81-76
NATIONAL CHAMPION

Louisville
March 16

Louisville 88-84

*Southwestern La.
March 11
Marshall
Las Cruces, NM

*S'western La. 112-101

Ames, IA
March 18

Louisville 72-65

Kansas St.
March 16

Kansas St. 66-55

Texas
March 11
Houston
Las Cruces, NM

Texas 85-74

WEST

Los Angeles, CA
March 25

UCLA 96-77

UCLA
March 18

UCLA 90-58

Weber St.
March 11
Hawaii
Pocatello, ID

Weber St. 91-64

Provo, UT
March 20

UCLA 73-57

*Long Beach St.
March 11
Brigham Young
Pocatello, ID

*Long Beach St. 95-90 (ot)

*Long Beach St. 75-55

San Francisco

North Caro.

Louisville

North Caro. 105-91
NATIONAL 3rd PLACE

Regional Third Place
March 18
at Dayton, OH
  South Caro. 90, Villanova 78
at Morgantown, WV
  *Minnesota 77, Marquette 72
at Ames, IA
  *Southwestern La. 100, Texas 70
March 20
at Provo, UT
  San Francisco 74, Weber St. 64

*Southwestern Louisiana's, Long Beach State's and Minnesota's participation in 1972 tournament vacated.

1973 Championship Bracket

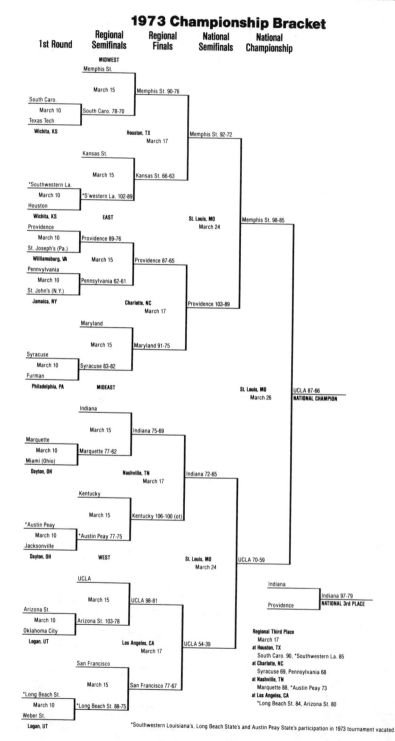

1st Round	Regional Semifinals	Regional Finals	National Semifinals	National Championship

MIDWEST
Memphis St.

March 15 — Memphis St. 90-76

South Caro.
March 10 — South Caro. 78-70
Texas Tech
Wichita, KS

Houston, TX
March 17 — Memphis St. 92-72

Kansas St.
March 15 — Kansas St. 66-63

*Southwestern La.
March 10 — *S'western La. 102-89
Houston
Wichita, KS

St. Louis, MO
March 24 — Memphis St. 98-85

EAST
Providence
March 10 — Providence 89-76
St. Joseph's (Pa.)
Williamsburg, VA

March 15 — Providence 87-65

Pennvylvania
March 10 — Pennsylvania 62-61
St. John's (N.Y.)
Jamaica, NY

Charlotte, NC
March 17 — Providence 103-89

Maryland
March 15 — Maryland 91-75

Syracuse
March 10 — Syracuse 83-82
Furman
Philadelphia, PA

MIDEAST
Indiana
March 15 — Indiana 75-69

Marquette
March 10 — Marquette 77-62
Miami (Ohio)
Dayton, OH

Nashville, TN
March 17 — Indiana 72-65

Kentucky
March 15 — Kentucky 106-100 (ot)

*Austin Peay
March 10 — *Austin Peay 77-75
Jacksonville
Dayton, OH

St. Louis, MO
March 24 — UCLA 70-59

WEST
UCLA
March 15 — UCLA 98-81

Arizona St.
March 10 — Arizona St. 103-78
Oklahoma City
Logan, UT

Los Angeles, CA
March 17 — UCLA 54-39

San Francisco
March 15 — San Francisco 77-67

*Long Beach St.
March 10 — *Long Beach St. 88-75
Weber St.
Logan, UT

St. Louis, MO
March 26 — UCLA 87-66
NATIONAL CHAMPION

Indiana
Providence — Indiana 97-79
NATIONAL 3rd PLACE

Regional Third Place
March 17
at Houston, TX
South Caro. 90, *Southwestern La. 85
at Charlotte, NC
Syracuse 69, Pennsylvania 68
at Nashville, TN
Marquette 88, *Austin Peay 73
at Los Angeles, CA
*Long Beach St. 84, Arizona St. 80

*Southwestern Louisiana's, Long Beach State's and Austin Peay State's participation in 1973 tournament vacated.

1974 Championship Bracket

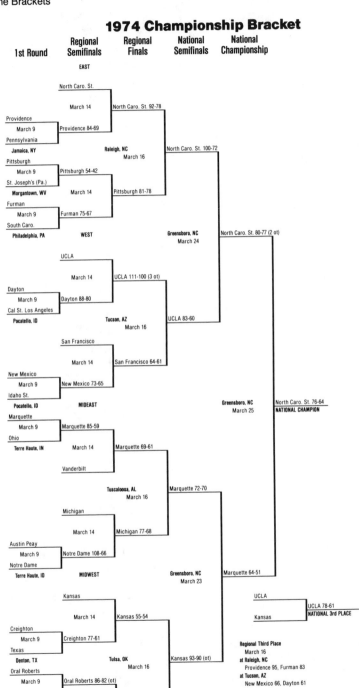

1st Round	Regional Semifinals	Regional Finals	National Semifinals	National Championship

EAST

North Caro. St.

March 14 — North Caro. St. 92-78

Providence
March 9 — Providence 84-69
Pennsylvania
Jamaica, NY

Raleigh, NC
March 16 — North Caro. St. 100-72

Pittsburgh
March 9 — Pittsburgh 54-42
St. Joseph's (Pa.)
Morgantown, WV — March 14 — Pittsburgh 81-78

Furman
March 9 — Furman 75-67
South Caro.
Philadelphia, PA

Greensboro, NC
March 24 — North Caro. St. 80-77 (2 ot)

WEST

UCLA
March 14 — UCLA 111-100 (3 ot)
Dayton
March 9 — Dayton 88-80
Cal St. Los Angeles
Pocatello, ID

Tucson, AZ
March 16 — UCLA 83-60

San Francisco
March 14 — San Francisco 64-61
New Mexico
March 9 — New Mexico 73-65
Idaho St.
Pocatello, ID

Greensboro, NC
March 25 — North Caro. St. 76-64
NATIONAL CHAMPION

MIDEAST

Marquette
March 9 — Marquette 85-59
Ohio
Terre Haute, IN — March 14 — Marquette 69-61

Vanderbilt

Tuscaloosa, AL
March 16 — Marquette 72-70

Michigan
March 14 — Michigan 77-68
Austin Peay
March 9 — Notre Dame 108-66
Notre Dame
Terre Haute, ID

Greensboro, NC
March 23 — Marquette 64-51

MIDWEST

Kansas
March 14 — Kansas 55-54
Creighton
March 9 — Creighton 77-61
Texas
Denton, TX

Tulsa, OK
March 16 — Kansas 93-90 (ot)

Oral Roberts
March 9 — Oral Roberts 86-82 (ot)
Syracuse
Denton, TX — March 14 — Oral Roberts 96-93

Louisville

UCLA
UCLA 78-61
NATIONAL 3rd PLACE
Kansas

Regional Third Place
March 16
at Raleigh, NC
Providence 95, Furman 83
at Tucson, AZ
New Mexico 66, Dayton 61
at Tuscaloosa, AL
Notre Dame 118, Vanderbilt 88
at Tulsa, OK
Creighton 80, Louisville 71

1975 Championship Bracket

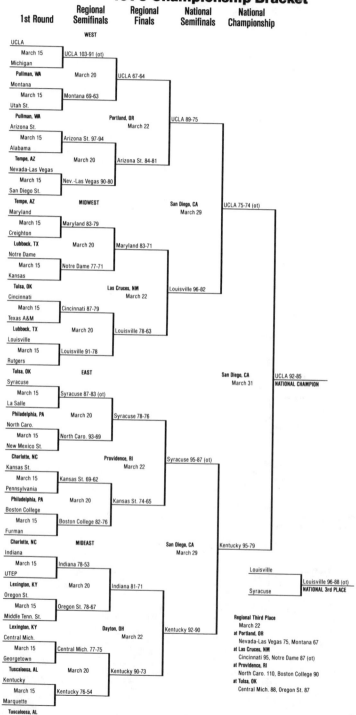

| 1st Round | Regional Semifinals | Regional Finals | National Semifinals | National Championship |

WEST

UCLA
March 15
Michigan
— UCLA 103-91 (ot)
Pullman, WA
March 20
— UCLA 67-64
Montana
March 15
Utah St.
— Montana 69-63
Pullman, WA
Portland, OR
March 22
— UCLA 89-75
Arizona St.
March 15
Alabama
— Arizona St. 97-94
Tempe, AZ
March 20
— Arizona St. 84-81
Nevada-Las Vegas
March 15
San Diego St.
— Nev.-Las Vegas 90-80
Tempe, AZ

San Diego, CA
March 29
— UCLA 75-74 (ot)

MIDWEST

Maryland
March 15
Creighton
— Maryland 83-79
Lubbock, TX
March 20
— Maryland 83-71
Notre Dame
March 15
Kansas
— Notre Dame 77-71
Tulsa, OK
Las Cruces, NM
March 22
— Louisville 96-82
Cincinnati
March 15
Texas A&M
— Cincinnati 87-79
Lubbock, TX
March 20
— Louisville 78-63
Louisville
March 15
Rutgers
— Louisville 91-78
Tulsa, OK

San Diego, CA
March 31
— UCLA 92-85
NATIONAL CHAMPION

EAST

Syracuse
March 15
La Salle
— Syracuse 87-83 (ot)
Philadelphia, PA
March 20
— Syracuse 78-76
North Caro.
March 15
New Mexico St.
— North Caro. 93-69
Charlotte, NC
Providence, RI
March 22
— Syracuse 95-87 (ot)
Kansas St.
March 15
Pennsylvania
— Kansas St. 69-62
Philadelphia, PA
March 20
— Kansas St. 74-65
Boston College
March 15
Furman
— Boston College 82-76
Charlotte, NC

San Diego, CA
March 29
— Kentucky 95-79

MIDEAST

Indiana
March 15
UTEP
— Indiana 78-53
Lexington, KY
March 20
— Indiana 81-71
Oregon St.
March 15
Middle Tenn. St.
— Oregon St. 78-67
Lexington, KY
Dayton, OH
March 22
— Kentucky 92-90
Central Mich.
March 15
Georgetown
— Central Mich. 77-75
Tuscaloosa, AL
March 20
— Kentucky 90-73
Kentucky
March 15
Marquette
— Kentucky 76-54
Tuscaloosa, AL

Louisville
— Louisville 96-88 (ot)
Syracuse
NATIONAL 3rd PLACE

Regional Third Place
March 22
at Portland, OR
Nevada-Las Vegas 75, Montana 67
at Las Cruces, NM
Cincinnati 95, Notre Dame 87 (ot)
at Providence, RI
North Caro. 110, Boston College 90
at Tulsa, OK
Central Mich. 88, Oregon St. 87

1976 Championship Bracket

1st Round	Regional Semifinals	Regional Finals	National Semifinals	National Championship

EAST

Virginia
March 13
DePaul — DePaul 69-60
Charlotte, NC — March 20 — Va. Military 71-66 (ot)
Va. Military
March 13
Tennessee — Va. Military 81-75
Charlotte, NC — Greensboro, NC — Rutgers 91-75
Princeton — March 22
March 13
Rutgers — Rutgers 54-53
Providence, RI — March 20 — Rutgers 93-79
Hofstra
March 13
Connecticut — Connecticut 80-78 (ot)
Providence, RI

MIDWEST

Wichita St.
March 13
Michigan — Michigan 74-73
Denton, TX — March 20 — Michigan 80-76
Cincinnati
March 13
Notre Dame — Notre Dame 79-78
Lawrence, KS — Louisville, KY — Michigan 95-88
Missouri — March 22
March 13
Washington — Missouri 69-67
Lawrence, KS — March 20 — Missouri 86-75
Texas Tech
March 13
Syracuse — Texas Tech 69-56
Denton, TX

Philadelphia, PA — March 29 — Michigan 86-70

MIDEAST

Alabama
March 13
North Caro. — Alabama 79-64
Dayton, OH — March 20 — Indiana 74-69
Indiana
March 13
St. John's (N.Y.) — Indiana 90-70
Notre Dame, IN — Baton Rouge, LA — Indiana 65-56
Western Ky. — March 22
March 13
Marquette — Marquette 79-60
Dayton, OH — March 20 — Marquette 62-57
Western Mich.
March 13
Virginia Tech — West. Mich. 77-67 (ot)
Notre Dame, IN

Philadelphia, PA — March 29 — Indiana 86-68 NATIONAL CHAMPION

Philadelphia, PA — March 27 — Indiana 65-51

WEST

Pepperdine
March 13
Memphis St. — Pepperdine 87-77
Tempe, AZ — March 20 — UCLA 70-61
San Diego St.
March 13
UCLA — UCLA 74-64
Eugene, OR — Los Angeles, CA — UCLA 82-66
Boise St. — March 20
March 13
Nevada-Las Vegas — Nevada-Las Vegas 103-78
Eugene, OR — March 18 — Arizona 114-109 (ot)
Arizona
March 13
Georgetown — Arizona 83-76
Tempe, AZ

UCLA
Rutgers — UCLA 106-92 NATIONAL 3rd PLACE

1977 Championship Bracket

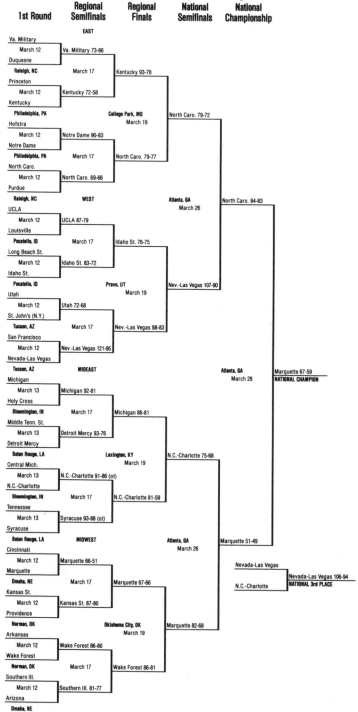

1st Round	Regional Semifinals	Regional Finals	National Semifinals	National Championship

EAST

Va. Military
March 12 — Va. Military 73-66
Duquesne
Raleigh, NC — March 17 — Kentucky 93-78
Princeton
March 12 — Kentucky 72-58
Kentucky
Philadelphia, PA — **College Park, MD** — North Caro. 79-72
Hofstra — March 19
March 12 — Notre Dame 90-83
Notre Dame
Philadelphia, PA — March 17 — North Caro. 79-77
North Caro.
March 12 — North Caro. 69-66
Purdue
Raleigh, NC — **WEST** — **Atlanta, GA** — North Caro. 84-83
UCLA — March 26
March 12 — UCLA 87-79
Louisville
Pocatello, ID — March 17 — Idaho St. 76-75
Long Beach St.
March 12 — Idaho St. 83-72
Idaho St.
Pocatello, ID — **Provo, UT** — Nev.-Las Vegas 107-90
Utah — March 19
March 12 — Utah 72-68
St. John's (N.Y.)
Tucson, AZ — March 17 — Nev.-Las Vegas 88-83
San Francisco
March 12 — Nev.-Las Vegas 121-95
Nevada-Las Vegas

Tucson, AZ — **MIDEAST** — **Atlanta, GA** — Marquette 67-59
Michigan — March 28 — **NATIONAL CHAMPION**
March 13 — Michigan 92-81
Holy Cross
Bloomington, IN — March 17 — Michigan 86-81
Middle Tenn. St.
March 13 — Detroit Mercy 93-76
Detroit Mercy
Baton Rouge, LA — **Lexington, KY** — N.C.-Charlotte 75-68
Central Mich. — March 19
March 13 — N.C.-Charlotte 91-86 (ot)
N.C.-Charlotte
Bloomington, IN — March 17 — N.C.-Charlotte 81-59
Tennessee
March 13 — Syracuse 93-88 (ot)
Syracuse
Baton Rouge, LA — **MIDWEST** — **Atlanta, GA** — Marquette 51-49
Cincinnati — March 26
March 12 — Marquette 66-51
Marquette — Nevada-Las Vegas
Omaha, NE — March 17 — Marquette 67-66 — Nevada-Las Vegas 106-94
Kansas St. — N.C.-Charlotte — **NATIONAL 3rd PLACE**
March 12 — Kansas St. 87-80
Providence
Norman, OK — **Oklahoma City, OK** — Marquette 82-68
Arkansas — March 19
March 12 — Wake Forest 86-80
Wake Forest
Norman, OK — March 17 — Wake Forest 86-81
Southern Ill.
March 12 — Southern Ill. 81-77
Arizona
Omaha, NE

1978 Championship Bracket

1st Round	Regional Semifinals	Regional Finals	National Semifinals	National Championship

MIDEAST

Michigan St.
March 11
Providence
Indianapolis, IN — Michigan St. 77-63
Western Ky.
March 11
Syracuse
Knoxville, TN — Western Ky. 87-86 (ot)

Michigan St. 90-69 (March 17)

Miami (Ohio)
March 11
Marquette
Indianapolis, IN — Miami (Ohio) 84-81 (ot)
Kentucky
March 11
Florida St.
Knoxville, TN — Kentucky 85-76

Kentucky 91-69 (March 16)

Dayton, OH — Kentucky 52-49 (March 18)

WEST

UCLA
March 11
Kansas
Eugene, OR — UCLA 83-76
Weber St.
March 11
Arkansas
Eugene, OR — Arkansas 73-52

Arkansas 74-70 (March 16)

San Francisco
March 11
North Caro.
Tempe, AZ — San Francisco 68-64
New Mexico
March 11
Cal St. Fullerton
Tempe, AZ — Cal St. Fullerton 90-85

Cal St. Fullerton 75-72 (March 16)

Albuquerque, NM — Arkansas 61-58 (March 18)

St. Louis, MO — Kentucky 64-59 (March 25)

EAST

Duke
March 12
Rhode Island
Charlotte, NC — Duke 63-62
Pennsylvania
March 12
St. Bonaventure
Philadelphia, PA — Pennsylvania 92-83

Duke 84-80 (March 17)

Furman
March 12
Indiana
Charlotte, NC — Indiana 63-62
Villanova
March 12
La Salle
Philadelphia, PA — Villanova 103-97

Villanova 61-60 (March 17)

Providence, RI — Duke 90-72 (March 19)

MIDWEST

Missouri
March 12
Utah
Wichita, KS — Utah 86-79 (2 ot)
Houston
March 12
Notre Dame
Tulsa, OK — Notre Dame 100-77

Notre Dame 69-56 (March 17)

Creighton
March 12
DePaul
Wichita, KS — DePaul 80-78
Louisville
March 12
St. John's (N.Y.)
Tulsa, OK — Louisville 76-68

DePaul 90-89 (2 ot) (March 17)

Lawrence, KS — Notre Dame 84-64 (March 19)

St. Louis, MO — Duke 90-86 (March 25)

St. Louis, MO — Kentucky 94-88 **NATIONAL CHAMPION** (March 27)

Arkansas
Notre Dame — Arkansas 71-69 **NATIONAL 3rd PLACE**

1979 Championship Bracket

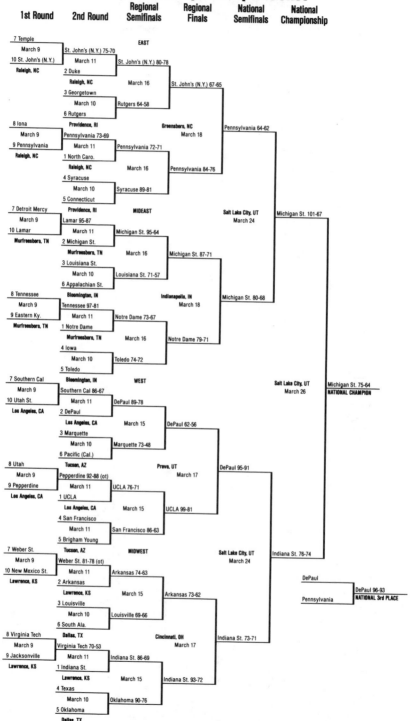

1980 Championship Bracket

1st Round	2nd Round	Regional Semifinals	Regional Finals	National Semifinals	National Championship

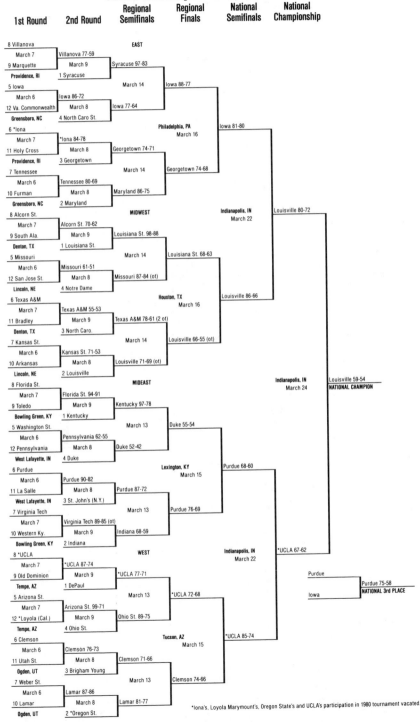

EAST

8 Villanova
March 7
9 Marquette
Providence, RI — Villanova 77-59 / March 9 / 1 Syracuse — Syracuse 97-83
5 Iowa
March 6
12 Va. Commonwealth
Greensboro, NC — Iowa 86-72 / March 8 / 4 North Caro St. — Iowa 77-64 / March 14 — Iowa 88-77
6 *Iona
March 7
11 Holy Cross
Providence, RI — *Iona 84-78 / March 8 / 3 Georgetown — Georgetown 74-71
7 Tennessee
March 6
10 Furman
Greensboro, NC — Tennessee 80-69 / March 8 / 2 Maryland — Maryland 86-75 / March 14 — Georgetown 74-68

Philadelphia, PA March 16 — Iowa 81-80

MIDWEST

8 Alcorn St.
March 7
9 South Ala.
Denton, TX — Alcorn St. 70-62 / March 9 / 1 Louisiana St. — Louisiana St. 98-88
5 Missouri
March 6
12 San Jose St.
Lincoln, NE — Missouri 61-51 / March 8 / 4 Notre Dame — Missouri 87-84 (ot) / March 14 — Louisiana St. 68-63
6 Texas A&M
March 7
11 Bradley
Denton, TX — Texas A&M 55-53 / March 9 / 3 North Caro. — Texas A&M 78-61 (2 ot)
7 Kansas St.
March 6
10 Arkansas
Lincoln, NE — Kansas St. 71-53 / March 8 / 2 Louisville — Louisville 71-69 (ot) / March 14 — Louisville 66-55 (ot)

Houston, TX March 16 — Louisville 86-66

Indianapolis, IN March 22 — Louisville 80-72

MIDEAST

8 Florida St.
March 7
9 Toledo
Bowling Green, KY — Florida St. 94-91 / March 9 / 1 Kentucky — Kentucky 97-78
5 Washington St.
March 6
12 Pennsylvania
West Lafayette, IN — Pennsylvania 62-55 / March 8 / 4 Duke — Duke 52-42 / March 13 — Duke 55-54
6 Purdue
March 6
11 La Salle
West Lafayette, IN — Purdue 90-82 / March 8 / 3 St. John's (N.Y.) — Purdue 87-72
7 Virginia Tech
March 7
10 Western Ky.
Bowling Green, KY — Virginia Tech 89-85 (ot) / March 9 / 2 Indiana — Indiana 68-59 / March 13 — Purdue 76-69

Lexington, KY March 15 — Purdue 68-60

WEST

8 *UCLA
March 7
9 Old Dominion
Tempe, AZ — *UCLA 87-74 / March 9 / 1 DePaul — *UCLA 77-71
5 Arizona St.
March 7
12 *Loyola (Cal.)
Tempe, AZ — Arizona St. 99-71 / March 9 / 4 Ohio St. — Ohio St. 89-75 / March 13 — *UCLA 72-68
6 Clemson
March 6
11 Utah St.
Ogden, UT — Clemson 76-73 / March 8 / 3 Brigham Young — Clemson 71-66
7 Weber St.
March 6
10 Lamar
Ogden, UT — Lamar 87-86 / March 8 / 2 *Oregon St. — Lamar 81-77 / March 13 — Clemson 74-66

Tucson, AZ March 15 — *UCLA 85-74

Indianapolis, IN March 22 — *UCLA 67-62

Indianapolis, IN March 24 — Louisville 59-54 NATIONAL CHAMPION

Purdue
Iowa — Purdue 75-58 NATIONAL 3rd PLACE

*Iona's, Loyola Marymount's, Oregon State's and UCLA's participation in 1980 tournament vacated.

1981 Championship Bracket

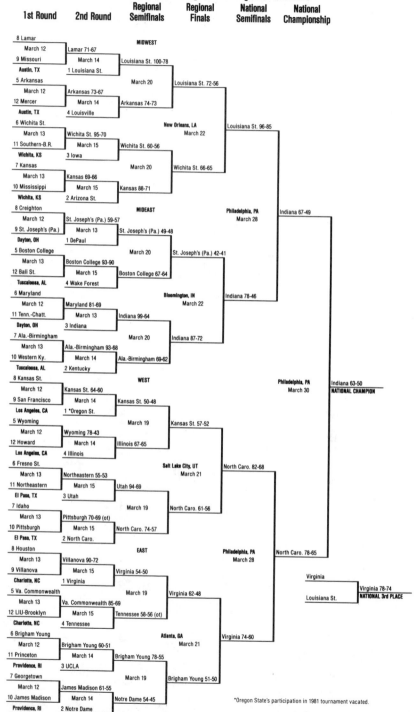

1st Round	2nd Round	Regional Semifinals	Regional Finals	National Semifinals	National Championship

MIDWEST

8 Lamar
March 12
Lamar 71-67
9 Missouri
March 14
Louisiana St. 100-78
Austin, TX
1 Louisiana St.
Louisiana St. 72-56
5 Arkansas
March 12
Arkansas 73-67
12 Mercer
March 14
Arkansas 74-73
Austin, TX
4 Louisville
New Orleans, LA
March 22
Louisiana St. 96-85
6 Wichita St.
March 13
Wichita St. 95-70
11 Southern-B.R.
March 15
Wichita St. 60-56
Wichita, KS
3 Iowa
Wichita St. 66-65
7 Kansas
March 13
Kansas 69-66
10 Mississippi
March 15
Kansas 88-71
Wichita, KS
2 Arizona St.

Indiana 67-49

MIDEAST

8 Creighton
March 12
St. Joseph's (Pa.) 59-57
9 St. Joseph's (Pa.)
March 13
St. Joseph's (Pa.) 49-48
Dayton, OH
1 DePaul
St. Joseph's (Pa.) 42-41
5 Boston College
March 13
Boston College 93-90
12 Ball St.
March 15
Boston College 67-64
Tuscaloosa, AL
4 Wake Forest
Bloomington, IN
March 22
Indiana 78-46
6 Maryland
March 12
Maryland 81-69
11 Tenn.-Chatt.
March 13
Indiana 99-64
Dayton, OH
3 Indiana
Indiana 87-72
7 Ala.-Birmingham
March 13
Ala.-Birmingham 93-68
10 Western Ky.
March 14
Ala.-Birmingham 69-62
Tuscaloosa, AL
2 Kentucky

Philadelphia, PA
March 28

Indiana 63-50
NATIONAL CHAMPION

WEST

8 Kansas St.
March 12
Kansas St. 64-60
9 San Francisco
March 14
Kansas St. 50-48
Los Angeles, CA
1 *Oregon St.
Kansas St. 57-52
5 Wyoming
March 12
Wyoming 78-43
12 Howard
March 14
Illinois 67-65
Los Angeles, CA
4 Illinois
Salt Lake City, UT
March 21
North Caro. 82-68
6 Fresno St.
March 13
Northeastern 55-53
11 Northeastern
March 15
Utah 94-69
El Paso, TX
3 Utah
North Caro. 61-56
7 Idaho
March 13
Pittsburgh 70-69 (ot)
10 Pittsburgh
March 15
North Caro. 74-57
El Paso, TX
2 North Caro.

Philadelphia, PA
March 30

North Caro. 78-65

EAST

8 Houston
March 13
Villanova 90-72
9 Villanova
March 15
Virginia 54-50
Charlotte, NC
1 Virginia
Virginia 62-48
5 Va. Commonwealth
March 13
Va. Commonwealth 85-69
12 LIU-Brooklyn
March 15
Tennessee 58-56 (ot)
Charlotte, NC
4 Tennessee
Atlanta, GA
March 21
Virginia 74-60
6 Brigham Young
March 12
Brigham Young 60-51
11 Princeton
March 14
Brigham Young 78-55
Providence, RI
3 UCLA
Brigham Young 51-50
7 Georgetown
March 12
James Madison 61-55
10 James Madison
March 14
Notre Dame 54-45
Providence, RI
2 Notre Dame

Philadelphia, PA
March 28

Virginia

Virginia 78-74
NATIONAL 3rd PLACE

Louisiana St.

*Oregon State's participation in 1981 tournament vacated.

1982 Championship Bracket

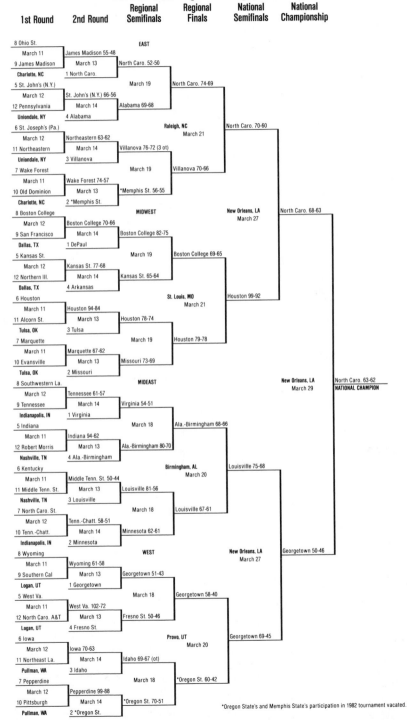

| 1st Round | 2nd Round | Regional Semifinals | Regional Finals | National Semifinals | National Championship |

EAST

8 Ohio St.
March 11 — James Madison 55-48
9 James Madison
March 13 — North Caro. 52-50
Charlotte, NC
1 North Caro.
5 St. John's (N.Y.)
March 12 — St. John's (N.Y.) 66-56
12 Pennsylvania
March 14 — Alabama 69-68
Uniondale, NY
4 Alabama

March 19 — North Caro. 74-69

6 St. Joseph's (Pa.)
March 12 — Northeastern 63-62
11 Northeastern
March 14 — Villanova 76-72 (3 ot)
Uniondale, NY
3 Villanova
7 Wake Forest
March 11 — Wake Forest 74-57
10 Old Dominion
March 13 — *Memphis St. 56-55
Charlotte, NC
2 *Memphis St.

March 19 — Villanova 70-66

Raleigh, NC — March 21 — North Caro. 70-60

North Caro. 68-63

MIDWEST

8 Boston College
March 12 — Boston College 70-66
9 San Francisco
March 14 — Boston College 82-75
Dallas, TX
1 DePaul
5 Kansas St.
March 12 — Kansas St. 77-68
12 Northern Ill.
March 14 — Kansas St. 65-64
Dallas, TX
4 Arkansas

March 19 — Boston College 69-65

6 Houston
March 11 — Houston 94-84
11 Alcorn St.
March 13 — Houston 78-74
Tulsa, OK
3 Tulsa
7 Marquette
March 11 — Marquette 67-62
10 Evansville
March 13 — Missouri 73-69
Tulsa, OK
2 Missouri

March 19 — Houston 79-78

St. Louis, MO — March 21 — Houston 99-92

New Orleans, LA — March 27 — North Caro. 68-63

MIDEAST

8 Southwestern La.
March 12 — Tennessee 61-57
9 Tennessee
March 14 — Virginia 54-51
Indianapolis, IN
1 Virginia
5 Indiana
March 11 — Indiana 94-62
12 Robert Morris
March 13 — Ala.-Birmingham 80-70
Nashville, TN
4 Ala.-Birmingham

March 18 — Ala.-Birmingham 68-66

6 Kentucky
March 11 — Middle Tenn. St. 50-44
11 Middle Tenn. St.
March 13 — Louisville 81-56
Nashville, TN
3 Louisville
7 North Caro. St.
March 12 — Tenn.-Chatt. 58-51
10 Tenn.-Chatt.
March 14 — Minnesota 62-61
Indianapolis, IN
2 Minnesota

March 18 — Louisville 67-61

Birmingham, AL — March 20 — Louisville 75-68

New Orleans, LA — March 27 — Georgetown 50-46

North Caro. 63-62 NATIONAL CHAMPION

New Orleans, LA — March 29

WEST

8 Wyoming
March 11 — Wyoming 61-58
9 Southern Cal
March 13 — Georgetown 51-43
Logan, UT
1 Georgetown
5 West Va.
March 11 — West Va. 102-72
12 North Caro. A&T
March 13 — Fresno St. 50-46
Logan, UT
4 Fresno St.

March 18 — Georgetown 58-40

6 Iowa
March 12 — Iowa 70-63
11 Northeast La.
March 14 — Idaho 69-67 (ot)
Pullman, WA
3 Idaho
7 Pepperdine
March 12 — Pepperdine 99-88
10 Pittsburgh
March 14 — *Oregon St. 70-51
Pullman, WA
2 *Oregon St.

March 18 — *Oregon St. 60-42

Provo, UT — March 20 — Georgetown 69-45

Georgetown 50-46

*Oregon State's and Memphis State's participation in 1982 tournament vacated.

1983 Championship Bracket

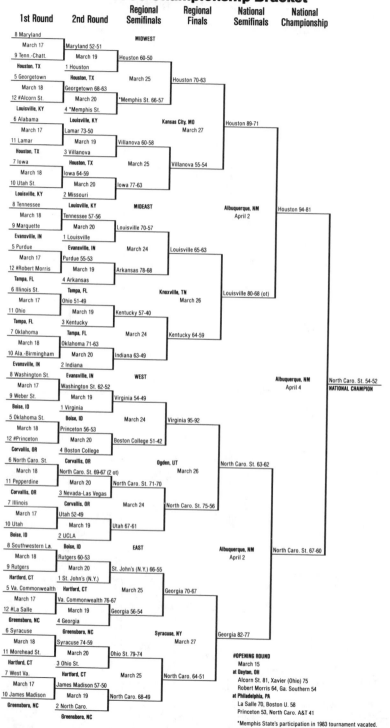

1st Round	2nd Round	Regional Semifinals	Regional Finals	National Semifinals	National Championship

MIDWEST

8 Maryland
March 17
9 Tenn.-Chatt.
Houston, TX
5 Georgetown
March 18
12 #Alcorn St.
Louisville, KY
6 Alabama
March 17
11 Lamar
Houston, TX
7 Iowa
March 18
10 Utah St.
Louisville, KY

Maryland 52-51
March 19
1 Houston
Houston, TX
Georgetown 68-63
March 20
4 *Memphis St.
Louisville, KY
Lamar 73-50
March 19
3 Villanova
Houston, TX
Iowa 64-59
March 20
2 Missouri

Houston 60-50
March 25
*Memphis St. 66-57
Villanova 60-58
March 25
Iowa 77-63

Houston 70-63
Kansas City, MO
March 27
Villanova 55-54

Houston 89-71

Houston 94-81

MIDEAST

8 Tennessee
March 18
9 Marquette
Evansville, IN
5 Purdue
March 17
12 #Robert Morris
Tampa, FL
6 Illinois St.
March 17
11 Ohio
Tampa, FL
7 Oklahoma
March 18
10 Ala.-Birmingham
Evansville, IN

Tennessee 57-56
March 20
1 Louisville
Evansville, IN
Purdue 55-53
March 19
4 Arkansas
Tampa, FL
Ohio 51-49
March 19
3 Kentucky
Tampa, FL
Oklahoma 71-63
March 20
2 Indiana

Louisville 70-57
March 24
Arkansas 78-68
Kentucky 57-40
March 24
Indiana 63-49

Louisville 65-63
Knoxville, TN
March 26
Kentucky 64-59

Louisville 80-68 (ot)

Albuquerque, NM
April 2

WEST

8 Washington St.
March 17
9 Weber St.
Boise, ID
5 Oklahoma St.
March 18
12 #Princeton
Corvallis, OR
6 North Caro. St.
March 18
11 Pepperdine
Corvallis, OR
7 Illinois
March 17
10 Utah
Boise, ID

Washington St. 62-52
March 19
1 Virginia
Boise, ID
Princeton 56-53
March 20
4 Boston College
Corvallis, OR
North Caro. St. 69-67 (2 ot)
March 20
3 Nevada-Las Vegas
Corvallis, OR
Utah 52-49
March 19
2 UCLA

Virginia 54-49
March 24
Boston College 51-42
North Caro. St. 71-70
March 24
Utah 67-61

Virginia 95-92
Ogden, UT
March 26
North Caro. St. 75-56

North Caro. St. 63-62

North Caro. St. 67-60

Albuquerque, NM
April 4

EAST

8 Southwestern La.
March 18
9 Rutgers
Hartford, CT
5 Va. Commonwealth
March 17
12 #La Salle
Greensboro, NC
6 Syracuse
March 18
11 Morehead St.
Hartford, CT
7 West Va.
March 17
10 James Madison
Greensboro, NC

Rutgers 60-53
March 20
1 St. John's (N.Y.)
Hartford, CT
Va. Commonwealth 76-67
March 19
4 Georgia
Greensboro, NC
Syracuse 74-59
March 20
3 Ohio St.
Hartford, CT
James Madison 57-50
March 19
2 North Caro.
Greensboro, NC

St. John's (N.Y.) 66-55
March 25
Georgia 56-54
Ohio St. 79-74
March 25
North Caro. 68-49

Georgia 70-67
Syracuse, NY
March 27
North Caro. 64-51

Georgia 82-77

Albuquerque, NM
April 2

Houston 89-71

Albuquerque, NM
April 2

Houston 94-81

North Caro. St. 54-52
NATIONAL CHAMPION

#OPENING ROUND
March 15
at Dayton, OH
Alcorn St. 81, Xavier (Ohio) 75
Robert Morris 64, Ga. Southern 54
at Philadelphia, PA
La Salle 70, Boston U. 58
Princeton 53, North Caro. A&T 41

*Memphis State's participation in 1983 tournament vacated.

1984 Championship Bracket

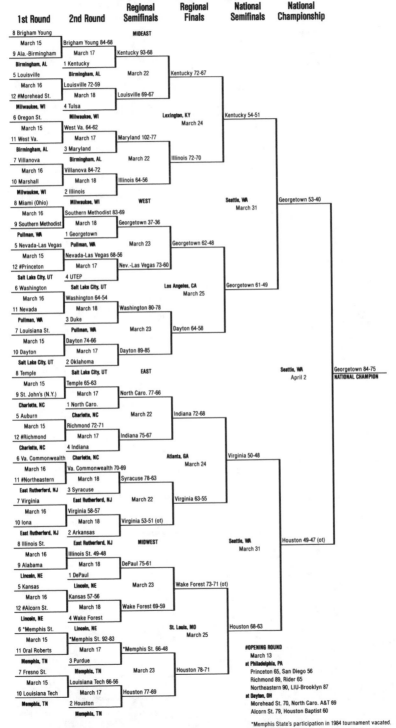

1st Round	2nd Round	Regional Semifinals	Regional Finals	National Semifinals	National Championship

MIDEAST

8 Brigham Young
March 15 — Brigham Young 84-68
9 Ala.-Birmingham — March 17 — Kentucky 93-68
Birmingham, AL — 1 Kentucky
5 Louisville — Birmingham, AL — March 22 — Kentucky 72-67
March 16 — Louisville 72-59
12 #Morehead St. — March 18 — Louisville 69-67
Milwaukee, WI — 4 Tulsa
6 Oregon St. — Milwaukee, WI — Lexington, KY — Kentucky 54-51
March 15 — West Va. 64-62 — March 24
11 West Va. — March 17 — Maryland 102-77
Birmingham, AL — 3 Maryland
7 Villanova — Birmingham, AL — March 22 — Illinois 72-70
March 16 — Villanova 84-72
10 Marshall — March 18 — Illinois 64-56
Milwaukee, WI — 2 Illinois

WEST

8 Miami (Ohio) — Milwaukee, WI — Seattle, WA — Georgetown 53-40
March 16 — Southern Methodist 83-69 — March 31
9 Southern Methodist — March 18 — Georgetown 37-36
Pullman, WA — 1 Georgetown
5 Nevada-Las Vegas — Pullman, WA — March 23 — Georgetown 62-48
March 15 — Nevada-Las Vegas 68-56
12 #Princeton — March 17 — Nev.-Las Vegas 73-60
Salt Lake City, UT — 4 UTEP
6 Washington — Salt Lake City, UT — Los Angeles, CA — Georgetown 61-49
March 16 — Washington 64-54 — March 25
11 Nevada — March 18 — Washington 80-78
Pullman, WA — 3 Duke
7 Louisiana St. — Pullman, WA — March 23 — Dayton 64-58
March 15 — Dayton 74-66
10 Dayton — March 17 — Dayton 89-85
Salt Lake City, UT — 2 Oklahoma

EAST

8 Temple — Salt Lake City, UT — Seattle, WA — Georgetown 84-75
March 15 — Temple 65-63 — April 2 — NATIONAL CHAMPION
9 St. John's (N.Y.) — March 17 — North Caro. 77-66
Charlotte, NC — 1 North Caro.
5 Auburn — Charlotte, NC — March 22 — Indiana 72-68
March 15 — Richmond 72-71
12 #Richmond — March 17 — Indiana 75-67
Charlotte, NC — 4 Indiana
6 Va. Commonwealth — Charlotte, NC — Atlanta, GA — Virginia 50-48
March 16 — Va. Commonwealth 70-69 — March 24
11 #Northeastern — March 18 — Syracuse 78-63
East Rutherford, NJ — 3 Syracuse
7 Virginia — East Rutherford, NJ — March 22 — Virginia 63-55
March 16 — Virginia 58-57
10 Iona — March 18 — Virginia 53-51 (ot)
East Rutherford, NJ — 2 Arkansas

MIDWEST

8 Illinois St. — East Rutherford, NJ — Seattle, WA — Houston 49-47 (ot)
March 16 — Illinois St. 49-48 — March 31
9 Alabama — March 18 — DePaul 75-61
Lincoln, NE — 1 DePaul
5 Kansas — Lincoln, NE — March 23 — Wake Forest 73-71 (ot)
March 16 — Kansas 57-56
12 #Alcorn St. — March 18 — Wake Forest 69-59
Lincoln, NE — 4 Wake Forest
6 *Memphis St. — Lincoln, NE — St. Louis, MO — Houston 68-63
March 15 — *Memphis St. 92-83 — March 25
11 Oral Roberts — March 17 — *Memphis St. 66-48
Memphis, TN — 3 Purdue
7 Fresno St. — Memphis, TN — March 23 — Houston 78-71
March 15 — Louisiana Tech 66-56
10 Louisiana Tech — March 17 — Houston 77-69
Memphis, TN — 2 Houston
Memphis, TN

#OPENING ROUND
March 13
at Philadelphia, PA
Princeton 65, San Diego 56
Richmond 89, Rider 65
Northeastern 90, LIU-Brooklyn 87
at Dayton, OH
Morehead St. 70, North Caro. A&T 69
Alcorn St. 79, Houston Baptist 60

*Memphis State's participation in 1984 tournament vacated.

1985 Championship Bracket

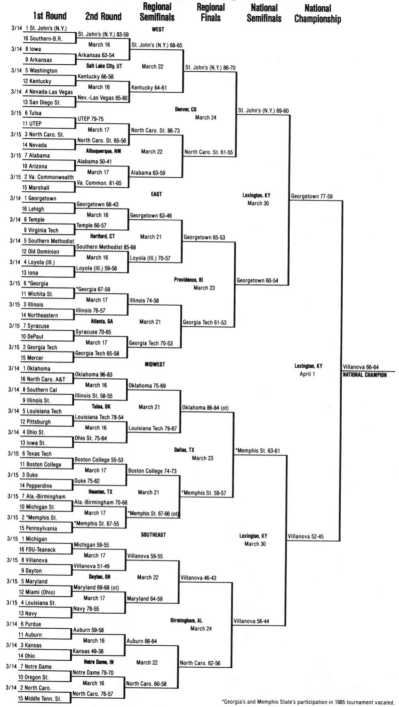

	1st Round	2nd Round	Regional Semifinals	Regional Finals	National Semifinals	National Championship

WEST

3/14 1 St. John's (N.Y.)
16 Southern-B.R.
 St. John's (N.Y.) 83-59
 March 16
3/14 8 Iowa
9 Arkansas
 Arkansas 63-54
 St. John's (N.Y.) 68-65
 Salt Lake City, UT
3/14 5 Washington
12 Kentucky
 Kentucky 66-58
 March 16
 March 22
3/14 4 Nevada-Las Vegas
13 San Diego St.
 Kentucky 64-61
 Nev.-Las Vegas 85-80
 St. John's (N.Y.) 86-70

3/15 6 Tulsa
11 UTEP
 UTEP 79-75
 March 17
3/15 3 North Caro. St.
14 Nevada
 North Caro. St. 65-56
 North Caro. St. 86-73
 Denver, CO
3/15 7 Alabama
10 Arizona
 Alabama 50-41
 March 17
 March 22
 March 24
3/15 2 Va. Commonwealth
15 Marshall
 Va. Common. 81-65
 Alabama 63-59
 North Caro. St. 61-55

St. John's (N.Y.) 69-60

EAST

3/14 1 Georgetown
16 Lehigh
 Georgetown 68-43
 March 16
3/14 8 Temple
9 Virginia Tech
 Temple 60-57
 Georgetown 63-46
 Hartford, CT
3/14 5 Southern Methodist
12 Old Dominion
 Southern Methodist 85-68
 March 16
 March 21
3/14 4 Loyola (Ill.)
13 Iona
 Loyola (Ill.) 59-58
 Loyola (Ill.) 70-57
 Georgetown 65-53

3/15 6 *Georgia
11 Wichita St.
 *Georgia 67-59
 March 17
3/15 3 Illinois
14 Northeastern
 Illinois 76-57
 Illinois 74-58
 Atlanta, GA
3/15 7 Syracuse
10 DePaul
 Syracuse 70-65
 March 17
 March 21
3/15 2 Georgia Tech
15 Mercer
 Georgia Tech 65-58
 Georgia Tech 70-53
 Georgia Tech 61-53

Lexington, KY
March 30

Georgetown 60-54

Georgetown 77-59

MIDWEST

3/14 1 Oklahoma
16 North Caro. A&T
 Oklahoma 96-83
 March 16
3/14 8 Southern Cal
9 Illinois St.
 Illinois St. 58-55
 Oklahoma 75-69
 Tulsa, OK
3/14 5 Louisiana Tech
12 Pittsburgh
 Louisiana Tech 78-54
 March 16
 March 21
3/14 4 Ohio St.
13 Iowa St.
 Ohio St. 75-64
 Louisiana Tech 79-67
 Oklahoma 86-84 (ot)

3/15 6 Texas Tech
11 Boston College
 Boston College 55-53
 March 17
3/15 3 Duke
14 Pepperdine
 Duke 75-62
 Boston College 74-73
 Houston, TX
3/15 7 Ala.-Birmingham
10 Michigan St.
 Ala.-Birmingham 70-68
 March 17
 March 21
3/15 2 *Memphis St.
15 Pennsylvania
 *Memphis St. 67-55
 *Memphis St. 67-66 (ot)
 *Memphis St. 59-57

Dallas, TX
March 23

*Memphis St. 63-61

SOUTHEAST

3/15 1 Michigan
16 FDU-Teaneck
 Michigan 59-55
 March 17
3/15 8 Villanova
9 Dayton
 Villanova 51-49
 Villanova 59-55
 Dayton, OH
3/15 5 Maryland
12 Miami (Ohio)
 Maryland 69-68 (ot)
 March 17
 March 22
3/15 4 Louisiana St.
13 Navy
 Navy 78-55
 Maryland 64-59
 Villanova 46-43

3/14 6 Purdue
11 Auburn
 Auburn 59-58
 March 16
3/14 3 Kansas
14 Ohio
 Kansas 49-38
 Auburn 66-64
 Notre Dame, IN
3/14 7 Notre Dame
10 Oregon St.
 Notre Dame 79-70
 March 16
 March 22
3/14 2 North Caro.
15 Middle Tenn. St.
 North Caro. 76-57
 North Caro. 60-58
 North Caro. 62-56

Birmingham, AL
March 24

Villanova 56-44

Villanova 52-45

Lexington, KY
April 1

Villanova 66-64
NATIONAL CHAMPION

*Georgia's and Memphis State's participation in 1985 tournament vacated.

1986 Championship Bracket

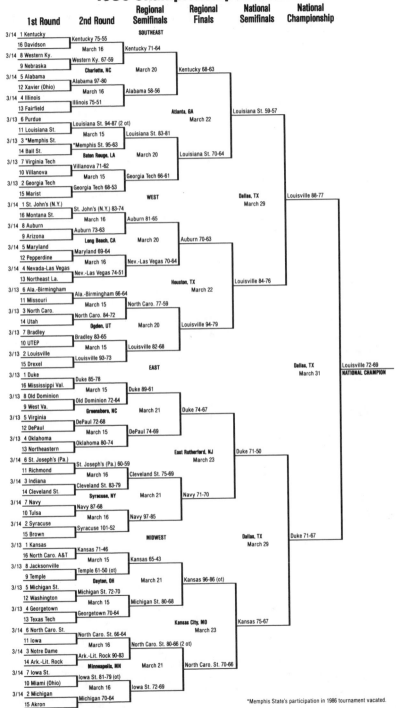

1st Round	2nd Round	Regional Semifinals	Regional Finals	National Semifinals	National Championship

SOUTHEAST

3/14 1 Kentucky
16 Davidson — Kentucky 75-55
March 16
3/14 8 Western Ky.
9 Nebraska — Western Ky. 67-59
Charlotte, NC — Kentucky 71-64
3/14 5 Alabama
12 Xavier (Ohio) — Alabama 97-80
March 16
3/14 4 Illinois
13 Fairfield — Illinois 75-51
Alabama 58-56
March 20 — Kentucky 68-63

Atlanta, GA
March 22 — Louisiana St. 59-57

3/13 6 Purdue
11 Louisiana St. — Louisiana St. 94-87 (2 ot)
March 15
3/13 3 *Memphis St.
14 Ball St. — *Memphis St. 95-63
Baton Rouge, LA — Louisiana St. 83-81
3/13 7 Virginia Tech
10 Villanova — Villanova 71-62
March 15
3/13 2 Georgia Tech
15 Marist — Georgia Tech 68-53
Georgia Tech 66-61
March 20 — Louisiana St. 70-64

Dallas, TX
March 29 — Louisville 88-77

WEST

3/14 1 St. John's (N.Y.)
16 Montana St. — St. John's (N.Y.) 83-74
March 16
3/14 8 Auburn
9 Arizona — Auburn 73-63
Long Beach, CA — Auburn 81-65
3/14 5 Maryland
12 Pepperdine — Maryland 69-64
March 16
3/14 4 Nevada-Las Vegas
13 Northeast La. — Nev.-Las Vegas 74-51
Nev.-Las Vegas 70-64
March 20 — Auburn 70-63

Houston, TX
March 22 — Louisville 84-76

3/13 6 Ala.-Birmingham
11 Missouri — Ala.-Birmingham 66-64
March 15
3/13 3 North Caro.
14 Utah — North Caro. 84-72
Ogden, UT — North Caro. 77-59
3/13 7 Bradley
10 UTEP — Bradley 83-65
March 15
3/13 2 Louisville
15 Drexel — Louisville 93-73
Louisville 82-68
March 20 — Louisville 94-79

Dallas, TX
March 31
NATIONAL CHAMPION — Louisville 72-69

EAST

3/13 1 Duke
16 Mississippi Val. — Duke 85-78
March 15
3/13 8 Old Dominion
9 West Va. — Old Dominion 72-64
Greensboro, NC — Duke 89-61
3/13 5 Virginia
12 DePaul — DePaul 72-68
March 15
3/13 4 Oklahoma
13 Northeastern — Oklahoma 80-74
DePaul 74-69
March 21 — Duke 74-67

East Rutherford, NJ
March 23 — Duke 71-50

3/14 6 St. Joseph's (Pa.)
11 Richmond — St. Joseph's (Pa.) 60-59
March 16
3/14 3 Indiana
14 Cleveland St. — Cleveland St. 83-79
Syracuse, NY — Cleveland St. 75-69
3/14 7 Navy
10 Tulsa — Navy 87-68
March 16
3/14 2 Syracuse
15 Brown — Syracuse 101-52
Navy 97-85
March 21 — Navy 71-70

Dallas, TX
March 29 — Duke 71-67

MIDWEST

3/13 1 Kansas
16 North Caro. A&T — Kansas 71-46
March 15
3/13 8 Jacksonville
9 Temple — Temple 61-50 (ot)
Dayton, OH — Kansas 65-43
3/13 5 Michigan St.
12 Washington — Michigan St. 72-70
March 15
3/13 4 Georgetown
13 Texas Tech — Georgetown 70-64
Michigan St. 80-68
March 21 — Kansas 96-86 (ot)

Kansas City, MO
March 23 — Kansas 75-67

3/14 6 North Caro. St.
11 Iowa — North Caro. St. 66-64
March 16
3/14 3 Notre Dame
14 Ark.-Lit. Rock — Ark.-Lit. Rock 90-83
Minneapolis, MN — North Caro. St. 80-66 (2 ot)
3/14 7 Iowa St.
10 Miami (Ohio) — Iowa St. 81-79 (ot)
March 16
3/14 2 Michigan
15 Akron — Michigan 70-64
Iowa St. 72-69
March 21 — North Caro. St. 70-66

Duke 71-50

Duke 71-67

*Memphis State's participation in 1986 tournament vacated.

1987 Championship Bracket

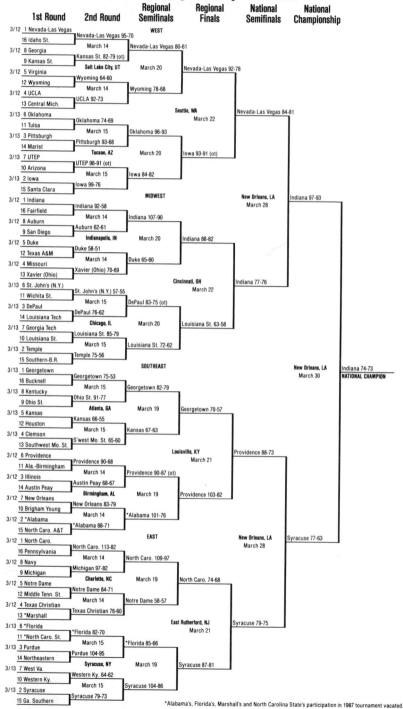

	1st Round	2nd Round	Regional Semifinals	Regional Finals	National Semifinals	National Championship

WEST

3/12 1 Nevada-Las Vegas
16 Idaho St. — Nevada-Las Vegas 95-70
March 14 — Nevada-Las Vegas 80-61
3/12 8 Georgia
9 Kansas St. — Kansas St. 82-79 (ot)
Salt Lake City, UT — March 20 — Nevada-Las Vegas 92-78
3/12 5 Virginia
12 Wyoming — Wyoming 64-60
March 14 — Wyoming 78-68
3/12 4 UCLA
13 Central Mich. — UCLA 92-73

Nevada-Las Vegas 84-81

Seattle, WA
March 22

3/13 6 Oklahoma
11 Tulsa — Oklahoma 74-69
March 15 — Oklahoma 96-93
3/13 3 Pittsburgh
14 Marist — Pittsburgh 93-68
Tucson, AZ — March 20 — Iowa 93-91 (ot)
3/13 7 UTEP
10 Arizona — UTEP 98-91 (ot)
March 15 — Iowa 84-82
3/13 2 Iowa
15 Santa Clara — Iowa 99-76

MIDWEST

New Orleans, LA
March 28

Indiana 97-93

3/12 1 Indiana
16 Fairfield — Indiana 92-58
March 14 — Indiana 107-90
3/12 8 Auburn
9 San Diego — Auburn 62-61
Indianapolis, IN — March 20 — Indiana 88-82
3/12 5 Duke
12 Texas A&M — Duke 58-51
March 14 — Duke 65-60
3/12 4 Missouri
13 Xavier (Ohio) — Xavier (Ohio) 70-69

Indiana 77-76

Cincinnati, OH
March 22

3/13 6 St. John's (N.Y.)
11 Wichita St. — St. John's (N.Y.) 57-55
March 15 — DePaul 83-75 (ot)
3/13 3 DePaul
14 Louisiana Tech — DePaul 76-62
Chicago, IL — March 20 — Louisiana St. 63-58
3/13 7 Georgia Tech
10 Louisiana St. — Louisiana St. 85-79
March 15 — Louisiana St. 72-62
3/13 2 Temple
15 Southern-B.R. — Temple 75-56

SOUTHEAST

New Orleans, LA
March 30

Indiana 74-73
NATIONAL CHAMPION

3/13 1 Georgetown
16 Bucknell — Georgetown 75-53
March 15 — Georgetown 82-79
3/13 8 Kentucky
9 Ohio St. — Ohio St. 91-77
Atlanta, GA — March 19 — Georgetown 70-57
3/13 5 Kansas
12 Houston — Kansas 66-55
March 15 — Kansas 67-63
3/13 4 Clemson
13 Southwest Mo. St. — S'west Mo. St. 65-60

Providence 88-73

Louisville, KY
March 21

3/12 6 Providence
11 Ala.-Birmingham — Providence 90-68
March 14 — Providence 90-87 (ot)
3/12 3 Illinois
14 Austin Peay — Austin Peay 68-67
Birmingham, AL — March 19 — Providence 103-82
3/12 7 New Orleans
10 Brigham Young — New Orleans 83-79
March 14 — *Alabama 101-76
3/12 2 *Alabama
15 North Caro. A&T — *Alabama 88-71

Syracuse 77-63

EAST

New Orleans, LA
March 28

3/12 1 North Caro.
16 Pennsylvania — North Caro. 113-82
March 14 — North Caro. 109-97
3/12 8 Navy
9 Michigan — Michigan 97-82
Charlotte, NC — March 19 — North Caro. 74-68
3/12 5 Notre Dame
12 Middle Tenn. St. — Notre Dame 84-71
March 14 — Notre Dame 58-57
3/12 4 Texas Christian
13 *Marshall — Texas Christian 76-60

Syracuse 79-75

East Rutherford, NJ
March 21

3/13 6 *Florida
11 *North Caro. St. — *Florida 82-70
March 15 — *Florida 85-66
3/13 3 Purdue
14 Northeastern — Purdue 104-95
Syracuse, NY — March 19 — Syracuse 87-81
3/13 7 West Va.
10 Western Ky. — Western Ky. 64-62
March 15 — Syracuse 104-86
3/13 2 Syracuse
15 Ga. Southern — Syracuse 79-73

*Alabama's, Florida's, Marshall's and North Carolina State's participation in 1987 tournament vacated.

1988 Championship Bracket

| 1st Round | 2nd Round | Regional Semifinals | Regional Finals | National Semifinals | National Championship |

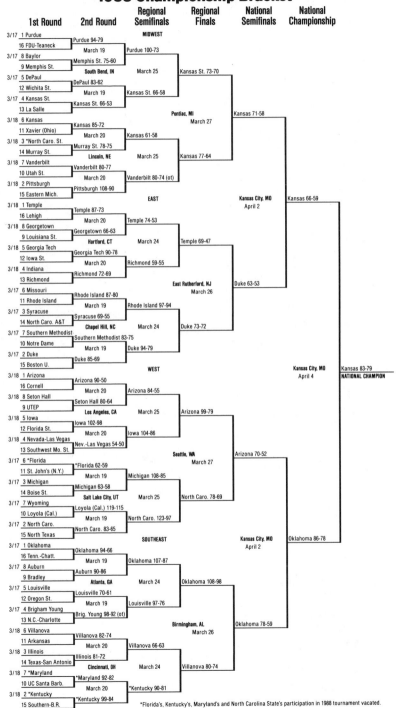

MIDWEST

3/17 1 Purdue
16 FDU-Teaneck
Purdue 94-79 — March 19
3/17 8 Baylor
9 Memphis St.
Memphis St. 75-60
Purdue 100-73
South Bend, IN — March 25
3/17 5 DePaul
12 Wichita St.
DePaul 83-62 — March 19
3/17 4 Kansas St.
13 La Salle
Kansas St. 66-53
Kansas St. 66-58
Kansas St. 73-70

3/18 6 Kansas
11 Xavier (Ohio)
Kansas 85-72 — March 20
3/18 3 *North Caro. St.
14 Murray St.
Murray St. 78-75
Kansas 61-58
Lincoln, NE — March 25
3/18 7 Vanderbilt
10 Utah St.
Vanderbilt 80-77 — March 20
3/18 2 Pittsburgh
15 Eastern Mich.
Pittsburgh 108-90
Vanderbilt 80-74 (ot)
Kansas 77-64

Pontiac, MI — March 27
Kansas 71-58

EAST

3/18 1 Temple
16 Lehigh
Temple 87-73 — March 20
3/18 8 Georgetown
9 Louisiana St.
Georgetown 66-63
Temple 74-53
Hartford, CT — March 24
3/18 5 Georgia Tech
12 Iowa St.
Georgia Tech 90-78 — March 20
3/18 4 Indiana
13 Richmond
Richmond 72-69
Richmond 59-55
Temple 69-47

3/17 6 Missouri
11 Rhode Island
Rhode Island 87-80 — March 19
3/17 3 Syracuse
14 North Caro. A&T
Syracuse 69-55
Rhode Island 97-94
Chapel Hill, NC — March 24
3/17 7 Southern Methodist
10 Notre Dame
Southern Methodist 83-75 — March 19
3/17 2 Duke
15 Boston U.
Duke 85-69
Duke 94-79
Duke 73-72

East Rutherford, NJ — March 26
Duke 63-53

Kansas City, MO — April 2
Kansas 66-59

WEST

3/18 1 Arizona
16 Cornell
Arizona 90-50 — March 20
3/18 8 Seton Hall
9 UTEP
Seton Hall 80-64
Arizona 84-55
Los Angeles, CA — March 25
3/18 5 Iowa
12 Florida St.
Iowa 102-98 — March 20
3/18 4 Nevada-Las Vegas
13 Southwest Mo. St.
Nev.-Las Vegas 54-50
Iowa 104-86
Arizona 99-79

3/17 6 *Florida
11 St. John's (N.Y.)
*Florida 62-59 — March 19
3/17 3 Michigan
14 Boise St.
Michigan 63-58
Michigan 108-85
Salt Lake City, UT — March 25
3/17 7 Wyoming
10 Loyola (Cal.)
Loyola (Cal.) 119-115 — March 19
3/17 2 North Caro.
15 North Texas
North Caro. 83-65
North Caro. 123-97
North Caro. 78-69

Seattle, WA — March 27
Arizona 70-52

Kansas City, MO — April 4
Kansas 83-79
NATIONAL CHAMPION

SOUTHEAST

3/17 1 Oklahoma
16 Tenn.-Chatt.
Oklahoma 94-66 — March 19
3/17 8 Auburn
9 Bradley
Auburn 90-86
Oklahoma 107-87
Atlanta, GA — March 24
3/17 5 Louisville
12 Oregon St.
Louisville 70-61 — March 19
3/17 4 Brigham Young
13 N.C.-Charlotte
Brig. Young 98-92 (ot)
Louisville 97-76
Oklahoma 108-98

3/18 6 Villanova
11 Arkansas
Villanova 82-74 — March 20
3/18 3 Illinois
14 Texas-San Antonio
Illinois 81-72
Villanova 66-63
Cincinnati, OH — March 24
3/18 7 *Maryland
10 UC Santa Barb.
*Maryland 92-82 — March 20
3/18 2 *Kentucky
15 Southern-B.R.
*Kentucky 99-84
*Kentucky 90-81
Villanova 80-74

Birmingham, AL — March 26
Oklahoma 78-59

Kansas City, MO — April 2
Oklahoma 86-78

*Florida's, Kentucky's, Maryland's and North Carolina State's participation in 1988 tournament vacated.

1989 Championship Bracket

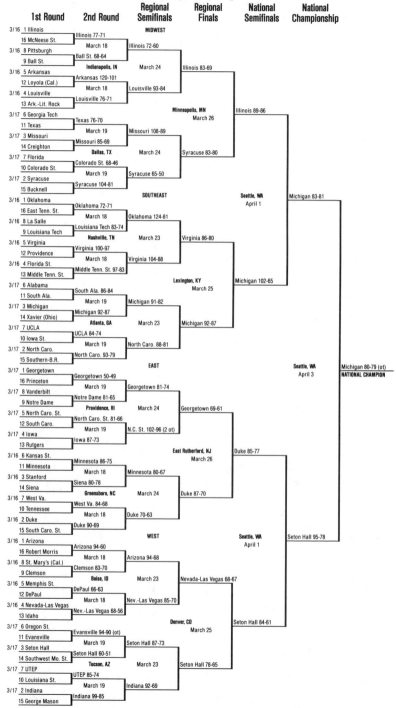

1st Round	2nd Round	Regional Semifinals	Regional Finals	National Semifinals	National Championship

MIDWEST

3/16 1 Illinois
Illinois 77-71
16 McNeese St.
March 18 — Illinois 72-60
3/16 8 Pittsburgh
Ball St. 68-64
9 Ball St.
Indianapolis, IN — March 24 — Illinois 83-69
3/16 5 Arkansas
Arkansas 120-101
12 Loyola (Cal.)
March 18 — Louisville 93-84
3/16 4 Louisville
Louisville 76-71
13 Ark.-Lit. Rock

Minneapolis, MN — March 26 — Illinois 89-86

3/17 6 Georgia Tech
Texas 76-70
11 Texas
March 19 — Missouri 108-89
3/17 3 Missouri
Missouri 85-69
14 Creighton
Dallas, TX — March 24 — Syracuse 83-80
3/17 7 Florida
Colorado St. 68-46
10 Colorado St.
March 19 — Syracuse 65-50
3/17 2 Syracuse
Syracuse 104-81
15 Bucknell

Seattle, WA — April 1 — Michigan 83-81

SOUTHEAST

3/16 1 Oklahoma
Oklahoma 72-71
16 East Tenn. St.
March 18 — Oklahoma 124-81
3/16 8 La Salle
Louisiana Tech 83-74
9 Louisiana Tech
Nashville, TN — March 23 — Virginia 86-80
3/16 5 Virginia
Virginia 100-97
12 Providence
March 18 — Virginia 104-88
3/16 4 Florida St.
Middle Tenn. St. 97-83
13 Middle Tenn. St.

Lexington, KY — March 25 — Michigan 102-65

3/17 6 Alabama
South Ala. 86-84
11 South Ala.
March 19 — Michigan 91-82
3/17 3 Michigan
Michigan 92-87
14 Xavier (Ohio)
Atlanta, GA — March 23 — Michigan 92-87
3/17 7 UCLA
UCLA 84-74
10 Iowa St.
March 19 — North Caro. 88-81
3/17 2 North Caro.
North Caro. 93-79
15 Southern-B.R.

Seattle, WA — April 3
NATIONAL CHAMPION
Michigan 80-79 (ot)

EAST

3/17 1 Georgetown
Georgetown 50-49
16 Princeton
March 19 — Georgetown 81-74
3/17 8 Vanderbilt
Notre Dame 81-65
9 Notre Dame
Providence, RI — March 24 — Georgetown 69-61
3/17 5 North Caro. St.
North Caro. St. 81-66
12 South Caro.
March 19 — N.C. St. 102-96 (2 ot)
3/17 4 Iowa
Iowa 87-73
13 Rutgers

East Rutherford, NJ — March 26 — Duke 85-77

3/16 6 Kansas St.
Minnesota 86-75
11 Minnesota
March 18 — Minnesota 80-67
3/16 3 Stanford
Siena 80-78
14 Siena
Greensboro, NC — March 24 — Duke 87-70
3/16 7 West Va.
West Va. 84-68
10 Tennessee
March 18 — Duke 70-63
3/16 2 Duke
Duke 90-69
15 South Caro. St.

Seattle, WA — April 1 — Seton Hall 95-78

WEST

3/16 1 Arizona
Arizona 94-60
16 Robert Morris
March 18 — Arizona 94-68
3/16 8 St. Mary's (Cal.)
Clemson 83-70
9 Clemson
Boise, ID — March 23 — Nevada-Las Vegas 68-67
3/16 5 Memphis St.
DePaul 66-63
12 DePaul
March 18 — Nev.-Las Vegas 85-70
3/16 4 Nevada-Las Vegas
Nev.-Las Vegas 68-56
13 Idaho

Denver, CO — March 25 — Seton Hall 84-61

3/17 6 Oregon St.
Evansville 94-90 (ot)
11 Evansville
March 19 — Seton Hall 87-73
3/17 3 Seton Hall
Seton Hall 60-51
14 Southwest Mo. St.
Tucson, AZ — March 23 — Seton Hall 78-65
3/17 7 UTEP
UTEP 85-74
10 Louisiana St.
March 19 — Indiana 92-69
3/17 2 Indiana
Indiana 99-85
15 George Mason

1990 Championship Bracket

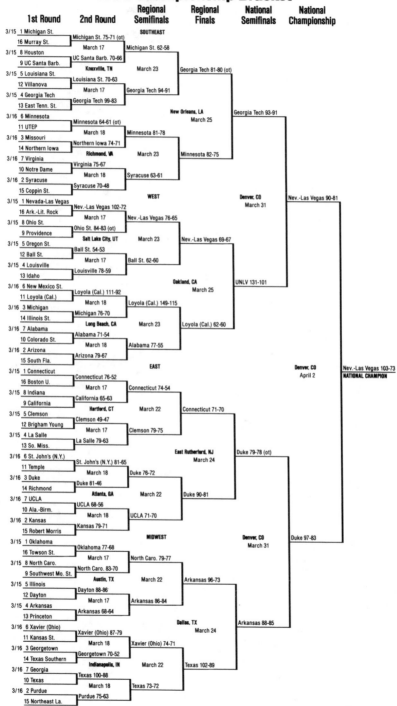

1st Round	2nd Round	Regional Semifinals	Regional Finals	National Semifinals	National Championship

SOUTHEAST

3/15 1 Michigan St.
16 Murray St.
— Michigan St. 75-71 (ot) — March 17 — Michigan St. 62-58
3/15 8 Houston
9 UC Santa Barb.
— UC Santa Barb. 70-66 — Knoxville, TN
— March 23 — Georgia Tech 81-80 (ot)
3/15 5 Louisiana St.
12 Villanova
— Louisiana St. 70-63 — March 17 — Georgia Tech 94-91
3/15 4 Georgia Tech
13 East Tenn. St.
— Georgia Tech 99-83

— New Orleans, LA — March 25 — Georgia Tech 93-91

3/16 6 Minnesota
11 UTEP
— Minnesota 64-61 (ot) — March 18 — Minnesota 81-78
3/16 3 Missouri
14 Northern Iowa
— Northern Iowa 74-71 — Richmond, VA
— March 23 — Minnesota 82-75
3/16 7 Virginia
10 Notre Dame
— Virginia 75-67 — March 18 — Syracuse 63-61
3/16 2 Syracuse
15 Coppin St.
— Syracuse 70-48

WEST

3/15 1 Nevada-Las Vegas
16 Ark.-Lit. Rock
— Nev.-Las Vegas 102-72 — March 17 — Nev.-Las Vegas 76-65
3/15 8 Ohio St.
9 Providence
— Ohio St. 84-83 (ot) — Salt Lake City, UT
— March 23 — Nev.-Las Vegas 69-67
3/15 5 Oregon St.
12 Ball St.
— Ball St. 54-53 — March 17 — Ball St. 62-60
3/15 4 Louisville
13 Idaho
— Louisville 78-59

— Oakland, CA — March 25 — UNLV 131-101

3/16 6 New Mexico St.
11 Loyola (Cal.)
— Loyola (Cal.) 111-92 — March 18 — Loyola (Cal.) 149-115
3/16 3 Michigan
14 Illinois St.
— Michigan 76-70 — Long Beach, CA
— March 23 — Loyola (Cal.) 62-60
3/16 7 Alabama
10 Colorado St.
— Alabama 71-54 — March 18 — Alabama 77-55
3/16 2 Arizona
15 South Fla.
— Arizona 79-67

EAST

3/15 1 Connecticut
16 Boston U.
— Connecticut 76-52 — March 17 — Connecticut 74-54
3/15 8 Indiana
9 California
— California 65-63 — Hartford, CT
— March 22 — Connecticut 71-70
3/15 5 Clemson
12 Brigham Young
— Clemson 49-47 — March 17 — Clemson 79-75
3/15 4 La Salle
13 So. Miss.
— La Salle 79-63

— East Rutherford, NJ — March 24 — Duke 79-78 (ot)

3/16 6 St. John's (N.Y.)
11 Temple
— St. John's (N.Y.) 81-65 — March 18 — Duke 76-72
3/16 3 Duke
14 Richmond
— Duke 81-46 — Atlanta, GA
— March 22 — Duke 90-81
3/16 7 UCLA
10 Ala.-Birm.
— UCLA 68-56 — March 18 — UCLA 71-70
3/16 2 Kansas
15 Robert Morris
— Kansas 79-71

MIDWEST

3/15 1 Oklahoma
16 Towson St.
— Oklahoma 77-68 — March 17 — North Caro. 79-77
3/15 8 North Caro.
9 Southwest Mo. St.
— North Caro. 83-70 — Austin, TX
— March 22 — Arkansas 96-73
3/15 5 Illinois
12 Dayton
— Dayton 88-86 — March 17 — Arkansas 86-84
3/15 4 Arkansas
13 Princeton
— Arkansas 68-64

— Dallas, TX — March 24 — Arkansas 88-85

3/16 6 Xavier (Ohio)
11 Kansas St.
— Xavier (Ohio) 87-79 — March 18 — Xavier (Ohio) 74-71
3/16 3 Georgetown
14 Texas Southern
— Georgetown 70-52 — Indianapolis, IN
— March 22 — Texas 102-89
3/16 7 Georgia
10 Texas
— Texas 100-88 — March 18 — Texas 73-72
3/16 2 Purdue
15 Northeast La.
— Purdue 75-63

Denver, CO — March 31 — Nev.-Las Vegas 90-81

Denver, CO — March 31 — Duke 97-83

Denver, CO — April 2 — Nev.-Las Vegas 103-73 — NATIONAL CHAMPION

1991 Championship Bracket

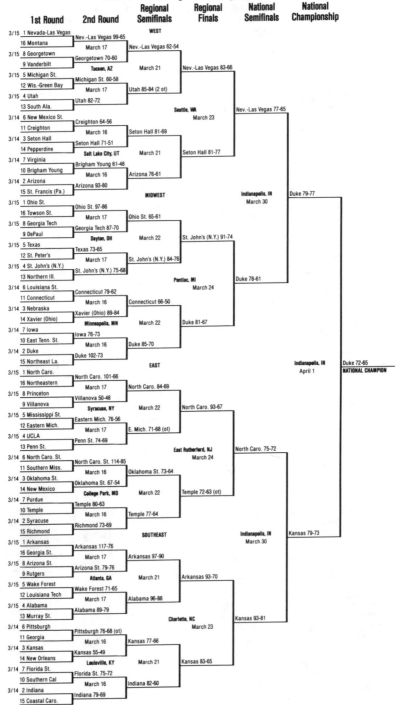

	1st Round	2nd Round	Regional Semifinals	Regional Finals	National Semifinals	National Championship

WEST

3/15 1 Nevada-Las Vegas — Nev.-Las Vegas 99-65 March 17
3/15 16 Montana
3/15 8 Georgetown — Georgetown 70-60
9 Vanderbilt
Nev.-Las Vegas 62-54
Tucson, AZ March 21
3/15 5 Michigan St. — Michigan St. 60-58 March 17
12 Wis.-Green Bay
3/15 4 Utah — Utah 82-72
13 South Ala.
Utah 85-84 (2 ot)
Nev.-Las Vegas 83-66
3/14 6 New Mexico St. — Creighton 64-56 March 16
11 Creighton
3/14 3 Seton Hall — Seton Hall 71-51
14 Pepperdine
Seton Hall 81-69
Salt Lake City, UT March 21
3/14 7 Virginia — Brigham Young 61-48 March 16
10 Brigham Young
3/14 2 Arizona — Arizona 93-80
15 St. Francis (Pa.)
Arizona 76-61
Seton Hall 81-77
Seattle, WA March 23

Nev.-Las Vegas 77-65

MIDWEST

3/15 1 Ohio St. — Ohio St. 97-86 March 17
16 Towson St.
3/15 8 Georgia Tech — Georgia Tech 87-70
9 DePaul
Ohio St. 65-61
Dayton, OH March 22
3/15 5 Texas — Texas 73-65 March 17
12 St. Peter's
3/15 4 St. John's (N.Y.) — St. John's (N.Y.) 75-68
13 Northern Ill.
St. John's (N.Y.) 84-76
St. John's (N.Y.) 91-74
3/14 6 Louisiana St. — Connecticut 79-62 March 16
11 Connecticut
3/14 3 Nebraska — Xavier (Ohio) 89-84
14 Xavier (Ohio)
Connecticut 66-50
Minneapolis, MN March 22
3/14 7 Iowa — Iowa 76-73 March 16
10 East Tenn. St.
3/14 2 Duke — Duke 102-73
15 Northeast La.
Duke 85-70
Duke 81-67
Pontiac, MI March 24

Duke 78-61

Indianapolis, IN March 30

Duke 79-77

EAST

3/15 1 North Caro. — North Caro. 101-66 March 17
16 Northeastern
3/15 8 Princeton — Villanova 50-48
9 Villanova
North Caro. 84-69
Syracuse, NY March 22
3/15 5 Mississippi St. — Eastern Mich. 76-56 March 17
12 Eastern Mich.
3/15 4 UCLA — Penn St. 74-69
13 Penn St.
E. Mich. 71-68 (ot)
North Caro. 93-67
3/14 6 North Caro. St. — North Caro. St. 114-85 March 16
11 Southern Miss.
3/14 3 Oklahoma St. — Oklahoma St. 67-54
14 New Mexico
Oklahoma St. 73-64
College Park, MD March 22
3/14 7 Purdue — Temple 80-63 March 16
10 Temple
3/14 2 Syracuse — Richmond 73-69
15 Richmond
Temple 77-64
Temple 72-63 (ot)
East Rutherford, NJ March 24

North Caro. 75-72

Indianapolis, IN April 1

Duke 72-65
NATIONAL CHAMPION

SOUTHEAST

3/15 1 Arkansas — Arkansas 117-76 March 17
16 Georgia St.
3/15 8 Arizona St. — Arizona St. 79-76
9 Rutgers
Arkansas 97-90
Atlanta, GA March 21
3/15 5 Wake Forest — Wake Forest 71-65 March 17
12 Louisiana Tech
3/15 4 Alabama — Alabama 89-79
13 Murray St.
Alabama 96-88
Arkansas 93-70
3/14 6 Pittsburgh — Pittsburgh 76-68 (ot) March 16
11 Georgia
3/14 3 Kansas — Kansas 55-49
14 New Orleans
Kansas 77-66
Louisville, KY March 21
3/14 7 Florida St. — Florida St. 75-72 March 16
10 Southern Cal
3/14 2 Indiana — Indiana 79-69
15 Coastal Caro.
Indiana 82-60
Kansas 83-65
Charlotte, NC March 23

Kansas 93-81

Indianapolis, IN March 30

Kansas 79-73

1992 Championship Bracket

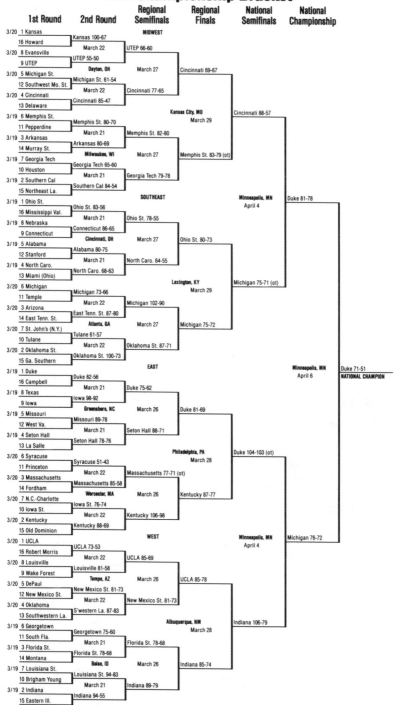

1st Round	2nd Round	Regional Semifinals	Regional Finals	National Semifinals	National Championship

MIDWEST

3/20 1 Kansas
Kansas 100-67
16 Howard
   March 22 — UTEP 66-60
3/20 8 Evansville
UTEP 55-50
9 UTEP
   Dayton, OH — March 27 — Cincinnati 69-67
3/20 5 Michigan St.
Michigan St. 61-54
12 Southwest Mo. St.
   March 22 — Cincinnati 77-65
3/20 4 Cincinnati
Cincinnati 85-47
13 Delaware
   Kansas City, MO — March 29 — Cincinnati 88-57
3/19 6 Memphis St.
Memphis St. 80-70
11 Pepperdine
   March 21 — Memphis St. 82-80
3/19 3 Arkansas
Arkansas 80-69
14 Murray St.
   Milwaukee, WI — March 27 — Memphis St. 83-79 (ot)
3/19 7 Georgia Tech
Georgia Tech 65-60
10 Houston
   March 21 — Georgia Tech 79-78
3/19 2 Southern Cal
Southern Cal 84-54
15 Northeast La.

SOUTHEAST

3/19 1 Ohio St.
Ohio St. 83-56
16 Mississippi Val.
   March 21 — Ohio St. 78-55
3/19 8 Nebraska
Connecticut 86-65
9 Connecticut
   Cincinnati, OH — March 27 — Ohio St. 80-73
3/19 5 Alabama
Alabama 80-75
12 Stanford
   March 21 — North Caro. 64-55
3/19 4 North Caro.
North Caro. 68-63
13 Miami (Ohio)
   Lexington, KY — March 29 — Michigan 75-71 (ot)
3/20 6 Michigan
Michigan 73-66
11 Temple
   March 22 — Michigan 102-90
3/20 3 Arizona
East Tenn. St. 87-80
14 East Tenn. St.
   Atlanta, GA — March 27 — Michigan 75-72
3/20 7 St. John's (N.Y.)
Tulane 61-57
10 Tulane
   March 22 — Oklahoma St. 87-71
3/20 2 Oklahoma St.
Oklahoma St. 100-73
15 Ga. Southern

EAST

3/19 1 Duke
Duke 82-56
16 Campbell
   March 21 — Duke 75-62
3/19 8 Texas
Iowa 98-92
9 Iowa
   Greensboro, NC — March 26 — Duke 81-69
3/19 5 Missouri
Missouri 89-78
12 West Va.
   March 21 — Seton Hall 88-71
3/19 4 Seton Hall
Seton Hall 78-76
13 La Salle
   Philadelphia, PA — March 28 — Duke 104-103 (ot)
3/20 6 Syracuse
Syracuse 51-43
11 Princeton
   March 22 — Massachusetts 77-71 (ot)
3/20 3 Massachusetts
Massachusetts 85-58
14 Fordham
   Worcester, MA — March 26 — Kentucky 87-77
3/20 7 N.C.-Charlotte
Iowa St. 76-74
10 Iowa St.
   March 22 — Kentucky 106-98
3/20 2 Kentucky
Kentucky 88-69
15 Old Dominion

WEST

3/20 1 UCLA
UCLA 73-53
16 Robert Morris
   March 22 — UCLA 85-69
3/20 8 Louisville
Louisville 81-58
9 Wake Forest
   Tempe, AZ — March 26 — UCLA 85-78
3/20 5 DePaul
New Mexico St. 81-73
12 New Mexico St.
   March 22 — New Mexico St. 81-73
3/20 4 Oklahoma
S'western La. 87-83
13 Southwestern La.
   Albuquerque, NM — March 28 — Indiana 106-79
3/19 6 Georgetown
Georgetown 75-60
11 South Fla.
   March 21 — Florida St. 78-68
3/19 3 Florida St.
Florida St. 78-68
14 Montana
   Boise, ID — March 26 — Indiana 85-74
3/19 7 Louisiana St.
Louisiana St. 94-83
10 Brigham Young
   March 21 — Indiana 89-79
3/19 2 Indiana
Indiana 94-55
15 Eastern Ill.

National Semifinals

Minneapolis, MN — April 4 — Duke 81-78

Minneapolis, MN — April 4 — Michigan 76-72

National Championship

Minneapolis, MN — April 6 — Duke 71-51
NATIONAL CHAMPION